Joseph Henry Allen, James Bradstreet Greenough

A Latin Grammar for Schools and Colleges

Founded on Comparative Grammar

Joseph Henry Allen, James Bradstreet Greenough

A Latin Grammar for Schools and Colleges
Founded on Comparative Grammar

ISBN/EAN: 9783337062743

Printed in Europe, USA, Canada, Australia, Japan

Cover: Foto ©Paul-Georg Meister /pixelio.de

More available books at **www.hansebooks.com**

A

LATIN GRAMMAR

FOR SCHOOLS AND COLLEGES

FOUNDED ON COMPARATIVE GRAMMAR

BY

JOSEPH H. ALLEN

AND

JAMES B. GREENOUGH

BOSTON

PUBLISHED BY GINN BROTHERS

3 BEACON STREET

1872

PREFACE.

Our aim has been to prepare, within moderate compass, a complete Latin grammar, to be used from the beginning of the study of Latin until the end of a college course. The whole has been composed from our own point of view, and is, in all essentials, a new and independent work. But we have used freely the standard authorities, as well those of the older scholastic as of the newer critical and scientific schools. In several points, particularly the topical arrangement of the Syntax, we have followed the outline sketched a few years ago by Professor Allen, of the University of Wisconsin.

We have endeavored to adapt the scientific (philological) method of inflection by stem and termination to the system used by the Romans themselves and handed down by general custom to our time. While the five Declensions are retained, with the old distinctions on which they are founded, at the same time the true philological difference, that of stems, is fully exhibited as the real basis of noun-forms. In the same way the true distinctions of verb-stems are adapted to the existing four Conjugations. We have preferred this to the "crude-form" system, partly because of the practical difficulty that our lexicons do not give stems, but words; chiefly, however, from the inherent difficulty of a crude-form system in a language so decayed as the Latin.

In respect to the actual forms of the language, we have not thought it necessary to go back of Neue's "Formenlehre," upon which we have relied, and which teachers will find digested so far as seems to come within the limits of a work like the present.

In the Syntax, our design has been to leave no principle untouched which a student needs during his school and college course. We have attempted to show, as far as possible, the reason and origin of constructions, for which purpose notes have been inserted where it seemed desirable. Many things in the treatment of the Subjunctive, of the Protasis and Apodosis (in which we have followed Professor Goodwin's analysis), of Temporal particles, of the Infinitive and Participles, and much of the matter of the notes, appear for the first time in a school-book, and are the results of the authors' own investigations in Comparative Grammar. The Syntax is illustrated by upwards of a thousand examples cited from classical authorities, principally from Cicero; besides nearly as many brief phrases in illustration of minor points, particularly the use of prepositions and cases.

In Prosody and Versification we have taken a little wider range than usual, so as to enable the student to read metrically any poetry he will meet in his college course.

In the typography and mechanical arrangement of the page, we have sought to give every aid that can be rendered in that way to the easy comprehension of the subject. The sub-sections in larger type (numbered 1, 2, 3, &c.) contain of themselves a complete outline, and we think will be found sufficient, with the accompanying paradigms or examples, for a course of elementary study. Details of form or structure, requiring to be committed to memory only as they occur in reading, are put in smaller type, marked *a, b, c,* &c. And the points of philology, or special criticism, which appear to throw valuable side-light upon the subject, interesting chiefly to teachers or special students, are contained in the form of Notes, not interfering at all with the treatment in the text. By paying attention to this subordination of topics, teachers will avoid the serious error of crowding upon the student, prematurely, a mass of details, which might only perplex and obscure his real understanding of the subject.

CAMBRIDGE, April, 1872.

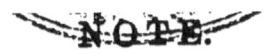

NOTE.

For the convenience of those who may wish to follow out special lines of study in general or comparative grammar, or to consult original sources on the history and development of the Latin, a list of works including the best and most recent authorities is here subjoined: —

Bopp: *Vergleichende Grammatik des Sanskrit, etc.* [Indo-European languages]. 4 vols. 3d Ed. Berlin, 1868-70.

The original standard work on Comparative Forms. Later researches have corrected some erroneous details. English translation (poor), London: 1862. The best form is a French translation, with Notes and Introductions by Michel Bréal. Paris: 1866.

Corssen: *Aussprache, Vokalismus und Betonung der Lateinischen Sprache.* 2 vols. 2d Ed. Leipzig, 1868.

The greatest work on Latin *alone*, treating the language in reference to its own individual development, particularly as to the sounds (*Lautlehre*). In the comparative portion, it needs the correction of other investigators.

Curtius, G.: *Grundzüge der Griechischen Etymologie.* 3d Ed. Leipsic: 1869.

Treats of Latin only by comparison; but is one of the most valuable works on the general subject.

——— *Erläuterungen zu meiner Griechischen Schul-grammatik.* 2d Ed. Prag. 1870. English translation ("Elucidations"), London: 1870.

Notes giving in connection with the Greek Grammar the simplest view of the doctrine of forms.

Delbruck: *Das Conjunctiv und Optativ, im Sanskrit und Griechischen.* Halle: 1871.

Origin of the Moods treated scientifically; should be read in connection with a notice in N. A. Review, Oct. 1871, and "Analysis of the Latin Subjunctive," by J. B. Greenough, Cambridge, 1870.

——— *Ablativ, Localis, Instrumentalis im indischen, etc.* Berlin, 1867.

Origin of the various Ablative constructions.

Ferrar: *Comparative Grammar of Sanskrit, Greek, and Latin.* London: 1869. Vol. I., including as far as Pronouns.

A convenient hand-book in English.

Fick: *Vergleichendes Wörterbuch der Indo-Germanischen Sprachen.* Göttingen: 1870.

A Dictionary of Roots and Words supposed to have existed in the Indo-European tongue, with the corresponding words and derivatives in the various languages. It can be used without a knowledge of German. No such book, however, is safe to use without careful study of the laws of consonant and vowel changes.

HOFFMANN: *Die Construction der Lateinischen Zeitpartikeln.* Vienna: 1860 (Pamphlet).

KUHN: See *Zeitschrift.*

LUBBERT: *Die Syntax von Quom.* Breslau: 1870.

NEUE: *Formenlehre der Lateinischen Sprache.* 2d Ed. Stuttgart, 1866.
Storehouse of all Latin forms, 1200 pages, containing the result of late textual criticism. The standard work.

PEILE: *Latin and Greek Etymology.* 2d Ed. Macmillan: London and Cambridge, 1872.

ROBY: *A Grammar of the Latin Language, from Plautus to Suetonius.* Macmillan: London and New York, 1871. Vol. I.
A thorough treatment of Latin Etymology on the principles of comparative grammar. Some errors have been pointed out in the N. A. Review, Jan. 1872.

SCHLEICHER: *Compendium der Vergleichenden Grammatik der Indo-Germanischen Sprachen.* 2d Ed. Weimar, 1866.

SCHWEIZER-SIDLER: *Elementar- und Formenlehre der Lateinischen Sprache, für Schulen.* Halle, 1869.
The best summary of the results of comparative grammar as applied to Latin in short compass (137 pages).

WILLIAMS: *A Practical Grammar of the Sanskrit Language.* 3d Ed. Oxford, 1864.
A very convenient Sanskrit grammar, without some knowledge of which it is difficult to pursue the study of comparative grammar to advantage.

Zeitschrift fur vergleichender Sprachforschung. Edited by Dr. A. KUHN. Vols. I. to XX. Berlin, 1851–1871, and still continued.
The best essays on all disputed points of comparative Philology. Indispensable to correct theories of individual investigators. Each volume has an Index; and there is also a general index to the first ten volumes.

CONTENTS.

PART I.—ETYMOLOGY.

Section	Page
1. Alphabet	1

    1. Classification; 2. Early Forms; 3. Changes; 4. Combinations; 5. Syllables.

2. Pronunciation 5
3. Quantity 6
4. Accent 7
5. Inflection 8

    1. Definition; 2. Root and Stem; Inflected parts of speech; 4. Particles.

6. Gender 9

    1. Natural and Grammatical; 2. Rules; 3. Common Gender; 4. Epicene.

7. Case 11
8. Declension 12

    1. Declensions; 2. Rules; 3. Case-Endings.

NOUNS.

9. First Declension 14

    1. Gender; 2. Case Forms; 3. Greek Nouns.

10. Second Declension 15

    1. Nominative; 2. Stems in **ro-**; 3. Gender; 4. Case Forms; 5, 6. Nouns in **er**; 7. Greek Nouns.

11. Third Declension 17

    I. Vowel Stems.—1. Stems; 2. Nominative; 3. Case Forms; 4. Greek Nouns.

    II. Liquid Stems 19

    III. Mute Stems.—1. Labial; 2. Lingual; 3. Palatal; 4. Peculiar Forms; 5. Greek Nouns 20

    IV. Rules of Gender.—1. Nominative endings; 2. Stems; 3. Classified List 23

xii   CONTENTS.

SECT.	PAGE
12. Fourth Declension	28
13. Fifth Declension	29
14. Irregular Nouns	30
1. Defective; 2. Variable.	
15. Proper Names	32

ADJECTIVES.

16. Inflection	33
1. Of the 1st and 2d Declension; 2. Of 3d Declension; 3. Consonant Stems, Comparatives.	
17. Comparison	38
1. Regular; 2. Irregular; 3. Defective; 4. Adverbs; 5. Signification.	
18. Numerals	41
1. Cardinal and Ordinal; 2. Distributives; 3. Numeral Adverbs; 4. Multiplicatives.	

PRONOUNS.

19. Personal and Reflexive	44
20. Demonstrative	45
21. Relative, Interrogative, and Indefinite	47
1. Case-Forms; 2. Compounds.	
22. Correlatives	49

VERBS.

23. Structure	50
24. Moods	51
25. Participles	51
26. Gerund and Supine	52
27. Tenses	52
1. Classification; 2. Meaning; 3. Perfect and Imperfect; 4. Passive Tenses; 5. Stems.	
28. Verb Forms	54
1. Personal Endings; 2. Changes of Stem; 3. Verb-Endings.	
29. **Esse** and its Compounds	57
30. Conjugation	60
1. First Conjugation; 2. Second Conjugation; 3. Third Conjugation; 4. Fourth Conjugation; 5. Principal Parts; 6. Special Forms; 7. Parallel Forms.	
31. First Conjugation	66
32. Second Conjugation	68
33. Third Conjugation	70
1. Regular; 2. Verbs in **io**; 3. Irregular Conjugation.	72

SECT.		PAGE.
34.	Fourth Conjugation	74
35.	Deponent Verbs	75
	1. Conjugation; 2. Semi-Deponents.	
36.	Derivative Verbs	77
37.	Irregular Verbs	78
38.	Defective Verbs	81
39.	Impersonal Verbs	82
40.	Periphrastic Forms	83

PARTICLES.

41.	Adverbs	84
	1. Derivation; 2. Classification; 3. Signification.	
42.	Prepositions	88
	1. With Cases; 2. Meaning and Use: Examples; 3. In Compounds.	
43.	Conjunctions	93
	1. Classification; 2. Classified List; 3. Special Meaning.	
44.	Derivation of Words	96
	1. Noun Forms; 2. Derivation of Verbs; 3. Compound Words.	

PART II. — SYNTAX.

45.	Definitions	101
	1. Sentence; 2. Subject and Predicate; 3. Modification; 4. Phrase; 5. Clause; 6. Connectives; 7. Agreement; 8. Government.	

1. SUBJECT AND PREDICATE.

46.	Of Nouns	103
	1. Appositive; 2. Predicate-Nominative.	
47.	Of Adjectives	105
	1. Number; 2. Gender; 3. As Nouns; 4. Use of Neuter; 5. Possessives; 6. As Adverbs; 7. Comparison; 8. Superlatives of Place; 9. Reciprocals.	
48.	Of Relatives	109
	1. Person of Verb; 2. Gender; 3. Antecedent; 4. As Connective; 5. Adverbs.	
49.	Verbs: Rules of Argument	112
	1. Plural with Collectives, &c.; 2. Nominative Subject.	

2. CONSTRUCTION OF CASES.

50.	Genitive	113
	1. Subjective, 114; 2. Partitive, 115; 3. Objective, 117; 4. After Verbs, 119.	

CONTENTS.

Sect.		Page.
51.	Dative	121

    1. With Transitives, 121; 2. With Intransitives, 122; 3. Of Possession, 126; 4. Of Agency, 127; 5. Of Service, 128; 6. Of Nearness, 128; 7. Of Advantage, 129; (Ethical Dative, 130).

52. Accusative 131

    1. General Use (Cognate Accusative, 131); 2. Two Accusatives; 3. Adverbial; 4. Special Uses.

53. Vocative 134

54. Ablative 134

    1. Of Separation, 135; 2. Of Source, 136; 3. Of Cause, 137; 4. Of Agent, 138; 5. Of Comparison, 138; 6. Of Means, 139; 7. Of Quality, 141; 8. Of Price, 141; 9. Of Specification, 142; 10. Locative, Ablative Absolute, 142.

55. Time and Place 143

    1. Time; 2. Space; 3. Place (Locative Form, 145); 4. Way by which.

56. Use of Prepositions 146

3. Syntax of the Verb.

57. Use of Moods 148

    1. Indicative; 2. Subjunctive (Independent or Dependent; 3. Hortatory; 4. Optative; 5. Concessive; 6. Dubitative); 7. Imperative; 8. Infinitive (Complementary, 154; With Subject-Accusative, 155; Historical, 156).

58. Use of Tenses 157

    1. Indicative; 2. Present (Conative, 157; Historical, 158); 3. Imperfect; 4. Future; 5. Perfect; 6. Pluperfect; 7. Future-Perfect; 8. Epistolary Tenses; 9. Of Subjunctive; 10. Sequence of Tenses (Primary and Secondary, 162); 11. Of Infinitive.

59. Conditional Sentences 166

    1. Protasis and Apodosis; 2. Particular and General Conditions; 3. Present and Past Conditions; 4. Future Conditions; 5. General Conditions.

60. Implied Conditions 172

    1. Condition Disguised; 2. Condition Omitted.

61. Conditional Particles 174

    1. Comparative; 2. Concessive; 3. Provisory; 4. Meaning and Use.

62. Relations of Time 176

    1. Use as in Protasis; 2. Absolute and Relative Time, (**Cum** *temporal*, 178; *causal*, 180).

63. Cause or Reason 181

    1. With Indicative; 2. With Subjunctive.

SECT.		PAGE.

64. Purpose (Final Clauses) 182
    1. Relatives or Conjunctions; 2. Forms.
65. Consequence or Result (Consecutive Clauses) 183
    1. Subjunctive with **ut** (ne); 2. Of Characteristic.
66. Intermediate Clauses 185
    1. Subjunctive of Citation; 2. Dependent Clauses.
67. Indirect Discourse 187
    1. Indirect Narrative (Subject-Accusative, Relative Clauses, Conditional Sentences, Questions), 188; 2. Indirect Questions, 190; 3. Indirect Commands, 191.
68. Wishes and Commands 192
69. Relative Clauses (Classification of) 193
70. Substantive Clauses 193
    1. Classification; 2. Accusative and Infinitive, 194; 3. Clauses of Purpose, 195; 4. Clauses of Result, 197; 5. Indicative with **quod**, 199.
71. Questions 200
    1. Interrogative Particles; 2. Double Questions; 3. Question and Answer.
72. Participles 202
    1. Distinctions of Tense; 2. Adjective use; 3. Predicate use; 4. Future Participle; 5. Gerundive.
73. Gerund and Gerundive 206
    1. Gerund; 2. Gerundive; 3. Construction of Cases.
74. Supine 209
75. General Rules of Syntax 210
76. Arrangement 212
    1. Normal Order; 2. Emphasis; 3. Structure (Periodic).

PART III. — PROSODY.

77. Rhythm 215
78. Rules of Quantity 215
    1. General Rules; 2. Final Syllables; 3. Penultimate Syllables (Increment of Nouns and Verbs).
79. Feet 220
80. Scanning 222
81. Metre 223
82. Forms of Verse 224
83. Early Prosody 232
84. Reckoning of Time 233
85. Measures of Value 235

APPENDIX 237

LATIN GRAMMAR.

PART FIRST.

FORMS OF WORDS (ETYMOLOGY).

1. Alphabet.

The Latin Alphabet is the same as the English, wanting **w**.

Note.—The letter **w** is found, however, in many modern Latin words, especially proper names.

1. *Classification*.—The letters of the alphabet are classified as follows:—

a. Vowels (litterae vocales, or *voice-letters*): a, e, i, o, u, y. The following are *Diphthongs* (double-vowels): ae (æ), au, eu, oe (œ), ei, ui.

b. Consonants (litterae consonantes, i.e., *sounding-with* the vowels):—

Mutes: *Labial* surd **p** sonant **b** spirant **f (v)** nasal **m**
        Lingual ,, **t** ,, **d**   ,, **n**
        Palatal ,, **c (k)** ,, **g** ,, **h** ,, **[ng]**
        Double Consonants, **x** (cs), **z** (ds).

Liquids: **l, m, n, r.**—Sibilants: surd **s**, sonant **z**.

The letters **i (j)** and **u (v)** at the beginning of a syllable before a vowel, also **u** in **quis, suadeo**, &c., are Semi-vowels.

The consonants **f, g, p, z**, are never used at the end of a word.

Note.—The Aspirate (or *breathing*) **h** follows in inflection the rule of palatals; and was originally, in many words, a harsh guttural (kh), like the Greek χ, or the Spanish **j**. Its later sound was very slight, and in most languages derived from Latin has quite disappeared. Sometimes, as in *aheneus* (= *aëneus*), it seems to be used only to separate two vowels. It is not reckoned as a consonant in Prosody.

2. Early Forms. — The alphabet in the time of Cicero (N. D. ii. 37) consisted of "one and twenty letters." These were, —

a, b, c, d, e, f, g, h, i, k, l, m, n, o, p, q, r, s, t, u, x.

y and **z** were added, in words derived from Greek. **i** and **u**, when used as consonants ("semi-vowels"), having the sound of **y** and **w**, are generally written **j** and **v**: as, **juvenis** for **iuuenis**.

a. In early use, **c** was not distinguished in form or sound from **g**. After the distinction was made, **C** was still used, conventionally, as the initial of names (**Gaius, Gnaeus**) beginning properly with **G**. It came, in later use, to take the place of **k**, which was retained only in abbreviations, or as the initial letter of a few words, as **Kalendae, Karthago**, in which it is followed by **a**.

b. Till after the age of Augustus, **u** was never, in good use, preceded in the same syllable by **u** or **v**. In many words, as in **volt, servos**, **o** was written where later custom allows **u**; while **c** was regularly used for **qu** in such words as **cum** (for **quum**), **ecus** (for **equus**), **relicus** (for **reliquus**), **locuntur** (for **loquuntur**), and the like; also in **cotidie** (for **quotidie**), and a few other words. The old forms **quom** (for **cum**) and **quor** (for **cur**) are also found.

c. At the end of a few words, — as **sed, apud, illud**, — **t** was anciently written instead of **d**. In words ending in **-s**, final **s** was often elided (Cic. Orat. 48), as in **qualist** (**qualis-est**); **plenu' fidei** (Senect. 1).

3. Changes. — Letters are often changed, according to general laws of inflection (*vowel-increase*), or to secure an easier or smoother sound (*euphonic change*); or have been altered or lost through long use (*phonetic decay*). Of such changes are the following: —

a. Vowels are strengthened in inflection and derivation (*vowel-increase*): as, **ăgo, ēgi** (cf. *tell, told*); **disco, dŏceo** (cf. *fall, fell; sit, set*); **pendo, pondus**; **persŏno, persōna**; **perfidus, fidus, foedus** (cf. *bind, band*).

NOTE. — The primitive vowel-sound may be assumed to be **a**, as in *father*. Starting with this, and gradually contracting the *palate*, we form in succession the sound of **e** (*ā*) and **i** (*ee*), leading to the semi-vowel **j** (*y*). By contracting the *lips*, we in like manner form the sound of **o** and **u** (*oo*), leading to the semi-vowel **v** (*w*). By contracting *both palate and lips*, we form the French sound of **u**, — in Greek **v**, and in Latin **y**. This, which is called the Vowel-Scale, is of great service in tracing the modifications of vowel-sounds. It may be represented thus: —

```
         a
      e     o
    i,j   y   v, u
```

b. Vowels are weakened by negligent pronunciation for long periods of time (*phonetic decay*). Thus, on one side of the scale, a becomes e, then i; or, on the other, becomes o, then u; while u and i meet in the French u (y): as, **agmen, agmĭnis; făcio, confĭcio, confectum; sălio, exsulto; sepĕlio, sepultus; ebur, ebŏris; maxŭmus, maxĭmus** (cf. *master, mister, mistress*).

c. Two vowels coming together are contracted into a single sound: as, **obit (obiit), cogo (co-ago), nil (nihil), debeo (dehĭbeo), coetus (coïtus), ingenī** (cf. *mayhem, maim*).

d. The semi-vowels **j** and **v** are lost before a vowel, contraction sometimes also taking place: as, **ōbicit (ŏbjicit), cōnicit (conjicit), cunctus (conjunctus), rursus (reversus), contio (conventio), mōtum (mŏvĭtum)**.

e. Between two vowels, or before **m** or **n**, **s** becomes **r**: as, **genus, generis; maereo, maestus; veternus (vetus-nus), carmen (casmen)**.

f. When two consonants come together by derivation, inflection, or composition, an easier pronunciation is secured thus:—

1. The first is entirely assimilated to the second. Thus, a liquid, — **m, n**, or (less frequently) **r** — before another liquid is changed to that liquid [but **r** is not changed to **m** or **n**]: as, *collego (con-lego), corrĭgo (com-rĕgo), illudo (in-ludo), illĭco (in lŏco), intellĕgo (inter-lĕgo), asellus (asin[u]lus)*. So **d** before **l**: as in *lapillus (lapĭdulus)*; and **b** (rarely) before a liquid: as, *summitto (submitto)*.

2. The former is assimilated in kind. Thus:—*a.* A sonant before a surd becomes surd: as, *tego, texi (x=cs), tectum; nubo, nupsi, nuptum; coquo, coxi, coctum*.—*b.* A surd before a sonant becomes sonant, as in *segmentum (seco)*.—*c.* A labial nasal before a dental mute sometimes becomes dental: *contendo (com-tendo), jandudum (jam dudum), quantus (quamtus)*.—*d.* A dental nasal before a labial sometimes becomes labial: as, *impono (in-pono)*.—*e.* **d** and **t** before **t** sometimes become **s** (see 4): as, *equester (equet-ter), est (edt)*.

3. The former is lost, having probably been first assimilated. Thus:—*a.* **d** and **t** are lost before **s**, but sometimes only assimilated: as, *pedes (pedets), vas (vads, vadis), esse (edse, edo)*.—*b.* **c** and **g** are lost before **t** and **s** when **l** or **r** precedes: as, *sartus (=sarctus, sarcio), mulsi (=mulgsi, mulgeo), indultus (=indulgtus, indulgeo)*.—*c.* **c** and **g** are sometimes lost before **m** and **n**: as, *exāmen (exagmen), luna (lucna), lumen (luc-men)*.

4. The second is partially assimilated to the first (as in English *wrecked* becomes, in pronouncing, *reckt*); in this case both are often changed. Thus, after **n** and **l**—rarely after other letters—**t** becomes **s** (the continued sound corresponding to the explosive **t**): as, *mansus (=mantus, maneo), pulsus (pello), casus (cado), passus (=pattus, patior), sparsus (=spargtus, spargo), tensus (tendo, but also tentus), fixus (figo, but fictus from fingo), maximus (for mag-timus), lapsus (labor), passus (pando)*.

NOTE.—After **m**, before **s** or **t**, **p** is inserted for euphony: as, *sumo, sumpsi, sumptum*. So *hiemps* for *hiems*.

g. Especially the final consonant of prepositi[ons]
to the initial consonant of verbs.

Thus, **ad** is assimilated before **c, g, p, t**; le[ss before]
l, r, s, and rarely before **m**; while before **f, n,**
to be preferred; — **ab** is not assimilated, but ma[y become]
au, or **abs;** — in **com (con, co), m** is retained [before]
assimilated before **l, n, r**; is changed to **n** bef[ore]
s, v; varies between **m** and **n** before **p**; is som[etimes]
(otherwise **n**) before **r** and **l**; and loses the fina[l in]
niveo, conitor, conubium; — **in** usually changes **n**
p; before **l** the better orthography retains **n**;
assimilated before **c, f, g, p**, and sometimes be[fore]
before **r**; and, in early Latin, **b** of these prep[ositions]
becomes **p** before **s** or **t**. The inseparable **am**[b is a]
consonant, and **m** is sometimes assimilated; — **cir[cum before]**
a vowel; — **s** of **dis** before a vowel becomes **r**, [before a conso-]
nant is lost or assimilated; — the **d** of **red** and **se**[d is assimilated]
before a consonant.

NOTE. — In most of these cases the later [writers preserve the]
unaltered forms throughout; but the changes giv[en have classical]
authority. Others, which are corruptions of tl[he original (as]
assum for *adsum*), would better be avoided.

h. The combinations **ci** and **ti** before a vow[el are inter-]
changed in many words: as in *nuntius* or *nunci[us, concio or con-]*
cio; but in these cases only one is correct: as, [etc.]

NOTE. — The substitution of **c** for **t** is an e[vidence of]
decay, and belongs to a later period of the langu[age;]
and in Spanish, **c,** has regularly taken the place [of ti in such]
nations: as in *nazione, nacion.* The sound of **s** (a[lways]
traceable in them led gradually to the adoption of [the]
sound of **c** before **e** or **i**.

i. The aspirate **h** is occasionally used to [harden the]
sound of **c,** as in **pulcher** for **pulcer.** Many [words are found]
sometimes with and sometimes without an in[itial h, as arena]
or **harena, ariolor** or **hariolor, erus** or **her**[us; the combina-]
tions **ph, th,** are found only in words taken fro[m the Greek.]

k. The following words are variously spelt ir [different authors,]
inferior or rejected forms being marked †: —

Adolescens, adulescens; ancora, †*anchora; ann[us,* †*anus;]*
artus; cæcus, cæcus; cælum, cœlum; cæruleus, cœrul[eus;]
cæspes, cespes; ceteri, †*cæteri; cœna, cæna, cena; co[njux,]*
junx, †*conjux; contio,* †*concio; dicio,* †*ditio; dumt[axat;]*
stola, epistula; eumdem, eundem; exsisto, existo (a[nd so]
of ex before s); femina, †*fœmina; fenus, fænus, f[ænus;]*
hædus, †*hœdus; hiems(ps),* †*hyems; idcirco,* †*iccirco;*
†*inclytus; intellego, intelligo; lacrima,* †*lacryma; lite[ra, lit-]*
tus; lubet, libet; mœror, mæror; milia, †*millia; m[ille;]*
nequidquam, nequiquam; numquam, nunquam; †*nu[mmus;]*
paulus; quicquid, quidquid; religio, relligio; retuli, r[

solennis, solemnis; solers, sollers; sulfur, †*sulphur; tamquam, tanquam; thesaurus, thensaurus; thus, tus; tiro,* †*tyro; umquam, unquam; ungo, unguo; verto, vorto;* also, the gerund-forms *-endus* or *-undus;* and the superlative *-imus* or *-umus.*

NOTE. — Many of the above variations are due to the practice of writing from dictation, or by the ear, by which most MS. copies of the classics were made, — a single reader often dictating to numerous copyists, whose spelling was often corrupt, and without authority.

4. *Combinations.* — Two words are often united in writing, and sometimes in sound.

a. Conjunctions or other particles are thus connected: as in **etenim, jamdiu, siquis,** and **siquidem**.

So the adverbial combinations **quare, quamobrem,** &c., as in English *nevertheless, notwithstanding.*

b. The verb **est,** *is,* is joined with the preceding word, especially in the old poets, or when the two would be united by elision: as, **homost, periculumst.**

c. Similar contractions are found in **vin' (visne), scin' (scisne), sis (si vis), sodes (si audes),** as in English, *don't, won't.*

5. *Syllables.* — In the division of syllables, a single consonant between two vowels is to be written with the latter.

a. This rule is usually extended to double consonants, or any combination of consonants which can be used to begin a word: as, **ho-spes, ma-gnus, di-xit.**

b. In compounds, the parts should be separated: as, **ab-est, ob-latus.**

NOTE. — Custom allows many other departures from the rule.

c. A syllable preceded by a vowel in the same word is called *pure;* when preceded by a consonant, *impure.*

d. An initial syllable ending, or a final syllable beginning, with a vowel, is called *open;* otherwise, it is called *close.*

2. PRONUNCIATION.

1. *Roman.* — The Roman pronunciation of the Vowels was, no doubt, nearly like the Italian; which, with little variation, is that found in most of the continental languages of Europe. That of some of the Consonants is more uncertain. In the system of pronunciation founded on ancient use, the long and short vowels are sounded respectively as follows:—

ā as in *father*.	ă as in *fast*.
ē ,, *rein*.	ĕ ,, *met*.
ī ,, *machine*.	ĭ ,, *pin*.
ō ,, *holy*.	ŏ ,, *wholly*.
ū ,, *rude*.	ŭ ,, *full*.

NOTE.— It is probable that y (also u in *maxŭmus*, &c.) was similar to the French u; it is usually, however, sounded like i.

a. The final or unaccented *open* sound of the vowels is nearly as in the last syllable of *comma, yesterday, pity, hollow, cuckoo*.

b. In Diphthongs, each vowel has its proper sound: thus, ae has nearly the sound of *ay*, au of *ow*, oe of *oy*, ui of *we*.

c. Of consonants, c and g are always hard, as in *can, give*; j has the sound of y, v of w, and n before palatals of ng; the combination bs is like ps, ch like k, and ph like f.

NOTE.— The sound of the vowels and diphthongs, as above given, has been generally adopted in this country. In regard to the consonants c, g, j, v, there is still considerable difference of usage.

2. *Modern*.— Modern custom has generally allowed Latin to be pronounced in each country according to the rules of its own language. What is known as the *English Method* adopts the following:—

a. The vowels and consonants have the same sound as in English. But there are no silent letters (except in scanning verse, by the usage called Elision); such words as **dies, mare, audiere, pauperiēi**, having each as many syllables as vowels or diphthongs.

b. By American custom, final a is pronounced in the Italian way, as in *comma*. But in the monosyllables **a, da, sta, qua**, some persons retain the English sound.

c. The diphthongs ae, oe, are pronounced like *ee*; au like *aw*; eu like *ew*; ei and ui like *i* in *kite*; es and (in plural words) os at the end of a word, as in the English *disease, morose*.

d. The consonants c and g are made *soft* (like s and j) before e, i, y, ae, oe, eu; ch is always hard, as in *chasm*.

3. QUANTITY.

1. Quantity is the *relative time* occupied in pronouncing a syllable,— a long syllable being equal to two short ones.

QUANTITY. — ACCENT.

NOTE. — The distinction of Quantity was carefully observed by the ancients, but came to be almost wholly disregarded in later times except in the composition of Latin verse.

2. Some of the most general rules of quantity are the following: —

a. A vowel before another vowel is short: as in **vĭa, nĭhil.**

b. A diphthong is long: as in **aedes, foedus.**

c. A syllable formed by contraction is long: as, **mī (mihi); nīl (nihil); intrārat (intraverat); nēmo (nĕ hŏmo).**

NOTE. — In many text-books and old editions, contraction is denoted by a circumflex: as, *mî, intrârat.*

d. A syllable in which a vowel is followed by two consonants, or a double consonant, is long: as in **rēctus, dūxit.** Sometimes the vowel itself is made long, as before **ns** in **praesēns.**

e. A syllable in which a short vowel is followed by a mute with l or r is *common,* — that is, it may be long in verse: as, **ălăcris.**

REMARK. — Many final syllables, originally long, are always found short in classic Latin: for example, the stem-vowel a of the first declension.

NOTE. — The sign (¯) denotes that a vowel is *long;* (˘) that it is *short;* (*) that it is common.

For particular rules of Quantity, see § **78.**

4. ACCENT.

1. The accent of Latin words never falls on the final syllable, but is confined to one of the two preceding.

2. The following are general rules of accent: —

a. Words of two syllables are always accented on the first syllable: as, **ĕ′rant,** *they were;* **dĭ′ēs,** *day.*

b. Words of more than two syllables are accented on the Penult, if that is long: as, **ămī′cus,** *friend;* if it is short or common, then on the Antepenult: as, **dŏ′mĭnus, ă′lacris.**

NOTE. — The Penult is the last syllable but one; the Antepenult, the last but two.

c. When an Enclitic is joined to a word, the accent falls on the syllable next before the enclitic, whether long or short: as, **dĕă′que, ămārĕ′ve, tĭbi′ne, ită′que,** *and so,* as distinguished from **i′tăque,** *therefore.*

NOTE. — The acute accent (´) is sometimes use[d]
voice; the grave (`), to mark an *adverb* or *conjunct*[ion]
(ˆ), the *ablative* in **a**, the perfect in **ēre**, or a contr[action]

5. INFLECTION.

1. Inflection is a change made in the fo[rm of a word, to]
show its grammatical relations.

a. Changes of inflection sometimes take pla[ce in the body of a]
word, but oftener in its termination: as, **vox**, *a [voice]*,
a voice; **vŏco**, *I call;* **vŏcat**, *he calls;* **vocāvi**[t, *he called.*]

b. Terminations of inflection had originall[y a]
meaning, and correspond nearly to the use of p[er]
sonal pronouns in English: thus, in **vŏcat**, [is]
equivalent to *he* or *she;* and in **vōcis**, to the pr[onoun]

c. Changes of inflection in the body of a v[erb denote]
relations of *time* or *manner*, and correspond to t[he auxiliary]
verbs in English: thus, in **frangit** (root **frag**[-], *he is*
breaking, the form of the word indicates Present
action; while in **frēgit**, *he broke* or *has broken*, it [denotes Past]
or Completed action.

2. The body of a word, to which the [termination is]
attached, is called the STEM.

a. The Stem contains the *idea* of the word [itself;]
but, in general, it cannot be used without so[me ending to]
express these. Thus the stem **vōc-** denotes *vo*[ice: with -s]
it becomes **vox**, *a voice* or *the voice*, as the subj[ect of an]
action; with **-is** it becomes **vōcis**, and signifie[s of a voice.]

b. A still more primitive form, expressing [the idea in]
definitely, and common also to other words, eith[er in Latin or]
other languages, is called a ROOT. For examp[le, the root is]
found in the Sanskrit *tíshṭhâmi*, Greek ἴστημι,
stare, German *stehen*, and English *stand*.

Again, the root of the stem **vōc-** is **vŏc**, w[hich does not]
call, or *I call*, or *calling*, but merely *call;* and [does not]
mean any thing without terminations. With **ā** [added it forms]
the stem of the present **vŏcāmus**, *we call;* w[ith **āvi**, the]
stem of the perfect **vŏcāvi**, *I called;* with **āt**[o, the]
stem of the participle **vocātos**, *called;* with [**ātio**,]
the stem of **vocationis**, *of a calling*. With its [short form]
it becomes the stem of **vox**, *a voice* (that by wh[ich we call);]
ālis added it means *belonging to a voice;* with **ŭ**[la]

NOTE. — Thus, in inflected languages, words are built up from Roots, which at a very early time, long before Latin was a distinct language, were used alone to express ideas, as is now done in Chinese. Roots are modified into Stems, which, by inflection, become Words. The process by which they are modified, in the various forms of derivatives and compounds, is called Stem-building.

c. The Stem is sometimes the same with the Root: as in **dŭc-is, fer-t;** but is more frequently formed from the root, either (1) by changing or lengthening its vowel, as in **rēg-is, dūc-o**; (2) by the addition or insertion of a consonant, as in **tendo, pango**; (3) by the addition of a terminal vowel, as in **fugis, fuga**; or (4) by derivation and composition, following the laws of development peculiar to the language.

d. The terminations of inflection are variously modified by combining with the final vowel or consonant of the Stem, leading to the various forms of Declension and Conjugation.

NOTE. — A termination beginning with a vowel is called an *open affix;* one beginning with a consonant, a *close affix.* When a close affix is joined to a consonant-stem, there is usually either a euphonic change, as *rexi* for *reg-si*, or a vowel appears, as *reg-i-bus*. But in most cases, what is called a connecting vowel really belongs to the stem, as in *voca-mus, regi-mus*.

3. Nouns, Adjectives, Pronouns, and Participles have inflections of *declension,* to denote gender, number, and case; Adjectives and Adverbs, of *comparison,* to denote degree; and Verbs of *conjugation,* to denote voice, mood, tense, number, and person.

4. Those parts of speech which are not inflected are called PARTICLES: these are Prepositions, Conjunctions, and Interjections, with Adverbs of *time, place,* and *manner.*

NOTE. — The term Particles is sometimes limited to such words as **num, -ne, an** (*interrogative*), **non, ne** (*negative*), **si** (*conditional*), &c., which are used simply to indicate the form or construction of a sentence. Interjections are not properly to be classed among parts of speech, and differ little from inarticulate sounds. For convenience, a list is given of those in most common use, following the conjunctions (p. 95).

6. GENDER.

1. The gender of Latin nouns is either *natural* or *grammatical.*

a. Natural gender is distinction as to the sex of the object denoted: as, **puer**, *boy*: **puella**, *girl*: **donum**, *gift*.

b. Many masculine nouns have a corresponding feminine form: as, **servus, serva,** *slave;* **cliens, clienta,** *client;* **victor, victrix,** *conqueror.* Most designations of persons (as, **nauta,** *sailor,* **miles,** *soldier*), usually though not necessarily male, are masculine.

c. Grammatical gender is a like distinction where no sex exists in the object, and is shown by the form of the adjective joined with it: as, **lapis magnus** (M.), *a great stone;* **manus mea** (F.), *my hand.*

d. A few neuter nouns are used to designate persons as belonging to a class: as, **mancipium tuum,** *your slave.* Names of *classes* or *bodies* of persons may be of either gender: as, **exercitus** (M.), **acies** (F.), and **agmen** (N.), *army;* and the feminine **operae,** *workmen,* **copiae,** *troops.*

NOTE. — What we call *grammatical gender* is in most cases the product of the imagination at a rude age, when language was in the course of growth. Thus a River was seen, or a Wind was felt, as *a living creature,* violent and strong, and so is masculine; a Month is a *guide* or *divider* of tasks, and so is masculine; and the fable of Atlas shows how similar living attributes were ascribed to Mountains, which, in the northern fables, are the bones of giants. Again, the Earth, or a country or city, seems the *mother* of its progeny; the Tree shelters and ripens its fruit, as a brooding bird its nest of eggs; and, to this day, a Ship is always referred to by a feminine pronoun.

Again, in the East and South, the Sun, from its fierce heat and splendor, is masculine, and its paler attendant, the Moon, feminine; while, among northern nations, the Sun (perhaps for its comforting warmth) is feminine, and the Moon (the appointer of works and days) masculine. The rules of grammatical gender only repeat and extend these early workings of the fancy.

2. Names of Male beings, together with Rivers, Winds, and Mountains are *masculine;* names of Female beings, Cities, Countries, Plants, of many Animals (especially Birds), and of most abstract Qualities, are *feminine.*

NOTE. — Most of the above may be recognized by their terminations, according to the rules of gender under the several declensions.

a. Names of Rivers are masculine, except a few, chiefly in **a.**

These are *Albula, Allia, Druentia, Duria, Garumna, Matrŏna, Mosella;* also *Lethe* and *Styx.* Many are variable.

NOTE. — Names of Months are properly Adjectives, the masculine noun *mensis* being understood.

b. Names of Towns, Islands, and Trees in **us** are feminine; also, many names of Plants and Gems in **us.**

c. Indeclinable nouns, Terms or Phrases used as nouns, and words quoted merely for their forms, are neuter: as, **nihil,** *nothing;* **gummi,** *gum;* **scire tuum,** *your knowing;* **triste vale,** *a sad farewell;* **hoc ipsum diu,** *this same word* diu; **illud ruisse, illud ardēre** (Plin.), *that crash, that blaze.*

3. Many nouns may be either masculine or feminine, according to the sex of the object. These are said to be of COMMON GENDER: as, **exsul,** *exile;* **bos,** *ox or cow.*

NOTE. — When a noun signifying a thing without life is both masculine and feminine, — as, **dies,** *day;* **finis,** *end,* — it is sometimes said to be of Doubtful Gender.

4. A few names of animals are always connected with adjectives of the same gender, either masculine or feminine, independent of sex. They are called EPICENE.

Thus **lepus,** *hare,* is always masculine, and **vulpes,** *fox,* feminine. To denote a male fox we may say, **vulpes mascula;** or a female hare, **lepus femina.**

7. CASE.

There are in Latin six Cases, which express the relations of nouns to other words. They are usually put in the following order: 1. Nominative; 2. Genitive; 3. Dative; 4. Accusative; 5. Vocative; 6. Ablative.

1. The NOMINATIVE is the case of the Subject of a proposition: as,

pater meus adest, *my father is here.*

2. The GENITIVE (*of*) is used like the English possessive; also with many adjectives and verbs, especially those of memory or feeling: as,

patris ejus amīcus miserētur mei, *his father's friend pities me.*

3. The DATIVE (*to* or *for*) is the case of the Indirect Object, and is used to denote the person whose interest is concerned: as,

dedit mihi cultellum: magno mihi usui erat, *he gave me a pocket-knife: it was of great service to me.*

4. The ACCUSATIVE (*objective*) is the case of the Direct Object, and is used after most prepositions: as,

pater me ad se vocavit et in hortum duxit, [my] *father called me to him, and led me into the garden.*

5. The VOCATIVE is used in address: as,

huc vĕni, care mi filiŏle, *come here, my dear little son.*

NOTE.— As the Vocative is independent of the other words in a sentence, it is by some grammarians not reckoned as a Case.

6. The ABLATIVE (*by, from, with*) is used with many verbs and prepositions, especially to denote separation or instrument: as,

in horto ludebāmus, et cultello me laesit, *we were playing in the garden, and he hurt me with a knife.*

NOTE.— All, excepting the nominative and vocative, are by the ancient grammarians called "Oblique Cases."

7. In names of towns and a few other words appear traces of another case (the LOCATIVE), denoting the *place where*,— generally the same in form as the dative (§ 55. 3. *c.*): as,

Rōmae vel Athēnis esse velim, *I should like to be at Rome or Athens.*

8. DECLENSION.

1. There are five Declensions, or modes of declining nouns. They are distinguished by the termination of the Genitive Singular, and by the final letter (characteristic) of the Stem.

DECL.		Gen. Sing.			Characteristic	
	1.		ae		ă	(anciently ā)
,,	2.	,,	i (ius)	,,	ŏ	
,,	3.	,,	ĭs	,,	ĭ or a Consonant	
,,	4.	,,	ūs (uis)	,,	ŭ	
,,	5.	,,	ēi	,,	ē	

a. The stem of a noun may be found, if a consonant-stem, by omitting the case-ending; if a vowel-stem, by substituting for the case-ending the characteristic vowel.

NOTE.— For the division of vowel and consonant-stems in the Third Declension, see § 11.

b. The Nominative of most masculine and feminine nouns (except in the first declension) is formed from the Stem by adding s.

NOTE 1.— Many, however, end in o, or in the liquids l, n, r,— the original s (sometimes with the final letter also) having been lost through phonetic decay. In some (as in *filius*) the stem-vowel is modified before the final s; and in some, as in *ager*, a vowel is inserted in the stem.

NOTE 2.— The s of the nominative is the remnant of an old demonstrative sa, which is found (with modifications) in the Sanskrit *personal pronoun*, in the Greek *article*, and in the English *she*.

2. The following are general Rules of Declension:—

a. The Vocative is always the same with the Nominative, except in the singular of nouns in **us** of the second declension.

NOTE.— In the first and second declensions the vocative ends in the (modified) stem-vowel. Most of the words likely to be used in address are of this form; and, in practice, few other words have a vocative.

b. In Neuters, the nominative and accusative are always alike, and in the plural end in **ă**.

c. Except in some neuters, the accusative singular always ends in **m**, and the accusative plural in **s**.

d. In the last three declensions (and in a few cases in the others) the dative singular ends in **i**.

e. The dative and ablative plural are always alike.

f. The genitive plural always ends in **um**.

3. *Case-Endings.* The original terminations of the Cases, in Latin, were probably the following:—

	Sing. M., F.	N.	Plur. M., F.	N.
Nom.	s (or lost)	m, –	es	ă
Gen.	os (is)		um, rum(sum)	
Dat.	i		ibus	
Acc.	m, em	m, –	es	ă
Abl.	ed		ibus	

NOTE.— These became so worn by use, and so united with the stem, that they are distinguishable only in consonant-stems. In some instances, one case was substituted for another, or two were merged in one. The combinations are given below as *case-endings*. The name "stem" is sometimes, conveniently though incorrectly, given to that part of the word — as serv- in servus — which precedes the case-ending.

DECL. I.	II.	III.	IV.	V.
Sing.				
N. a *ĕ, as, es*	us, um os, on *eus*	s – (See p. 23.)	ŭs, ū	ēs
G. æ (ai) *es*	ī (ius) *es* o, u *ei*	ĭs *yos, ŏs*	ūs (uis)	ēi (e)
D. æ (ai)	ō (i) . *ei, eo*	ī	uī (ū)	ēi (e)
A. am *an, en*	um on *ea*	em (im) *in, yn* ă	um, ū	em
V. ă *e*	ĕ *a* *eu*	(as nom.) *ĭ, y*	ŭs, ū	ēs
A. ā *ē*	ō *eo*	e (i), ī	ū	ē
Plur.				
N. V. æ	ī ă	ēs, a, ia *ĕs*	ūs, ua	ēs
G. ārum (um)	ōrum (um, om) *ōn*	um, ium	uum	ērum
D. A. īs (ābus)	īs (ōbus)	ĭbus	ĭbus (ūbus)	ēbus
A. ās	ōs	ēs (īs), a, ia *ăs*	ūs, ua	ēs

N.B. Rare forms in *parenthesis*; Greek forms in *italics*.

NOUNS.

9. First Declension.

The Stem of nouns of the First Declension ends in **a**. Latin nouns have the Nominative like the stem.

	SINGULAR.	PLURAL.
Nom.	stellă, *a star.*	stellae, *stars.*
Gen.	stellae, *of a star.*	stellārum, *of stars.*
Dat.	stellae, *to a star.*	stellīs, *to stars.*
Acc.	stellam, *a star.*	stellās, *stars.*
Voc.	stellă, *thou star!*	stellae, *ye stars!*
Abl.	stellā *with a star.*	stellīs, *with stars.*

1. Gender. Most nouns of the first declension are Feminine. Nearly all the exceptions are such as are masculine from their signification: as, **nauta**, *sailor.* Also, **Hadria**, *the Adriatic.*

2. Case Forms. — *a.* The genitive singular anciently ended in āi, which is occasionally found in a few authors: as, **aulāi**. The same ending occurs in the dative, but only as a diphthong.

b. There is also an old genitive in ās, found in the word **familias** used in certain combinations, as, **păter (māter, filius, filia) familias**, *father of a family, &c.*

c. The Locative form for the singular ends in **ae**, and for the plural in **is**: as, **Romae, Athēnis**.

d. The genitive plural is sometimes found in **um** instead of **ārum**, especially in compounds with -cŏla and -gĕna, signifying *dwelling* and *descent:* as, **caelicŏlum**, *of the heavenly ones.*

e. The dative and ablative plural of **dea**, *goddess*, **filia**, *daughter*, **liberta**, *freed-woman*, **equa**, *mare*, **mula**, *she-mule*, end in an older form **-ābus**. But, except when the two sexes (as in wills, &c.) are mentioned together, the form in **is** is also used.

3. Greek Nouns. — Some Greek nouns (chiefly proper names) end in ās, ēs (M.), and ē (F.) in the nominative, and ān or ēn in the accusative; those in ē have the genitive in ēs (stem ā or ē): as,

	comet (M.)	*laurel* (F.)		
N.	comētes (a)	daphnē	Ænēās	Anchīses
G.	comētæ	daphnēs (æ)	Ænēæ	Anchīsæ
D.	comētæ	daphnē (æ)	Ænēæ	Anchīsæ
Ac.	comēten(am)	daphnēn	Ænēān (am)	Anchīsēn
V.	comētă	daphnē	Ænēă (ā)	Anchīsē (ă)
Ab.	comētā (ē)	daphnē (ā)	Ænēā	Anchīsē (ā)

NOTE. — This form is found only in the singular; the plural is regular: as, *cometæ, arum*, &c. It includes (besides proper names) about thirty-five words, several being names of plants; among others the following, those marked † having also regular forms in **a**: — bule, *council;* geometres, *geometer;* † grammatice, *grammar;* harpe, *sickle;* magice, *magic;* † musice, *music;* † ode, *ode;* pandectes, *repertory;* † patriarches, *patriarch;* † prophetes, *prophet;* sophistes, *sophist;* † tetrarches, *tetrarch;* thymele, *leader's-stand;* † tiaras, *tiara.*

10. SECOND DECLENSION.

The Stem of nouns of the Second Declension ends in **o** (as of *vir, viro-*, and of *servus, servo-*).

NOTE. — This form is an original ă-stem, to which the ā-stem of the first declension is the corresponding feminine.

1. The Nominative is formed from the Stem by adding **s** (in neuters **m**), the characteristic ŏ being weakened to ŭ.

2. In most nouns whose stem ends in **ro-**, the **s** is not added, but the **o** is lost, **e** being inserted before **r**.

Thus **ager**, *field* (stem **agro-**), is the same as the Greek ἀγρός. The exceptions are, *hesperus, humerus, juniperus, morus, numerus, uterus.*

SINGULAR.

	Boy.	*Book.*	*Slave.*	*Gift.*
Nom.	puĕr	lĭbĕr	servŭs (ŏs)	dōnum
Gen.	puĕrī	librī	servī	donī
Dat.	puĕrō	librō	servō	donō
Acc.	puĕrum	librŭm	servum (om)	donum
Voc.	puĕr	liber	servĕ	donum
Abl.	puĕrō	librō	servō	donō

PLURAL.

Nom.	puĕrī	librī	servī	donă
Gen.	puĕrōrum	librōrum	servōrum	donōrum
Dat.	puĕrīs	librīs	servīs	donīs
Acc.	puĕrōs	librōs	servōs	donă
Voc.	puĕrī	librī	servī	donă
Abl.	puĕrīs	librīs	servīs	donīs

NOTE. — The old form **os, om** (for **us, um**), is sometimes used after **u** or **v**: as, *servos, servom* (§ 1. 2. *b.*).

3. Gender. — Nouns ending in **us (os), er, ir**, are Masculine (exc. on p. 16); those ending in **um (on)** are Neuter. (But which stems are M. or N. can only be learned from the Dictionary.)

a. But names of towns in **us (os)** are Feminine: as, **Corinthus**. Also, **arctus (os)**, *the Polar Bear;* **alvus**, *belly;* **carbăsus**, *linen* (plural **carbăsa**, *sails*, N.); **cŏlus**, *distaff;* **hŭmus**, *ground;* **vannus**, *winnowing-shovel;* with many names of Plants and Gems.

b. The following are Neuter: **pelăgus**, *sea;* **vīrus**, *poison;* **vulgus** (rarely M.), *the crowd.* Their accusative, as of all neuters, is the same as the nominative.

4. *Case Forms.* *a.* The Locative form for the singular of this declension ends in **i**: as, **humi**, *on the ground;* **Corinthi**, *at Corinth.* For the plural, **is**: as, **Philippis**, *at Philippi*.

b. The genitive of nouns in **ius** or **ium** is correctly written with a single **i**: as, **fĭlī**, *of a son;* **ingĕ'ni**, *of genius.*
The same contraction occurs with the gen. sing. and the dat. and abl. plur. of nouns in **āius** and **ēius**: as, **Grāis, Pompēī**.

c. Proper names in **ius** lose **e** in the vocative: as, **Vergĭ'li**; also, **filius**, *son*, **genius**, *divine guardian;* and the possessive **meus**, *my*: as, **audi, mi fili**, *hear, my son.*

d. Greek names in **īus** have the vocative **īe**; and adjectives derived from proper names — as **Lacedaemonius** — also form the vocative in **ie**.

e. In the genitive plural, **um** (or, after **v**, **om**) is often found for **ōrum**, especially in poets.

f. **Deus**, *god*, has vocative **deus**; plural, nominative and vocative **dei** or **di** (**dii**); dative and ablative **deis** or **dis** (**diis**).
For the genitive plural **deorum, divum** or **divom** (from **divus**) is often used.

5. The following stems in **ĕro**, in which **e** belongs to the stem, retain **e** throughout: **puer**, *boy;* **gener**, *son-in-law;* **socer**, *father-in-law;* **vesper**, *evening;* with compounds in **-fer** and **-ger**: as, **lūcĭfer, -fĕri**, *light-bringer;* **armĭger, -gĕri**, *armor-bearer.*

a. **Vir**, *man*, has the genitive **vĭri**; the adjective **satur**, *sated*, has **satŭri**; **vesper** has abl. **vespere** (loc. **vesperi**).

b. **Lĭber**, a name of Bacchus, also has **Lĭbĕri**; so, too, the plur. **līberi**, *children.*

6. The following, which insert **e**, are declined like **līber**: **ager**, *field;* **aper**, *boar;* **arbiter**, *judge;* **auster**, *south-wind;* **caper**, *goat;* **coluber**, *snake;* **conger**, *sea-eel;* **culter**, *knife;* **faber**, *smith;* **fiber**, *beaver;* **geometer**, *geometer;* **magister**, *master;* **minister**, *servant;* **oleaster**, *wild-olive;* **onager** (**grus**), *wild-ass;* **scomber** (**brus**), *mackerel.*

7. Greek Nouns. *a.* Many Greek names in **eus**, as **Orpheus** (being of the third declension in Greek), have gen. **ei** or **eos**, dat. **ei**; acc. **ea**; voc. **eu**; abl. **eo**.

b. Many in **es**, belonging to the third declension, have also a gen. in **i**: as, **Thucydidi**.

c. Some Greek names in **er** have a form in **us**: as, **Teucer, Teucrus**.

d. About twenty words have the Greek ending **ŏs** (M. or F.) or **ŏn** (N.): as, **lōtos**, *water-lily*; **parēlion**, *mock-sun*. Among these are the following: —

Barbitos (on), *lyre*; miltos, *cinnabar*; mythos, *fable*; nomos, *district*; rhythmos, *rhythm*; scopos, *aim*; spodos (F.), *dross*.

11. Third Declension.

Nouns of the Third Declension are most conveniently classed according to their Stems, whether ending in a *vowel*, a *liquid*, or a *mute*.

I. Vowel-Stems.

1. Vowel-stems of this declension end in **i**. Thus that of **turris** is **turri-**; and that of **mare, mari-**.

a. Nouns of this class are *parisyllabic*; that is, the oblique cases of the singular have no more syllables than the nominative. (For exceptions in **al, ar**, see 2, *c*.)

b. A few stems ending in **u-**, as of **grus, sus**, were treated as consonant-stems. (See III. 4, *a*.)

2. The Nominative, except in neuters, is formed from the stem by adding **s**.

a. About thirty nouns (as **nubes**) change **ĭ** to **ē** in the nominative (Compare Note, p. 22).

These are *acinăces, alces, cædes, cautes, clades, compăges, contăges, crates, fames, feles, fides, labes, meles, moles, nubes, proles, propăges, sedes, sepes, sordes, strages, subŏles, sudes, tabes, torques, tudes, vates, vehes, verres.*

b. The nominative of a few stems in **ri-** does not add **s**, but loses **i**, inserting **e** before **r**. These are **imber, linter, uter, venter**.

c. The nominative of neuters is the same as the stem, with the change of **ĭ** to **ĕ**. But, when **i** is preceded by **al** or **ar**, the **e** is lost (except in **collare, mare, navale, tibiale**).

Note. — This latter class were originally neuters of adjectives in **alis, aris**; and, when used as adjectives, retain the **e**. They are the following: *anĭmal, cervĭcal, cubĭtal, putĕal, toral, tribūnal; calcar, cochlear, exemplar, lacūnar, laquear, lumĭnar, palear, pulvĭnar, torcŭlar, vectĭgal*.

THIRD DECLENSION.

SINGULAR.

	Tower (F.).	Cloud (F.).	Sea (N.).	Spur (N.).
Nom.	turrĭs	nūbēs	mărĕ	calcăr
Gen.	turrĭs	nubĭs	marĭs	calcărĭs
Dat.	turrī	nubī	marī	calcārī
Acc.	turrim (em)	nubem	mărĕ	calcăr
Voc.	turrĭs	nubēs	marĕ	calcăr
Abl.	turrī (ĕ)	nubĕ	marī	calcārī

PLURAL.

	Tower	Cloud	Sea	Spur
Nom.	turrēs	nubēs	maria	calcaria
Gen.	turrium	nubium	marium	calcarium
Dat.	turrĭbus	nubĭbus	marĭbus	calcarĭbus
Acc.	turrīs (ēs)	nubēs	maria	calcaria
Voc.	turrēs	nubēs	maria	calcaria
Abl.	turrĭbus	nubĭbus	marĭbus	calcarĭbus

3. *Case Forms.* *a.* The regular form of the accusative singular, M. and F., is **im** (as **am, um, em** of the other vowel-declensions). But, in most nouns, this was supplanted by the consonant-form **em**; and it is only retained in the following: —

1. Exclusively (1) in Greek nouns and names of rivers; (2) in *buris, cucŭmis, ravis, sitis, tussis, vis*; (3) in adverbs in **tim** (being acc. of nouns in **tis**), with *partim* and *amussim;*

2. Along with **em** in *febris, restis, turris, secŭris, sementis,* and (in one or two passages) in many other words.

b. The regular form of the ablative singular is **ī** (as in the other declensions ā, ō, ū, ē, with loss of the original **d**). This was also supplanted by **ĕ**, and retained only —

1. Exclusively (1) in those above having accusative in **im**; also *securis*, and the following adjectives used as nouns: *æqualis, annalis, aqualis, consularis, gentilis, molaris, primipilaris, tribulis;* (2) in neuters (as above), except *baccar, jubar,* and sometimes (in verse) *mare, rete;*

2. Along with **e** in *avis, clavis, febris, finis, ignis* (always *aquâ et igni interdici*), *imber, navis, ovis, pelvis, puppis, sementis, strigĭlis, turris;* and the following adjectives used as nouns: *affinis, bipennis, canalis, familiaris, natalis, rivalis, sapiens, triremis, vocalis.*

3. The ablative of **fames**, *hunger*, is always of the Fifth declension. The defective **mane**, *morning*, has sometimes abl. **mani**.

4. Most names of towns in **e** — as *Præneste, Cære* — and the mountain *Soracte,* have the ablative in **e.**

c. The regular nominative plural would be **īs**, but this is rarely found. The regular accusative **īs** is common, but not exclusively used in any word.

d. The regular genitive plural **ium** is retained by all except the following: —

(1) *ambāges* and *volucris* (always *um*); (2) *vates* (commonly *um*); (3) *apis, cædes, clades, subŏles* (rarely *um*); (4) *canis, juvĕnis, mensis*, had not originally vowel-stems, and retain *um*; but *mensis* has both.

4. *Greek Nouns*. — A few Greek nouns in **is** have the acc. im or in, voc. ĭ, abl. ī.

Many in **ēs** have forms of the First or Second Declension: as, **Achilles**, gen. ei or i, dat. i, acc. ēn, ea, voc. ĕ, abl. ī.

NOTE. — Nouns such as *urbs, pars*, having the genitive plural **ium** and the accusative (occasionally) **īs**, were originally vowel-stems.

II. LIQUID STEMS.

In nouns whose stem ends in a liquid (**l, n, r**), the nominative has no termination, but is the same as the stem, except when modified as follows: —

a. Final **n** of the stem is dropped in masculines and feminines, except some Greek nouns: as, **leōn-is, leo**; **legiōn-is, legio**.

b. Stems ending in **dĭn-, gĭn-** (mostly feminine) retain in the nominative an original **o**: as, **virgo**. Those in **ĭn-** preceded by any other consonant retain an original **ĕ**: as, **carmĕn, ĭnis**, N.; **cornicen, ĭnis**, M. (Exceptions IV. 2, *b*.)

c. Nouns whose stem ends in **tr** retain in the nominative an original **e**: as, **pater** (compare I. 2, *b*.).

d. In neuters whose stem ends in **ĕr, ŏr, ŭr**, the **r** was originally **s**, which is retained in the nominative, **ŏ** of the stem being weakened into **ŭ**: as, **opŭs, ĕris**: **corpŭs, ŏris**. A few masc. and fem. stems also retain **s**. (Exceptions IV. 2, *b*.)

e. Stems in **ll, rr**, lose one of these liquids in the nominative.

f. The following have gen. plur. **ium**: **glis, mas, ren, mus**.

	SING. *Consul.*	PLUR.	SING. *Name.*	PLUR.
Nom.	consŭl	consŭlēs	nōmĕn	nomĭna
Gen.	consŭlis	consŭlum	nomĭnis	nomĭnum
Dat.	consŭli	consŭlĭbus	nomĭni	nominibus
Acc.	consŭlem	consŭlēs	nomen	nomĭna
Voc.	consŭl	consŭlēs	nomen	nomĭna
Abl.	consŭle	consŭlĭbus	nomĭne	nominibus

	Honor, M.	Lion, M.	Father, M.	Tree, F.	Maiden, F.	Work, N.
Sing.						
N. V.	hŏnŏr	leo	păter	arbor	virgo	opus
G.	honōris	leōnis	patris	arbŏris	virgĭnis	opĕris
D.	honōri	leōni	patri	arbŏri	virgĭni	opĕri
A.	honōrem	leōnem	patrem	arbŏrem	virgĭnem	opus
A.	honōre	leōne	patre	arbŏre	virgĭne	opĕre
Plur.						
N. A. V.	honōres	leōnes	patres	arbŏres	virgĭnes	opĕra
G.	honōrum	leōnum	patrum	arbŏrum	virgĭnum	opĕrum
D. Ab.	honoribus	leonibus	patribus	arboribus	virginibus	operibus

III. Mute Stems.

Masculine or feminine nouns whose stem ends in a Mute form the nominative by adding **s**. Neuters have for nominative the simple stem.

NOTE. — If the stem ends in two consonants, the genitive plural generally has **ium** (II. 8, N.). Some of these, originally i-stems, have also an old nominative in **is**: as, *trabis, urbis*.

1. *Labial.* If the mute is a *labial* (**b, p**), **s** is simply added to the stem.

a. Stems in ĭp- retain in the nominative an original **e**, the vowel having been weakened in the other cases: as, **princeps, ĭpis**.

b. Most stems in cĭp- (M.) are compounds of the root căp (in capio) *take:* as, **auceps (avi-ceps)**, *bird-catcher*.

In these the stem sometimes has the form **cup-**, as *aucŭpis*.

c. The only noun whose stem ends in **m** is **hiemps**, *winter*. (For the insertion of p, see note, foot of p. 3.)

	SING. *City*, F.	PLUR.	SING. *Chief*.	PLUR.
Nom.	urbs	urbes	princeps	princĭpes
Gen.	urbis	urbium	princĭpis	princĭpum
Dat.	urbi	urbibus	princĭpi	principĭbus
Acc.	urbem	urbes	princĭpem	princĭpes
Voc.	urbs	urbes	princeps	princĭpes
Abl.	urbe	urbibus	princĭpe	principĭbus

2. *Lingual.* If the mute is a *lingual* (**d, t**), it is suppressed before **s**.

a. Stems in ĭt- (M. or F.) retain in the nominative an original **e**: as, **hospĕs, ĭtis**. (In a few, as **comes**, the e is not original.)

NOTE. — The only nominative in **t** is *caput, ĭtis*.

b. Neuter stems ending in two consonants, and those ending in ăt- (Greek nouns), drop the final lingual in the nominative: as, **cor, cordis; poēma, ătis**.

	SING.	*Guard.*	PLUR.	SING.	*Companion.*	PLUR.
Nom.		custōs	custōdes		comĕs	comĭtes
Gen.		custōdis	custōdum		comĭtis	comĭtum
Dat.		custōdi	custōdibus		comĭti	comĭtibus
Acc.		custōdem	custōdes		comĭtem	comĭtes
Voc.		custōs	custōdes		comes	comĭtes
Abl.		custōde	custodibus		comĭte	comitĭbus

Sing.	*Age,* F.	*Heart,* M.	*Stone,* M.	*Family,* F.	*Head,* N.	*Poem,* N.
N. V.	ætas	cor	lapis	gens	caput	poēma
G.	ætātis	cordis	lapĭdis	gentis	capĭtis	poēmătis
D.	ætāti	cordi	lapĭdi	genti	capĭti	poēmăti
A.	ætātem	cor	lapĭdem	gentem	caput	poēma
A.	ætāte (i)	corde	lapĭde	gente	capĭte	poēmăte
Plur.						
N. A. V.	ætātes	corda	lapĭdes	gentes	capĭta	poēmăta
G.	ætātum (ium)		lapĭdum	gentium	capĭtum	poēmătum
D. Ab.	ætatibus	cordibus	lapĭdibus	gentibus	capitibus	poēmătis (or ĭbus)

c. Case-forms. Some nouns of lingual stems have forms of the vowel-declension.

1. Participles used as nouns, and a few others originally i-stems, occasionally have the ablative in **i**: as, *continenti, ætati, parti, sorti.*

2. Stems in **tat-** (originally i-stems), **nt-** (participles used as nouns), **d** or **t** preceded by a consonant, — also **dis, lis,** and **pons,** — regularly have the genitive plural **ium.**

3. Names denoting birth or abode, with stems in **at-, it-** (originally adjectives), with *penates, optimates,* regularly have the gen. plur. **ium.**

d. Greek neuters (as **poëma**), with nom. sing. in **a**, frequently end the dat. and abl. plur. in **ĭs**, and rarely the gen. in **ōrum**.

3. *Palatal.* If the mute is a *palatal* (**c, g**), it unites with **s** in the nominative, forming **x.**

a. Stems in **ĭc-** (short i) have nom. in **ex**, and are chiefly masculine; those in **īc-** (long i) retain **i**, and are feminine.

b. In **nix, nĭvis,** *snow,* the nom. retains a palatal lost in the other cases (original stem **snig-,** compare **ningit**); **supellex** (-ectĭlis) is partly a lingual, partly an i-stem.

	SING.	*Peak,* M.	PLUR.	SING.	*Raven,* F.	PLUR.
Nom.		apex	apĭces		cornix	cornīces
Gen.		apĭcis	apĭcum		cornĭcis	cornĭcum
Dat.		apĭci	apĭcibus		cornĭci	cornĭcibus
Acc.		apĭcem	apĭces		cornīcem	cornīces
Voc.		apex	apĭces		cornix	cornīces
Abl.		apĭce	apĭcibus		cornīce	cornīcibus

Sing.	Peace, F.	King, M.	Light, F.	Fruit, F.	Citadel, F.	Throat.
N.	pax	rex	lux	[frux]	arx	
G.	pācis	rēgis	lūcis	frūgis	arcis	—
D.	paci	regi	luci	frugi	arci	—
Ac.	pacem	regem	lucem	frugem	arcem	—
Ab.	pace	rege	luce	fruge	arce	fauce
Plur.						
N. A. V.	paces	reges	luces	fruges	arces	fauces
G.	—	regum	—	frugum	arcium	faucium
D. Ab.	pacibus	regibus	lucibus	frugibus	arcibus	faucibus

c. **Case-forms.** A few monosyllables, as **faux** (def.), **arx**, have gen. plur. **ium**; in **lux**, an abl. **luci** occurs rarely.

4. *Peculiar Forms.* In many nouns the stem is variously modified in the nominative.

a. The vowel-stems **gru-**, **su-**, simply add **s**, retaining the original **ū**; **grūs** has also a nom. **grŭis**; **sus** has in pl. **subus**.

b. In **bov-** (**bou-**), the diphthong **ou** becomes **ō** (**bōs**, **bŏvis**); in **nav-** (**nau-**) an **i** is added (**nāvis, is**); in **Jŏv-**(=Ζεύς) the diphthong becomes **ū** in **Jū-pĭter** (**păter**), gen. **Jŏvis**, &c.

c. In **Ĭtĕr, Ĭtĭnĕris** (N.), **jĕcur, jecinŏris** (N.), the nom. has been formed from a shorter stem; so that these words show a combination of two distinct forms.

d. Of the many original **s**-stems, only **vas, vasis** (pl. **vasa, ōrum**) retains its proper declension.

NOTE.—Of apparent s-stems, **as** (**assis**) is an i-stem; of **os, ossis**, the original stem is **osti-** (cf. ὀστέον and Sanskrit *asthi*); while the others have either (1) passed into **r**-stems (changed from s) in most of the cases, as **honor, ōris, corpus, ŏris** (see *liquid stems*); or (2) have broken down into i-stems, as **moles** (cf. *molestus*), **nubes** (Sanskrit *nabhas*), **sedes** (cf. ἕδος), **vis** (*vīres*), &c.

Sing.	Ox, C.	Snow, F.	Old Man, M.	Flesh, F.	Bone, N.	Force, F.
N.	bōs	nix	sĕnex	cāro	ŏs	vīs
G.	bŏvis	nĭvis	sĕnis	carnis	ossis	vīs
D.	bŏvi	nivi	sĕni	carni	ossi	—
A.	bŏvem	nivem	sĕnem	carne	ŏs	vim
A.	bŏve	nivĕ	sĕnĕ	carne	osse	vī
Plur.						
N. A. V.	bŏves	nives	sĕnes	carnes	ossa	vīres
G.	bŏum	—	sĕnum	—	ossium	vīrium
D. A.	bōbus (būbus)	nivĭbus	sĕnĭbus	carnibus	ossĭbus	vīrĭbus

5. The Locative form for nouns of the Third declension ends, like the dative, in **ī**; sometimes, like the ablative, in **ĕ**: as, **ruri**, *in the country;* **Karthagini**, *at Carthage;* **Tibŭre** (Hor.), *at Tibur;* — plural in **ĭbus**: as, **Trallibus**, *at Tralles.*

6. *Greek Nouns.* Many nouns, originally Greek, — mostly proper names, — retain Greek forms of inflection.

a. Stems in **īn-** (i long) add **s** in the nominative, omitting **n**: as, **delphis** (but also **delphin**), **Salamis**. So **Phorcys**.

b. Most stems in **ĭd-** (nom. **is**) often have also the forms of i-stems: as, **tigris, ĭdis (ĭdos)** or **is**; acc. **ĭdem (ĭda)** or **im**; abl. **ĭde** or **ĭ**. But many, including most feminine proper names, have acc. **idem (ida)**, abl. **ĭde**, — not **im** and **ĭ**. These follow the forms in Greek, which depend on the place of the *accent*.

c. Stems in **ŏn-** sometimes retain **n**: as, **Agamemnon** (or **Agamemno), ŏnis**, acc. **ŏna**.

d. Stems in **ont-** form the nom. in **ōn**: as, **horĭzon, Xenŏphon**; but a few are occasionally latinized into **ōn-** (nom. **o**): as, **Draco, ōnis**.

e. Stems in **ant-, ent-**, have nom. in **ās, ĭs**: as, **adămās, antĭs; Simoĭs, entis**. So a few in **unt-** (contr. from **oent-**) have **ūs**: as, **Trapēzus, untis**. Occasionally the Latin form of nominative is also found: as, **Atlans, elephans**.

f. Case-Forms. — Many Greek nouns (especially in the poets) have gen. **ŏs**, acc. **ă**; plur. nom. **ĕs**, acc. **ăs**: as, **aēr, aethēr, cratēr, hēro (ōis), lampas (ădis** or **ădos), lynx (cis** or **cŏs), naĭs (idos), Orpheus (eos)**.

g. A few in **ys** have acc. **yn**, voc. **y**; abl. **yĕ**: as, **chelys, yn, y; Capys, yos, yn, y, yē**.

h. Several feminine names in **ō** have gen. sing. **ūs**, all the other cases ending in **ō**; they may also have regular forms: as, **Dido;** gen. **Didōnis** or **Didūs;** dat. **Didōni** or **Dido**, &c.

IV. Rules of Gender.

1. The following are general Rules of Gender of nouns of the third declension, classed according to the *termination of the nominative*.

NOTE. — Rules of gender are mostly only rules of memory, as there is no necessary connection between the form and gender. In fact, most nouns could originally be inflected in all genders.

a. Masculine endings are **o, or, os, er, es (ĭdis, ĭtis)**.

b. Feminine endings are **as (ātis), es (is), is, ys, x, s** (following a consonant); also, **do, go, io** (abstract and collective), and **ūs (ūdis, ūtis)**.

c. Neuter endings are **a, e, i, y; c, l, t; men (mĭnis); ar, ur, us (ĕris, ŏris)**.

2. The following are general Rules of Gender of nouns of the third declension, classed *according to their stems*.

NOTE. — See the Note above. But the preference of masc. and fem. (especially fem.) for long vowels cannot be accidental (compare long **a** of 1st declension). Some affixes also prefer one or another gender: as, **tor** (originally **tar**), *masculine;* **ti,** *feminine;* **men** (originally **man**), *neuter*.

a. Vowel Stems. Stems in i, having s in the nominative are *feminine*, except those mentioned below (3, *a*). Those having nominative in ĕ, or which drop the e, are *neuter*.

b. Liquid Stems. Stems in l are *masculine*, except sil, fel, mel, and sometimes sal (N). Those in mĭn are *neuter*, except homo, nemo, flamen (M.). Others in in are *masculine* except pollen, unguen (N.). Those in ēn are *masculine*. Those in dĭn, gĭn, iōn (abstract and collective) are *feminine*. Other in ōn, with cardo, margo, ordo, unio, senio, quaternio, are *masculine*. Those in r preceded by a short vowel are *neuter* except nearly 30 given below. Those in r preceded by a long vowel are *masculine*, except soror, uxor, glos, tellus, F.; crus, jus, pus, rus, tus (in which the long vowel is due to contraction), N.

c. Labial Stems (no *neuters*). Stems in b and m are *feminine*, except chalybs. Those in p are chiefly *masculine* (exceptions below).

d. Lingual Stems. Stems in ăd, ĕd, ĭd, nd, ūd, aud, are *feminine*, except dromas, pes, quadrupes, obses, præses, lapis (M.). Those in āt, ūt, are *feminine*, except patrials (as Arpīnas), with penātes and optimātes. Those in ēd, ēt, are *masculine*, except merces and quies with its compounds. Those in ĕt, ĭt, are *masculine*, except abies, merges, seges, teges (F.) and those which are *common* from signification. Those in ăt are *neuter*; those in nt *various* (see List); those in lt, rt, *feminine* (For a few isolated forms, see List.)

e. Palatal Stems. Stems in c preceded by a consonant or long vowel are *feminine*, except calx (*stone* or *heel*), decunx, phoenix, storax, vervex, M. Those in c preceded by a short vowel are chiefly *masculine* (for exceptions, see List); those in g *masculine*, except frux, lex, phalanx, syrinx (also nix, nĭvis)

3. The following are the Forms of Inflection of nouns of the Third Declension, classed according to their Stems.

a. Vowel-Stems.

ēs, is:— about 35 nouns (original s-stems, list p. 17), *feminine*, except tudes, *hammer*; vates, *prophet*; verres, *pig* (M.).

ĭs, ĭs:— about 100 nouns, chiefly *feminine*.

Exc.— ædilis, *edile*; amnis, *river*; anguis, *snake*; antes (pl.), *ranks*; assis, *a coin*; axis, *axle*; callis (c.), *by-path*; canalis (c.), *canal*; canis (c.), *dog*; caulis, *stalk*; civis (c.), *citizen*; clunis (c.), *haunch*; collis, *hill*; crinis (c.), *hair*; ensis, *sword*; fascis, *fagot*; finis (c.), *end*; follis, *bellows*; funis (c.), *rope*; fustis, *club*; hostis (c.), *enemy*; ignis, *fire*; juvenis (c.), *youth*; lactes (pl.), *entrails*; lares, *gods*; manes, *departed spirits*; mensis, *month*; orbis, *circle*; panis, *bread*; piscis, *fish*; sentis (c.), *brier*; testis (c.), *witness*; torris, *brand*; unguis, *claw*; vectis, *bar*; vepres (c., pl.), *brambles*; vermis, *worm* (M.).

ĕ, is: — upwards of 20 nouns, all *neuter*.

ăl, ālis; ăr, āris: — 16, *neuter* (see list, page 17; and for those in **ăr, ăris**, see Liquid Stems).

ĕr, ris: — imber, *shower;* linter, *boat;* uter, *bag;* venter, *stomach,* — all M. except **linter**, which is commonly F.

PECULIAR: — grus, gruis, *crane,* F.; rhus, rhois (acc. rhum), sumach, M.; sus, suis, *hog,* C.; heros, herōis, *hero,* M.; misy, yos, *truffle,* F.; oxys, yos, *sorrel,* F.; cinnibări, *vermilion;* gummi, *gum;* sināpi, *mustard* (indecl.), N.

b. Liquid Stems.

l, lis: — 9 nouns, *masculine,* except **sil**, *ochre,* and (sometimes) **sal**, *salt,* N.

en, ĕnis: — hymen, *marriage;* ren, *kidney;* splen (ēnis), *spleen,* M.

ĕn, ĭnis: — 10 nouns, M. except **pollen**, *flour;* **unguen**, *ointment,* N.

mĕn, mĭnĭs (verbal): — about 30 nouns, *neuter;* but **flamen**, *priest,* M.

ōn, ŏnis (Greek): — canon, *rule;* dæmon, *divinity;* gnomon, *index,* M.; — aēdon, *nightingale;* alcyon, *kingfisher;* ancon, *corner;* sindon, *fine linen,* F.

o, ŏnis: — nearly 60 nouns, all *masculine.*

io, iōnis (material objects, &c.): — about 30 nouns, *masculine.*

io, iōnis (abstract and collective): — upwards of 50, *feminine.*

o, ĭnis: — homo, *man;* turbo, *whirlwind,* M.; nemo, *no one,* C.

do, dĭnis: — nearly 50 nouns, *feminine* excepting **cardo**, *hinge;* **ordo**, *rank,* M.

go, gĭnis: — about 30 nouns, *feminine.*

ar, ăris: — baccar, *valerian;* jubar, *sunbeam;* nectar, *nectar,* N.; lar, *household god;* salar, *trout,* M.

ĕr, ris: — accipiter, *hawk;* frater, *brother;* pater, *father,* M.; mater, *mother.*

ēr, ēris (Greek): — crater, *cup;* halter, *dumb-bell;* prester, *waterspout,* M.

ĕr, ĕris: — acipenser, *hawk;* aër, *air;* æther, *ether;* anser, *goose;* asser, *stake;* aster, *star;* cancer, *crab;* carcer, *dungeon;* later, *brick;* passer, *sparrow,* M.; — mulier, *woman,* F.; — acer, *maple;* cadāver, *corpse;* cicer, *vetch;* papāver, *poppy;* piper, *pepper;* tūber, *hump;* uber, *udder;* verber, *lash,* N.

ĭs, ĕris: — cinis, *ashes;* cucŭmis, *cucumber;* pulvis, *dust;* vomis, *ploughshare,* M.

ŏr (ōs), ōris: — nearly 70 nouns (besides many denoting the *agent,* formed upon verb-stems), all *masculine,* except **soror**, *sister;* **uxor**, *wife.*

ŏr, ŏris: — castor, *beaver;* rhetor, *rhetorician,* M.; — arbor, *tree,* F.; — ador, *fine-wheat;* æquor, *level;* marmor, *marble,* N.

ōs, ōris: — flos, *flower;* mos, *custom;* ros, *dew,* M.; — glos, *sister-in-law,* F.; — os, *mouth,* N.

ŭr, ŏris: — ebur, *ivory;* femur, *thigh;* jecur, *liver;* robur (or), *strength,* N.

ŭr, ŭris: — 9 *masculine;* with fulgur, *thunderbolt;* murmur, *murmur;* sulphur, *brimstone,* N.

us, ĕris: — 13 *neuter;* also, *Venus,* F.

us, ŏris: — 14 nouns, *neuter,* except lĕpus, *hare,* M.

us, ūris: — mus, *mouse,* M.; — tellus, *earth,* F.; — crus, *leg;* jus, *right;* pus, *fester;* rus, *country;* tus, *incense,* N.

PECULIAR: — delphin, ĭnis, *dolphin;* sanguis (en) ĭnis, *blood;* senex, senis, *old man,* N.; caro, carnis, *flesh,* F.; æs, æris, *copper;* far, farris, *corn;* fel, fellis, *gall;* mel, mellis, *honey;* iter, itineris, *journey;* jecur, jecinŏris (jecŏris), *liver,* N.; glis, -īris, *dormouse,* M.

c. Labial.

bs, bis: — chalybs, *steel,* M.; — plebs, *people;* scrobs, *ditch;* trabs, *beam;* urbs, *city,* F. (original i-stems).

ms, mis: — hiemps, *winter,* F.

ps, pis: — 15 nouns, *masculine,* except forceps, *pincers;* merops, *bee-eater;* ops, *help;* stips, *gift;* stirps, *stock,* F.

d. Lingual.

ăs, ădis (Greek): — 14 nouns, *feminine,* except dromas, *dromedary;* vas, *surety,* M.

ēs, ēdis: — cupes, *epicure;* heres, *heir;* præs, *surety,* M.; — merces, *pay,* F.

ēs, ĕdis: — pes, *foot;* quadrupes, *quadruped,* M.; — compes, *fetter,* F.

ēs, ĭdis: — obses, *hostage;* præses, *chief,* C.

ĭs, ĭdis: — nearly 40 nouns, mostly Greek, *feminine,* except lapis, *stone,* M.

ōs, ōdis: — custos, *guardian,* M.

ōs, ōtis: — nepos, *grandson,* M.; cos, *whetstone;* dos, *dowry,* F.

ūs, ūdis: — incus, *anvil;* palus, *marsh;* subscus, *dovetail;* with fraus, *fraud;* laus, *praise;* pecŭs, ŭdis, *sheep,* F.

ă, ătis (Greek): — nearly 20 nouns, *neuter.*

ās, ātis: — about 20 nouns (besides derivatives), *feminine;* also, anas, ătis, *duck.*

ēs, ētis: — celes, *race-horse;* lebes, *kettle;* magnes, *magnet,* M.; — quies, requies, *rest;* inquies, *unrest,* F.

es, ĕtis:—aries, *ram;* interpres, *interpreter;* paries, *house-wall,* M.;—abies, *fir;* seges, *crop;* teges, *mat,* F.

ĕs, ĭtis:—about 20 nouns, *masculine* (or *common* from signification).

ūs, ūtis:—juventus, *youth;* senectus, *old age;* servitus, *slavery;* virtus, *virtue,* F.

ns, ndis:—frons, *leaf;* glans, *acorn;* juglans, *walnut,* F.

ns, ntis:—nearly 20 (besides many participial nouns), *common,* except dens, *tooth;* fons, *fountain;* mons, *mountain;* pons, *bridge,* M.;—frons, *brow;* gens, *nation;* lens, *lentile;* mens, *mind,* F.

rs, rtis (originally i-stems):—ars, *art;* cohors, *cohort;* fors, *chance;* mors, *death;* sors, *lot,* F.

ys, ydis:—chelys, *tortoise;* chlamys, *cloak,* F.

PECULIAR:—as, assis, *penny,* M.;—lis, litis, *lawsuit;* nox, noctis, *night;* puls, pultis, *pottage,* F.;—caput, itis, *head;* cor, cordis, *heart;* hepar, ătis, *liver;* os, ossis, *bone;* vas, vasis, *vessel,* N.; also, compounds of **-pūs, -pŏdis** (M.), Gr. for **pes,** *foot.*

e. Palatal.

ax, ăcis:—anthrax, *coal;* corax, *raven;* frax (pl.), *dregs;* panax, *panacea;* scolopax, *woodcock,* M.;—fax, *torch;* styrax, *a gum,* F.

ax, ācis:—cnodax, *pivot;* cordax, *a dance;* thorax, *breastplate,* M.;—pax, *peace,* F.

ex, ĭcis:—upwards of 40 nouns, *masculine,* except carex, *sedge;* forfex, *shears;* ilex, *holm;* imbrex, *tile;* nex (nĕcis), *violent death;* pellex, *concubine,* F.

ix, īcis:—about 30 nouns (also, larix, ĭcis, *larch*), *feminine;* besides many in **trix,** regular feminines of nouns in **tor.**

ox, ōcis:—celox, *cutter,* F.

ux, ŭcis:—dux, *leader,* C.;—crux, *cross;* nux, *nut,* F.

ux, ūcis:—balux, *gold-dust;* lux, *light,* F.

x, cis:—arx, *tower;* calx, *lime;* falx, *pruning-knife;* lynx, *lynx;* merx (def.), *ware,* F.;—calyx, *cup;* calx, *heel,* M.

x, gis:—conjux (nx), *spouse;* grex, *herd;* remex, *rower;* rex, *king,* M. or C.;—frux (def.), *fruit;* lex, *law;* phalanx, *phalanx,* F., with a few rare names of animals.

Other nouns in **x** are nix, nivis, *snow;* nox, noctis, *night;* supellex, ectilis, F.;—onyx, ychis, *onyx,* M.

12. Fourth Declension.

The Stem of nouns of the Fourth Declension ends in **u**. (Usually this is weakened to *i* before *-bus*).

1. Masculine and feminine nouns form the nominative by adding **s**; neuters have for nominative the simple stem, but with **ū** (long).

NOTE. — The **u** in neuters is lengthened, probably on account of the loss of **m**.

	SING. *Car* (M.)	PLUR.	SING. *Knee* (N.)	PLUR.
Nom.	currŭs	currūs	gĕnū	genua
Gen.	currūs (uis)	curruum	genū (ūs)	genuum
Dat.	currui (ū)	currĭbus	genū	genĭbus
Acc.	currum	currūs	genū	genua
Voc.	currŭs	currūs	genū	genua
Abl.	currū	currĭbus	genū	genĭbus

NOTE. — The Genitive singular is contracted from the old form in **uis**. It is sometimes written with a circumflex: as, *currûs*.

2. Gender. — a. Most nouns in **us** are masculine. The following are feminine: — ăcus, *needle*; ănus, *old woman*; cŏlus, *distaff*; dŏmus, *house*; īdus (pl.), *the Ides*; mănus, *hand*; nurus, *daughter-in-law*; portĭcus, *gallery*; quinquātrus, *feast of Minerva*; socrus, *mother-in-law*; trĭbus, *tribe*; with a few names of plants and trees. Also, rarely, arcus, penus, specus.

b. The only neuters are cornu, *horn*; genu, *knee*; pecu (def.), *cattle*; veru, *spit*. (Some others are mentioned by grammarians, and the form ossua, as from ossu, occurs in inscriptions.)

3. Case-Forms. — a. An original genitive in **os** is sometimes found: as, senatuos; and an old (but not original) genitive in **i** is used by some writers.

b. The nominative plural has rarely the form **uus**.

c. The genitive plural is sometimes contracted into **ūm**.

d. The following retain the regular dative and ablative plural in **ŭbus**: artus, partus, portus, tribus, veru; with dissyllables in -cus, as lacus.

e. Dŏmus, *house*, has also the following forms of the second declension: domi (locative; less frequently domuï), *at home*; dative (rarely) domō; ablative domō (rarely domū); plural gen. domorum (rarely domuum); accusative domōs (or domūs).

f. Most names of plants, with **colus**, *distaff*, have also forms of the second declension.

4. Most nouns of the fourth declension are formed from verb-stems, with the suffix -tus: as, **cantus**, *song*, from **căno**.

a. The Supines of verbs are the accusative and ablative (or dative, perhaps both) of these nouns.

b. Many have only the genitive, or the genitive and ablative: as, **jussu (meo)**, *by my command;* so **injussu (populi)**, *without the people's order.* Some only the dative, **memoratui, divisui**.

c. The remaining nouns of this declension are the following: —

æstus, *heat;* arcus, *bow;* artus, *joint;* cœtus, *meeting;* fetus, *produce;* ficus, *fig;* gradus, *step;* incestus, *incest;* lacus, *lake;* laurus, *laurel;* myrtus, *myrtle;* penus (def.), *provision;* pinus, *pine;* portus, *port;* rictus, *gape;* senatus, *senate;* sinus, *fold, bay;* situs, *dust;* specus, *den;* tonitrus, *thunder;* tumultus, *tumult.* vultus

NOTE. — Several of these are formed upon verb-stems not in use, or obsolete.

13. FIFTH DECLENSION.

The Stem of nouns of the Fifth Declension ends in **ē**, which appears in all the cases.

1. The nominative is formed from the stem by adding **s**.

	SING. *Thing* (F.) PLUR.		SING. *Day* (M.) PLUR.		*Faith* (F.)
Nom.	rēs	rēs	diēs	diēs	fĭdes
Gen.	rĕi	rērum	diēī (diē)	diērum	fidĕi
Dat.	rĕi	rēbus	diēī (diē)	diēbus	fidĕi
Acc.	rem	rēs	diēm	diēs	fidem
Voc.	rēs	rēs	diēs	diēs	fidēs
Abl.	rē	rēbus	diē	diēbus	fidē

NOTE. — The e is shortened in the genitive and dative singular, when not preceded by **i**; viz., in *fides, plebes, spes, res*.

2. *Gender.* All nouns of this declension are feminine, except **dies** and **meridies**, M.

NOTE. — **Dies** is sometimes feminine in the singular, especially in phrases indicating a fixed time, or time in general: as, longa dies, *a long time;* constitutâ die, *on the set day;* also in the poets: pulcra dies, *a fair day.*

3. Case-Forms. The genitive singular anciently ended in ēs (cf. ās of first declension); and ei was sometimes contracted into i or e, as in the phrase **plebi-scītum,** *people's decree* (Fr. *plébiscite*). An old dative in i or e also occurs.

4. Several nouns of the fifth declension have also forms of the first, of which this is only a variety: as, **materia, -ies,** *timber*; **saevitia, -ies,** *cruelty*.

Note.— Nouns in **ies** (except **dies**) are original a-stems. The others are probably (excepting **res**) corrupted s-stems, like *moles, moles-tus; dies, diurnus; spes, spero. Requies* (*ĕtis*) has also forms of this declension: with others, as *saties* (for *satietas*), &c.

5. The Locative form of this declension is represented by -e, as in **hodie,** *to-day*; **perendie,** *day-after-to-morrow*; **die quarti,** *the fourth day*.

6. Of about forty nouns of this declension, the only ones complete in all their parts are **dies** and **res.** Most want the plural, which is, however, found in the nominative, accusative, and vocative, in the following: **acies, effigies, eluvies, facies, glacies, progenies, series, species, spes.**

14. Irregular Nouns.

1. Defective. Many nouns are defective in their forms of declension, either from signification or by accident of use.

a. Some are found only in the singular (**singularia tantum**), chiefly abstract nouns: as, **pietas,** *piety*; names of materials and things weighed or measured (not counted): as, **aes,** *copper,* **far,** *coin*; and proper names, as **Cicero.**

Abstract nouns in the plural may denote *repetitions* or *instances,* as **paces**:— names of things measured, &c., *kinds* or *samples,* as **vina,** *wines,* **aera,** *brazen utensils;* proper names, two or more of the same, as **Scipiones.** So **Galliae,** *the two Gauls,* **Castŏres,** *Castor and Pollux,* **nives,** *snowflakes,* **soles,** *days,* **Joves,** *images of Jupiter,* **palatia,** the *buildings* on the hill.

b. Some are found only in the Plural (**pluralia tantum**): these include (1) many *proper names,* including those of Festivals and Games; (2) names of *classes:* as, **majores,** *ancestors;* **liberi,** *children;* **penates,** *household gods;* (3) the following from signification: **arma,** *weapons;* **artus,** *joints;* **divitiae,** *riches;* **excubiae,** *night-guard;* **insidiae,** *ambush;* **manes,** *departed spirits;* **minae,** *threats;* **moenia,** *fortifications,* and a few others, which are very rare.

c. The following are defective in Case:—

ambage, § F.; *astus* (s. and p.), *astu*, M.; *cassem, e*, § M.; *dapis, i, em, e*, § F.; *dicam, as*, F.; *dicionis, i, em, e*, § F.; *fauce*, § F.; *foras, is* (pl.), F.; *fors, forte*, F.; *frugis, i, em, e*, § F.; *glos*, F.; *gratiæ, as, is*, F.; *impetus, um, u*, M.; *infitias*, F.; *jugera, um, ibus*, N.; *lues, em, e*, F.; *mane* (nom., acc., and abl.), N.; *nauci*, N.; *ohice*, § C.; *opis, em, e*, § F., *pondo* (abl. or in.lec.), N.; *precem, e*, § F.; *sentis, em, es, ibus*, M.; *sordem, e*, § F.; *spontis, e*, F.; *suppetias*, F.; *venui, um*, M. (o, N.); *vicis, em, e, es, ibus*, F. The gen. plur. is also wanting in *cor, cos, fax, fæx, lux, nex, os* (*oris*), *pax, præs, ros, sal, sol, tus, vas, ver; jura, rura*, have only nom. and acc. plur.

§ **Plural complete.**

Many nouns of the fourth declension occur only in the dative, or in the acc. and abl. (supines).

The following neuters are indeclinable: *fas, nefas, instar, necesse, nihil, opus, secus.*

Nouns found only in one case are called *monoptotes;* in two cases, *diptotes;* in three cases, *triptotes.*

2. *Variable.* Many nouns vary in their form of *declension*, their *gender*, or their *signification* under different forms.

a. Some have two or more forms of Declension, and are called *heteroclites:* as,

Balnea or *æ; carbasus* (F.), pl., *a* (N.); *colus* (1st and 4th), F.; *femur, ŏris* or *ĭnis; jugerum, i*, or abl. *e*, pl. *a, um*, N.; *margarita, æ* (F.), or *um, i* (N.); *Mulciber, bri* or *beris; munus, ĕris*, pl. *munia* (*mœnia*), *orum; pubes, eris; em, e; penus, i*, or *ŏris; sævitia, æ; -ies, iei; -itudo, inis*, F.; *sequester, tri*, or *tris;* with many found in the 1st and 5th declensions, and a few other rare forms.

b. Some nouns vary in Gender (*heterogeneous*): as,

cælum (N.), pl. cæli (M.). *sky;* clipeus (M.), or clipeum (N.), *shield;* frenum (M.), pl. freni (M.), *rein.*

c. Many nouns vary in meaning as they are found in the singular or plural : as,

 ædes, is (F.), *temple;* ædes, ium, *house.*
 auxilium (N.), *help;* auxilia, *auxiliaries.*
 carcer (M.), *dungeon;* carcĕres, *barriers* (of a race-course).
 castrum (M.), *fort;* castra, *camp.*
 copia (F.), *plenty;* copiæ, *troops.*
 finis (M.), *end;* fines, *bounds, territories.*
 forum, *market-place;* fori, *gang-ways.*
 gratia (F.), *favor;* gratiæ, *thanks.*
 impedimentum (N.), *hinderance;* impedimenta, *baggage.*
 littĕra (F.), *letter* (of alphabet); littĕræ, *epistle.*
 lŏcus (M.), *place* [pl. loca (N.)]; loci, *passages in books.* (In early
  writers this is the regular plural.)
 ludus, *sport;* ludi, *public games.*
 opera, *task;* operæ, *day-laborers* ("hands").

opis (F. gen.), *help;* opes, *resources, wealth.*
plăga (F.), *region* [plăga, *blow*]; plăgæ, *snares.*
rostrum, *beak of a ship;* rostra, *speaker's platform.*
săl (M. or N.), *salt;* sales, *witticisms.*
tabella, *tablet;* tabellæ, *documents.*

sestertius (M.) means the sum of 2½ asses, = about 4 cents.
sestertium (N.) means the sum of 1000 sestertii, = about $40.
decies sestertium means the sum of 1000 sestertia, = $40,000.

d. Sometimes a noun in combination with an adjective takes a special signification, both parts being regularly inflected: as, jusjūrandum, jūrisjurandi, *oath;* respublica, reipublicae, *commonwealth.*

15. Proper Names.

1. A Roman had regularly three names. Thus, in the name *Marcus Tullius Cicero,* we have —

Marcus, the *prænomen,* or personal name;

Tullius, the *nomen;* i.e., name of the Gens, or house, whose original head was **Tullus**; this name is properly an adjective;

Cicero, the *cognomen,* or family name, often in its origin a nickname, — in this case from **cĭcer,** a *vetch,* or small pea.

2. A fourth or fifth name, called the *agnomen,* was sometimes given.

Thus the complete name of Scipio the Younger was *Publius Cornelius Scipio Africanus Æmilianus; Africanus* from his exploits in Africa; *Æmilianus* as adopted from the Æmilian gens.

3. Women had no personal names, but were known only by that of their gens.

Thus the wife of Cicero was *Terentia,* and his daughter *Tullia.* A younger sister would have been called *Tullia secunda* or *minor,* and so on.

4. The commonest prænomens are thus abbreviated: —

A. Aulus.	L. Lucius.	Q. Quintus.
C. (G.) Gaius (*Caius*).	M. Marcus.	Ser. Servius.
Cn. (Gn.) Gnæus (*Cneius*).	M'. Manius.	Sex. Sextus.
D. Decimus.	Mam. Mamercus.	Sp. Spurius.
K. Kæso.	N. Numerius.	T. Titus.
App. Appius.	P. Publius.	Ti. Tiberius.

ADJECTIVES.

16. Inflection of Adjectives.

ADJECTIVES and Participles are in general formed and declined like Nouns, differing from nouns only in their use. In accordance with their use, they distinguish gender by different forms in the same word. They are (1) of the *first and second declensions*, or (2) of the *third declension*.

NOTE. — Latin adjectives and participles are either o-stems with the corresponding feminine a-stems (originally ă and ā), or i-stems. Many, however, were originally stems in u or a consonant, which passed over, in all or most of their cases, into the i-declension, for which Latin had a special fondness. (Compare the endings ēs and īs of the Third declension with Greek ες and ᾱς; navis (nom.) with the Greek ναῦς; *animus* with *exanimis*; *cornu* with *bicornis*; *lingua* with *bilinguis*; *cor, corde, corda*, with *discors, -di, -dia, -dium*; *suāvis* with ἡδύς; *ferens, -entia*, with φέρων, -οντα.) A few, which in other languages are nouns, retain the consonant-form: as, *vetus* = ἔτος, *uber* = οὖθαρ. Comparatives also retain the consonant form in most of their cases.

1. Stems in **o** have the feminine **ă** (originally **ā**). They are declined like **servus** (M.), **stella** (F.), **donum** (N.): as,

		M.	F.	N.
SING.	Nom.	cărŭs	cără	cărum, *Dear.*
	Gen.	carī	carae	carī
	Dat.	carō	carae	carō
	Acc.	carum	caram	carum
	Voc.	carĕ	cară	carum
	Abl.	carō	carā	carō
PLUR.	Nom.	carī	carae	cară
	Gen.	carōrum	carārum	carōrum
	Dat.	carīs	carīs	carīs
	Acc.	carōs	carās	cară
	Voc.	carī	carae	cară
	Abl.	carīs	carīs	carīs

NOTE. — The masc. gen. of adjectives in **ius** ends in **ii**, and the vocative in **ie**; not in **i** as in nouns.

a. In adjectives of stems ending in **ro-** preceded by **ĕ** or a consonant (also **satur**), the masculine nominative is formed like **puer** or **liber** (§ **10**): as,

Sing.   Miser, *wretched.*   Ater, *black.*

	M.	F.	N.	M.	F.	N.
N.	mĭser	mĭsĕra	mĭsĕrum	ater	atra	atrum
G.	miseri	miseræ	miseri	atri	atræ	atri
D.	misero	miseræ	misero	atro	atræ	atro
Ac.	miserum	miseram	miserum	atrum	atram	atrum
V.	miser	misera	miserum	ater	atra	atrum
Ab	misero	miserā	misero	atro	atra	atro

Plur.

	M.	F.	N.	M.	F.	N.
N.	miseri	miseræ	misera	atri	atræ	atra
G.	miserorum	miserarum	miserorum	atrorum	atrarum	atrorum
D.	miseris	miseris	miseris	atris	atris	atris
Ac.	miseros	miseras	misera	atros	atras	atra
V.	miseri	miseræ	misera	atri	atræ	atra
Ab.	miseris	miseris	miseris	atris	atris	atris

Stems in **ēro**, with **morigĕrus, propĕrus, postĕrus**, have the regular nominative in **us**.

Like **miser** are declined — asper, *rough;* gibber, *hunched;* lacer, *torn;* liber, *free;* prosper (erus), *favoring;* satur (ura, urum), *sated;* tener, *tender;* with compounds of -fer and -ger; also, usually, dexter, *right.* In these the e belongs to the stem; but in dexter it is often syncopated.

Like **ater** are declined — æger, *sick;* creber, *close;* faber, *skilled;* glaber, *sleek;* integer, *whole;* ludicer, *sportive;* macer, *lean;* niger, *dark;* noster, *our;* piger, *sluggish;* ruber, *red;* sacer, *sacred;* sinister, *left;* teter, *foul;* vafer, *shrewd;* vester, *your.*

The following feminines lack a masculine singular nominative: — cetĕra, infĕra, postĕra, supĕra. They are rarely found in the singular except in certain phrases: as, *postero die.* A feminine ablative in **o** is found in a few Greek adjectives, as *lectīcā octophŏro* (Verr. v. 11.).

b. The following (o-stems) with their compounds have the genitive singular in **īus** and the dative in **ī** in all the genders: —

ălius (N. aliud), *other.*   nullus, *none.*   ullus, *any* (with negatives).
alter, *other* (of two).   sōlus, *alone.*   ūnus, *one.*
neuter, -trīus, *neither.*   tōtus, *whole.*   ŭter, -trīus, *which* (of two).

Note. — The suffix **ter**, in *alter, uter, neuter,* is the same as the Greek comparative suffix -τερο(ς). The stem of *aliud* appears in early Latin and in derivatives as **ali-**, in the forms *alis, alid* (for *aliud*), *aliter,* &c.

Of these the singular is thus declined: —

	M.	F.	N.	M.	F.	N.
N.	solus	sola	solum	uter	utra	utrum
G.	solīus	solīus	solīus	utrīus	utrīus	utrīus
D.	soli	soli	soli	utri	utri	utri
A.	solum	solam	solum	utrum	utram	utrum
A.	solo	solā	solo	utro	utrā	utro

	M.	F.	N.	M.	F.	N.
N.	alius	alia	aliud	alter	altĕra	alterum
G.	alīus	alīus	alius	alterius	alterius	alterius
D.	alii	alii	alii	alteri	alteri	alteri
A.	alium	aliam	aliud	alterum	alteram	alterum
A.	alio	aliā	alio	altero	alterā	altero

NOTE. — These words, in Greek and Sanskrit, are treated as pronouns; which accords with the pronominal forms of the genitive in **ius**, the dative in **i**, and the neuter **d** in **aliud**. The **i** in the genitive **-ius**, though long, may be made short in verse; and *alterius* is generally accented on the antepenult. Instead of *alīus* (gen.), *alterius* is more commonly used. In compounds — as *alteruter* — sometimes both parts are declined, sometimes only the latter.

2. Stems in **i** — distinguished by being *parisyllabic* — have properly no form for the feminine, and hence are called *adjectives of two terminations*. In the neuter, **i** is changed to **e**. They are declined like **turris** (acc. **em**) and **mare**.

Sing.	M., F.	*Light.* N.	M.	*Keen.* F.	N.
N.V.	lĕvis	lĕve	acer	acris	acre
G.	lĕvis	lĕvis	acris	acris	acris
D.	lĕvi	lĕvi	acri	acri	acri
Ac.	lĕvem	lĕve	acrem	acrem	acre
Ab.	lĕvi	lĕvi	acri	acri	acri
Plur.					
N.V.	lĕvēs	lĕvia	acres	acres	acria
G.	lĕvium	lĕvium	acrium	acrium	acrium
D.	lĕvibus	lĕvibus	acribus	acribus	acribus
Ac.	lĕvēs (īs)	lĕvia	acres (īs)	acres (īs)	acria
Ab.	lĕvibus	lĕvibus	acribus	acribus	acribus

a. Several stems in **ri-** form the masc. nom. in **er** (as **acer**, compare § **11**, I. 2, *b.*). These are the following: —

acer, *keen.*
alacer, *eager.*
campester, *of the plain.*
celeber, *famous.*
equester, *of horsemen.*
paluster, *marshy.*

pedester, *on foot.*
puter, *rotten.*
salūber, *wholesome.*
silvester, *wooded.*
terrester, *of the land.*
volŭcer, *winged.*

Also **celer, celĕris, celĕre,** *swift;* and, in certain phrases, the names of months in **-ber**.

NOTE. — This formation is not original; and hence, in the poets, and in early Latin, either the masculine or feminine form of these adjectives was used for both genders. In others, as *illustris, lugubris, mediŏcris, muliebris,* there is no separate masculine form.

b. **Case-Forms.** These adjectives, as true **i**-stems, retain **i** in the abl. singular, the neut. plural **ia**, the gen. plur. **ium**, and often in the acc. plur. **īs**, but never **im** in the acc. sing. For metrical reasons, an abl. in **e** sometimes occurs in poetry. When **celer** is used as an adjective, it has the regular gen. plur. in **ium**; as a noun, denoting a military rank, it is **celĕrum**; as a proper name, it has the abl. in **e**.

3. The remaining adjectives of the third declension have the form of **i**-stems in the ablative singular **ī**, the plural neuter **ia**, and genitive **ium**. In other cases they follow the rule of consonant-stems.

a. In adjectives of consonant-stems (except comparatives) the nominative singular is alike for all genders: hence they are called *adjectives of one termination.* Except of stems in **l** and **r**, it is formed from the stem by adding **s**: as,

Sing.	M. F.	*Happy.* N.	M. F.	*Calling.* N.
N.V.	fēlix	fēlix	vocans	vocans
Gen.	felīcis	felīcis	vocantis	vocantis
Dat.	felīci	felīci	vocanti	vocanti
Acc.	felīcem	felix	vocantem	vocans
Abl.	felīce or	felīci	vocante or	vocanti
Plur.				
N.V.	felīces	felīcia	vocantes	vocantia
Gen.	felīcium	felīcium	vocantium	vocantium
Dat.	felīcibus	felīcibus	vocantibus	vocantibus
Acc.	felīces (īs)	felīcia	vocantes (īs)	vocantia
Abl.	felīcibus	felīcibus	vocantibus	vocantibus

Other examples are the following: —

Sing.	M. F.	N.	M. F.	N.	M. F.	N.
N.V.	iens, *going*		par, *equal*		præceps, *headlong*	
Gen.	euntis		paris		præcipĭtis	
Dat.	eunti		pari		præcipiti	
Acc.	euntem	iens	parem	par	præcipitem	præceps
Abl.	eunte (i)		pari		præcipite	
Plur.						
N.A.V.	euntes	euntia	pares	paria	præcipites	præcipitia
Gen.	euntium		parium		præcipitium	
D. Ab.	euntibus		paribus		præcipitibus	

Sing.	M. F.	N.	M. F.	N.	M. F.	N.
N.V.	dives, *rich*		uber, *fertile*		vetus, *old*	
Gen.	divĭtis		ubĕris		vetĕris	
Dat.	divĭti		ubĕri		vetĕri	
Acc.	divitem	dives	ubĕrem	uber	veterem	vetus
Abl.	divĭte (i)		ubere (i)		vetere (i)	
Plur.						
N.A.V.	divĭtes (ditia)		ubĕres	ubĕra	vetĕres	vetĕra
Gen	divĭtum		ubĕrum		veterum	
D Ab.	divitibus		uberibus		veteribus	

NOTE. — The regular feminine of these adjectives, by analogy of cognate languages, would end in **ia**: this form is found in the abstracts *amentia, desidia, socordia, &c.*, and in proper names, as *Florentia* (cf. Greek φέρουσα). The neuter would regularly have the simple stem (as *caput, cor, allec,* Greek φέρον); but in all except liquid stems, the masc. form in **s** has forced itself not only upon the neuter nominative, but upon the accusative also, where it is wholly abnormal.

16: 3.]   ADJECTIVES: INFLECTION.   37

A few of these forms, used as nouns, have a feminine in a: as, *clienta, hospita, inhospita*, with the appellation *Juno Sospita*.

b. The stem of Comparatives properly ended in ŏs, which became or in all cases except the neuter singular (N. A. V.), where s is retained, and ŏ is changed to ŭ (compare honōr, ōris; corpus, ŏris). Thus they appear to have two terminations.

Sing.	M. F. *Dearer.*	F.	M. F. *More.*	N.
N.V.	carior	carius	—	plus
Gen.	cariōris	cariōris	—	plūris
Dat.	cariōri	cariōri	—	plūri
Acc.	cariōrem	carius	—	plus
Abl.	cariōre or	cariori	—	plūre
Plur.				
N.V.	cariōres	cariōra	plūres	plūra (ia)
Gen.	cariōrum	cariōrum	plurium	plurium
Dat.	carioribus	carioribus	pluribus	pluribus
Acc.	cariōres	cariōra	plures	plura
Abl.	carioribus	carioribus	pluribus	pluribus

NOTE. — The neuter sing. **plus** is used only as a noun. Its derivative **complures**, *several*, has sometimes neut. plur. **compluria**. All other comparatives are declined like **carior**.

c. Case Forms. **1.** The ablative singular of these adjectives commonly ends in **i**; but, when used as nouns, — as **superstes**, *survivor*, — they have **e**. Participles in **ns** used *as such*, — especially in the Ablative Absolute, — or as nouns, regularly have **e**; but as adjectives, regularly **i**. (So adjectives in **ns** as in the phrase, **me imprudente**.)

In the following, e is the regular form: — *cæles, compos, deses, dives, hospes, pauper, particeps, præceps, princeps, superstes, supplex;* also in patrials (see § 44), with stems in **at-, it-, nt-, rt-**, when used as nouns, and sometimes as adjectives.

2. The genitive plural ends commonly in **ium**, and the accusative often in **īs**, even in comparatives, which are less inclined to the i-declension.

In the following, the gen. plur. ends in **um**: — always in *dives, compos, inops, præpes, supplex*, and compounds of **pes**; — sometimes, in poetry, participles in **ns**. In *vetus* (ĕris), *pubes* (ĕris), *uber* (ĕris), which did not become i-stems, the forms e, a, um, are regular; but *uber* and *vetus* rarely have the abl. in **i**.

3. Several are declined in more than one form: as, **gracĭlis (us), hilaris (us), inermis (us)**. A few are indecl. or defective: as,

damnas (esto, sunto), frugi (dat. of advantage), *exspes* (only nom.), *exlex* (nom. and acc.), *mactus* (nom. and voc.), *nequam* (indecl.), *pernox* (pernoctu), *potis, pote* (indecl. or M. F. *potis*, N. *pote*), *primōris, seminĕci*, &c.

d. Many adjectives, from their signification, are used only in the masculine or feminine, and may be called *adjectives of common gender*. Such are **adolescens,** *youthful;* **deses, ĭdis,** *slothful;* **inops, ŏpis,** *poor;* **sospes, ĭtis,** *safe.* So **senex** and **juvenis** may be called *masculine adjectives.*

e. Many nouns may be also used as adjectives (compare § **47**, 3) : as, **pedes,** *a footman* or *on foot ;* especially nouns in **tor** (M.) and **trix** (F.), denoting the *agent :* as, **victor exercitus,** *the conquering army ;* **victrix causa,** *the winning cause.*

f. Certain cases of adjectives are regularly used as Adverbs. These are, the acc. and abl. of the neuter singular: as, **multum, multo,** *much ; —* the neuter of comparatives (regularly) : as, **carius,** *more dearly ;* **lĕvius,** *more lightly ; —* together with those ending in **ē** for o-stems, and **ter** for i-stems: as, **carē,** *dearly ;* **levĭter,** *lightly ;* **acerrime,** *most eagerly.*

17. Comparison.

1. *Regular Comparison.* The Comparative is formed by adding, for the nominative, **ior** (old stem **ios**), neuter **ius**, and the Superlative by adding **issĭmus, a, um** (old **issŭmus**), to the stem of the Positive, which loses its final vowel : as,

carus, *dear ;* **carior,** *dearer ;* **carissimus,** *dearest.*
lĕvis, *light ;* **levior,** *lighter ;* **levissimus,** *lightest.*
fēlix, *happy ;* **felicior,** *happier ;* **felicissimus,** *happiest.*
hebes, *dull ;* **hebetior,** *duller ;* **hebetissimus,** *dullest.*

Note. — The comparative suffix is the same as the Greek ιων, or the Sanskrit *iyans.* That of the superlative (**issimus**) is a double form, but what is the combination is not certain ; perhaps it stands for **ios-timus** (comp. and sup.), or possibly for **ist-timus** (two superlatives). Strictly, new stems are thus formed.

a. Adjectives in **er** form the superlative by adding **-rimus** to the nominative (comparative regular) : as,

miser, miserior, miserrimus ; acer, acrior, acerrimus.

So **vetus, veterrimus** (for comparative, **vetustior**) from the old form **veter**; and, rarely, **maturrimus** (for **maturissimus**).

b. The following in **lis** add **-limus** to the stem clipped of its vowel : **facilis,** *easy ;* **difficilis,** *hard ;* **similis,** *like ;* **dissimilis,** *unlike ;* **gracilis,** *slender ;* **humilis,** *low.*

Note. — The endings **-limus** and **-rimus,** the regular superlatives, are formed by assimilation from **-timus** and **-simus.**

c. Compounds in -dĭcus (*saying*), -fĭcus (*doing*), -vŏlus (*willing*), take the forms of corresponding participles in ns, which were anciently used as adjectives: as,

    maledĭcus, *slanderous*, maledīcentior, maledīcentissimus.
    malevŏlus, *spiteful*, malevŏlentior, malevolentissimus.

d. Adjectives in us preceded by a vowel (except u) rarely have forms of comparison, but are compared by the adverbs magis, *more*; maxime, *most*: as,

    idoneus, *fit*; magis idoneus, maxime idoneus.

Most derivatives in -ĭcus, -ĭdus, -ālis, -āris, -īlis, -ŭlus, -undus, -timus, -īnus, -īvus, -ōrus, with compounds, as degener, inops, are also thus compared.

e. Participles when used as adjectives are regularly compared: as, patientior, patientissimus; apertior, apertissimus.

NOTE.—Many adjectives—as aureus, *golden*—are from their meaning incapable of comparison; but each language has its own usage in this respect. Thus niger, *black*, and candidus, *white*, are compared; but not ater or albus, meaning *absolute* black or white.

2. *Irregular Comparison.* Several adjectives are compared from different stems, or contain irregular forms: as,

    bŏnus, mělior, optĭmus, *good, better, best.*
    mălus, pējor, pessimus, *bad, worse, worst.*
    magnus, mājor, maximus, *great, greater, greatest.*
    parvus, mĭnŏr, minimus, *small, less, least.*
    multum, plūs (N.), plurimum, *much, more, most.*
    multi, plūres, plurimi, *many, more, most.*
    nēquam (indecl.), nequior, nequissimus, *worthless,*
    frūgi (indecl.), frugālior, frugalissimus, *useful, worthy.*
    dexter, dextěrior, dextĭmus, *on the right, handy.*

3. *Defective Comparison.* The following are formed from roots or stems not used as adjectives:—

    [cis, citra] citěrior, citĭmus, *hither, hithermost.*
    [in, intra] intěrior, intĭmus, *inner, inmost.*
    [prae, pro] prior, prīmus, *former, first.*
    [prope] propior, proxĭmus, *nearer, next.*
    [ultra] ulterior, ultĭmus, *farther, farthest.*

a. Of the following the positive forms (originally comparative) are rare, except when used as nouns, generally in the plural:—

    [extěrus] exterior, extrēmus (extimus), *outer, outmost.*
    [infěrus] inferior, infimus (īmus), *lower, lowest.*
    [postěrus] posterior, postrēmus, *latter, last.*
    [supěrus] superior, supremus or summus, *higher, highest.*

The plurals, exteri, *foreigners*; posteri, *posterity*; superi, *the heavenly gods*; inferi, *those below*, are common.

b. From **juvenis,** *youth,* **sĕnex,** *old man,* are formed the comparatives **junior,** *younger,* **senior,** *older.* Instead of the superlative, the phrase **minimus** or **maximus natu** is used (**natu** being often understood): as,

maximus fratrum, *the eldest of the brothers;* but,
senior fratrum, *the elder of the* [two] *brothers.*

c. In the following, one of the forms of comparison is wanting: —

1. The Positive is wanting in deterior, deterrimus, *worse, worst;* ocior, ocissimus, *swifter, swiftest;* potior, potissimus, *more* and *most preferable* [from potis, *able*].

2. The Comparative is wanting in bellus, *pretty;* caesius, *gray;* falsus, *false;* inclŭtus (or inclītus), *famous;* invictus, *unsurpassed;* invītus, *reluctant;* novus, *new* (novissimum agmen, *rear guard*); pius, *pious;* sacer, *sacred;* vetus, *old;* and most derivatives in **Ilis** and **bĭlis.**

3. The Superlative is not found in actuōsus, *energetic;* alăcer, *eager;* arcānus, *secret;* diuturnus, *long-continued;* exīlis, *slender;* ingens, *huge;* jejūnus, *sterile;* longinquus, *distant;* opīmus, *rich;* proclīvis, *inclined;* satur, *sated;* segnis, *sluggish;* serus, *late;* supinus, *supine;* taciturnus, *silent;* tempestīvus, *seasonable;* vicīnus, *neighboring.*

4. ***Adverbs.*** Adverbs formed from adjectives are compared in like manner: as,

carus, *dear;* carē, carius, carissimē.
miser, *wretched;* miserē (iter), miserius, miserrimē.
lĕvis, *light;* levĭter, levius, levissimē.
audax, *bold;* audacter, audăcius, audacissimē.
bŏnus, *good;* bĕnĕ, mĕlius, optimē.
mălus, *bad;* malĕ, pējus, pessimē.

Also, diu, *long* (in time), diutius diutissime; — potius, *rather,* potissimum, *first-of-all;* — saepe, *often,* saepius; — satis, *enough,* satius, *preferable;* — sĕcus, *otherwise,* sēcius, *worse;* — multum (multo), măgis, maxime, *much, more, most.*

5. ***Signification.*** Besides their regular signification, the forms of comparison are used as follows: —

a. The Comparative denotes a *considerable* or *excessive* degree of a quality: as, **brevior,** *rather short;* **audacior,** *too bold.* It is used instead of the superlative where only two are spoken of: as, **melior imperatorum,** *the best of the* (two) *commanders.*

b. The Superlative (of eminence) denotes a *very high degree* of a quality: as, **maximus numerus,** *a very great number.* With **quam,** it indicates the highest degree: as, **quam plurimi,** *as many as possible;* **quam maxime potest** (**quam potest**), *as much as can be.*

c. With **quisque**, the superlative has a peculiar signification: thus the phrase **ditissimus quisque** means, *all the richest;* **primus quisque,** *all the first* (each in his order).

d. A high degree of a quality is denoted by such adverbs as **admodum, valde,** *very;* or by **per** or **prae** in composition: as, **permagnus,** *very great;* **praealtus,** *very high* (or *deep*).

e. A low degree is indicated by **sub** in composition: as, **subrusticus,** *rather countrified;* or by **minus,** *not very;* **minime,** *not at all;* **parum,** *not enough;* **non satis,** *not much.*

18. NUMERALS.

1. *Cardinal and Ordinal.* Cardinal Numbers answer to the interrogative **quot,** *how many;* Ordinal Numbers to **quotus,** *which in order,* or *one of how many.*

	CARDINAL.	ORDINAL.	ROMAN NUMERALS.
1.	unus, una, unum, *one.*	primus, a, um, *first.*	I.
2.	duo, duæ, duo, *two.*	secundus (alter), *second.*	II.
3.	tres, tria, *three, &c.*	tertius, *third, &c.*	III.
4.	quattuor	quartus	IV.
5.	quinque	quintus	V.
6.	sex	sextus	VI.
7.	septem	septĭmus	VII.
8.	octo	octāvus	VIII.
9.	novem	nonus	IX.
10.	decem	decĭmus	X.
11.	undĕcim	undecĭmus	XI.
12.	duodĕcim	duodecĭmus	XII.
13.	tredĕcim	tertius decĭmus	XIII.
14.	quattuordĕcim	quartus decĭmus	XIV.
15.	quindĕcim	quintus decĭmus	XV.
16.	sedĕcim	sextus decĭmus	XVI.
17.	septĕndecim	septimus decĭmus	XVII.
18.	duodeviginti (octodĕcim)	duodevicesĭmus	XVIII.
19.	undeviginti (novendĕcim)	undevicesĭmus	XIX.
20.	viginti	vicesĭmus (vigesĭmus)	XX.
21.	viginti unus *or* unus et viginti	vicesimus primus, &c.	XXI.
30.	triginta	tricesimus	XXX.
40.	quadraginta	quadragesimus	XL.
50.	quinquaginta	quinquagesimus	Ł. or L.
60.	sexaginta	sexagesimus	LX.
70.	septuaginta	septuagesimus	LXX.
80.	octoginta	octogesimus	LXXX.
90.	nonaginta	nonagesimus	XC.
100.	centum	centesimus	C.

CARDINAL.		ORDINAL.	ROMAN NUMERALS.
200.	ducenti, æ, a	ducentesimus	CC.
300.	trecenti	trecentesimus	CCC.
400.	quadringenti	quadringentesimus	CCCC.
500.	quingenti	quingentesimus	IƆ, *or* D.
600.	sexcenti	sexcentesimus	DC.
700.	septingenti	septingentesimus	DCC.
800.	octingenti	octingentesimus	DCCC.
900.	nongenti	nongentesimus	DCCCC.
1000.	mille	millesimus	CIƆ, *or* M.
5000.	quinque millia (milia)	quinquies millesimus	IƆƆ.
10,000.	decem millia (milia)	decies millesimus	CCIƆƆ.
100,000.	centum millia (milia)	centies millesimus	CCCIƆƆƆ.

NOTE. — The Ordinals (except *secundus, tertius, octavus*) are formed by means of the same suffixes as superlatives. Thus *decimus* (compare the form *infimus*) may be regarded as the last of a series of ten; *primus* is a superlative of *pro*; the forms in -tus (*quartus, quintus, sextus*) may be compared with the corresponding Greek forms in -τος and πρῶτος, superlative of πρό; *nonus* is contracted from *novimus*; while the others have the regular superlative ending -s▪. Of the exceptions, *secundus* is a participle of *sequor*; and *alter* is ▪ ▪parative form (compare -τερος in Greek).

a. **Unus, una, unum,** *one*, is declined like **solus** (§ 16, 1.), gen. **unīus** and dat. **uni** in all genders. It often has the meaning of *same*, or *only*. It is used in the plural in this sense, as also to agree with a plural noun of a singular meaning: as, **una castra,** *one camp*. So **uni et alteri**, *one party and the other*.

b. **Duo,** *two* (also **ambo,** *both*), is thus declined: —

Nom.	duo	duae	duo
Gen.	duorum	duarum	duorum
Dat.	duobus	duabus	duobus
Acc.	duos (duo)	duas	duo
Abl.	duobus	duabus	duobus

NOTE. — This form in -o is a remnant of the *dual number*, which was lost in Latin, but is found in cognate languages.

c. **Tres, tria,** *three*, is an i-stem, and is regularly declined like the plural of **lĕvis**. The other cardinal numbers, up to **centum** (100), are indeclinable. The multiples of ten are compounds of the multiple, with a fragment of **decem**: as, **viginti** = dui-ginta.

NOTE. — The forms *octodecim* (18), *novendecim* (19), are rare, *undeviginti, duodeviginti*, &c., being commonly employed.

d. The hundreds, up to 1000, and all the ordinals, are o-stems, and are regularly declined like adjectives of the first and second declension.

f. To the personal (and sometimes to the adjective) pronouns enclitics are joined for emphasis: — **met** to all the pronouns; **-te** to **tu**; **-pte** to the abl. sing. of the adjectives, and in early Latin to the others: as, **vosmetipsos prodĭtis,** *you betray your own very selves;* **suopte pondere,** *by its own weight.*

20. Demonstrative.

1. The Demonstrative Pronouns are **hic,** *this;* **is, ille, iste,** *that;* with the Intensive **ipse,** *self,* and **idem,** *same.*

Note. — These are combinations of **o** and **i**-stems, which are not clearly distinguishable. **Hic** is a compound of the stem **ho-** with the demonstrative **-ce,** which appears in full in early Latin (**hice**), and when followed by the enclitic **-ne** (**hicine**). In most of the cases it is shortened to **c,** and in many lost; but it is appended for emphasis to those that do not regularly retain it (**hujusce**). In early Latin **c** alone is retained in some of these (**horunc**). **Ille** and **iste** are sometimes found with the same enclitic (**illic, istuc**).

a. **Ille** is a later form of **ollus (olle),** which is sometimes used by the poets; a gen. sing. in **i, ae, i,** occurs in **ille** and **iste.**

b. **Iste** is sometimes found in early writers in the form **ste,** &c., with the entire loss of the first syllable; and the **i** of **ipse** and **ille** is very often found *shortened.*

c. **Ipse** is compounded of **is** and **-pse** (for **pte,** from the same root as **potis**), meaning *self.* The first part was originally declined, as in **reāpse** (for **re eapse**), *in fact.* An old form **ipsus** occurs. **Idem** is the demonstrative **is** with the affix **-dem.**

2. These demonstratives are used either with nouns as Adjectives, or alone as Pronouns; and, from their signification, cannot (except **ipse**) have a vocative.

	This.			*That.*		
Sing.	M.	F.	N.	M.	F.	N.
Nom.	hic	haec	hoc	is	ea	id
Gen.	hujus	hujus	hujus	ejus	ejus	ejus
Dat.	huic	huic	huic	ei	ei	ei
Acc.	hunc	hanc	hoc	eum	eam	id
Abl.	hoc	hac	hoc	eo	eā	eo
Plur.		*These.*			*Those.*	
Nom.	hi	hae	haec	ii (ei)	eae	ea
Gen.	horum	harum	horum	eorum	earum	eorum
Dat.	his	his	his		eis or iis	
Acc.	hos	has	haec	eos	eas	ea
Abl.	his	his	his		eis or iis	

DEMONSTRATIVE PRONOUNS.

That.

	SING. M.	F.	N.
N.	ille	illa	illud
G.	illīus	illīus	illīus
D.	illi	illi	illi
A.	illum	illam	illud
V.	—	—	
A.	illo	illā	illo

Self.

	M.	F.	N.
	ipse	ipsa	ipsum
	ipsīus	ipsīus	ipsīus
	ipsi	ipsi	ipsi
	ipsum	ipsam	ipsum
	ipse	ipsa	ipsum
	ipso	ipso	ipso

Those.

PLUR.			
N.	illi	illae	illa
G.	illorum	illarum	illorum
D.	illis	illis	illis
A.	illos	illas	illa
V.	—	—	
A.	illis	illis	illis

Selves.

ipsi	ipsae	ipsa
ipsorum	ipsarum	ipsorum
ipsis	ipsis	ipsis
ipsos	ipsas	ipsa
ipsi	ipsae	ipsa
ipsis	ipsis	ipsis

The Same.

SING.		
N.	Idem	eădem	Idem
G.	ejusdem	ejusdem	ejusdem
D.	eidem	eidem	eidem
A.	eundem	eandem	Idem
A.	eodem	eădem	eodem

PLUR.		
iidem	eaedem	eădem
eorundem	earundem	eorundem
eisdem or iisdem		
eosdem	easdem	eădem
eisdem or iisdem		

a. **Hic** is used of what is *near the speaker* (in time, place, thought, or on the written page); hence called the *demonstrative of the first person*. It is sometimes used of the speaker himself; sometimes for "the latter" of two things mentioned.

b. **Ille** is used of what is *remote* (in time, &c.); hence called the *demonstrative of the third person*. It is sometimes used to mean "the former"; also (usually following its noun) of what is *famous* or *well-known*; often (especially the neuter **illud**) to mean "the following."

c. **Iste** is used of what is *between the two others* in remoteness; often of the person addressed, — hence called the *demonstrative of the second person*; especially of one's opponent, frequently implying contempt.

d. **Is** is a weaker demonstrative than the others, not denoting any special object, but referring to one just mentioned, or to be explained by a relative. It is used oftener than the others as a personal pronoun; and is often merely a correlative to the relative **qui**: as, **eum quem**, *one whom*; **eum consulem qui non dubitet** (Cic.), *a consul who will not hesitate*.

e. **Ipse**, may be used with a personal pronoun, as **nos ipsi** (nosmetipsi), *we ourselves*; or independently (the verb containing the pronoun), as, **ipsi adestis**, *you are yourselves present*; or with a noun, as **ipsi fontes** (Virg.), *the very fountains*.

NOTE. — In English, the pronouns *himself*, &c., are used both intensively (as, *he will come himself*), or reflexively (as, *he will kill himself*): in Latin the former would be translated **ipse**; the latter **se**, or **sese**.

21. Relative, Interrogative, and Indefinite.

1. The Relative, Interrogative, and Indefinite pronouns are the same; viz., **qui, quis** (*who, who? any*), with their compounds and derivatives.

NOTE. — The stem has two forms, **quo-** and **qui-**. From the latter are formed *quis, quid, quem, quibus, quī* (abl.), while *qui, quae,* are probably lengthened forms of *quŏ, quā,* made by the addition of the demonstrative particle **i**.

Sing.	M.	F.	N.
Nom.	qui, quis	quae	quŏd, quĭd
Gen.	cūjus	cūjus	cūjus
Dat.	cui (quoi)	cui	cui
Acc.	quem	quam	quod
Abl.	quo (quī)	quā	quo
Plur.			
Nom.	qui	quae	quae (quă)
Gen.	quorum	quarum	quorum
Dat.		quibus or quīs (queis)	
Acc.	quos	quas	quae (quă)
Abl.		quibus or quīs (queis)	

Case Forms. **a.** The Relative has always **qui** and **quod** in the nom. sing. The Interrogative and Indefinite have **quis, quid** *substantive,* and **qui, quod** *adjective.* But **quis** and **qui** are sometimes used for each other.

b. Old forms for the gen. and dat. are **quoius, quoi**. A locative **cui** occurs only in the form **cuicuimŏdi,** *of whatever sort.*

c. The form **quī** is used for the ablative of both numbers and all genders; but especially as an adverb (*how, by which way, in any way*), and in the combination **quicum,** as interrogative or indefinite relative.

d. A nom. plur. **quēs** (stem quĭ-) is found in early Latin. The dat. and abl. **quīs** (stem quŏ-) is old, but not infrequent.

e. The preposition **cum** is joined enclitically to all forms of the ablative, as with the personal pronouns.

2. The stems **quo** and **qui** are variously compounded.

a. The suffix **-cunque** (**-cumque**) added to the relative makes an Indefinite-relative, which is declined as the simple word: as,

quicumque, quaecumque, quodcumque, *whoever, whatever.*

NOTE. — This suffix, with the same meaning, may be used with any relative: as, **qualiscunque,** *of whatever sort;* **quandocunque (quandoque),** *whenever;* **ubicunque,** *wherever.*

b. The interrogative form doubled also makes an indefinite-relative: as, **quisquis**, *whoever* (so **utut**, *however*, **ubiubi**, *wherever*). Of **quisquis** both parts are declined, but the feminine is wanting: as,

Nom.	quisquis (quiqui)	quidquid (quicquid)
Gen.		cujuscujus
Dat.		cuicui
Acc.	quemquem	quidquid (quicquid)
Abl.		quoquo
Plur. Nom. quiqui		Dat., Abl. quibusquibus

This compound is rare, except in the forms **quisquis**, **quicquid**, and **quoquo**. The case-form **quamquam** is used as a conjunction, *although* (lit. *however*). **Quiqui** is an early form.

c. Indefinite Compounds are the following: **quispiam**, *any*; **quisquam**, *any-at-all*; **quivis**, **quilibet**, *any-you-please*; **quidam**, *a, a certain*. Of these the first part is inflected like **quis**, **qui**, with **quid** or **quod** in the neuter.

Note. — The form -**quam** is from the stem **quo-**, perhaps -**piam** also; but if so it must be dialectic (compare Oscan **pam** for **quam**). In **quivis**, **quilibet**, the second part is a verb (**vis**, *you wish*; **libet**, *it pleases*). They have the accusative case-forms **quamvis**, **quamlibet** (*however, although*), used as adverbs or conjunctions.

d. In **aliquis**, *any*, **siquis**, *if any*, **nequis**, *lest any*, **ecquis**, **numquis**, *whether any*, the second part is declined like **quis**, but having **quă** for **quae**, except in the nom. plur. feminine. **Si quis**, **ne quis**, **num quis**, are better written separately. The simple form **quis** is rare except in these combinations; and the compounds **quispiam**, **aliquis** (**si quis**, *if any one*; **si aliquis**, *if some one*), are often used in these, being rather more emphatic.

Note. — **Aliquis** is compounded with **ali-**, old stem of **alius**, but with weakened meaning. **Ecquis** is compounded with **en**.

e. The enclitic -**que** added to the indefinite gives a Universal: as, **quisque**, *every one*; **ubique**, *everywhere* (so **uterque**, *either of two*, or *both*). Of **quisque** the first part is declined. · In the compound **unusquisque**, both parts are declined, and sometimes separated by other words.

f. The relative and interrogative have a possessive adjective **cujus** (stem **cujo-**), *whose*; and a patrial **cujas** (stem **cujat-**), *of what country*.

g. **Quantus**, *how great*, **qualis**, *of what sort*, are derivative adjectives from the same stem, and are used as interrogative or relative, corresponding to the demonstratives **tantus**, **talis**. **Quam**, *how*, is an accusative of the same stem, corresponding to the case-form **tam**, *so*.

h. **Quisquam**, with **ullus**, *any*, **unquam**, *ever*, **usquam**, *anywhere*, are chiefly used in negative, interrogative, or conditional sentences, or after **quam**, *than*; **sine**, *without*; **vix**, *scarcely*.

22. Correlatives.

Many adjectives, pronouns, and adverbs are found in several corresponding forms, as, *demonstrative, relative, interrogative,* and *indefinite.* These are called Correlatives. Their forms are seen in the following Table: —

DEMONSTR.	RELAT.	INTERROG.	INDEF. REL.	INDEF.
is, *that*	qui	quis?	quisquis	aliquis
tantus, *so great*	quantus	quantus?	*	aliquantus
talis, *such*	qualis	qualis?	*	——
ibi, *there*	ubi	ubi?	ubiŭbi	alicŭbi
eo, *thither*	quo	quo?	quoquo	aliquo
eā, *that way*	quā	quā?	quāquā	aliquā
inde, *thence*	unde	unde?	*	alicunde
tum, *then*	quum, cum	quando?	*	aliquando
tot, *so many*	quot	quot?	quotquot	aliquot
toties, *so often*	quoties	quoties?	*	aliquoties

* Compounds with -cumque.

a. The forms **tot, quot, aliquot, totidem** (originally **toti**), are indeclinable, and may take any gender, number, or case: as,

   per tot annos, tot prœliis, tot imperatores (Cic.), *so many commanders, for so many years, in so many battles.*

b. The correlative of the second member is often to be rendered simply *as:* thus,

   tantum argenti quantum aeris, *as much silver as copper.*

c. A frequent form of correlative is found in the ablatives **quo** or **quanto,** *by how much;* **eo** or **tanto,** *by so much,* used with comparatives (rendered in English *the . . the*) : as,

   quo magis conatur, eo minus discit, *the more he tries the less he learns.*

d. Certain adverbs and conjunctions are often used correlatively: as,

   et . . . et, *both . . . and.*
   ut . . . ita (sic), *as (while) . . . so (yet).*
   aut (vel) . . . aut (vel), *either . . . or.*
   sive (seu) . . . sive, *whether . . . or.*
   tam . . . quam, *so (as) . . . as.*
   cum (tum) . . . tum, *both . . . and; not only . . . but also.*
   idem . . . qui, *the same . . . as.*

Note. — For the reciprocal use of **alius** and **alter,** see Syntax (§ 47, 9).

VERBS.

23. STRUCTURE.

1. The forms of a Latin verb are the following:—

a. VOICES: Active and Passive.
b. MOODS: Indicative, Subjunctive, Imperative, Infinitive.
c. PARTICIPLES: *Active*, Present and Future.
   Passive, Perfect and Gerundive.
d. VERBAL NOUNS: Gerund and Supine.
e. TENSES: Present, Imperfect, Future; Perfect, Pluperfect, Future-Perfect.
f. There are also separate terminations of inflection for each of the three Persons, Singular and Plural (§ **28**).

NOTE.— The Infinitives, Participles, Gerund, and Supine are not strictly parts of the verb, as having no personal terminations, but having the form and (in general) the construction of nouns. They were, however, regarded and used as verbal forms by the Romans.

2. Special forms for the following tenses are wanting in certain parts of the verb:—

a. In the Subjunctive mood, the *future* and *future-perfect*.

NOTE.— These are wanting, because the original meaning and most of the uses of this mood are future. In some cases, the future participle with the corresponding tense of esse is used.

b. In the Passive voice, the *perfect*, *pluperfect*, and *future-perfect*, which are supplied by corresponding tenses of **esse**, *to be*, with the Perfect Participle.

c. In the Imperative mood only two tenses are found,— *present* and *future*. In the Infinitive only the *present*, *perfect*, and *future*.

3. The Active and Passive voices are equivalent to the corresponding English forms, except that the tenses of the passive are used with more exactness. Thus **vocātur** means, *he is* [being] *called*, i.e., some one is now calling him; **vocātus est**, *he is called*, i.e., the action is now over.

NOTE. — The passive voice often has a *reflexive* meaning, as, **induitur vestem**, *he puts on his clothes;* and many verbs are active in meaning though passive in form. (See § 35, "Deponents.")

24. Moods.

1. The Indicative is used for direct assertion or interrogation.

2. The Subjunctive is used chiefly in commands, conditions, and dependent clauses.

NOTE. — The Latin Subjunctive is usually translated, in grammars, by the English potential forms, *may, might, could, would,* &c., to distinguish it from the Indicative, because the English has no subjunctive in general use. But the subjunctive is used in many cases where we use the indicative; and we use the potential in many cases where the Latin employs a separate verb. Thus *I may write* (except when it follows **ut**, *in order that*) is not **scribam** (subj.), but **licet mihi scribere**; *I can write* is **possum scribere**; *I would write* is **scribam, scriberem**, or **scribere velim** (**vellem**); *I should write, if, &c.*, **scriberem si** . . . or (implying duty) **oportet me scribere**. A few examples of the use of the subjunctive may be seen in the following: —

eamus, *let us go.* ne cunctemur, *let us not linger.*
quid morer, *why should I delay?*
si tardior sim iratus sit, *if I should be too late he would be angry.*
adsum ut videam, *I am here to see* [that I may see].
imperat ut scribam, *he orders me to write.*
nescio quid scribam, *I know not what to write.*
licet eas, *you may go;* cave cadas, *don't fall.*
vereor ne eat, *I fear he will go* (vereor ut, *I fear he will not*).
sunt qui putent, *there are some who think.*
si ita esset non manerem, *if it were so I would not stay.*
quæ cum dixisset abiit, *when he had said this he went away.*

3. The Imperative is used for exhortation or command; but its place is often supplied by the Subjunctive.

4. The Infinitive is used as an indeclinable noun, as the subject or object of another verb; but often takes the place of one of the other moods.

NOTE. — For the Syntax of the Moods, see § 57.

25. Participles.

1. The Present participle has the same meaning as the English participle in *-ing:* as, **vocans,** *calling;* **regentes,** *those ruling.* (For its inflection, see § **16,** 2.)

2. The Future participle is rarely used, except with tenses of **esse,** *to be* (see § **40**), or to express purpose: as, **urbs est casura,** *the city is about to fall;* **venit auditurus,** *he came to hear.*

3. The Perfect participle is used to form certain tenses of the passive, and often has simply an adjective meaning: as, **vocatus est,** *he was (has been) called;* **tectus,** *sheltered;* **acceptus,** *acceptable.*

> NOTE. — There is no perfect active or present passive participle in Latin. The perfect participle of deponents, however, is generally used in an active sense, as **secutus,** *having followed.* In other cases some different construction is used: as, **cum venisset,** *having come (when he had come)* ; **equitatu praemisso,** *having sent forward the cavalry (the cavalry having been sent forward)* ; **dum verberatur,** *while being struck* (= τυπτόμενος).
> For the Syntax of these participles, see § 72.

4. The Gerundive (sometimes called the *future passive participle*) has, with tenses of **esse,** the meaning *ought* or *must* (see § 40): as, **audiendus est,** *he must be heard.* But, in the oblique cases, it is oftener to be translated as if it were an active participle, and governed the word it agrees with: as, **ad petendam pacem,** *to seek peace* (§ 73).

26. GERUND AND SUPINE.

1. The Gerund is the neuter singular of the Gerundive. It is a verbal noun, corresponding to the English participial noun in *-ing:* as, **loquendi causā,** *for the sake of speaking.*

2. The Supines are the accusative and ablative (or dative) of a verbal noun of the fourth declension (§ 12, 4, *a*). They are generally translated by the English Infinitive *of purpose:* as, **venit spectatum,** *he came to see;* **mirabile dictu,** *wonderful to tell.*

> NOTE. — The Supine in **tum** is the regular Infinitive in Sanskrit.

27. TENSES.

1. The tenses of a Latin verb are of two classes: (1) those denoting *incomplete action*, the Present, Imperfect, and Future; (2) those denoting *completed action*, the Perfect, Pluperfect, and Future-Perfect.

Those of the former class, together with the Perfect, are also used to denote *indefinite action*.

2. The Present, Future, Pluperfect, and Future-Perfect have the same meaning as the corresponding tenses in English, but are distinguished more accurately in their use: as,

diu aegrōto, *I have long been* [and still am] *sick.*
cum venero scribam, *when I come* [shall have come] *I will write.*

3. The Perfect and Imperfect are both used to denote past time, the former usually to tell *a simple fact;* the latter, a *continued action,* or a *condition of things.* The Imperfect is variously rendered in English: as,

dīcēbat, *he said, he was saying,* or *he used to say;* saepe dīcēbat, *he would often say;* dictitabat, *he kept saying.*

The Perfect has two separate uses, distinguished as *definite* and *historical,* corresponding to the English perfect (compound) and preterite (imperfect) : as,

vocāvit, *he has called* (definite), or *he called* (historical).

NOTE. — In Latin, and in the languages derived from Latin (as Italian and French), there are two past tenses, — the Perfect or Preterite (*aorist*), which merely states that *the fact took place;* and the Imperfect, which is used for *description,* or to indicate that *the action was in progress.* In the Northern languages (Germanic or Gothic, including English), the same tense serves for both: as,

longius prosequi vetuit, quod loci naturam ignorabat, *he forbade to follow farther, because he was ignorant of the nature of the ground* (B. G. v. 9.).

4. The tenses of *completed action* are supplied in the Passive voice by adding the corresponding tenses of *incomplete action* of esse to the Perfect Participle : as, occisus est, *he was slain,* or, *he has been slain.*

5. The tenses of a Latin verb are formed upon three different stems, called the *present,* the *perfect,* and the *supine* stems.

a. The tenses of *incomplete action,* both active and passive, are formed upon the Present stem.

b. The tenses of *completed action* in the active voice are formed upon the Perfect stem.

c. The *perfect participle,* which is used in the tenses of completed action in the passive voice, is formed upon the Supine

28. Verb Forms.

1. *Personal endings*. Verbs have terminations for each of the three persons, both singular and plural, active and passive. These terminations are fragments of old pronouns, whose signification is thus added to that of the verb-stem.

	ACTIVE.		PASSIVE.	
	SINGULAR.	PLURAL.	SINGULAR.	PLURAL.
1.	m	mus	r	mur
2.	s	tis	ris	mĭni
3.	t	nt	tur	ntur

a. The present and perfect indicative have lost the **m**, and end in the modified stem-vowels **o** and **i**. Except **sum**, *I am*, and **inquam**, *I say*.

b. The second person of the perfect indicative has for the singular **sti**, and for the plural **stis**. The third person plural has an ending of verbal origin, **ērunt**.

c. The Imperative has special terminations:

ACTIVE.		PASSIVE.	
Sing. 2. [lost]	Plur. 2. **te, tote**	Sing. 2. **re**	Plur. 2. **mĭni**
3. **to**	3. **nto**	3. **tor**	3. **ntor**

NOTE. — The Passive is a peculiar Latin *middle* (or reflexive) form, made by adding **se** to the forms of the active voice, with some abrasion of their endings (the original form of **se**, **sva**, was not limited to the third person). Thus *amor* = *amo-se*, *amaris* = *amasise*, *amatur* = *amatise*. The above view seems the most probable, in spite of some objections. The ending **mini** in the second person plural of the passive is a remnant of the participial form found in the Greek -μενος.

All Latin words ending in **t**, except a few in **ot**, **ut**, with **et**, **at**, **sat**, are third persons of verbs; all in **nt** are third persons plural. In **dumtaxat**, *however*, **licet**, *although*, and the indefinite pronouns in **-libet**, the meanings of the verbs are disguised.

2. *Changes of Stem*. These terminations appear in all the tenses of the verb; but the Stem in many parts is variously modified to receive them, sometimes by changes in its form, and sometimes by additions at the end.

a. The Present indicative and subjunctive, the Imperative, and sometimes the Future, add the personal endings directly to the *present stem*, with or without change of vowel: as, **do**, **dăs**, **dat** (stem **dă-**); **vŏcem** (stem **vŏcā-**).

b. The Perfect indicative also sometimes adds them directly; but to another form of the root called the *perfect stem:* as, **dedi, dedisti, dedit.**

NOTE. — The **i** of the Perfect, which in early Latin is always *long* (ei, i, e) except before **mus**, is of doubtful origin. It is treated for convenience as part of the stem, as it is in **dedi, steti**, where it takes the place of the vowel **a**. .In the suffixes **vi** (= **fui**) and **si** (= Skr. *āsa*), and in the perfects of consonant-roots, it seems to be, but probably is not, a mere connecting vowel. The **s** before **ti** and **tis** is also anomalous. Most scholars regard it as a remnant of **es**; but it may be, like the others, of pronominal origin.

c. All other true verbal forms are compounded with a suffix — originally a verb — which contains the personal endings: as, **vocav-eram, vocav-ĕro, voca-bo.** The first person of the Perfect, thus compounded, produces another form of *perfect stem:* as, **vocā-vi.**

d. The Present Infinitive Active, Present Participle, and Gerundive, add nominal (noun or adjective) suffixes to the *present stem:* as, **vocāre, vocans (antis), vocandus.**

e. The Perfect infinitive adds an infinitive (**esse**) already formed to the *perfect stem:* as, **vocavisse** (= **vocavi-esse**).

f. The Perfect and Future Participles and the Supine are formed upon what is called a *supine stem*, which adds **t-** either to the Present stem or to the Root: as, **vocāt-, tect-** (root **tĕg-**).

NOTE. — Strictly, these have no common stem, but are formed with special suffixes (**to-, turo-, tu-**). As, however, the form to which they are added is the same for each, and as the suffixes all begin with **t**, it is convenient to give the name *supine stem* to the form in **t**. The participle in **to-** corresponds to the Greek verbal -τος; that in **turo-** is a development of the noun of *agency* ending in **-tor** (as **victor, victurus**); that in **tu-** is an abstract noun of the fourth declension (§ 12, 4, *a*).

g. The Present Infinitive Passive is an anomalous form, made by adding **-ri** or **i** to the *present stem:* as, **voco, vocāri; tego, tĕgi.** (When **i** is added, the final vowel of the stem disappears.) It was anciently followed by **-ĕr.**

h. The Future Infinitive Passive is supplied by the *supine in* **tum** with the infinitive passive of **eo**, *to go,* used impersonally: as, **vocatum iri,** *to be about to be called.*

NOTE. — The construction of this infinitive is different from the others, the form in **tum** being invariable, and the apparent subject accusative being really the *object* of the supine taken actively. Few verbs in fact have this form, for which **fore ut** with the subjunctive is often found.

3. *Verb-Endings.* The scheme of Verb-Endings, as they are formed by suffixes or personal endings, is as follows: —

a. Verbal Forms.

ACTIVE VOICE.		PASSIVE VOICE.	
INDICATIVE.	SUBJUNCTIVE.	INDICATIVE.	SUBJUNCTIVE.

PRESENT.

INDICATIVE.	SUBJUNCTIVE.	INDICATIVE.	SUBJUNCTIVE.
[o]	m (vowel-change)	[or]	r (vowel-change)
s	s	ris or re	ris or re
t	t	tur	tur
mus	mus	mur	mur
tis	tis	mĭni	mĭni
nt	nt	ntur	ntur

IMPERFECT.

bam	rem	bar	rer
bas	res	bāris(re)	rēris(re)
bat	ret	bātur	rētur
bāmus	rēmus	bāmur	rēmur
bātis	rētis	bamĭni	remĭni
bant	rent	bantŭr	rentur

FUTURE.

bo, or am (vowel-change)		bor, or ar (vowel-change)	
bis	es	bĕris(re)	ēris(re)
bit	et	bĭtur	ētur
bĭmus	ēmus	bĭmur	ēmur
bĭtis	ētis	bimĭni	emĭni
bunt	ent	buntur	entur

PERFECT.

i	ĕrim	tus (ta, tum) { sum / es / est	sim / sis / sit
isti	ĕris		
it	ĕrit		
ĭmus	erĭmus	ti (tae, ta) { sŭmus / estis / sunt	sīmus / sītis / sint
istis	erĭtis		
ērunt or ēre	ĕrint		

PLUPERFECT.

ĕram	issem	tus (ta, tum) { ĕram / ĕras / ĕrat	essem / esses / esset
ĕras	isses		
ĕrat	isset		
erāmus	issēmus	ti (tae, ta) { erāmus / erātis / erant	essēmus / essētis / essent
erātis	issētis		
ĕrant	issent		

FUT. PERFECT.

ĕro		⎧ ero
ĕris	tus (ta,	⎨ eris
ĕrit	tum)	⎩ erit
erĭmus		⎧ erĭmus
erĭtis	ti (tae,	⎨ erĭtis
ĕrint	ta)	⎩ erunt

IMPERATIVE.

—	re
to	tor
te, tōte	mĭni
nto	ntor

b. *Nominal Forms.*

INFINITIVE.

PRESENT.	re (Pres. stem)	ri or i (old rier, ier)
PERFECT.	sse (Perf. stem)	tus (a, um) esse
FUTURE.	turus (a, um) esse	tum iri.

PARTICIPLE.

PRESENT.	ns, ntis	—
PERFECT.	—	tus, a, um
FUTURE.	turus, a, um	GERUNDIVE. ndus, a, um
SUPINE.	tum, tu	

NOTE. — The origin and meaning of some of the above verb-endings may be given as follows. The suffix **bam** is an imperfect of BHU, which appears in *fui, futurus, fio,* the Greek φύω, and English *be;* — **rem** (for **sem**) is an optative or subjunctive imperfect of ES, which appears in *sum,* εἰμί, *am,* &c.; — **bo** is a future, and **vi** a perfect, of BHU; — **si** is a perfect of ES, and is kindred with the aorist-ending σα, though not of the same formation; — **erim** is an optative form of ES corresponding to **sim**; — **ero** is the future of **es** (for **es-io**).

29. Esse AND ITS COMPOUNDS.

The verb **esse**, *to be*, is both irregular and defective, having no gerund or supine, and no participle but the future.

NOTE. — The present participle, which should be **sens** (compare Sanskrit *sunt*), appears in that form in **ab-sens, præ-sens**; and as **ens** (compare ὤν) in **pot-ens**. The simple form **ens** is sometimes found in late or philosophical Latin as a participle or abstract noun, in the forms **ens**, *Being;* **entia**, *things which are.*

PRINCIPAL PARTS: *Present*, **sum**, *I am*.
Infinitive, **esse**, *to be*.
Perfect, **fui**, *I was* or *have been*.
Future Participle, **futūrus**, *about to be*.

PRESENT.

	INDICATIVE.	SUBJUNCTIVE.
SING. 1.	**sum**, *I am*.	**sim**, *I am, may be, &c.* (see
2.	**ĕs**, *thou art*.	**sis** [examples on p. 51).
3.	**est**, *he (she, it) is*.	**sit**
PLUR. 1.	**sŭmus**, *we are*.	**sīmus**
2.	**estis**, *you are*.	**sītis**
3.	**sunt**, *they are*.	**sint**

IMPERFECT.

SING. 1.	**ĕram**, *I was*.	**essem**, *was (would* or	**fŏrem**
2.	**ĕras**, *thou wast*.	**esses**, *might be, &c.*).	**fŏres**
3.	**ĕrat**, *he was*.	**esset**	**fŏret**
PLUR. 1.	**erāmus**, *we were*.	**essēmus**	
2.	**erātis**, *you were*.	**essētis**	
3.	**erant**, *they were*.	**essent**	**fŏrent**

FUTURE.

SING. 1. **ĕro**, *I shall be*.
2. **ĕris**, *thou wilt be*.
3. **ĕrit**, *he will be*.

PLUR. 1. **erĭmus**, *we shall be*.
2. **erĭtis**, *you will be*.
3. **ĕrunt**, *they will be*.

PERFECT.

SING. 1.	**fui**, *I was (have been)*.	**fuĕrim**, *was (have been, may*
2.	**fuisti**, *thou wast*.	**fuĕris** [*have been*).
3.	**fuit**, *he was*.	**fuĕrit**
PLUR. 1.	**fuĭmus**, *we were*.	**fuerĭmus**
2.	**fuistis**, *you were*.	**fuerĭtis**
3.	**fuērunt**, *they were*. or **fuēre**.	**fuĕrint**

PLUPERFECT.

SING. 1. fŭĕram, *I had been.*   fuissem, *had been (might or*
     2. fŭĕras, *thou hadst been.*   fuisses   *would have been).*
     3. fŭĕrat, *he had been.*   fuisset
PLUR. 1. fuerāmus, *we had been.*   fuissēmus
     2. fuerātis, *you had been.*   fuissētis
     3. fŭĕrant, *they had been.*   fuissent

FUTURE PERFECT.

SING. 1. fŭĕro, *I shall have been.*
     2. fŭĕris, *thou wilt have been.*
     3. fŭĕrit, *he will have been.*
PLUR. 1. fuerĭmus, *we shall have been.*
     2. fuerĭtis, *you will have been.*
     3. fuerint, *they will have been.*

IMPERATIVE.

PRESENT. ĕs, *be thou.*   este, *be ye.*
FUTURE. esto, *thou shalt be.*   estote, *ye shall be.*
      esto, *he shall be.*   sunto, *they shall be.*

INFINITIVE.

PRESENT. esse, *to be.*
PERFECT. fuisse, *to have been.*
FUTURE. fŏre *or* futurus esse, *to be about to be.*
FUTURE PARTICIPLE. futurus, a, um, *about to be.*

RARE FORMS. Fut. Indic. escit, escunt (strictly inchoative pres., § 39). Pres. Subj. siem, fuam.

NOTE. — The root of the verb esse is es-, which in the imperfect is changed to er- (§ 1, 3, *e*), and in many cases is shortened to s-. Some of its modifications, as found in several languages more or less distantly related to Latin, may be seen in the following Table; — the "Indo-European" being the primitive or theoretic form, and the form *syām* corresponding to the Latin siem, sim:—

Ind.-Eur.	Sanskrit.		Greek.	Slavonic.	Lithuanian.
as-mi	as-mi	syām (opt.)	ἐμμι †	yes-mi	es-mi
as-si	as-i	syās	ἐσσί †	yes-si	es-i
as-ti	as-ti	syāt	ἐστί	yes-ti	es-ti
as-masi	s-mas	syāma	ἐσμέν	yes-mu	es-me
as-tasi	s-tha	syāta	ἐστέ	yes-te	es-te
as-anti	s-anti	syus	ἐντί †	s-unti	es-ti

† Old Form.

The Perfect and Supine stems, fui, futu-, are kindred with the Greek (ἔφυ, *was*), and with the English *be*.

a. The verb **esse** is compounded, without any change of its inflection, with many prepositions. In the compound **prodesse**, *to profit*, **pro** retains its original d where followed by e: as, **prosum, prodes, prodest, prosŭmus, prodestis, prosunt**.

b. **Esse** is also compounded with the adjective **potis** or **pote**, *able*, in the verb **posse**. Its inflection, with that of **prodesse**, is given in the following:—

PRESENT.

INDIC.	SUBJ.	INDIC.	SUBJ.
possum, *I can.*	possim	prosum	prosim
potes, *thou canst.*	possis	prodes	prosis
potest, *he can.*	possit	prodest	prosit
possŭmus, *we can.*	possīmus	prosŭmus	prosīmus
potestis, *you can.*	possītis	prodestis	prosītis
possunt, *they can.*	possint	prosunt	prosint

IMPERFECT.

potĕram	possem	prodĕram	prodessem

FUTURE.

potĕro		prodĕro

PERFECT.

potui	potuĕrim	profui	profuĕrim

PLUPERFECT.

potuĕram	potuissem	profuĕram	profuissem

FUTURE PERFECT.

potuĕro		profuĕro

IMPERATIVE.

——   prodes, prodesto, &c.

INFINITIVE.

PR. **posse**   PERF. **potuisse**   PR. **prodesse**   PERF. **profuisse**

PARTICIPLES.

[**potens**, *powerful*.]   **profuturus**, *about to help*.

30. CONJUGATION.

There are in Latin four principal forms of Present Stems, ending respectively in ā, ē, ĕ, ī. With this difference of stem most of the other differences of conjugation coincide.

Verbs are accordingly classed in *four regular conjugations*, distinguished by the vowel before **re** in the Present Infinitive Active, which is the same in each case as those given above.

Note. — This mode of classification was invented by the Roman grammarians, and has been generally adopted by the moderns. In fact, however, thé vowels a, e, i (*long*), found in the First, Second, and Fourth Conjugations, are different corruptions of the form AYA, which in the original language was added to roots in one form of present stems. All other forms of present stems, except a few unmodified, had originally, or received in Latin, a suffix ending in (or consisting of) a *short*, which was corrupted to e or i *short*. These are collected in the Third Conjugation. A few roots ending in a vowel were drawn — perhaps by *vowel-increase* — into the analogy of the other conjugations; and a few of the fourth conjugation had IYA instead of AYA.

1. *First Conjugation*. Most verbs of the first conjugation retain the stem-vowel (ā) throughout, except in the *present indicative*, which loses it before **o**, and the *present subjunctive*, where it is changed to **ē**.

Note. — Dare, *to give* — stem originally dă — retains a *short*, except in da and das. The Subjunctive with *changed vowel* (e) corresponds to the Greek and Sanskrit Optative, and is formed by the addition of a tense of i, *to go*, a + i becoming e.

a. In the Future, the ending -bo, &c., is added to the present stem: as, **vocābo**.

b. The Perfect stem adds **vi** to that of the present: as, **vocāvi**. But

1. A few verbs, either always or occasionally, add **vi** not to the present stem, but to the root, **v** becoming **u**: as, **sono, sonui** (see p. 67).

2. Two verbs, **do, sto**, form their perfect stem by *reduplication:* **dĕdi, stĕti**.

c. The Supine stem adds **t** to the *present stem;* but verbs that add **vi** to the *root* add **t** in like manner, sometimes with a connecting vowel: as, **seco, sectus; domo, domitus.**

2. *Second Conjugation*. Only a few verbs of the second conjugation retain **ē** throughout.

a. The Present Indicative has e before o in the first person; in the Present Subjunctive a (originally ā) is inserted after e: as, **deleo, deleam.**

Note. — The a in the present subjunctive is borrowed from the *third conjugation.* (See next head, 3, *e*, N.)

b. The Future (as in the first conjugation) adds -bo, &c., to the present stem: as, **delēbo.**

c. In a few verbs, the Perfect stem adds **vi** to the present, as **deleo, delēvi;** but in most this termination is added to the root, as **moneo, monui** (see p. 69).

d. In a few, the root is reduplicated, and in several -si is added to the root, or its vowel is strengthened: as, **tondeo, totondi; măneo, mansi; lugeo, luxi; căveo, cāvi.**

e. For the Supine stem, those which add **-vi** to the *stem* add **t** also to the stem; those which add **vi** to the *root* add **t** to the root, with the connecting-vowel **i**; those which form the perfect otherwise add **t** (or its weakened form **s**) to the *root:* as, **delētus, monĭtus, tonsus, mansus, cautus.**

3. *Third Conjugation.*

To the third conjugation belong those verbs which form the present stem in any other way than by adding a long vowel to the root.

a. The Present Stem is formed in eight different ways, in all of which **ĕ** (originál **ă**), or else a suffix containing it, is added to the Root. Besides this addition, —

1. The vowel of the root is *lengthened* (vowel-increase): as in **dūco, fīdo, nūbo** (compare **dŭcis, perfĭdus, pronŭba**; also Gr. λείπω, root λιπ-).

2. The root is *reduplicated:* as in **sisto, bĭbo, gigno**, from the root **stă-** (in **stătus**), **pă-** (in **pŏtus**), **gĕn-** (in **gĕnus**; compare γίγνομαι, root γεν-).

3. The root is *strengthened* by the insertion of **n** (**m**) before its final consonant: as in **findo, frango, cumbo** (compare *think, thought;* μανθάνω, root μαθ-).

4. Final **l** or **r** of the root is doubled by assimilation of an added consonant: as in **fello, pello** (compare στέλλω, root στελ-), **verro.**

5. The consonant **n** is added to the root: as in **cerno, lino, temno** (compare τέμνω, root τεμ-).

6. The root adds **sc** or **isc** (originally and often still inceptive): as in **disco** (= **dicsco**, root **dĭc**), **nascor** (root **gnă**), **nanciscor** (root **năc**, compare φάσκω, εὑρίσκω).

7. The root adds **t**: as in **pecto, plecto, mitto** (compare κόπτω).

8. The root adds **ĭ** (originally **y**) in the following: **căpio, cŭpio, -cŭtio, făcio, fŏdio, fŭgio, jăcio, -lĭcio, părio, quătio** (**-cŭtio**), **răpio, săpio, -spĭcio.**

NOTE. — Verbal stems in **u** add merely the vowel **e**, and are of the third conjugation. The **u** may be *radical*, as in **suo, pluo, fluo**; or developed from a *palatal*, as in **loquor, stinguo** (cf. στίζω); or may belong to the *noun* in denominatives, as **statuo** (**statu-s**), **acuo** (**acu-s**). Stems in **o** are lost, as **po-** (cf. **potum**); or have become of the first conjugation, as **boo, boare.**

b. The stem-vowel ĕ is weakened to ĭ in several forms of the Present indicative and imperative; is lengthened to ē in the Imperfect; and undergoes other changes exhibited in the paradigm.

c. The Future is formed (without the suffix bo) by vowel-changes to a and e before the personal endings.

NOTE. — The a (properly long) of the future is borrowed from the present subjunctive; the forms in e have the same origin as the present subjunctive of the first conjugation, and are properly optative.

d. The Perfect stem is formed in five different ways: —

1. The root is *reduplicated:* as in cădo, cecĭdi; curro, cŭcurri; disco, didĭci.

2. The root-vowel is *increased*, ă becoming ē, and ĭ, ŏ, ŭ being simply lengthened: as in căpio, cēpi; fŏdio, fōdi; fŭgio, fūgi.

3. The same form appears in the perfect as in the present stem: this is regular with verbs of this conjugation in uo (vo): as, acuo, acui; solvo, solvi.

NOTE. — It is probable that in the last two cases the root was originally reduplicated; but that the reduplication was retained only where vowel-increase did not take place.

4. The suffix si is added to the root: as in carpo, carpsi; gĕro, gessi; sūmo, sumpsi; dīco, dixi; tĕgo, texi.

5. The suffix ui (vi) is added to the root: as in cŏlo, colui; frĕmo, fremui; gigno, genui; rapio, rapui. Before this suffix a long vowel of various origin is often found: as in cŭpio, cupīvi; peto, petīvi; sperno, sprēvi.

NOTE. — Both suffixes are combined in the following: necto, nexui; plecto, plexui. A few verbs vary: as, pango, panxi (pegi or pepigi); vello, velli or vulsi.

e. The Present Subjunctive changes ĕ to ā: as, vehĕre, vehās.

NOTE. — This form with ā corresponds to the Greek and Sanskrit subjunctive with long vowel, and proceeds from the addition of another a (*short*): compare ἔχῃς, *vahāsi*.

f. The Supine stem is formed by adding to the root t-, which in many cases takes euphonically the form s- (§ 1, 3, *f.* 4).

NOTE. — A few roots take a connecting vowel before this affix, and some have both forms. When this is the case, the future participle and derivative verb take the longer form: as, ortus, oriturus; actus (ago), agito.

g. Some verbs of the third conjugation form the other parts upon the (modified) present stem as a root: as, fingo, finxi, fict- (fĭg); jungo, junxi, junct- (jŭg).

h. In verbs which add i to the root in the present stem, this vowel is lost where it would be followed by ĕ or ĭ (except in the future third person singular): as in capit, capĕret, capiet.

4. Fourth Conjugation. Verbs of the fourth conjugation retain **i** throughout, except before another vowel.

a. Several forms of the present stem have in addition the final vowels of the third conjugation. In the Imperfect the regular form (retained in **ībam**, from **eo**) is often found in early Latin.

b. The Future does not take **bo**, but has **ia** and **ie** (from the third conjugation) before the personal endings. In early Latin the form in **bo** (retained in **ībo**) sometimes occurs.

c. The Perfect stem adds **vi** to the present stem: as, **finio, finīvi**. A few verbs add it to the root, as **aperio, aperui**; several add **si**, as **sentio, sensi**; and in a few the perfect is the same as the present stem, with or without vowel-increase: as, **repĕrio, repĕri**; **vĕnio, vēni**.

d. The Supine stem adds **t-** to the present: as, **finio, finītus**. A few add it to the root: as, **salio, saltus**; **sepĕlio, sepultus**.

5. Principal Parts. The principal parts of a verb, which determine its conjugation throughout, are the following: 1. Present Indicative (showing the *present stem*); 2. Present Infinitive (the *conjugation*); 3. Perfect (the *perfect stem*); 4. Supine (the *supine stem*).

a. The regular forms of conjugation are seen in the following:—

  1. vŏco, vocāre, vocāvi, vocātum, *call*.
  2. dĕleo, delēre, delēvi, delētum, *destroy*.
  3. carpo, carpĕre, carpsi, carptum, *gather*.
  4. audio, audīre, audīvi, audītum, *hear*.

In the second conjugation, however, the characteristic **ē** rarely appears in the perfect and supine: thus the type of this conjugation is —

  mŏneo, monēre, monui, monĭtum, *warn*.

b. What is called the Synopsis of a verb consists of the *first person singular* of each tense, with infinitive and participles, given in regular order: as, of **ămo**, *I love* —

Indic. amo, amābam, amābo, amāvi, amavĕram, amavĕro.
Subj. amem, amārem, amavĕrim, amavissem.
Imp. ama, amāto.
Inf. amāre, amavisse.
Part. amans, amatūrus, amātus, amandus.

Notice that in all verbs the *Imperf.* and *Pluperfect Subjunctive* may be formed by adding the personal-endings to the *present* and *perfect infinitive;* and the Imperative Passive (second person) is the same in form with the *present infinitive active.*

c. In many verbs the principal parts take the form of two or more different conjugations: as,

1, 2. dŏmo, domāre, domui, domĭtum, *subdue.*
2, 3. augeo, augēre, auxi, auctum, *increase.*
3, 4. pĕto, petĕre, petīvi, petītum, *seek.*
4, 3. vincio, vincīre, vinxi, vinctum, *bind.*

In these the conjugation is said to be denoted by the *first* or *present stem.*

d. The compounds of many verbs vary from the forms of the primitive. This variation is seen especially (1) in the change of the vowel of the root, ă in open syllables becoming ĭ and in close syllables ĕ, while ē becomes ī: as, căpio, captum, concĭpio, conceptum; tĕneo, contĭneo; (2) in the loss of the reduplication: as, concĭdo, concĭdi. (This is, however, retained in compounds of **disco, do, posco, sto,** and in some of those of **curro**).

6. *Special Forms.* The following special forms are found in the conjugation of many verbs: —

a. In tenses formed upon the Perfect stem, **v** between two vowels is often suppressed, and the second vowel merged in the first (unless **a** or **e** follows **i** or **u**): as, **amasse** = **amavisse; flestis** = **flevistis; audieram** = **audiveram; nosse** = **novisse; noram** = **noveram.** This is especially frequent in verbs of the fourth conjugation, and is regular in the compounds of **eo**: as, **abiit** for **abivit.**

b. In many forms **s** with its vowel is suppressed in like manner when it would be repeated: as, **dixti** for **dixisti.**

c. Four verbs — **dīco, dūco, făcio, fĕro** — with several of their compounds, drop the vowel-termination of the Imperative, making **dīc, dūc, făc, fĕr** (but **effĭce, confĭce**). The forms **dice, duce, face** (never **fere**) occur in early Latin.

d. For the imperative of **scio**, the future form **scito** is always used in the singular, and **scitote** usually in the plural.

e. The following are ancient forms, rarely found except in poetry: —

1. In the fourth conjugation -ībam, -ībo for -iebam, -iam (fut.);
2. In the present subjunctive **-im**: as in **duim, perduim** (retained also in religious formulas);
3. In the perf. subj. and fut. perf. **-so, -sim**: as, **faxo, faxim**;
4. In the passive infinitive **-ier**: as, **vocarier** for **vocari.**

7. *Parallel Forms.* Many verbs have more than one set of forms, of which only one is generally found in classic use: as,

lavo, lavāre or **lavĕre,** *to wash.*
scateo, scatēre or **scatĕre,** *to gush.*
ludifico, āre or **ludifĭcor, āri,** *to mock.*

31. First Conjugation.

ACTIVE VOICE.

INDICATIVE.	SUBJUNCTIVE.
Present, *I love or am loving.*	
ămo, *I love.*	amem
amas, *thou lovest.*	ames
amat, *he loves.*	amet
amāmus, *we love.*	amēmus
amātis, *you love.*	amētis
amant, *they love.*	ament
Imperfect, *I loved (used to love).*	
amābam, *I loved.*	amārem
amābas	amāres
amābat	amāret
amabāmus	amarēmus
amabātis	amarētis
amābant	amārent
Future, *I shall love.*	
amābo, *I shall love.*	
amābis	
amābit	
amabĭmus	
amabĭtis	
amābunt	
Perfect, *I loved (have loved).*	
amāvi, *I loved.*	amavĕrim
amavisti	amavĕris
amavit	amavĕrit
amavĭmus	amaverĭmus
amavistis	amaverĭtis
amavērunt (ēre)	amavĕrint
Pluperfect, *I had loved.*	
amavĕram, *I had*	amavissem
amavĕras [*loved.*	amavisses
amavĕrat	amavisset
amaverāmus	amavissēmus
amaverātis	amavissētis
amavĕrant	amavissent
Future Perfect, *I shall have loved.*	
amavĕro, *I shall have loved.*	
amavĕris	
amavĕrit	
amaverĭmus	
amaverĭtis	
amavĕrint	

PASSIVE VOICE.

INDICATIVE.	SUBJUNCTIVE.
I am beloved.	
amor	amer
amāris (re)	amēris (re)
amātur	amētur
amāmur	amēmur
amamĭni	amemĭni
amantur	amentur
I was loved.	
amābar	amārer
amabāris (re)	amarēris (re)
amabātur	amarētur
amabāmur	amarēmur
amabamĭni	amaremĭni
amabantur	amarentur
I shall be loved.	
amābor	
amabĕris (re)	
amabĭtur	
amabĭmur	
amabimĭni	
amabuntur	
I was (have been) loved.	
amātus sum	amatus sim
amatus es	amatus sis
amatus est	amatus sit
amati sumus	amati sīmus
amati estis	amati sītis
amati sunt	amati sint
I had been loved.	
amatus eram	amatus essem
amatus eras	amatus esses
amatus erat	amatus esset
amati erāmus	amati essēmus
amati erātis	amati essētis
amati erant	amati essent
I shall have been loved.	
amatus ero	
amatus eris	
amatus erit	
amati erĭmus	
amati erĭtis	
amati erunt	

	ACTIVE.	IMPERATIVE.	PASSIVE.
Pr.	ămā, *love thou.*		amāre, *be thou loved.*
	amāte, *love ye.*		amamĭni, *be ye loved.*
Fut.	amāto, *he shall love.*		amātor, *he shall be loved.*
	amatote, *ye shall love.*		
	amanto, *they shall love.*		amantor, *they shall be loved.*

Noun and Adjective Forms.

INFINITIVE.

Pres.	amāre, *to love.*	amāri, *to be loved.*
Perf.	amavisse, *to have loved.*	amātus esse, *to have been loved.*
Fut.	amatūrus esse, *to be about to love.*	amātum īri, amātus fore.

PARTICIPLES.

Pres.	**amans,** *loving.*	
Perf.	———	**amatus,** *beloved.*
Fut.	**amaturus,** *about to love.*	———

Gerundive.	amandus, a, um, *to be loved (lovely).*
Gerund.	amandum, -di, -do, *loving.*
Supines.	amātum, amātu, *to love.*

1. There are about 360 simple verbs of this conjugation, most of them formed directly upon a noun or adjective-stem, to which they generally give the force and meaning of an *active verb:* as, **armo,** *to arm* (**arma**); **caeco,** *to blind* (**caecus**); **exsulo,** *to be in exile* (**exsul**). Their conjugation is usually regular, like **amo**; though of many only a few parts are found in use.

2. Those which form their Perfect and Supine stems differently are the following, — those marked † having also regular forms; and those preceded by a hyphen being found only in compounds: —

crepo, crepui, crepit-, *resound.*
cubo, cubui, cubit-, *lie down.*
do, dare, dedi, dat-, *give.*
domo, domui, domit-, *subdue.*
frico, fricui, † frict-, *rub.*
juvo, juvi, jut-, *help.*
mico, micui, *glitter.*
neco, † necui, † nect-, *kill.*

plico, plicui, -plicit-, *fold.*
poto, potavi, † pot-, *drink.*
seco, secui, sect-, *cut.*
sono, sonui, sonit-, *sound.*
sto, steti, stat-, *stand.*
tono, tonui, tonit-, *thunder.*
veto, vetui, vetit-, *forbid.*

32. Second Conjugation.

ACTIVE VOICE.		PASSIVE VOICE.	
INDICATIVE.	SUBJUNCTIVE.	INDICATIVE.	SUBJUNCTIVE.

Present, *I warn.*   *I am warned.*

mŏneo, *I warn.*	moneam	moneor	monear
mones, *you warn.*	moneas	monēris (re)	moneāris (re)
monet, *he warns.*	moneat	monētur	moneātur
monēmus	moneāmus	monēmur	moneāmur
monētis	moneātis	monemĭni	moneamĭni
monent	moneant	monentur	moneantur

Imperfect, *I warned (was warning).*   *I was warned.*

monēbam	monērem	monēbar	monērer
monēbas	monēres	monebāris (re)	monerēris (re)
monēbat	monēret	monebātur	monerētur
monebāmus	monerēmus	monebāmur	monerēmur
monebātis	monerētis	monebamĭni	moneremĭni
monēbant	monērent	monebantur	monerentur

Future, *I shall warn.*   *I shall be warned.*

monēbo		monēbor
monēbis		monebĕris (re)
monēbit		monebĭtur
monebĭmus		monebĭmur
monebĭtis		monebimĭni
monēbunt		monebuntur

Perfect, *I warned (have warned).*   *I was (have been) warned.*

monui	monuĕrim	monĭtus sum	monitus sim
monuisti	monuĕris	monitus es	monitus sis
monuit	monuĕrit	monitus est	monitus sit
monuĭmus	monuerĭmus	moniti sumus	moniti simus
monuistis	monuerĭtis	moniti estis	moniti sitis
monuērunt (re)	monuerint	moniti sunt	moniti sint

Pluperfect, *I had warned.*   *I had been warned.*

monuĕram	monuissem	monitus eram	monitus essem
monueras	monuisses	monitus eras	monitus esses
monuerat	monuisset	monitus erat	monitus esset
monueramus	monuissēmus	moniti eramus	moniti essemus
monueratis	monuissētis	moniti eratis	moniti essetis
monuerant	monuissent	moniti erant	moniti essent

Fut. Perfect, *I shall have warned.*   *I shall have been warned.*

monuĕro		monitus ero
monuĕris		monitus eris
monuĕrit		monitus erit
monuerĭmus		moniti erimus
monuerĭtis		moniti eritis
monuĕrint		moniti erunt

[32: 1, 2.] SECOND CONJUGATION. 69

	ACTIVE.		IMPERATIVE.	PASSIVE.	
	Sing.	Plur.	Sing.		Plur.
Pr.	mone, *warn.*	monēte	monēre		monemĭni
F.	monēto	monetote	—		—
	monēto	monento	monētor		monentor

INFINITIVE.

Pr. monēre Pf. monuisse Pr. monēri Pf. monitus esse
F. monitūrus esse   F. monĭtum iri (monitus fore)

PARTICIPLES.

monens   moniturus   monĭtus   monendus
Ger. monendum, di, &c.   Sup. monĭtum monĭtu

1. There are nearly 120 simple verbs of this conjugation, most of them denominative verbs of *condition*, having a corresponding noun and adjective from the same root, and an inceptive form in -sco: as, **caleo, calor, calĭdus, calesco; timeo, timor, timĭdus.**

2. Most verbs of the second conjugation form their perfect and supine like **moneo.** The following have **vi** and **ĕtum: deleo,** *destroy;* **fleo,** *weep;* **neo,** *spin;* and compounds of **-pleo,** *fill.* The remainder are —

algeo, alsi, —, —.   moveo, movi, mot-, *move.*
ardeo, arsi, ars-, *burn.*   mulceo, mulsi, muls-, *soothe.*
audeo, ausus sum, *dare.*   mulgeo, si (xi), muls- (mulct-),
augeo, auxi, auct-, *increase.*   *milk.*
caveo, cavi, caut-, *care.* niveo, nivi (nixi), *wink.*
censeo, censui, cens-, *value.* paveo, pavi. *fear.*
cieo, civi, cit-, *excite.* pendeo, pependi, *hang.*
doceo, docui, doct-, *teach.* prandeo, prandi, prans-, *dine.*
faveo, favi, faut-, *favor.* rideo, risi, ris-, *laugh.*
ferveo, fervi (ferbui), *glow.* sedeo, sedi, sess-, *sit.*
foveo, fovi, fot-, *cherish.* soleo, solitus sum, *be wont.*
frigeo, frixi, *be cold.*   sorbeo, sorbui (sorpsi), *suck.*
fulgeo, fulsi, *shine.*   spondeo, spopondi, spons-, *to*
gaudeo, gavisus sum, *rejoice.* strideo, stridi, *whiz.* [*pledge.*
haereo, haesi, haes-, *cling.* suadeo, suasi, suas-, *urge.*
indulgeo, indulsi, indult-, *in-* teneo, tenui, tent-, *hold*
jubeo, jussi, juss-, *order.* [*dulge.* tergeo, tersi, ters-, *wipe.*
langueo, langui. *be faint.* tondeo, totondi, tons-, *shear.*
liqueo, liqui (licui), *melt.* torqueo, torsi, tort-, *twist.*
luceo, luxi, *shine.*   torreo, torrui, tost-, *roast.*
lugeo, luxi, luct-, *mourn.* turgeo, tursi, *swell.*
maneo, mansi, mans-, *wait.* urgeo, ursi, *urge.*
misceo, cui, mixt- (mist-), *mix.* video, vidi, vis-, *see.*
mordeo, momordi, mors-, *bite.* voveo, vovi, vot-, *vow.*

33. THIRD CONJUGATION.

ACTIVE VOICE.

INDICATIVE.	SUBJUNCTIVE.
Present, *I rule.*	
rĕgo, *I rule.*	regam
regis, *thou rulest.*	regas
regit, *he rules.*	regat
regĭmus, *we rule.*	regāmus
regĭtis, *you rule.*	regātis
regunt, *they rule.*	regant
Imperfect, *I ruled (was ruling).*	
regēbam, *I ruled.*	regĕrem
regēbas	regĕres
regēbat	regĕret
regēbamus	regĕremus
regēbatis	regĕretis
regēbant	regĕrent
Future, *I shall rule.*	
regam, *I shall rule.*	
reges	
reget	
regēmus	
regētis	
regent	
Perfect, *I ruled (have ruled).*	
rexi, *I ruled.*	rexĕrim
rexisti	rexĕris
rexit	rexĕrit
reximus	rexerĭmus
rexistis	rexerĭtis
rexērunt (re)	rexĕrint
Pluperfect, *I had ruled.*	
rexĕram, *I had*	rexissem
rexĕras [*ruled.*	rexisses
rexĕrat	rexisset
rexerāmus	rexissemus
rexerātis	rexissetis
rexĕrant	rexissent
Fut. Perfect, *I shall have ruled.*	
rexĕro, *I shall have ruled.*	
rexĕris	
rexĕrit	
rexerĭmus	
rexerĭtis	
rexĕrint	

PASSIVE VOICE.

INDICATIVE.	SUBJUNCTIVE.
I am ruled.	
regor	regar
regĕris (re)	regāris (re)
regĭtur	regātur
regĭmur	regāmur
regimĭni	regamĭni
reguntur	regantur
I was ruled.	
regēbar	regĕrer
regebāris (re)	regerēris (re)
regebātur	regerētur
regebāmur	regerēmur
regebamĭni	regeremĭni
regebantur	regerentur
I shall be ruled.	
regar	
regēris (re)	
regētur	
regēmur	
regemĭni	
regentur	
I was (have been) ruled.	
rectus sum	rectus sim
rectus es	rectus sis
rectus est	rectus sit
recti sumus	recti simus
recti estis	recti sitis
recti sunt	recti sint
I had been ruled.	
rectus eram	rectus essem
rectus eras	rectus esses
rectus erat	rectus esset
recti eramus	recti essemus
recti eratis	recti essetis
recti erant	recti essent
I shall have been ruled.	
rectus ero	
rectus eris	
rectus erit	
recti erĭmus	
recti erĭtis	
recti erunt	

	ACTIVE.		IMPERATIVE.	PASSIVE.	
	Sing.	Plur.	Sing.		Plur.
Pr. 2.	rege, *rule*.	regĭte	regĕre		regimĭni
F. 2.	regĭto	regitōte	——		——
3.	regĭto	regunto	regĭtor		reguntor

INFINITIVE.

Pr. regĕre   Pf. rexisse   Pr. regi   Pf. rectus esse
F. recturus esse   F. rectum iri (rectus fore)

PARTICIPLES.

regens   recturus   rectus   regendus
Ger. regendum, di, &c.   Sup. rectum, rectu

Verbs in **io** (*present stem*) are inflected as follows:—

INDICATIVE.	SUBJUNCTIVE.	INDICATIVE.	SUBJUNCTIVE.
Present, *I take.*		*I am taken.*	
căpio, *I take.*	capiam	capior	capiar
capis, *thou takest.*	capias	capĕris (re)	capiāris (re)
capit, *he takes.*	capiat	capĭtur	capiātur
capĭmus, *we take.*	capiāmus	capĭmur	capiāmur
capĭtis, *you take.*	capiātis	capimĭni	capiamĭni
capiunt, *they take.*	capiant	capiuntur	capiantur
Imperfect, *I took (was taking).*		*I was taken.*	
capiēbam, *I took.*	capĕrem	capiēbar	capĕrer
capiēbas	capĕres	capiebāris (re)	caperēris (re)
capiēbat	capĕret	capiebātur	caperētur
capiebāmus	caperēmus	capiebāmur	caperēmur
capiebātis	caperētis	capiebamĭni	caperemĭni
capiēbant	capĕrent	capiebantur	caperentur
Future, *I shall take.*		*I shall be taken.*	
capiam	capiēmus	capiar	capiēmur
capies	capiētis	capiēris (re)	capiemĭni
capiet	capient	capiētur	capientur
Perf. cepi	ceperim	captus sum	captus sim
Plup. ceperam	cepissem	captus sim	captus essem
F. P. cepero		captus ero	

IMPERATIVE.

cape	capĭte	capĕre	capimĭni
capĭto	capitote	——	——
capĭto	capiunto	capĭtor	capiuntor
Infin. capĕre	cepisse	capi	captus esse
Part. capiens	capturus	captus	capiendus

THIRD CONJUGATION. [33: 1, 2, 3.

1. The following simple verbs of this conjugation form the perfect and supine stems like **rego**, by adding **s** and **t** to the root. Those marked ‡ take **s** in the supine:—

ango, *choke;* carpo, *pluck;* cingo, *bind;* ‡ claudo, *shut;* clĕpo, *steal;* cōmo, *comb;* cŏquo, *cook;* dēmo, *take away;* dīco, *say;* dūco, *guide;* ‡ figo, *fix;* ‡ flecto, *bend;* frīgo, *fry;* ‡ laedo, *hurt;* lingo, *lick;* ‡ lūdo, *play;* nūbo, *marry;* ‡ pecto, *comb;* ‡ plaudo, *applaud;* plecto, *twine;* prōmo, *bring out;* ‡ rādo, *scrape;* rĕgo, *rule;* rēpo, *creep;* ‡ rōdo, *gnaw;* sarpo, *prune;* scalpo, *scrape;* scrībo, *write;* serpo, *crawl;* sūmo, *take;* tĕgo, *shelter;* tingo, *stain;* traho, *drag;* ‡ trūdo, *thrust;* ‡ vādo, *go;* veho, *draw;* vivo, *live.*

NOTE.—In these verbs, h and v are treated as *palatals*, becoming x and ct; p takes the place of b, and is inserted euphonically after m, before s and t; while d and t are omitted: as in **scripsi, sumpsi, flexi, plausi**; demo, promo, sumo, are old compounds.

2. Verbs in **io** of the third conjugation are conjugated as follows:—

capio, cepi, capt-, *take.*
cupio, cupivi, cupīt-, *desire.*
-cutio, -cussi, -cuss-, *shake.*
facio, feci, fact-, *make.*
fodio, fodi, foss-, *dig.*
fugio, fugi, fugit-, *flee.*
jacio, jeci, jact-, *throw.*

-licio, -lexi, -lect-, *entice.*
pario, peperi, part- (pariturus), *bring forth.*
quatio, —, quass-, *shake.*
rapio, rapui, rapt-, *seize.*
sapio, sapivi, or sapui, *be wise.*
-spicio, -spexi, -spect-, *view.*

3. Those otherwise conjugated are the following (see § **30**, 3, *a, b*).

ago, egi, act-, *drive.*
alo, alui, alt- (alit-), *nourish.*
arcesso, ivi, arcessīt-, *summon.*
bibo, bibi, bibit-, *drink.*
cado, cecidi, cas-, *fall.*
cædo, cecidi, cæs-, *cut.*
cano, cecini, cant-, *sing.*
capesso, capessivi, *undertake.*
cedo, cessi, cess-, *yield.*
-cello, -cellui(-culi), -cels-, *push.*
-cendo, -cendi, -cens-, *kindle.*
cerno, -crevi, -cret-, *decree.*
colo, colui, cult-, *dwell, till.*
compesco, compescui, *restrain.*
consulo, lui, consult-, *consult.*
cresco, crevi, cret-, *increase.*

cudo, -cudi, -cus-, *forge.* [*down.*
-cumbo [CUB], cubui, cubit-, *lie*
curro, cucurri, curs-, *run.*
depso, depsui, depst-, *knead.*
disco [DIC], didici(discit-), *learn.*
divido, divisi, divis-, *divide.*
-do, -didi, -dit- (as in abdo, &c., with credo, vendo), *put* [DHA]
edo, edi, esum, *eat* (§ **37**, 5).
emo, emi, empt-, *buy.*
facesso, facessi, facessīt-, *execute.*
fallo, fefelli, fals-, *deceive.*
-fendo, -fendi, -fens-, *ward off.*
fero, ferre, tuli, lat-, *bear* (§ **37**,
findo [FID], fidi, fiss-, *split.* [4).
fido, fisus sum, *trust.*

THIRD CONJUGATION.

fingo [FIG], finxi, fict-, *fashion.*
fluo, fluxi, flux-, *flow.*
frango [FRAG], fregi, fract-, *to break.*
fremo, fremui, fremit-, *roar.*
frendo, -fresi, fress-, *gnash.*
fundo [FUD], fudi, fus-, *pour.*
furo, furui, *rage.*
gemo, gemui, gemit-, *groan.*
gero, gessi, gest-, *carry.*
gigno [GEN], genui, genit-, *beget.*
ico, ici, ict-, *hit.*
incesso, incessivi, *attack.*
lacesso, lacessivi, lacessit-, *pro-voke.*
lambo, lambi, lambit-, *lap.*
lavo, lavi, lot- (laut-), *wash* (reg. of 1st conj.).
lego, legi(intellexi), lect-, *gather.*
lino [LI], levi (livi), lit-, *smear.*
linquo [LIC], -liqui, -lict-, *leave.*
luo, lui, luit-, *wash.*
mando, mansi, mans-, *chew.*
mergo, mersi, mers-, *plunge.*
meto, messui, mess-, *reap.*
mitto, misi, miss-, *send.*
molo, molui, molit-, *grind.*
necto [NEC], nexi (nexui), nex-, *weave.*
nosco[GNO], novi, not-(cognit-), *know.*
nuo, nui, nuit-, *nod.*
occulo, occului, occult-, *hide.*
pando, pandi, pans- (pass-), *open.*
pango [PAG], †pegi (pepigi), †pact-, *fasten.*
parco, peperci, parcit-, *spare.*
pasco, pavi, past-, *feed.*
pello, pepuli, puls-, *drive.*
pendo, pependi, pens-, *weigh.*
pergo, perrexi, perrect-, *go on.*
peto, petivi, petīt-, *seek.*
pingo [PIG], pinxi, pict-, *paint.*
pinso, pinsi, pins-(pinst-, pist-), *bruise.*
pono [POS], posui, posit-, *put.*
posco, poposci (posciturus,) *de-mand.*
prehendo, di, prehens-, *seize.*

premo, pressi, press-, *press.*
pungo [PUG], pupugi, punct-, *prick.*
quæro, quæsivi, quæsīt-, *seek.*
quiesco, quievi, quiet-, *rest.*
rudo, rudivi, rudīt-, *bray.*
rumpo [RUP], rupi, rupt-, *burst.*
ruo, rui, rut- (ruit-), *fall.*
scabo, scabi, *scratch.*
scando, scansi, scans-, *climb.*
scindo [SCID], scidi, sciss-, *tear.*
scisco, scivi, scīt-, *decree.*
sero, sevi, sat-, *sow.*
sero, serui, sert-, *entwine.*
sido, sidi (sedi), sess-, *settle.*
sino, sivi, sit-, *permit.*
sisto [STA], stiti, stat-, *stop.*
solvo, solvi, solut-, *pay, loose.*
spargo, sparsi, spars-, *scatter.*
sperno, sprevi, spret-, *scorn.*
sterno, stravi, strat-, *strew.*
sterto, stertui, *snore.*
strepo, strepui, strepit-, *sound.*
-stinguo, -stinxi, -stinct-, *quench.*
stringo, strinxi, strict-, *bind.*
struo, struxi, struct-, *build.*
suesco, suevi, suet-, *be wont.*
surgo, surrexi, surrect-, *rise.*
tango [TAG], tetigi, tact-, *touch.*
tendo, tetendi (-tendi), tens- (tent-), *stretch.*
tergo, tersi, ters-, *wipe.*
tero, trivi, trīt-, *rub.*
texo, texui, text-, *weave.*
tollo [TOL] (sustuli, sublat-), tremo, tremui, *tremble.* [*raise.*
tundo [TUD], tutudi, tuns-, *beat.*
uro, ussi, ust-, *burn.*
vello, velli (vulsi), vuls-, *pluck.*
verro, verri, vers-, *sweep.*
verto, verti, vers-, *turn.*
vinco [VIC], vici, vict-, *conquer.*
viso [VID], visi, vis-, *visit.*
vivo, vixi, vict-, *live.*
volvo, volvi, volut-, *turn.*
vomo, vomui, vomit-, *vomit.*

Those reduplicated in the perfect are — *cado, cædo, curro, disco, fallo, pango, parco, pello, pendo, posco, pungo, tendo, tundo.*

34. Fourth Conjugation.

ACTIVE VOICE.
INDICATIVE.	SUBJUNCTIVE.

Present, *I hear.*

audio, *I hear.*	audiam
audis, *thou hearest.*	audias
audit, *he hears.*	audiat
audĭmus, *we hear.*	audiāmus
audītis, *you hear.*	audiātis
audiunt, *they hear.*	audiant

Imperfect, *I heard (was hearing).*

audiēbam	audīrem
audiēbas	audīres
audiēbat	audīret
audiebāmus	audīrēmus
audiebātis	audirētis
audiēbant	audīrent

Future, *I shall hear.*

audiam, *I shall hear.*	
audies	
audiet	
audiēmus	
audiētis	
audient	

Perfect, *I heard (have heard).*

audīvi, *I heard.*	audivĕrim
audivisti	audivĕris
audivit	audivĕrit
audivĭmus	audiverĭmus
audivistis	audiverītis
audivērunt (re)	audivĕrint

Pluperfect, *I had heard.*

audivĕram, *I had*	audivissem
audivĕras [*heard.*	audivisses
audivĕrat	audivisset
audiverāmus	audivissēmus
audiverātis	audivissētis
audivĕrant	audivissent

Fut. Perfect, *I shall have heard.*

audivĕro, *I shall have heard.*
audivĕris
audivĕrit
audiverĭmus
audiverītis
audivĕrint

PASSIVE VOICE.
INDICATIVE.	SUBJUNCTIVE.

I am heard.

audior	audiar
audīris (re)	audiāris (re)
audītur	audiātur
audīmur	audiāmur
audimĭni	audiamĭni
audiuntur	audiantur

I was heard.

audiēbar	audīrer
audiebāris (re)	audirēris (re)
audiebātur	audirētur
audiebāmur	audirēmur
audiebamĭni	audiremĭni
audiebantur	audirentur

I shall be heard.

audiar
audiēris (re)
audiētur
audiēmur
audiemĭni
audientur

I was (have been) heard.

audītus sum	audītus sim
audĭtus es	auditus sis
auditus est	auditus sit
auditi sumus	auditi simus
auditi estis	auditi sitis
auditi sunt	auditi sint

I had been heard.

auditus eram	auditus essem
auditus eras	auditus esses
auditus erat	auditus esset
auditi eramus	auditi essemus
auditi eratis	auditi essetis
auditi erant	auditi essent

I shall have been heard.

auditus ero
auditus eris
auditus erit
auditi erĭmus
auditi erītis
auditi erunt

	ACTIVE.		IMPERATIVE.	PASSIVE.
	Sing.	Plur.	Sing.	Plur.
Pr. 2.	audī, hear.	audīte	audīre	audimĭni
F. 2.	audīto	auditōte	—	—
3.	audīto	audiunto	audītor	audiuntor

INFINITIVE.

Pr. audīre   Pf. audivisse   Pr. audīri   Pf. audītus esse
F. auditūrus esse   F. audītum iri (auditus fore)

PARTICIPLES.

audiens   auditūrus   audītus   audiendus
Ger. audiendum, di, &c.   Sup. audītum, audītu

1. There are — besides a few deponents and regular derivatives in -ūrio — about 60 verbs of this conjugation, a large proportion of them being *descriptive* verbs: viz.,

barrio, *roar* (as an elephant); crocio, *croak;* cūcūrio, *crow;* dentio, *teethe;* ebullio, *bubble;* effutio, *drivel;* frigutio, *stutter;* fritinnio, *twitter;* gannio, *yelp;* glutio, *gulp;* grunnio, *grunt;* hinnio, *neigh;* hirrio, *snarl;* ligūrio, *lick;* lipio, *scream* (as a hawk); lippio, *blink;* mugio, *bellow;* muttio, *mutter;* pavio, *trample;* scalptūrio, *scratch;* scatūrio, *gush;* singultio, *hiccup;* tinnio, *tinkle;* tussio, *cough;* vagio, *cry.*

2. Those not conjugated regularly, like audio, are the following:—

amicio, amixi (amicui), amict-, *clothe.*
aperio, aperui, apert-, *open..*
comperio, peri, compert-, *find.*
farcio, farsi (farct-) (-tum), *stuff.*
fulcio, fulsi, fult-, *prop.*
haurio, hausi, haust-, *drain.*
operio, operui, opert-, *cover.*
raucio, rausi, raus-, *be hoarse.*
reperio, reperi, repert-, *find.*
salio, salui, salt-, *leap.*
sancio, sanxi, sanct-, *sanction.*
sarcio, sarsi, sart-, *patch.*
sentio, sensi, sens-, *feel.*
sepelio, sepelivi, sepult-, *bury.*
sepio, sepsi, sept-, *hedge in.*
venio, veni, vent-, *come.*
vincio, vinxi, vinct-, *bind.*

35. Deponent Verbs.

1. Deponent Verbs have the form of the *Passive voice*, with an active or reflexive signification: as,

    1. mīror, mirāri, mirātus, *admire.*
    2. vĕreor, verēri, verĭtus, *fear.*
    3. sĕquor, sequi, secūtus, *follow.*
    4. pŏtior, potīri, potītus, *possess.*

The synopsis of these verbs is given as follows:—

INDICATIVE.

PRES.	miror	vereor	sequor	potior
IMP.	mirābar	verēbar	sequēbar	potiēbar
FUT.	mirabor	verēbor	sequar	potiar
PERF.	mirātus sum	verĭtus sum	secūtus sum	potītus sum
PLUP.	,, eram	,, eram	,, eram	,, eram
FUT. P.	,, ero	,, ero	,, ero	,, ero

SUBJUNCTIVE.

PRES.	mirer	verear	sequar	potiar
IMP.	mirārer	verērer	sequĕrer	potīrer
PERF.	miratus sim	verĭtus sim	secūtus sim	potītus sim
PLUP.	,, essem	,, essem	,, essem	,, essem

IMPERAT.	mirāre, ātor	verēre, ētor	sequĕre, ĭtor	potīre, ītor
INFIN.	mirāri	verēri	sequi	potīri
PART. PR.	mirans	verens	sequens	potiens
FUT.	miraturus	verĭturus	secuturus	potiturus
PERF.	mirātus	verĭtus	secūtus	potītus
GER.	mirandus	verendus	sequendus	potiendus

a. These verbs have the participles of both voices: as, **mirans**, *admiring;* **miraturus**, *about to admire;* **miratus**, *having admired;* **mirandus**, *to-be-admired (admirable).*

b. The participle in **dus** (gerundive) has necessarily a passive meaning, and hence is found only in transitive verbs, or of neuter verbs used impersonally (§ **39**, *c*): as, **potienda est tellus**, *the land must be won;* **pugnandum est nobis**, *we must fight.*

c. Most deponents are neuter or reflexive in their meaning, corresponding to what in Greek is called the *middle voice.*

d. More than half of all deponents are of the *first conjugation*, and all of these are *regular.*

e. About twenty verbs of active signification are found in both active and passive forms: as, **mereo** or **mereor**, *deserve.*

f. Some deponents are occasionally used in a passive signification: as, **criminor**, *I accuse* or *I am accused.*

g. The perfect participle of verbs otherwise deponent is often passive: as, **mercatus**, *bought;* **adeptus**, *obtained.*

h. The following list contains all the *irregular* deponents:—

adipiscor, i, adeptus, *obtain.*
expergiscor, i, -perrectus, *rouse.*
experior, iri, expertus, *try.*
fateor, eri, fassus, *confess.*
fruor, i, fructus, *enjoy.*
fungor, i, functus, *fulfil.*
gradior, i, gressus, *step.*
irascor, i, iratus, *be angry.*
labor, i, lapsus, *fall.*
loquor, i, locutus, *speak.*
-miniscor, i, -mentus, *think.*
metior, iri, mensus, *measure.*
morior, i (iri), mortuus (moriturus, moribundus), *die.*
nanciscor, i, nactus (nanctus), *find.*
nascor, i, natus, *be born.*
nitor, i, nisus (nixus), *strive.*
obliviscor, i, oblītus, *forget.*
opperior, iri, oppertus, *await.*

ordior, iri, orsus, *begin.* [*rise.* queror, i, questus, *complain.*
orior, i (iri), ortus (oriturus), reor, reri, ratus, *think.*
paciscor, i, pactus, *bargain.* sequor, i, secutus, *follow.*
patior, i, passus, *suffer.* tueor, eri, tuitus (tutus), *defend.*
-plector, i, -plexus, *clasp.* ulciscor, i, ultus, *avenge.*
proficiscor, i, profectus, *set-out.* utor, i, usus, *use, employ.*

2. Semi-Deponents. A few verbs, having no perfect stem, form the tenses of completed action like the passive: these are called *semi-deponents* or *neuter passives.* They are the following:—

    audeo, audēre, ausus, *dare.*
    fido, fidĕre, fisus, *trust.*
    gaudeo, gaudēre, gavīsus, *rejoice.*
    soleo, solēre, solĭtus, *be wont.*

a. From **audeo** there is an old subjunctive **ausim**. The form **sōdes** (for **si audes**), *an thou wilt*, is frequent in the dramatists.

b. The active forms **vapulāre**, *to be flogged*, and **venīre**, *to be sold* (**venum īre**, *go to sale*), having a passive meaning, are sometimes called *neutral passives.* To these may be added **fiĕri** (**fio**), *to be made*, and **exsulare**, *to be banished* (live in exile).

36. Derivative Verbs.

Several classes of verbs have derivative meanings corresponding to their form. (For their formation, see § **44**.)

a. INCEPTIVES or INCHOATIVES end in -sco, and denote the *beginning of an action:* as, **calesco**, *I grow warm* (**caleo**); **vesperascit**, *it is getting late* (**vesper**). They are of the third conjugation, and have only the Present stem, though often completed by forms of simple verbs.

b. INTENSIVES or ITERATIVES end in -to or -ĭto, and denote a *forcible* or *repeated* action: as, **jactat**, *he hurls* (**jacio**); **dictitabat**, *he kept saying* (**dico**). They are of the first conjugation.

NOTE.— Iteratives (or Frequentatives), though distinct in meaning from Intensives, are not always distinguished from them in form.

c. Another form of Intensives (sometimes called MEDITATIVES, or verbs of *practice*) ends in **-sso**, denoting a certain *energy* or *eagerness* of action: as, **facessit**, *he makes haste to do.* They are of the third conjugation, with perfect and supine of the fourth: as, **lacesso, lacessīvi, lacessītum,** *to provoke.*

d. DIMINUTIVES end in -illo, and denote a *feeble* or *petty* action: as, **cantillāre**, *to chirp* or *warble* (**cano**, *sing*).

e. **Desideratives** end in **ŭrio**, expressing *longing* or *wish*, and are of the fourth conjugation. Only these three are in common use, **emptŭrio** (**emo,** *buy*), **esŭrio** (**ĕdo,** *eat*), **parturio** (**pario,** *bring forth*). Others occur for comic effect in the dramatists.

37. Irregular Verbs.

[For **esse** and its compounds, see § 29.]

Several verbs retain older forms in the tenses of the present stem, or combine two roots in their inflection. These are called Irregular Verbs.

The most common verbs of this class are —

1. Vŏlo, velle, volui, *to wish* (the supine stem appears in **vultus,** *countenance*).

2. Nōlo (non volo), **nolle, nolui,** *to be unwilling.*

3. Mālo (mage-volo), **malle, malui,** *to prefer.*

[For the inflection of **volo, nolo, malo,** see opposite page.]

4. Fĕro, ferre, tŭli, lātum, *to bear.*

Note. — The perfect **tuli** is for **tetuli** (which sometimes occurs), from TUL in **tollo**; the Supine **latum** for **tlatum** (cf. τλητός).

	ACTIVE.		PASSIVE.	
	INDIC.	SUBJ.	INDIC.	SUBJ.
Pres.	fĕro	feram	feror	ferar
	fers	feras	ferris	feraris (re)
	fert	ferat	fertur	feratur
	ferimus	feramus	ferĭmur	feramur
	fertis	feratis	ferimini	feramini
	ferunt	ferant	feruntur	ferantur
Imp.	ferēbam	ferrem	ferēbar	ferrer
Fut.	feram		ferar	
Perf.	tŭlí	tulerim	latus sum	latus sim
Plup.	tuleram	tulissem	latus eram	latus essem
F. Perf.	tulero		latus ero	

	IMPERATIVE.			
	Sing.	*Plur.*	*Sing.*	*Plur.*
Pres.	fer	ferte	ferre	ferimini
Fut.	ferto	fertote		
	ferto	ferunto	fertor	feruntor

	INFINITIVE.			
	Pres.	Perf.	Pres.	Perf.
	ferre	tulisse	ferri	latus esse

	PARTICIPLES.			
	Pres.	Fut.	Perf.	Ger.
	ferens	laturus	latus	ferendus

Inflection of volo and its Compounds.

VOLO, *will.*   **NOLO,** *will not.*   **MALO,** *prefer.*

INDIC.	SUBJ.	INDIC.	SUBJ.	INDIC.	SUBJ.
			PRESENT.		
volo	velim	nolo	nolim	malo	malim
vis	velis	nonvis	nolis	mavis	malis
vult	velit	nonvult	nolit	mavult	malit
vol'umus	veli'mus	nol'umus	noli'mus	mal'umus	mali'mus
vultis	velitis	nonvultis	nolitis	mavultis	malitis
volunt	velint	nolunt	nolint	malunt	malint
			IMPERFECT.		
volebam	vellem	nolebam	nollem	malebam	mallem
volebas	velles	nolebas	nolles	malebas	malles
volebat	vellet	nolebat	nollet	malebat	mallet
volebamus	vellemus	nolebamus	nollemus	malebamus	mallemus
volebatis	velletis	nolebatis	nolletis	malebatis	malletis
volebant	vellent	nolebant	nollent	malebant	mallent
			FUTURE.		
volam		nolam †		malam †	
voles		noles		males	
volet		nolet		malet	
volemus		nolemus		malemus	
voletis		noletis		maletis	
volent		nolent		malent	
			PERFECT.		
volui	-erim	nolui	-erim	malui	-erim
voluisti	-eris	noluisti	-eris	maluisti	-eris
voluit	-erit	noluit	-erit	maluit	-erit
voluimus	-erimus	noluimus	-erimus	maluimus	-erimus
voluistis	-eritis	noluistis	-eritis	maluistis	-eritis
voluerunt	-erint	noluerunt	-erint	maluerunt	-erint
			PLUPERFECT.		
volueram	-issem	nolueram	-issem	malueram	-issem
volueras	-isses	nolueras	-isses	malueras	-isses
voluerat	-isset	noluerat	-isset	maluerat	-isset
volueramus	-issemus	nolueramus	-issemus	malueramus	-issemus
volueratis	-issetis	nolueratis	-issetis	malueratis	-issetis
voluerant	-issent	noluerant	-issent	maluerant	-issent
			FUTURE PERFECT.		
voluero		noluero		maluero	
volueris		nolueris		malueris	
voluerit		noluerit		maluerit	
voluerimus		noluerimus		maluerimus	
volueritis		nolueritis		malueritis	
voluerint		noluerint		maluerint	

IMPERATIVE.

PR.   noli, noli'te, *do not.*
FUT.   noli'to, nolito'te, *thou shalt not, ye shall not.*
        noli'to, nolunto, *he shall not, they shall not.*

INFINITIVE.

PRES.	velle	nolle	malle
PERF.	voluisse	noluisse	maluisse

PARTICIPLE.

PRESENT,   volens, *willing.*   nolens, *unwilling.*
GERUND,   volendi, volendo   nolendi

† Rare.

5. Edo, *to eat* (regular of third conjugation), has also some forms directly from the root without a characteristic vowel: viz.,

Ind. Pres. **ēs, est, estis**; Subj. Pres. **edim,** Imperf. **essem**; Imperat. **ēs, esto, este**; Infin. **esse**; Passive, **estur, essētur**; and, in compounds, **comes, comest, comestum, comēsum; exest, exesset, exesse.**

6. Eo, īre, īvi, ĭtum, *to go* (root **I**, cf. εἶμι; the e stands for ei produced by vowel-increase from i). The forms of **eo** are found in **veneo,** *to be sold* (**venum eo,** *go to sale*).

	INDICATIVE.	SUBJUNCTIVE.
Pres. S.	eo, is, it	eam, eas, eat
P.	īmus, ītis, eunt	eamus, eatis, eant
Imp.	ībam, ības, ībat	irem, ires, iret
	ibamus, ibatis, ibant	iremus, iretis, irent
Fut.	ibo, ibis, ibit	
	ibĭmus, ibĭtis, ibunt	
Perf.	ivi (ii)	iverim (ierim)
Plup.	iveram (ieram)	ivissem (issem)
Fut. P.	ivero	

Imperat. **i, ite; itote, eunto**

Infin.	Pr. ire	Per. ivisse (isse)
Part.	P. iens, euntis	F. iturus

7. Făcio, facĕre, fēci, factum, *to make,* — regular, with the peculiar forms fut. perf. **faxo,** perf. subj. **faxim,** imperat. **fac.** It has for its passive

fīo, fĭĕri, factus sum, *to be made,* or *become,*

of which the tenses of the first stem are regular of the fourth conjugation, but with subj. imperf. **fiĕrem.**

	INDICATIVE.	SUBJUNCTIVE.
Pres. S.	fio, fis, fit	fiam, fias, fiat
P.	fimus, fitis, fiunt	fiamus, fiatis, fiant
Imp.	fiebam	fiĕrem
Fut.	fiam, fies, &c.	
Perf.	factus sum	factus sim
Plup.	factus eram	factus essem
Fut. P.	factus ero	

Imperat. **fi, fite; fito, fitote, fiunto**

Infin.	Pres. fiĕri	P. factus esse
Part.	Perf. factus	faciendus

Most compounds of **facio** with prepositions change ă to ĭ or e, and form the passive and imperative regularly: as,

confĭcio, confĭcĕre, confēci, confectum, *to finish.*

Other compounds retain **a**, and have **-fio** in the passive: as,

bĕnĕ-facio (-fă′cis), -fēci, -factum; pass. **benefīo,** *to benefit.*

A few isolated forms of **-fio** occur with prepositions (see § **38,** *h*).

38. Defective Verbs.

1. Some verbs have lost their Present stem, and use only tenses of the Perfect (sometimes with the meaning of the present), in which they are inflected regularly.

a. **Coepi** (root CO-AP as in **apiscor**), *I began.* Infin. **coepisse;** Fut. Part. **coepturus.** A passive participle **coeptus** is used with the *passive infinitive.* For the Present, **incipio** is used.

b. **Odi,** *I hate* (root ŏd- in **odium**); with the participles **ōsus,** *hating* or *hated* (**perōsus,** *utterly hateful*), **osurus,** *likely to hate.*

c. **Memĭni,** *I remember* (root MEN, as in **mens, remĭniscor**), with the imperative **memento** and **mementote.**

NOTE.— **Odi** and **memini,** having a Perfect form with a present meaning, are called *preteritive verbs.*

2. Many verbs have only the Present stem, and in many the simple verb is incomplete, but the parts appear in the compounds. Some occur very commonly, but only in a few forms: as,

a. **Aio** (root AGH found in **adagium** and in **nego,** which has passed into the first conjugation):

IND. PRES. *Sing.* **aio,** *I say.*   *Plur.* ——
              ais   ——
              ait   **aiunt**

IMPERF. **aiēbam (aībam), aiebas,** &c.
SUBJ. PRES. **aias, aiat, aiant.**
IMPERAT. **ai.** — PART. **aiens.**

b. **Inquam,** *say* (used only in quotations, as the English *quoth,* which is from the same root):

IND. PRES. *Sing.* **inquam**   *Plur.* **inquĭmus**
              inquis   **inquĭtis**
              inquit   **inqueunt**

IMPERF. **inquībat.** — FUT. **inquiet.** — PERF. **inquisti.**
IMPERAT. **inque, inquĭto.**

c. **Fari**, *to speak*, forms the periphrastic tenses regularly: as, **fatus sum, eram**, &c. It has also

 IND. PRES. fatur, fantur. — FUT. fabor, fabĭtur.
 IMPERAT. fare. — INFIN. fari. — PART. fanti (with the compound **infans**, as noun).
 GERUND. fandus, *to be spoken of* (with the compounds **infandus, nefandus,** *abominable*). — SUPINE, fatu.

The compounds **affamur, affabimur, præfamini**, &c., occur.

d. **Quaeso**, *I ask, beg* (an original form of **quaero**), has quaeso, quaesŭmus, quaesere, quaesens.

e. **Ovare**, *to triumph*, has the following:
 ovat, ovet, ovāret; ovans, ovandi, ovatus, ovaturus.

f. A few are found chiefly in the Imperative: as,
salve, salvete, *hail!* also **salvēre** (from **salvus**).
ăve (or hăve), avēte, avēto, *hail*, or *farewell*.
cĕdo, cedĭte (cette), *give, tell*.
apăge! *begone!* (properly a Greek word).

g. **Queo**, *I can*, **nequeo**, *I cannot*, are conjugated like **eo**. They are rarely used except in the Present.

IND. PRES.	queo, quis, quit, quimus, quitis, queunt.
IMP.	quībam, quībat, quibant. — FUT. quibo, quibunt.
PERF.	quivi, quivit, quiverunt.
SUBJ. PRES.	queam, &c. — IMP. quirem, quiret, quirent.
PERF.	quiverit. — PLUP. quissent.
INFIN.	quīre, quivisse (quisse). — PART. quiens, queuntis.

IND. PRES.	nequeo (often **non queo**), nonquis, nequit, nequīmus, nequītis, nequeunt.
IMP.	nequībam, -ībat, -ibant. — FUT. nequībunt.
PERF.	nequivi, nequivisti, nequivit, nequiverunt.
SUBJ. PRES.	nequeam, &c. — IMP. nequīrem.
PERF.	nequiverim. — PLUP. nequisset.
INFIN.	nequire, nequivisse. — PART. nequiens.

h. The following compounds of **fio** have only the forms **confit**, *it comes to pass*; **defit**, *it lacks*; **infit**, *he begins* (to speak).

39. IMPERSONAL VERBS.

Many verbs, from their meaning, appear only in the *third person singular*, with the *infinitive* and *gerund*. These are called Impersonal Verbs.

NOTE. — With impersonal verbs the word IT is used in English, having usually no representative in Latin, though **id, hoc, illud,** are often used nearly in the same way.

Impersonal Verbs may be classified as follows : —

a. Verbs expressing the *operations of nature:* as, **pluit**, *it rains;* **ningit**, *it snows;* **grandĭnat**, *it hails;* **fulgurat**, *it lightens.*

In these, no subject is distinctly thought of; though sometimes the name of a deity is expressed; and, in poetic use, of other agents also: as, **fundae saxa pluunt**, *the slings rain stones.*

b. Verbs of *feeling,* where the person who is the proper subject becomes the object, as if himself affected by the feeling expressed in the verb. Such are, **miseret**, *it grieves;* **poenĭtet**, *it repents;* **piget**, *it disgusts;* **pudet**, *it shames;* **taedet**, *it wearies:* as, **miseret me**, *I pity* (*it distresses me*).

Such verbs often have also a passive form: as, **misereor**, *I pity* (*am moved by pity*); and occasionally other parts: as, **libens, licens, poeniturus, poenitendus, pudendus.**

c. By a similar construction, the *passive of intransitive verbs* is very often used impersonally: as, **pugnatur**, *there is fighting;* **dicĭtur**, *it is said;* **parcĭtur mihi**, *I am spared.*

NOTE. — This use of the passive proceeds from its original *reflexive* meaning, the action being regarded as *accomplishing itself* (compare the French *cela se fait*).

d. Verbs which have a *phrase* or *clause* as their subject: as, **libet**, *it pleases;* **licet**, *it is permitted;* **certum est**, *it is resolved;* **constat**, *it is clear;* **placet, videtur**, *it seems good;* **decet**, *it is becoming;* **delectat, juvat**, *it delights;* **oportet, necesse est**, *it is needful;* **praestat**, *it is better;* **interest, refert**, *it concerns;* **vacat**, *there is leisure;* with verbs of *happening* and the like. Many of these are also used personally.

40. PERIPHRASTIC FORMS.

When the tenses of **esse** are used with a Participle, this use is called *periphrastic conjugation.* It is most frequent—

a. With the participle in **urus**, to express *intention*, or *simple futurity;* this is sometimes necessary in the subjunctive: as, **cum venturus sit**, *since he is about to come.* This form is sometimes called the *first periphrastic conjugation;* and, when used with **sim**, the *future subjunctive.*

b. With the gerundive to denote *duty* or *propriety:* as, **vera dicenda sunt**, *the truth must be told.* This form is sometimes called the *second periphrastic conjugation.*

c. With the perfect participle, in the regular inflection of the tenses of *completed action* in passives and deponents.

NOTE. — The participle in **tus** frequently, and that in **ns** regularly, is used with **esse** simply as an adjective: as, **sapiens est**, *he is wise;* **acceptus est**, *he is welcome.*

PARTICLES.

41. Adverbs.

What are called PARTICLES — that is, all Adverbs, Prepositions, and Conjunctions — are real or extinct *case-forms*, or else *compounds* and *phrases*.

In classification Particles cannot always be distinguished; many prepositions and conjunctions being also reckoned among adverbs.

1. *Derivation.* The regular adverbs of manner are formed from Adjectives.

[For the comparison of these adverbs, see § **17**, 4.]

a. Adjectives of the *first and second declensions* change the characteristic vowel of the stem into **ē** (originally an ablative in **d**): as, from **carus**, *dear*, **carē**, *dearly*.

So **abunde, sæpe, prope**, from adjectives not in use; as also **prod (pro), re- (red-), se-, (sed-).**

b. Adjectives of the *third declension* add **-ter** to the stem (most being treated as i-stems): as, **fortĭter**, *bravely*; **vigilanter**, *watchfully*.

NOTE. — This suffix is of uncertain origin, probably the same as in the Greek -τερος, and in *alter, uter;* and, if so, these are *neuter accusatives.*

c. Some adverbs of the former class have both forms: as, **dure, durĭter; misere, miseriter.** (So **alĭter** from **alius** — old stem **ali-**.)

d. The *neuter accusative* of adjectives and pronouns is often used as an adverb (strictly a *cognate accusative,* see § **52**, 1, *d*): as, **multum**, *much;* **actutum**, *at once;* **facile**, *easily;* **non** (= **ne unum**), *not;* **iterum** (comparative of **is**), *again.*

e. The *ablative neuter* or (less commonly) *feminine* is used adverbially: as, **falso**, *falsely;* **cito**, *quickly;* **rectā (viā)**, *straight (straightway)* ; **contrā**, *on the other hand;* **quā (parte)**, *where;* **quī**, *how;* **alioqui**, *otherwise.*

f. A few adverbs are *datives* of adjectives and pronouns: as, quo, *whither;* adeo, *so;* ultra, *beyond;* citro, *this side;* retro, *back* (compar. of uls, cis, re); illoc (illo-ce, weakened to illuc), *thither.*

g. Some *locative* forms are used as adverbs: as, ibi, *there;* ubi, *where,* &c.; peregre, *abroad;* hic, *here;* interim, *meanwhile;* deinde, *then;* tamen, *yet;* and the compounds extrinsecus, *outside;* perendie, *day after to-morrow.*

h. Several *feminine accusatives* are used as adverbs: as, statim, *on the spot;* saltim, *with a leap* (generally in the form saltem, *at least*); palam, *openly;* perpĕram, *wholly otherwise* (i.e., changed for the worse); tam, quam, nam (which may be neuters).

i. Several *plural accusatives,* neuter and feminine, are used adverbially, as frustra, *vainly;* alias, *otherwise;* foras, *out of doors.*

k. Some adverbs are of uncertain formation: (1) those in -tus (usually preceded by i): as, penitus, funditus, *from the bottom* (*utterly*); divinitus, *providentially,* — which are ablative in meaning; (2) those in -dem, -dam, -do (in quan-do, *when;* do-nec, *until*), dum, perhaps jam (from the same root with dies, diu, &c.).

l. Many *phrases* or *clauses* have grown into adverbs: as, antea, *before;* postmŏdo, *a little after;* denuo (de nŏvo), *again;* prorsus, *utterly;* quotannis, *every year;* quamobrem, *wherefore;* obviam, *in the way;* pridem, *before the day* (i.e., before this time); forsan, *a chance whether;* forsitan (fors sit an), *perhaps;* scilĭcet (scire licet), *to be sure.*

(For Numeral Adverbs, see § **18**, 3.)

2. *Classification.* Adverbs, other than those directly formed from adjectives, are classified as follows:—

a. Adverbs of Place.

ubi, *where.*	quo, *whither.*	unde, *whence.*	quâ, *by what way.*
hic, *here.*	huc, *hither.*	hinc, *hence.*	hac, *by this way.*
ibi, *there.*	eo, *thither.*	inde, *thence.*	eâ, *by the way.*
istic ,,	istuc ,,	istinc ,,	istâ ,,
illic ,,	illuc ,,	illinc ,,	illâ (illac) ,,
alicubi, *somewhere;*	aliquo	alicunde	aliquâ.
ibidem, *in the same place;*	eodem	indidem	eâdem.
alibi, *elsewhere;*	alio	aliunde	aliâ.
ubiubi, *wherever;*	quoquo	undecunque	quâquâ.
ubivis, *anywhere;*	quovis	undique	quâvis.
sicubi, *if anywhere;*	siquo	sicunde	siquâ.
necubi, *lest anywhere;*	nequo	necunde	nequâ.

nusquam, *nowhere;* ultro, *beyond* (or *freely*); citro, *to this side;* intro, *inwardly;* porro, *further on.*

quorsum (quo versum), *to what end?* horsum, *this way;* prorsum, *forward* (prorsus, *utterly*); introrsum, *inwardly;* retrorsum, *backward;* sursum, *upward;* deorsum, *downward;* seorsum, *apart;* aliorsum, *another way.*

b. Adverbs of Time.

quando? *when?* cum (quom, quum), *when* (relat.).
nunc, *now;* tunc (tum), *then;* mox, *presently.*
primum (primo), *first;* deinde (postea), *next after;* postremum, (postremo), *finally.*
umquam (unquam), *ever;* numquam, *never;* semper, *always.*
aliquando, *some time, at length;* quandoque (quandocumque), *whenever.*
quotiens (quoties), *how often;* totiens, aliquotiens.
quotidie, *every day;* in dies, *from day to day.*
nondum, *not yet;* necdum, *nor yet;* vixdum, *scarce yet;* quam primum, *as soon as possible.*

c. Adverbs of Degree or Cause.

quam, *how, as;* tam, *so;* quamvis, *however much.*
cur, quare, *why;* quod, quia, *because;* eo, *therefore.*
ita, sic, *so;* ut (uti), *as, how;* utut, utcumque, *however.*
quamquam (quanquam), *although;* etiam, quoque, *even, also.*

d. Interrogative Particles.

an, -ne, anne, utrum, num, *whether.*
nonne, *whether not;* numquid, ecquid, *whether at all;* (ecquid intellegis? *have you any idea?*)
utrum (num), -ne, *whether;* ... an (annon, necne), *or.*
— ,, an, -ne ,,

NOTE. — The word *whether* is not now used in English, except in Indirect Questions (See § 71).

e. Negative Particles.

non, *not* in simple denial; **haud** (hau, haut), or **minime,** *not* in contradiction; **ne,** *not* in prohibition.
ne, *lest;* neque, nec, *nor;* ne ... quidem, *not even.*
non modo ... verum (sed) etiam, *not only ... but also.*
non modo ... sed ne ... quidem, *not only* NOT *... but not even.*
si minus, *if not;* quo minus, *so as not.*
quin (relat.), *but that;* (interrog.) *why not? who (what) not?*
ne (in compos.), *not:* as, nescio, *I know not;* nego (ne-aio), *I say no* (aio, *I say yes*); nēmo (ne hŏmo), *no one;* ne quis, *lest any one.*

REMARK. — Two negatives are equivalent to an affirmative: as, **nemo non audiet,** *every one will hear.*

This is especially frequent with compounds of **non**: as, **nonnullus** (= **aliquis**), *some;* **nonnihil** (= **aliquid**), *something;* **nonnemo** (= **aliquot**), *sundry persons;* **nonnumquam** (= **aliquotiens**), *sometimes;* **necnon,** *also.*

On the other hand, **nemo non, nulli non,** *every one;* **nihil non,** *every thing;* **numquam non,** *always,* &c.

3. *Signification.* The following adverbs require special explanation: —

a. **Etiam,** *also,* is stronger than **quŏque,** and usually precedes the emphatic word, while **quoque** follows it: as,

terret etiam nos, ac minatur (Rosc. Am. 40), *us also he terrifies and threatens.*
hoc quoque maleficium (id.), *this crime too.*

b. **Nunc,** *now,* means definitely *the present time;* **jam,** *already,* — or, with the future, *presently;* with negatives, *no longer,* — has reference to the past. **Tunc,** *then,* is a strengthened form of **tum,** which is correlative with **cum,** *when:* as,

nunc jam confiteris, *now at length you confess.*
non est jam lenitati locus, *there is no longer room for mercy.*
quod jam erat institutum, *which had come to be a practice.*
nunc quidem deleta est, tunc florebat (Læl. 4), *now ('tis true) she* [Greece] *is ruined, then she was in her glory.*
tum cum regnabat, *at the time he reigned.*

c. **Certō** means *certainly;* **certe** (usually), *at any rate:* as,

certo scio, *I know for a certainty.*
aut jam urgentis aut certe adventantis senectutis (C. M. 1.), *of old age, which is already pressing or at least approaching.*

d. **Prīmum,** *first (first in order,* or *for the first time),* is usually followed by **deinde, tum,** . . . **denique; primo,** *at first,* by **posteā (post)** or **mox,** *afterwards.* (The adjective form is preferred in such phrases as **nos primi,** *we first,* &c.) Thus,

primum de genere belli, **deinde** de magnitudine, **tum** de imperatore deligendo (Manil. 2), *first of the kind of war, next of its greatness, then of the choice of commander.*

e. **Quidem,** *indeed,* is emphatic, and often has a *concessive* meaning, especially when followed by **sed, autem,** &c. (see above **nunc quidem,** &c.). With **ne** . . . **quidem,** *not even* or *not either,* the emphatic word must stand between: as,

senex ne quod speret quidem habet (C. M. 19), *an old man has* NOT EVEN *any thing to hope for.*
ne Jugurtha quidem quietus erat (Jug. 51), NOR *was Jugurtha quiet* EITHER.

42. Prepositions.

1. Prepositions are not originally distinguished from adverbs in form or meaning. They are, however, distinguished in their use, requiring to be followed by some *special case* of a noun or pronoun.

a. The following Prepositions require the *accusative*:—

ad, *to.*
adversus, or
adversum, *towards.*
ante, *before.*
apud, *at, near.*
circā, or
circum, *around.*
circĭter, *about.*
cis, citrā, *this side.*
contrā, *against.*

ergā, *towards.*
extrā, *outside.*
infrā, *below.*
inter, *among.*
intrā, *inside.*
juxtā, *near.*
ŏb, *on account of.*
penes, *in the power.*
per, *through.*
pōne, *behind.*

post, *after.*
praeter, *beyond.*
prope, *near.*
propter, *on account of.*
secundum, *next to.*
suprā, *above.*
trans, *across.*
ultrā, *on the further side.*
versus, *towards.*

b. The following require the *ablative*:—

ā, ăb, abs, *from, by.*
absque, *but for, without.*
cōram, *in presence of.*
cum, *with.*
dē, *from.*

ē, ex, *out of.*
prae, *in comparison with.*
pro, *in front of, for.*
sine, *without.*
tenus, *up to,* or *as far as.*

c. The following may take either case, but usually with a difference in meaning:—

in, *into, in;* sub, *under;* subter, *beneath;* super, *above.*

In and **sub,** when followed by the Accusative, signify *motion to,* when by the Ablative, *rest in,* a place.

(For the Syntax of Prepositions, see § 56.)

2. The meaning and use of these prepositions may be seen in the following examples, which include many *adverbial phrases*:—

A, ab, *away from* (opposite of **ad**): ab eo loco, *from that place;* a nobis, *from our house;* prope ab urbe, *near* (not far from) *the city;* secundus a rege, *next the king;* liberare ab, *to set free from;* occisus ab hoste (periit ab hoste), *slain by an enemy;* a fronte, *in front;* ab hac parte, *on this side;* a primo, *at first;* ab re, *afterwards;* dolet ab animo, *he grieves at heart;* ab initio ordiri, *to begin at the beginning;* stat ab amicis, *he stands by his friends;* ab hac contione, *after this speech;* ab re ejus, *to his advantage;* servus a manu, *an amanuensis;* a pedibus, *a footman.*

NOTE.— **ab** signifies direction *from* the object, but *towards* the speaker; compare **de** and **ex**.

Absque, *without:* — absque argumento, *without argument;* absque paucis, *except a few;* absque me, *but for me.*

Ad, *to, towards, at* (place or time): — eo ad patrem, *I go to my father;* ad pedes ejus, *at his feet;* ad flumen, *near the river;* ad ripas, *on the banks;* ad meridiem, *towards the south;* ad vesperum, *near evening;* ad tempus, *at the* (fit) *time;* adiit ad rempublicam, *he went into public life;* ad manus, *to blows;* ad petendam pacem, *to seek peace;* ad communem salutem, *for the common safety;* nihil ad Cæsarem, *nothing in comparison with Cæsar;* ad hunc modum, *in this way;* quem ad modum, *how, as;* ad nuptias, *for the wedding;* ad auxilium, *for aid;* ad hos casus, *for these emergencies;* ad centum, *near a hundred;* ad primum nuntium, *at the first message;* ad hoc, *besides;* ad speciem, *in respect to form;* ad praesens, *for the moment;* ad verbum, *word for word;* ad summum, *in short, at most;* ad ultimum, *wholly, finally;* ad unum, *to a man.*

Adversus (-sum), *opposite, towards, against:* — adversus montem, *over against the mountain;* te adversum, *to your face;* adversus eum, *in comparison with him;* adversus ea, *in reply to this;* adversus deos, *towards the gods.*

Ante, *in front, before* (place or time): — ante oculos, *before his eyes;* ante urbem captam, *before the city was taken;* ante diem quintum (A.D.V.) Kal, *the fifth day before the Calends* (third day before the end of the month); ante quadriennium, *four years before* or *ago;* ante alios carissimus, *dearest of all;* ante tempus, *too soon;* ante omnia, *first of all;* ante Ciceronem, *before Cicero's time.*

Apud, *at* or *by* (rarely of places): — apud forum, *in the forum;* apud populum, *before the people;* apud exercitum, *with the army;* apud aliquem, *at one's house;* apud se, *at home*, or *in his senses;* apud Ciceronem, *in Cicero* (in his works); apud antiquos, *among the ancients.*

Circum (acc.), **circa** (abl.), **circiter** (stem as in **circus**, *circle*), *about, around:* — circum axem vertitur, *it turns about the axle;* circum haec loca, *hereabout;* circa se habent, *they have with them;* (of *time* or *number*, circa or circiter, not circum): — circa eandem horam, *about the same hour;* circiter passus mille, *about a mile;* circa bonas artes (late), *in reference to good arts;* loca haec circiter, *hereabout.*

Cis, citra (abl. of comparative, compare Greek -τερος), *this side of* (both motion towards and rest in; opposite to **ultra**): — cis Padum, *this side the Po;* citra flumen, *this side the river;* citra rustici operam, *within the labor of a farmer;* citra usum, *without regard to use;* citra satietatem, *not to fulness;* paucos cis dies, *within a few days.*

Contra (abl. comp of **cum**), *opposite, against:* — contra Italiam, *over against Italy;* contra hostem, *against the enemy;* contra munera, *as a set-off to the gifts;* haec contra, *this in reply;* contra autem, *but on the other hand,* adv.; quod contra, *whereas on the other hand,* adv.; non pro me sed contra me, *not for but against me;* contra fas, *contrary to right.*

Coram, *in presence of* (only of persons) : — coram judicibus, *before the judges;* Germanico coram (Tac.), usually an adverb.

Cum, *with* (together in place or time) : — cum fratre, *with his brother;* abi cum donis, *away with your gifts;* cum malo suo, *to his own hurt;* cum labore, *with toil;* cum dis volentibus, *with favor of the gods;* cum decimo, *tenfold;* confligere cum hoste, *to fight with the enemy;* cum armis, *in arms;* cum imperio, *in power;* cum pallio, *in a cloak;* esse cum telo, *to go armed;* cum silentio, *in silence.*

De, *from, away, down from:* — de domo, *out of the house;* de sella, *down from his seat;* unus de plebe, *one of the people* (the whole, from which a part is taken); emi domum de Crasso, *I bought a house of Crassus* (also **ab**); de tuo (de te), *out of your property;* qua de re, *concerning which thing;* qua de causa, *for which reason;* de summo genere, *of high birth;* de improviso, *of a sudden;* de industria, *on purpose;* de integro, *anew;* de nocte, *at night;* de tertia vigilia, *just at midnight* (starting at the third watch); de mense Dec. navigare, *to sail in December;* de amicorum sententia, *in accordance with the views of friends;* triumphare de, *to triumph over;* de schola, *of that sect.*

Erga, *towards* (usually of persons): — erga aedes, *opposite the house;* benevolentia erga nos, *kindness towards us;* malus erga me, *spiteful towards me* (but more generally used of a favorable inclination).

Ex, e, *from* (the midst, opposed to **in**), *out of:* — ex urbe, *from the city;* ex hoc die, *from this day forth;* statua ex aere, *a statue of brass;* ex fuga, *during flight;* ex consulatu. *right after his consulship;* ex aere alieno, *by reason of debt;* ex ejus sententia. *after his opinion;* ex aequo, *justly;* ex improviso, *unexpectedly;* ex tua re, *to your advantage;* ex voluntate ejus, *by his good will;* magna ex parte, *in a great degree;* ex pede Herculem, *to know one by a slight token;* felix ex misero. *bettering one's condition;* ex Metello consule, *beginning with Metellus's consulship;* ex pedibus laborare, *to be lame in the feet;* ex equo pugnare, *to fight on horseback.*

Extra, *outside of* (opposed to **intra**): — extra provinciam, *beyond the province;* extra causam, *beside the case;* extra te unum, *except you alone* (not used of time).

In, *into* (acc. opp. to **ex**), *in* (abl. of time or place): — in urbem ire, *to go to town;* in mentem venit, *it comes to mind;* amor in (erga or adversus) patrem, *love for his father;* in aram confugit, *he fled to the altar* (on the steps or merely *to*); in diem, *to the set day;* in dies, *from day to day;* vi. pedes in longitudinem, *six feet long;* in vi. partes fractus, *broken in six parts;*

in hæc verba jurare, *to swear to these words;* in alicujus verba jurare, *to take an oath of allegiance to one;* in silvam deponere, *to* (carry and) *place in the wood;* hunc in modum, *in this way;* oratio in Catilinam, *a speech against Catiline;* in universum (in planum), *on the whole;* in totum, *wholly;* in reliquum, *for the rest;* in perpetuum, *for ever;* in majus, *too much;* in pejus, *for the worse;* in quantum, *so far as;* in magnam partem, *in great part;* in utramque partem, *on either side;* nos in diem vivimus (Tusc. v. 11), *we live from hand to mouth;* — in urbe esse, *to be in the city;* in tempore, *in season;* in scribendo, *while writing;* est mihi in animo, *I have it in mind;* in collo, *on the neck;* in arbore, *up the tree;* in ancoris (Cæs.), *at anchor;* in altera parte, *on the other side;* in sapientibus, *among the wise;* in hoc homine, *in the case of this man;* in bonis artibus (Sall.), *in good behavior.*

Infra, *below:* — infra caelum, *under the sky;* infra nos, *beneath us;* infra Homerum, *later than Homer;* infra iii. pedes, *less than three feet.*

Inter, *between* (of two limits) : — inter flumen et montem, *between the river and hill* (so of time); inter noctem, *in the course of the night;* inter bibendum, *while drinking;* interest inter, *there is a difference between;* inter se amant, *they love each other;* inter se loquuntur, *they talk together;* inter nos, *between ourselves;* inter ceteram planitiem, *in a district elsewhere level.*

Intra, *within* (surrounded on all sides) : — intra parietes, *inside the house;* (of time), intra v. dies, *within five days;* intra legem, *inside the law.*

Juxta, *hard by* (superl. from **jungo**) : — juxta murum, *close to the wall;* juxta se, *alike with himself;* juxta deos, *next the gods;* juxta vicinitatem (Liv.), *by reason of nearness;* juxta quam, *nearly as;* juxta ac si, *about as if.*

Ob, *towards* (in place) : — ob Romam (early), *towards Rome;* ob oculos, *before the eyes;* ob eam causam, *for that reason;* ob rem, *to the purpose;* ob hoc, *therefore;* quam ob rem, *wherefore.*

Penes, *with, in possession of* (same root as **penitus**) : — est penes me, *he is with me* (at my house); non est penes me, *it is not in my power.*

Per, *through* (in any direction) : — per urbem ire, *to go through the city;* licet per me, *you may for all me;* juro per leges, *I swear by the laws;* per literas, *by letter;* per jocum, *in jest;* per longum tempus, *for a long time;* per somnum, *during sleep.*

Pone, *behind* (only in space) : — pone tergum, *behind the back.*

Post, *after* (space or time) : — post iii. dies, *after three days;* post tergum, *behind the back;* post me, *after me* (in time).

Prae, *in front:* — prae se ferre, *to carry before him (exhibit or make known);* prae gaudio conticuit, *he was silent for joy* (used only of an objection or hindrance); prae fratre egens est, *he is poor compared to his brother.*

Praeter, *by, on the outside:* — praeter spem, *beyond hope;* praeter hoc, *besides this;* praeter oculos, *before the eyes;* nil praeter saxa, *nothing but stones.*

Pro, *in front* (facing the same way): — pro populo, *in presence of the people;* pro lege, *in defence of the law;* argentum pro vino, *money for wine;* pro hac vice, *for this once;* pro consule, *in place of consul;* pro viribus, *considering his strength.*

Prope, *near:* — prope (propius, proxime) urbem, *or* ab urbe, *near the city;* prope lucem, *towards daybreak.*

Propter, *near:* — propter te sedet, *he sits next you;* propter quos vivit (Mil. 22), *through whose means he lives;* propter metum, *through fear;* propter frigora (Cæs.), *by reason of cold.*

Secundum, *just behind, following along* (part. of sequor): — ite secundum me (Plaut.), *go behind me;* secundum litus, *near the shore;* secundum flumen, *along the stream;* secundum ludos, *after the games;* secundum naturam, *according to nature;* secundum causam nostram, *to the advantage of our cause.*

Sine, *apart from:* — urbs sine regibus, *a city without kings;* non sine lacrimis, *with tears;* sine sanguine, *bloodless.*

Sub, *under:* — sub jugum mittere, *to send under the yoke;* sub montem succedere, *to come close to the hill;* sub noctem, *towards night;* sub lucem, *near daylight;* sub hæc dicta, *at these words;* — sub terra, *underground;* sub Jove, *in the open air;* sub monte, *at the foot of a hill;* sub castris, *near the camp;* sub terra eximere (Plaut.), *to take from under ground;* sub profectione (Cæs.), *during the march;* sub eodem tempore, *about that time;* sub oculis domini, *under the master's eye;* sub regno, *under royal power;* sub lege, *liable to the law.*

Subter (rarely with abl.), *beneath:* — subter fastigia tecti, *under the house-roof;* subter præcordia, *close to the heart;* subter murum, *beneath the wall;* subter se, *below itself;* subter testudine, *under the shed* (of shields).

Super, *above, over:* — super tumulum, *on the hillock;* super ipsum, *above him* (at table); super Indos, *beyond the Hindoos;* super cenam loqui, *to talk during supper;* super morbum fames etiam, *besides sickness famine also;* super omnes, *above all;* — super cervice (Hor.), *over his head;* super arbore sidunt, *they perch on a tree;* nocte super media (Vir.), *about midnight;* super tali re, *about such an affair;* satis superque, *more than enough.*

Supra, *on the top:* — supra terram, *above ground;* supra caput (Sall.), *imminent;* supra Alexandriam, *beyond Alexandria;* supra hanc memoriam, *before our remembrance;* supra mille, *above a thousand;* supra morem, *more than usual;* supra quod, *besides.*

Tenus, *as far as:* — capulo tenus, *up to the hilt;* verbo (nomine) tenus, *in name, nominally;* aurium tenus, *as far as the ears* (only); labrorum tenus, *along the lips.*

Trans, *beyond:* — trans mare, *over sea;* trans flumen, *beyond the river* (rest or motion).

Ultra, *on the further side:* — ultra eum, *beyond him*; portas ultra, *beyond the gates;* ultra pueritiam, *later than childhood;* ultra eum numerum, *more than that number;* ultra fidem, *incredible;* ultra modum, *immoderate.*

Versus, *turned to* (Eng. -*ward*): — Italiam versus, *towards Italy* (usually with another prep.); modo ad urbem modo in Galliam versus (Sall.), *now towards the city, now towards Gaul.*

3. Prepositions are frequently compounded with verbs, retaining their original meaning as Adverbs: as,

a, ab, *away* (aufero, *bear off*); **ad,** *towards* (affero, *bring*); **ante,** *before;* **circum,** *around* (urbem circumire = ire circum urbem); **con** (**cum**), *together;* **de,** *down;* **di** or **dis** (insep.), *apart;* **ex,** *out, completely;* **in,** *in, on, against;* **inter,** *between, into, to pieces;* **ob,** *towards, in the way of;* **per,** *through, thoroughly;* **re, red** (insep.), *back, again;* **se, sed** (insep.), *apart;* **sub,** *under, near;* **super,** *over, in place of.* (For the assimilation of the final consonant, see page 4.)

43. Conjunctions.

1. *Classification.* Conjunctions are more numerous, and their use is much more accurately distinguished, in Latin than in English. They are divided into two classes, viz.: —

a. **Co-ordinate:** — these include Copulative (AND), Disjunctive (OR), Adversative (BUT), Causal (FOR), Illative (THEREFORE).

b. **Subordinate:** — these are Conditional (IF), — including Comparative (AS IF), Concessive (THOUGH, EVEN IF), — Temporal (WHEN), Causal (BECAUSE, SINCE), Consecutive (SO THAT), Final (IN ORDER THAT).

2. The following list includes most of the conjunctions and conjunctive phrases in common use.

NOTE. — Some of these have been included in the classification of Adverbs, and a list of Interjections has been added. See also list of Correlatives, page 49.

a. Copulative and Disjunctive.

et, -que, atque (ac), *and.*
etiam, quoque, neque non (necnon), quinetiam, itidem (item), *also.*
cum ... tum; tum ... tum, *both ... and; not only ... but also.*
quâ ... quâ, *on one hand, on the other hand.*
modo ... modo, *now ... now.*
aut ... aut; vel ... vel (-ve), *either ... or.*
sive (seu) ... sive, *whether ... or.*

et . . . et; et . . . -que (atque); -que . . . et; -que . . . -que (poet.),
both . . . and.
nec (neque) . . . nec (neque); neque . . . nec; nec . . . neque (rare),
neither . . . nor.
et . . . neque, *both . . . and not.*
nec (neque) . . . -que, *neither . . . and.*

b. Adversative.

sed, autem, verum, vero, at, atqui, *but.*
tamen, attamen, sed tamen, verumtamen, *but yet, nevertheless.*
nihilominus, *none the less.*
at vero, enimvero, *but (for) in truth.*
ceterum, *on the other hand, but.*

c. Causal.

nam, namque, enim, etenim, *for.*
quia, quod, *because.*
quoniam, quippe, cum (quom), quando, quandoquidem, siquidem,
utpote, *since, inasmuch as.*

d. Illative.

ergo, igitur, itaque, ideo, idcirco, proinde, *therefore.*
propterea (. . . quod), *for this reason (. . . that).*
quapropter, quare, quamobrem, quocirca, unde, *wherefore,
whence.*

e. Comparative.

ut, uti, sicut, velut, prout, praeut, ceu, *as, like as.*
tamquam (tanquam), quasi, utsi, acsi, *as if.*
quam, atque (ac), *as, than.*

f. Conditional.

si, *if;* sin, *but if;* nisi (ni), *unless, if not;* quod si, *but if.*
modo, dum, dummodo, si modo, *if only, provided.*
dummodo ne (dum ne, modo ne), *provided only not.*

g. Concessive.

etsi, etiamsi, tametsi, tamenetsi, quamquam, *although.*
quamvis, quantumvis, quamlibet, *however much.*
licet, ut, cum (quom), *though.*

NOTE. — A *concessive* is often followed by an *adversative:* as, **tamenetsi . . . tamen nihilominus,** *though . . . yet none the less.*

h. Temporal.

cum (quom), cum primum, ubi, ut, ut primum, postquam, *when.*
prius . . . quam, ante . . . quam, *before* (non ante . . . quam, *not
. . . until*).
quando, simulatque (simul ac), simul, *as soon as.*
dum, usque dum, donec, quoad, *until.*

i. Final.

ut (uti), quo, *in order that.*
ne, ut ne, *lest (in order that not)*; neve (neu), *nor.*
quin (after negatives), quominus, *but that (so as to prevent).*

k. *Interjections.*

O, en, ecce, ehem, papae, vah (of *astonishment*).
io, evae, evoe (of *joy*).
heu, eheu, vae, *alas!* (of *sorrow*).
heus, eho, ehodum, *ho!* (of *calling*).
eia, euge (of *praise*).
proh (of *attestation*): as, proh pudor, *shame!*

3. Special Meaning. The following list includes most of the conjunctions whose meaning or use requires special notice: —

a. **Et,** *and,* connects independent words or clauses; **-que** (enclitic) combines closely into one connected whole; **atque** (sometimes **ac** before consonants) adds with emphasis. In the second member, *and not* is expressed by **neque** or **nec.**

Atque (ac), *as,* is also used after words of comparison and likeness, as **idem,** *the same,* **simul,** *as soon,* **aliter,** *otherwise.*

b. **Sed** and **vērum** or **vero** (more forcible), *but,* are used to contradict what precedes, — always after negatives; **at,** *yet,* introduces with emphasis a new point, especially in argument (**at enim** almost always) alluding to a *supposed* statement on the other side; **autem** is used in the same way, especially in transitions, but with less force.

c. **Aut,** *or,* excludes the alternative; **vel (-ve)** gives a choice; **sive (seu)** is properly used in disjunctive conditions, but is also used with single words, — especially two names for the same thing. (But of **aut** and **vel** the use is not always clearly distinguished.)

d. **Nam (namque),** *for,* introduces a sufficient reason; **ĕnim,** an explanatory circumstance; **etenim** (*for, you see; for, you know*), something self-evident, or needing no proof.

e. **Ergo,** *therefore,* is used of things proved logically; **ităque,** in proofs from the nature of things; **igĭtur,** *then* (a weak **ergo**), in passing from one stage of the argument to another, often merely to resume; **idcirco,** *for this reason,* to call attention to a special point.

f. **Quia,** *because,* regularly introduces a fact; **quod,** either a fact or a statement or allegation; **quoniam,** *since,* has reference to motives.

g. **Quom (cum),** *when,* is always a relative conjunction, often a correlative with **tum**; **quando** is also used as interrogative or indefinite (**quando?** *when?* **si quando,** *if ever*).

h. **Et . . . et,** means simply *both . . . and;* **cum** (less frequently **tum**) **. . . tum** has also the meaning *not only . . . but also,* emphasizing the second member.

i. **Autem, enim, vero,** always follow one or two words in their clause; the same is generally true of **igitur,** and often of **tamen.**

k. Conjunctions are often *doubled,* for the sake of emphasis, or to bind a sentence more closely to the preceding : as, **at vero, itaque ergo (namque, etenim).** The same is true of Relatives, which are equivalent to a conjunction and demonstrative combined : as, **qui ubi sit nescio,** *for where he is I know not.*

44. Derivation of Words.

The ROOT is a primitive element of speech. All roots are monosyllabic, and have a short vowel. STEMS are formed from roots, and are divided into two main groups; viz., *noun-stems* (including adjectives) and *verb-stems.*

1. *Noun Forms.* Derivative Nominal forms include (1) nouns of *agency,* (2) names of *actions,* (3) active and passive *adjectives.*

NOTE. — Examples of roots are ES, *be;* I, *go;* STA, *stand;* CAP, *take;* DUC, *lead;* FAC, *make;* FER, *bear;* RAP, *seize;* SED, *sit;* TEN, *stretch* (see also pp. 72, 73).

a. **Roots and Stems.** Roots may be used as stems (1) without change, as in dŭc-is, nĕc-is; (2) with vowel-increase, as in lūc-is, pāc-is; (3) with reduplication, as in **furfur, marmor;** (4) compounded, as in **judic-is (jus, dico), conjug-is (con-jugo).** But Stems are more commonly formed by means of suffixes added to the root (primary), or to a stem (secondary), either with or without the above changes.

b. **Primary Suffixes.** The simplest suffixes are the vowels a (in Latin o, a), i, u. Other primary suffixes are ta, ti, tu; na, ni, nu; va, ra, ya, ka, an.

NOTE. — The vowel-suffixes a, i, u, are sometimes regarded as if merely added to the root to fit it for inflection; but they are, in fact, true pronominal roots, and must be regarded as formative suffixes. The first is found in nouns and adjectives of **a-** and **o-**stems, as *ludus, vagus, scriba, toga* (root TEG); — **i** is less common, and in Latin has frequently disappeared, especially in the nominative, as in *scobs* (*scobis,* root SCAB); — **u** is disguised in most adjectives by an additional **i,** as in *suavis* (for *suadvis,* cf. ἡδύς), *tenuis* (root TEN in *tendo*), and remains alone only in nouns of the fourth declension, as *acus* (root AK, *sharp,* in *acer, acies,* ὠκύς), *pecu* (root PAK, *bind,* in *paciscor*).

The signification of the other primary suffixes is as follows: — **ta** (in the form **to-**) makes the regular perfect participle, as *tectus, tectum;* sometimes active, as in *potus, pransus;* and is found in a few not recognized as participles, as *putus, altus* (*alo*); — **ti** forms abstracts, rarely nouns of agency, as *messis, vestis, pars, mens;* — **tu** forms abstracts (including supines), sometimes becoming concretes, as *actus, luctus;* — **na**, forming perfect participles in other languages, in Latin makes adjectives of like meaning, which often become nouns, as *magnus* (= *mactus*, root MAG), *plenus, regnum;* — **ni**, nouns of agency and adjectives, as *ignis, segnis;* — **nu**, rare, as in *manus, sinus;* — **ma**, various, as in *animus, almus, firmus, forma;* — **va** (commonly **uo**), of active or passive meaning, as in *equus, arvum, conspicuus, exiguus, vacivos* (*vacuus*); — **ra** (or **la**, a passive participle termination in other languages), usually passive, as in *ager, integer, pleri-que* (= *plenus* = ·*plētus*), *sella* (for *sed-la*, cf. ἕδρα); — **ya** (gerundives in other languages), adjectives and abstracts, including many of the first and fifth declensions, as *eximius, audacia, Florentia, pernicies;* — **ka**, sometimes primary, as in *pauci* (cf. παῦρος), *locus* (for *stlocus*, cf. Sk. *sthara, sthala*, Ger. *Stelle*, Eng. *stall*); — **an** (*in, ŏn*), in nouns of agency and abstracts: as *aspergo, compago* (*ĭnis*), *gero* (*ōnis*).

The above, with some compound suffixes given below, belong to the original language, and most of them were not felt as living formations in the literary period. But developed forms of these, with a few other primary suffixes, were used consciously, — generally as secondary suffixes. The old primary suffixes thus used are (along with **ta** and **tu**, given above) **man, ant, vant, tar, tro, as.** (Observe that it is the *stem*, not the *nominative*, that is formed by the suffix, although the nominative is given for convenience of reference.)

c. **Significant Endings.** The principal classes of regular derivate nouns and adjectives, as indicated by their nominative-ending, are the following: —

1. **Nouns of Agency** (active adjectives or appellatives), ending in —

tor (lengthened from **tăr**, M.), **trix** (**trīc-** = **tar** + **ic**, F.), added to the same form of stem that precedes **t** of the supine (which for convenience may be called the *supine-base*), or to noun-stems by analogy: as *ductor, victrix, viator*. Earlier formations with **tar** are *patĕr, matĕr*.

es (-**ĭtis**), descriptive nouns, as *miles, comes*. *M.M: 61*

2. **Names of Actions** (passing into abstracts, instruments, results): —

or (M.), **es** (-**is**, F. — all from **as**): as *timor, sedes, decus*.

io (added to pres. stem), **tio, tura, tus** (to supine base), verbal abstracts: as *legio, actio, pictura, cultus* (those in **tus** more concrete). *M.M. 19*

ium (**ya**) from neuter abstracts (with verb-stems), as *gaudium;* or from nouns meaning offices or groups: as *hospitium, servitium, collegium.*

men (man), **mentum** (man + ta), **monia, monium** (man + ya), denoting act, means, or result: as *flumen, carmen, ornamentum, querimonia, matrimonium.*

ia, tia, tas, tus, tudo, do, go, feminine abstracts, often passing into concretes: as *audacia, militia, duritia (ies), bonitas, servitus, altitudo, dulcedo, lanugo.*

brum, crum, trum, bŭlum, cŭlum, nouns of means, usually from verb-stems: as *claustrum, lavacrum, vehiculum, turibulum.*

3. Adjective forms, passing frequently into names of persons or things:—

ŭlus (following a vowel, **ŏlus**; following s or r, **cŭlus**), **ellus, illus,** DIMINUTIVES (with endings for gender), forming nouns or adjectives, meaning *little* or *tender:* as *puerculus, puella (puerula), puellula, asellus (asinulus), misellus (miserulus).* Rare diminutive forms are *eculeus, homuncio.*

ădes (F. **as**), **ĭdes, īdes** (F. **is, ēis**), PATRONYMICS, denoting parentage, &c., as *Æneădes, Priamĭdes, Priamēis.*

ānus, ēnus, īnus; as (-atis), **ensis; ius, iăcus, ācius,** GENTILE names, denoting country—with other rare forms—several being derived from the same word: as *Cres, Creticus, Cretæus, Cressus, Cretensis.*

ax, ulus (rare), **vus** (**uus, īvus**), denote tendency or inclination, those in **ax** being often faulty or aggressive, those in **īvus** rather passive: as *pugnax, bibulus, protervus, nocuus, captivus.*

āris, ālis, ēlis, īlis, ūlis (all from **ra**), with **īnus, ōrius,** and several of the above gentile forms, denote various ideas of relation or possession. Several neuters of derivatives in **īlis** signify place, as *ovile;* and many of those in **ālis, āris** (usually with loss of **e**), also become nouns (regular i-stems); those in **īnus,** from names of animals, are often used of flesh.

eus, ĭnus, āceus, ĭcius, denote material, &c.: as *fraxineus.*

ōsus (old **onsus,** *vant*), **olens, ŏlentus** (root **ŏl** in **adolesco**), denote full of, or inclined to, as *fluctuosus, bellicosus;* so **ĭdus** (generally verbal) with similar meaning: as *cupidus, gelidus;* **bundus, cundus,** participial, but denoting persistence of quality: as *iracundus.*

ātus, ītus, ūtus (from imaginary verb-stems), denote provided with: as *galeātus, aurītus, cornūtus.*

ter (-tris), tĭmus (a superl. form) from noun-stems: as *campester, maritimus;* **ternus,** from adverbs of time: as *sempiternus, hesternus* (from *heri,* old *hesi,* cf. *yesterday*).

mĭnus, mnus, mna (Gr. -μενος), participles, but no longer significant as such: as *terminus, alumnus, autumnus, lamina, ærumna, femina.*

ndus, the gerund-ending, forms a few words of active meaning, as *secundus, rotundus* (cf. *volvendis annis*).

2. *Derivation of Verbs.* Verbs of the third conjugation, with irregular verbs and vowel-stems **dă, stă,** are *primitive.* All others are either *causative* or *denominative* (formed from nouns).

NOTE.— The consciousness of *roots* was lost in Latin, so that in forming the parts of verbs only *stems* are dealt with. Thus *moneo, monui* (not *menui*), from root *men*, as in *mens; cædo, cecĭdi* (not *cecĭdi*), from root (*căd*, as in *cădo*). For modifications of the root in verb-stems, see §§ **28, 30.** The derivative suffix in the regular conjugations is original **ya** added either to the *root*, the *present stem* in **a**, or the *noun-stem*.

a. The following are the regular conjugational forms : —

1. Verbs of the first conjugation (generally active) may be formed from almost any noun or adjective of the first or second declension, by changing the stem-vowel into the characteristic **ā**. A few add this vowel to the stem, as **vigĭlare, exsulare.**

2. A few verbs of the second conjugation are formed in like manner from noun-stems; but most add the characteristic **ē** to the root, and are intransitive or neuter in their meaning.

3. A few **u**-stems simply add the characteristic of the third conjugation, becoming either active or intransitive, as **acuo, fluo.**

4. Most verbs of the fourth conjugation add the characteristic **ī** to the root, as **scio, salio**; many are formed from **ĭ**-stems, as **sitio, finio, polio** (see § **34**).

b. The following are regular derivative suffixes : —

sco or **isco** (§ **36,** I) inchoative, denoting the *beginning* of an action; they imply a primitive verb-stem, which is sometimes found only in the perfect and supine stems.

asso, esso, denote *attempt* to do a thing; they are of the third conjugation in the present stem, and of the fourth in the perfect and supine.

NOTE. — These are probably *denominative,* from nouns originally in **as** (Latin **es** or **us**), but seem as if formed upon verb-roots.

to, ĭto (first conjugation) denote *frequent* action, being added to the actual supine, or to another form of it, with a connecting vowel **i,** changing **u** to the characteristic **a** of the first conjugation.

illo (first conjugation) denotes *feeble* or *trifling* action like that of some simpler verb, but is formed from some real or supposed diminutive noun.

ŭrio (fourth conjugation), added to the supine-base, denotes *desire* to do the act expressed by some simple verb; but is formed from some noun of agency in **tor** (**sor**). **Viso** is a regular inherited desiderative of an earlier formation.

3. *Compound Words.* In compound words, either (1) the second part is merely *added* to the first; (2) the first part *modifies* the second as an adjective; (3) the first part is *governed* by the second as a verb; or (4) a verb is modified by a preposition or adverb prefixed. In all, only the second part receives inflection.

NOTE. — The Indo-European family had great power of forming compounds with mere stems. This power the Latin for the most part lost, as has English compared with German. Many compounds attempted by poets failed to become established in the language; but there remain many traces of the old usage.

The most usual compounds may be classed as follows: —

a. Meanings added: as *suovetaurilia, undecim.*

b. Noun with modifying adjective: as *latifundium, pœninsula, tergeminus.*

c. Noun and Verb, as *armiger, cornicen, manifestus, carnufex, mantele.*

d. Compound adjectives, in which the last word is a noun, the compound acquiring the meaning of *possessed of* the property denoted, as *alipes, magnanimus, concors, anceps* (having a head at both ends), *obvius, multiformis, multiplex.*

e. Compounds of **facio**, with an actual or formerly existing verbal stem in **e**. These are causative in force, as *consuefacio, calefacto.*

f. Adverbs (of manner) and Verb, which have grown together: as *benedico, satago.*

g. Verbs with Prepositions, usually having their original adverbial sense: as, **ab**, *away;* **ex**, *out.* In those with **circum, praeter, trans,** and sometimes **ad** and **per**, the compound retains the force of the preposition.

h. Verbs with the following inseparable Particles, which no longer appear as prepositions in Latin: **amb** (**am, an**), *around;* **dis, di,** *asunder* (*in two*); **por,** *forward;* **red, re,** *back;* **sed, se,** *apart.*

PART SECOND.

USE OF WORDS (SYNTAX).

45. DEFINITIONS.

1. *Sentence.* A SENTENCE is a form of words which contains either a Statement, a Question, an Exclamation, or a Command.

a. A sentence in the form of a Statement is called a DECLARATORY SENTENCE: as, **puer vēnit,** *the boy came.*

b. A sentence in the form of a Question is called an INTERROGATIVE SENTENCE: as, **venitne puer,** *did the boy come?*

c. A sentence in the form of an Exclamation is called an EXCLAMATORY SENTENCE: as, **quam celerĭter venit!** *how fast he came!*

d. A sentence in the form of a Command is called an IMPERATIVE SENTENCE: as, **vĕni, puer, ad me,** *come to me, boy.*

2. *Subject and Predicate.* The Subject of a sentence is the person or thing spoken of; the Predicate is that which is stated of the Subject.

a. The Predicate may be either a neuter verb, a noun or adjective with the *Copula* (**esse, fĭĕri,** &c.), or a Transitive verb with its Object.

b. The verb **esse,** *to be,* when it connects an attribute with its subject, is called the *Copula;* otherwise, it is called the *Substantive Verb.*
Thus in the sentence **sunt viri fortes,** *there are brave men,* **sunt** is a substantive verb; in **viri sunt fortes,** *the men are brave,* it is a copula.

c. The Object of a verb is that on which its action is exerted: thus in the sentence **pater vocat filium,** *the father calls his son,* **pater** is subject, and **filium** object, of **vocat.**

d. One or more words, essential to the grammatical completeness of a sentence, may be unexpressed: this is called ELLIPSIS, and the sentence is called an *elliptical sentence.*

3. *Modification.* The Subject or Predicate of a sentence may be modified by single words, or by a phrase or clause. The modifying word may itself be modified in the same way.

a. A single modifying word is generally either an Adjective, an Adverb, an Appositive (§ 46), or the oblique case of a Noun. Thus in the sentence **puer formosus venit**, *a handsome boy came*, the adjective **formosus** modifies the subject **puer**; in the sentence **celeriter venit**, *he came quickly*, the adverb **celeriter** modifies the predicate **venit**.

b. The modifying word is in some cases said to *limit* the word to which it belongs: thus in the sentence **video pueri patrem**, *I see the boy's father*, the genitive **pueri** limits **patrem**.

4. *Phrase.* A Phrase is a group of words, without subject or predicate of its own, which may be used as an Adjective or Adverb.

Thus in the sentence **puer erat eximiae formae**, *he was a boy of remarkable beauty*, the words **eximiae formae** are used for the adjective **formosus** (or **formosissimus**), and are called an ADJECTIVE PHRASE; in the sentence **magnā celeritate venit**, *he came with great speed*, the words **magna celeritate** are used for the adverb **celeriter** (or **celerrime**), and are called an ADVERBIAL PHRASE.

5. *Clause.* A Clause is a group of words forming part of a sentence, and having a subject and predicate of its own.

Thus in the sentence **puer qui heri venit formosus erat**, *the boy who came yesterday was handsome*, the words **qui heri venit** are a RELATIVE CLAUSE; in the sentence **puer si cras veniat acceptus sit**, *if the boy should come to-morrow he would be welcome*, the words **si cras veniat**, are a CONDITIONAL CLAUSE.

a. When a Clause is used as the Subject or Object of a verb, it is called a *Substantive Clause* (see § 70).

b. When a clause is used to modify the subject or predicate of a sentence, it is called a *Subordinate Clause*. Subordinate Clauses are *Conditional, Temporal, Causal, Consecutive,* and *Final*, like the conjunctions which introduce them (§ 43, 1, *b*).

c. When two or more clauses in the same sentence are independent of one another, they are said to be *Coördinate.*

d. Any clause introduced by a Relative is called a *Relative Clause;* when used simply by way of explanation, and not otherwise connected with the form of the sentence, it is called an *Intermediate Clause* (§ 66).

e. A clause expressing the *purpose* of an action is called a *Final Clause;* one expressing its *result* is called a *Consecutive Clause* (see §§ 64, 65).

NOTE.—In English, a Consecutive clause is introduced by the phrase *so that;* a Final clause by the phrase *in order that.*

f. A clause containing a *condition,* introduced by IF or some equivalent (§ 59), is called a *Conditional Clause.* A sentence modified by a conditional clause is called a *Conditional Sentence.*

NOTE.—Observe that these classes are not exclusive, but that a single clause may belong to several of them at once. Thus a relative clause may be subordinate, conditional, or intermediate; and two subordinate clauses may be coördinate with each other.

6. Connectives. Sentences or coördinate clauses are regularly connected by means of *Conjunctions;* but frequently in Latin — very rarely in English — sentences are connected by *Relatives.*

In this case, the relative is often best translated in English by a conjunction with a demonstrative: as, **quo cum venisset,** *and when he had come there;* **quae cum ita sint,** *but since these things are so* (§ 43, 3, *k*).

7. Agreement. A word is said to AGREE with another when it is required to be in the same *gender, number, case,* or *person.*

When a word takes the gender or number of some other word *implied* in that with which it should agree, this use is called SYNESIS, or *constructio ad sensum.*

8. Government. A word is said to GOVERN another, when it requires the latter to be in a particular *case.*

I. Subject and Predicate.

46. OF NOUNS.

A noun used to describe another, and meaning the same thing, agrees with it in *Case:* as,

    Servius rex, *Servius the king.*
    ad urbem Solos, *to the city Soli.*
    spes nostra Cicero, *Cicero our hope.*
    homo nata fuerat, *she had been born human.*

1. When the noun thus used is in the same part of the sentence (subject or predicate) it is called an *appositive*, and the use is called *apposition*.

2. When the noun is used to form a predicate with **esse** or a verb of similar meaning, it is called a *predicate-nominative* (or *accusative* as the case may be).

externus timor, maximum concordiæ vinculum, jungebat animos (Liv. ii. 39), *fear of the foreigner, the chief bond of harmony, united hearts.* [Here both nouns belong to the *subject*.]

quattuor hic, primum omen, equos vidi (Æn. iii. 537), *I saw here four horses, the first omen.* [Here both nouns are in the *predicate*.]

Ancum Marcium regem populus creavit (Liv. i. 32), *the people made Ancus Marcius king.* [Here **regem** is called the *complementary accusative*.]

consules creantur Cæsar et Servilius (B. C. iii. 1), *Cæsar and Servilius are made consuls.* [Here **consules** is *predicate-nominative* after **creantur**.]

litteras Græcas senex didici (Cat. M. 8), *I learned Greek when an old man.* [Here **senex** is in apposition with the subject of **didici**, expressing the *time, condition*, &c., of the act.]

Gnæus et Publius Scipiones, *the Scipios, Cneius and Publius.* [Here the appositive is *plural*, as referring to more than one subject.]

gloria virtutem tanquam umbra sequitur (Tusc. i. 45). [Here the appositive is introduced by way of *comparison*.]

a. The appositive will agree in *gender* when it can; sometimes also in *number:* as,

Aristæus, olivæ inventor (N. D. iii. 18), *Aristæus, discoverer of the olive.*
oleæ Minerva inventrix (G. i. 18), *Minerva, inventress of the olive.*
quia sequuntur naturam, optimam ducem (Læl. 19), *because they follow nature, the best guide.*
omnium doctrinarum inventrices Athenas (De Or. i. 4), *Athens, discoverer of all learning.*

b. A common noun in apposition with a *locative* is put in the Ablative, with or without the preposition **in**: as,

Antiochiæ, celebri quondam urbe (Arch. 3), *at Antioch, once a famous city.*
Albæ constiterunt in urbe munitâ (Phil. iv. 2), *they halted at Alba, a fortified town.*

c. The genitive is used in apposition with *possessives*, taking the gender and number of the implied subject: as,

> in nostro omnium fletu (Mil. 34), *amid the tears of us all.*
> ex Anniană Milonis domo (Att. iv. 3), *out of Annius Milo's house.*

NOTE. — The proper appositive is sometimes put in the Genitive. See § **50**, 1, *f.*

47. OF ADJECTIVES.

Adjectives agree with their nouns in *gender, number,* and *case.* This rule applies also to adjective pronouns and participles.

> **vir fortis,** *a brave man.*
> **cum ducentis militibus,** *with* 200 *men.*
> **consularia munera,** *the duties of consul.*
> **hac lege,** *by this law.*
> **uno interfecto,** *one being slain.*

REMARK. — The adjective may be either *attributive* or *predicate.* An attributive adjective simply qualifies the noun without the intervention of a verb; a predicate adjective is connected with its noun by **esse,** or a verb of similar meaning, expressed or implied.

An adjective may also be used in apposition like a noun: as,

> Hortensium vivum amavi (Off. iii. 18), *I loved Hortensius when living.*

1. With two or more nouns the adjective is plural (also, rarely, when they are connected with **cum**): as,

> Nisus et Euryalus primi (Æn. v. 394), *Nisus and Euryalus first.*
> Juba cum Labieno capti (B. Afr. 52), *Juba and Labienus were taken.*

2. When nouns are of different genders, an attributive adjective agrees with the nearest: as,

> multæ operæ ac laboris, *of much trouble and toil.*
> vita moresque mei, *my life and character.*
> si res, si vir, si tempus ullum dignum fuit (Mil. 7), *if any thing, if any man, if any time, was fit.*

a. A predicate adjective may follow the same rule if the subjects form one connected idea: as,

> factus est strepitus et admurmuratio (Verr. i. 15), *a noise of assent was made.*

b. Generally, a predicate adjective will be masculine, if nouns of different genders mean *living beings;* neuter, if *things without life:* as,

> uxor deinde ac liberi amplexi (Liv. ii. 40), *then his wife and children embraced him.*
> labor (M.) voluptasque (F.) societate quâdam inter se naturali sunt juncta (N.) (id. v. 4), *labor and delight are bound together by a certain natural alliance.*

c. Abstract nouns of the same gender may have a neuter adjective: as,

> stultitia et temeritas et injustitia ... sunt fugienda (Fin. iii. 11), *folly, rashness, and injustice must be shunned.*
> pax et concordia jactata sunt (Tac. Hist. ii. 20), *peace and harmony were talked of.*

d. A masculine or femine adjective may belong (by *Synesis*) to a noun of different gender or number, when the existence of persons is implied: as,

> duo milia relicti (Liv. xxxvii. 39), *two thousand were left.*
> pars certare parati (Æn. v. 108), *a part ready to contend.*
> magna pars raptæ (Liv. i. 9), *a large part* [of the women] *were seized.*
> coloniæ aliquot deductæ, Prisci Latini appellati (id. i. 3), *several colonies were led out* [of men] *called Old Latins.*

e. An adjective pronoun agrees in gender with a word *in apposition* rather than with its antecedent: as, *Hoc opus, hic labor,*

> rerum caput hoc erat, hic fons (Hor. Ep. i. 17), *this was the head of things, this the source.*
> eam sapientiam interpretantur quam adhuc mortalis nemo est consecutus [for id ... quod] (Læl. 5), *they explain that* [thing] *to be wisdom which no man ever yet attained.*

f. Occasionally, an adjective takes the gender of a partitive genitive: as,

> velocissimum animalium delphinus est (Plin.), *the dolphin is the swiftest of creatures.*

3. Adjectives are often used as nouns, the masculine to denote *men,* and the feminine *women:* as,

omnes, *all men,* or *everybody;* **majores,** *ancestors;* **veteres,** *the ancients;* **barbari,** *barbarians;* **amīcus,** *a friend.*

> instinctu purpuratorum (Curt. iii. 9), *at the instigation of the courtiers* [those clad in purple].
> iniquus noster (Planc. 2.), *our foe.*
> didicit jam dives avarus laudare disertos (Juv. vii. 30), *the rich miser has now learned to flatter the eloquent.*

NOTE. — The singular of adjectives in this use is more rare; the plural is very frequent, and may be used of any adjective or participle, to denote those in general described by it.

a. This is especially frequent with possessives: as,

nostri, *our countrymen*, or *men of our party.*
Sullani, *the veterans of Sulla's army.*
suos continebat (B. C. i. 15), *he held his men in check.*

b. The demonstratives **is**, **ille**, &c., used in this way, have nearly the force of personal pronouns. They are often thus used in apposition with a noun, or a clause: as,

vincula, eaque sempiterna (Cat. iv. 4), *chains, and that for ever.*
exspectabam tuas litteras, idque cum multis (Fam. x. 14), *I, with many others, am expecting your letter.*

c. On the other hand, a noun is sometimes used as an adjective, and may be qualified by an adverb (compare § 16, 3, *e*): as,

victor exercitus, *the victorious army.*
servum pecus, *a servile troop.*
admodum puer, *quite a boy.*
magis vir, *more of a man.*
fautor inepte (Hor.), *a stupid admirer.*

4. A neuter adjective may be used as a noun —

a. In the *singular*, to denote either a single object or an abstract quality: as,

rapto vivere, *to live by plunder.*
in arido, *on dry ground.*
honestum, *an honorable act*, or *honor* (as a quality).

b. In the *plural*, to signify objects in general having the quality denoted, and hence the abstract idea: as,

honesta, *honorable deeds* (in general), or *honor* (in the abstract).
omnium ignarus, *ignorant of all.*
justis solutis, *the due rites being paid.*

c. In *apposition*, or as *predicate*, to a noun of different gender: as,

turpitudo pejus est quam dolor (Tusc. ii. 13), *disgrace is worse than pain.*
labor bonum non est (Sen. Ep. 31), *toil is no good thing.*

d. In agreement with an *infinitive* or a *substantive clause*: as,

aliud est errare Caesarem nolle, aliud nolle misereri (Lig. 5), *it is one thing to be unwilling that Caesar should err, another to be unwilling that he should pity.*

REMARK. — The neuter of an adjective is ordinarily used as a noun only in the nominative and accusative: as,

> omnia, *all things (everything)*; but, omnium rerum, *of all things* (omnium is usually *of all persons*); — loquitur de omnibus rebus, *he talks about everything* (de omnibus, *about everybody*).

5. Adjectives denoting source or possession may be used for the genitive: as,

> Pompeiana acies, *Pompey's line.*
> video herilem filium (Ter.), *I spy master's son.*
> æs alienum, *another's money*, i.e. DEBT.

a. Possessives are thus regularly used for the genitive of the personal pronouns: as,

> domus mea, *my house;* nostra patria, *our country.*

b. A possessive in any case may have a genitive in apposition (§ **46**, *c*): as,

> mea solius causa, *for my sake.*
> nostra omnium patria, *the country of us all.*

c. An adjective is occasionally thus used for the *objective genitive* (§ **50**, 3, *b*): as,

> metus hostilis (Jug. 41), *fear of the enemy.*
> feminâ in pœnâ (Virg.), *in punishing a woman.*
> periculo invidiæ meæ (Cat. ii. 2), *at the risk of odium against me.*
> studiosus cædis ferinæ (Ov. M. vii. 675), *eager to slaughter game.*

6. An adjective, with the subject or object, is often used to qualify the *act*, having the force of an adverb: as,

> primus venit, *he came first (was the first to come).*
> nullus dubito, *I no way doubt.*
> læti audiêre, *they were glad to hear.*
> patre invito discessit, *he departed against his father's wishes.*
> erat Romæ frequens (Rosc. Am. 6), *he was often at Rome.*
> serus in cœlum redeas (Hor. Od. i. 2), *may'st thou return late to heaven.*

7. When two qualities of an object are compared, both adjectives (or adverbs) are in the comparative: as,

> longior quam latior acies erat (Liv. xxvii. 48), *the line was longer than it was broad* (or, *rather long than broad*).

a. But not where **magis** is used: as,

clari magis quam honesti (Jug. 8), *more renowned than honorable.*

b. A comparative with a positive, or even two positives, may be thus connected by **quam** (a rare and less elegant use): as,

vehementius quam caute (Agric. 4), *with more fury than good heed.*
claris majoribus quam vetustis (Ann. iv. 61), *of a family more famous than old.*

8. Superlatives denoting order and succession often designate not *what object*, but *what part of it*, is meant: as,

summus mons, *the top of the hill.*
in ultima platæa, *at the end of the avenue.* So,
prior actio, *the earlier part of an action.*

Also, **medius**, *midst;* **ceterus**, *other;* **reliquus**, *remaining:* as,

reliqui captivi, *the rest of the prisoners.*
in colle medio (B. G. i. 24), *on the middle of the hill.*
inter ceteram planitiem (Jug. 92), *in a region elsewhere level.*

Similarly, **serā nocte**, *late at night;* **nos omnes**, *all of us* (§ 50, 2).

9. The expressions **alter ... alter, alius ... alius** (as also the adverbs derived from them), may be used *reciprocally;* or may imply a change of *predicate* as well as of subject: as,

hi fratres alter alterum amant, *these brothers love each other.*
alius aliud petit, *one man seeks one thing, one another.*
alius aliâ ex navi, *out of different ships.*
alius aliâ viâ civitatem auxerunt (Liv. i. 21), *they enlarged the State each in his own way.*

For the use of Adjectives as Adverbs, see § 16, 3, *f.*

For the ablative used adverbially with Comparatives, see § 54, 6, *e.*

48. OF RELATIVES.

A Relative agrees with its Antecedent in *gender and number;* but its *case* depends on the construction of the clause in which it stands: as,

puer qui vēnit, *the boy who came;* liber quem legis, *the book you are reading;* via quā ambulat, *the way he walks in.*

NOTE. — A Relative is properly an *adjective pronoun*, of which the proper noun (the Antecedent) is usually omitted. The full construction would require a corresponding *demonstrative*, to which the relative refers. Hence, relatives serve two uses: — 1. As Nouns in their own clause; 2. As Connectives, and are thus often equivalent to a *demonstrative* and *conjunction* combined (see § 69). The connective force is not original, but is developed from a demonstrative or indefinite meaning; the relative and the antecedent clause being originally co-ordinate.

1. A Verb having a relative as its subject takes the person of the expressed or implied *antecedent:* as,

>adsum qui feci (Æn. ix. 427), *here am I who did it.*

2. A relative generally agrees in gender with a noun (appositive) in its own clause, rather than with an antecedent of different gender : as,

>mare etiam quem Neptunum esse dicebas (N. D. iii. 20), *the sea, too, which you said was Neptune.*

a. A relative may (rarely) by Attraction agree with its antecedent in *case:* as,

>si aliquid agas eorum quorum consuêsti (Fam. v. 14), *if you do something of what you are used to.*

b. A relative may agree in gender and number with an *implied* antecedent: as,

>quartum genus ... qui premuntur (Cat. ii. 10), *a fourth class, that are sinking.*
>unus ex eo numero qui parati erant (Jug. 35), *one of the number* [of those] *who were ready.*
>conjuravêre pauci... de quâ [conjuratione] dicam (Sall. C. 18), *a few have conspired....of which* [conspiracy] *I will speak.*

3. The antecedent noun sometimes appears in both clauses; usually only in the one that precedes; sometimes it is wholly omitted: thus —

a. The noun may be repeated in the relative clause: as,

>loci natura erat haec quem locum nostri delegerant (B. G. ii. 18), *the nature of the ground which our men had chosen was this.*

b. The noun may appear only in the relative clause: as,

>quas res in consulatu nostro gessimus attigit hic versibus (Arch. 11), *he has touched in verse the things which we did in our consulship.*
>urbem quam statuo vestra est (Æn. i. 573), *yours is the city which I found.*

48: 3, 4, 5.] RELATIVES. 111

In such cases the demonstrative **is** or **hic** usually stands in the antecedent clause: as,

> quæ pars civitatis calamitatem populo Romano intulerat, ea princeps pœnas persolvit (B. G. i. 12), *that part of the State which had brought disaster on the Roman people was the first to pay the penalty.*

REMARK.— In a sentence of this class, the relative clause in Latin usually stands first; but, in translating, the noun should be transferred, in its proper case, to the antecedent clause, as in the example just quoted.

c. The antecedent noun may be omitted: as,

> qui decimæ legionis aquilam ferebat (B. G. iv. 25), [the man] *who bore the eagle of the tenth legion.*
> qui cognoscerent misit (id. i. 21), *he sent men to reconnoitre.*

d. A predicate adjective (especially a superlative) agreeing with the antecedent may stand in the relative clause: as,

> vasa ea quæ pulcherrima apud eum viderat (Verr. iv. 27), *those most beautiful vessels which he had seen at his house.*

e. The phrase **id quod** or **quae res** is used (instead of **quod** alone): to relate to an idea or group of words before expressed as,

> [obtrectatum est] Gabinio dicam anne Pompeio? an utrique — id quod est verius? (Manil. 19), *an affront is offered shall I say to Gabinius or Pompey? or — which is truer — to both?*

4. A relative often stands at the beginning of a clause or sentence, where in English a demonstrative must be used: as,

> quæ cum ita sint, *since these things are so.*
> quorum quod simile factum? (Cat. iv. 8), *what ever happened like this?*
> qui illius in te amor fuit (Fam. iv. 5), *such was his love for you.*

5. A Relative Adverb is often equivalent to the relative pronoun with a preposition: as,

quo (= ad quem), *to whom*; **unde** (= a quo), *from whom*, &c.: as,

> apud eos quo se contulit (Verr. iv. 18), *among those to whom he resorted.*
> qui eum necâsset unde ipse natus esset (Rosc. Am. 26), *one who should have slain his own father.*

A similar use is found with the demonstratives **eo, inde,** &c: as,

> eo imponit vasa (Jug. 75), *upon them* [the beasts] *he puts the baggage.*

49. Verbs.

A Verb agrees with its subject-nominative in *number* and *person:* as,

ego statuo, *I resolve;* **oratio est habita,** *the plea was spoken.*

REMARK.—The verb in the periphrastic forms sometimes agrees in gender and number with the *predicate*, or with a noun in *apposition:* as,

non omnis error stultitia est dicenda (Parad. vi. 3), *not every error should be called folly.*
Corinthus lumen Græciæ exstinctum est, *Corinth the light of Greece is put out.*
deliciæ meæ Dicearchus disseruit (Tusc. i. 31), *my pet Dicearchus discoursed.*

1. Two or more singular subjects take a verb in the plural; also, rarely, when one is in the ablative with **cum:** as,

pater et avus mortui sunt, *his father and grandfather are dead.*
dux cum aliquot principibus capiuntur (Liv. xxi. 60), *the general and several chiefs are taken.*

a. When the subjects are of different *persons*, the verb will be in the first and the second rather than the third: as,

si tu et Tullia valetis ego et Cicero valemus (Fam. xiv. 5), *if you and Tullia are well, Cicero and I are well.*

b. If the subjects are joined by disjunctives, or if they are considered as a single whole, the verb is singular: as,

neque fides neque jusjurandum neque illum misericordia repressit (Ter. Ad.), *not faith nor oath, nay, nor mercy, checked him.*
Senatus populusque Romanus intellegit (Fam. v. 8), *the Roman Senate and people understand.*

c. A collective noun — also such distributives as **quisque,** *every;* **uterque,** *each* — may take a plural verb: as,

pars prædas agebant (Jug. 32), *a part brought in booty.*
suum quisque habeant quod suum est (Plaut. Curc.), *let every one keep his own.*

This is most common in poetry.

d. When the action of the verb belongs to the subjects *separately*, it may agree with one and be understood with the others: as,

intercedit M. Antonius et Cassius tribuni plebis (B. C. i. 2),
Antony and Cassius, tribunes of the people, interpose.

2. The Subject of a finite verb is in the *nominative*.

DEFIN.—A Finite Verb is a verb in any mood except the Infinitive.

a. The *personal pronoun*, as subject, is usually omitted unless emphatic: thus,

loquor, *I speak;* ego loquor, *it is I that speak.*

b. An *indefinite* subject is often omitted: as,

dicunt (ferunt, perhibent), *they say.*

c. The verb is sometimes omitted in certain phrases: as,

quorsum hæc [spectant]? *what does this aim at?*
ex ungue leonem [cognosces], *you will know a lion by his claw.*

The indicative and infinitive of **esse** are most frequently omitted.

(For the HISTORICAL INFINITIVE, see § **57**, 8, *h*.)

II. Construction of Cases.

NOTE.—The Oblique Cases of nouns express their relations to other words in the sentence. Originally, the family of languages to which Latin belongs had at least seven cases, besides the vocative, all expressing different relations. Of these the Locative and Instrumental cases were lost, and their functions divided among the others.

The names of the cases, except the Ablative, are of Greek origin. The name *genitive*— Gr. γενική, from γένος — refers, originally, to the *class* to which anything belongs. The *dative*— δοτική — is the case of *giving*. The name *accusative* is a mistranslation of αἰτιατική, signifying that which is *effected* or *caused* (αἰτία).

50. GENITIVE.

A noun used to limit or define another, and *not* meaning the same thing, is put in the genitive.

NOTE.—This relation is most frequently expressed in English by the preposition OF. The genitive seems originally to have meant *that from which something springs;* hence, *that to which it belongs.* From this signification most of its others may be deduced.

1. Subjective Genitive. The Genitive is used to denote the Author, Owner, Source, and (with an adjective) Measure or Quality: as,

  libri Ciceronis, *the books of Cicero.*
  Cæsaris horti, *Cæsar's gardens.*
  culmen tecti, *the roof of the house.*

a. For the genitive of possession a possessive adjective is often used, — regularly for that of the personal pronouns: as,

  liber meus, *my book.*
  aliena pericula, *other men's dangers.*
  Sullana tempora, *the times of Sulla.*

b. The noun limited is understood in a few expressions: as,

  Castoris [ædes], *the* [temple] *of Castor.*
  Hectoris Andromache, *Hector's* [wife] *Andromache.*

c. The genitive is often in the predicate, connected with its noun by a verb, like a predicate appositive: as,

  hæc domus est patris mei, *this house is my father's.*
  tutelæ nostræ [eos] duximus (Liv.), *we held them to be in our protection.*
  Thrasybuli facta lucri fecit (Nep. viii. 1), *he made profit of the deeds of Thrasybulus.*
  Tyros mare dicionis suæ fecit (Curt. iv. 4), *Tyre brought the sea under her sway.*
  hominum non causarum toti erant (Liv. iii. 36), *they belonged wholly to the men, not to the cause.*

d. A phrase or clause often stands for the limited noun; this is most frequent with the genitive of adjectives or abstract nouns: as,

  neque sui judici [erat] decernere (B. C. i. 35), *it was not for his judgment to decide.*
  timidi est optare necem (Ov. M. iv. 15), *it is for the coward to wish for death.*

REMARK. — The genitive of an adjective (especially of the third declension) is thus used instead of the neuter nominative: as,

  sapientis [*not* sapiens] est pauca loqui, *it is wise* [the part of a wise man] *to say little.*

The neuter of possessives is used in the same way: as,

  mentiri non est meum, *it is not for me to lie.*
  humanum [*for* hominis] est errare, *it is man's to err.*

e. A genitive may denote the *substance* of which a thing consists (a modified form of the idea of *source*): as,

  talentum auri, *a talent of gold.*
  flumina lactis, *rivers of milk.*
  navis auri (compare Part. Gen.), *a shipload of gold.*

f. A limiting genitive is sometimes used instead of a noun in apposition: as,

>nomen insaniæ, *the word madness.*
>oppidum Antiochiæ, *the city of Antioch.*

g. The genitive is used to denote *quality*, but only when the quality is modified by an adjective (usually an indefinite one): as,

>vir summæ virtutis, *a man of the highest courage.*
>magnæ est deliberationis, *it is an affair of great deliberation.*
>magni formica laboris, *the ant*, [a creature] *of great toil.*

So **ejus modi,** *of that sort.*

>(Compare the Ablative of Quality, § **54**, 7.)

h. The genitive (of quality), with numerals, is used to define measures of *length, depth,* &c.: as,

>fossa trium pedum, *a trench of three feet* [depth].
>murus sedecim pedum, *a wall sixteen feet* [high].
>minor nulla erat duûm milium amphorûm (Fam. xii. 15), *none held less than* 2000 *jars.*

i. Certain adjectives of Quantity — as **magni, pluris,** and the like — are used in the genitive to express indefinite *value.* (Also the nouns **nihili, flocci, nauci, pili, pensi, terunci, assis,** see Ablative of Price, § **54**, 8.)

REMARK. — The genitive is often followed by the ablatives **causā, gratiā,** *for the sake of;* **ergo,** *because of;* and the indeclinable **instar,** *like.*

2. *Partitive Genitive.* Words denoting a *part* are followed by the genitive of the *whole* to which the part belongs. Partitive words are the following:—

a. Nouns or Pronouns: as,

pars militum, *part of the soldiers.*
quis nostrum, *which of us?* (*but* nos omnes, *all of us*).
nihil erat reliqui, *there was nothing left.*
vastatur agri [id] quod ... (Liv. i. 14), *so much of the land is wasted as,* &c.

b. Numerals, Comparatives, and Superlatives: as,

alter consulum, *one of the* [two] *consuls.*
unus tribunorum, *one of the tribunes.*
plurimum totius Galliæ equitatu valet (B. G. v. 3), *is strongest in cavalry of all Gaul.*

c. Neuter adjectives and pronouns used as nouns: as,

>tantum spati, *so much space.*
>aliquid nummorum, *a few pence.*
>id loci (*or* locorum), *that spot of ground.*

id temporis, *at that time.*
plana urbis, *the level parts of the town.*
quid novi, *what news?*

REMARK.—Of adjectives of the *third declension* the genitive is only rarely used in this way: thus,

nihil novi (gen.), *nothing new;* but
nihil memorabile (nom.), *nothing worth mention.*

d. Adverbs, especially of Quantity and Place: as,

satis pecuniæ, *money enough.*
parum oti, *not much ease.*
ubinam gentium sumus, *where in the world are we?*
inde loci, *next in order.*
istuc æqui bonique, *to that degree of equity and goodness.*
tum temporis, *at that point of time.*
eo miseriarum (Sall.), *to that pitch of misery.*

e. The poets and later writers often use the partitive genitive after adjectives, instead of a noun in its proper case: as,

sequimur te sancte deorum (Æn. iv. 576), *we follow thee, O holy deity.*
nigræ lanarum (Plin. H. N. viii. 48), *black wools.*
electi juvenum (Liv. xxx. 9), *the choice of the young men.*

REMARK.—**1.** Cardinal numbers, with **quidam**, *a certain one,* more commonly, other words rarely, take the ablative with **e (ex)** or **de**, instead of the genitive: as,

unus ex tribunis, *one of the tribunes.*
minumus ex illis (Jug. 11), *the youngest of them.*
medius ex tribus (ib.), *the midst of the three.*

2. With nouns **uterque** generally agrees as an adjective; but with pronouns it always takes a genitive: as,

uterque consul, *both the consuls.*
uterque nostrum, *both of us.*

3. Numbers and words of quantity including the *whole* of anything—as **omnes**, *all;* **quot**, *how many*—take a case in agreement, and not the partitive genitive: as,

nos omnes, *all of us.*
qui omnes, *all of whom.*
quot sunt hostes, *how many of the enemy are there?*
cave inimicos qui multi sunt, *beware of your enemies, of whom you have many.*

So when no others are thought of, although such exist: as,

multi milites, *many of the soldiers.*
nemo Romanus, *not one Roman.*

4. Rarely two genitives are used with one noun: as,

animi multarum rerum percursio (Tusc. iv. 13), *the mind's traversing of many things.*

3. *Objective Genitive.* With many nouns and adjectives implying *action*, the genitive is used to denote the *object*.

NOTE. — This is an extension of the idea of *belonging to;* as in the phrase **odium Caesaris**, *hate of Cæsar*, the hate in a passive sense *belongs* to Cæsar, though in its active sense he is the *object* of it.

a. Nouns of *action*, *agency*, and *feeling* govern the genitive of the object: as,

desiderium oti, *longing for rest.*
vacatio militiæ, *a respite of military service.*
gratia benefici, *gratitude for a kindness.*
fuga malorum, *refuge from disaster.*
laudator temporis acti, *a praiser of the past.*
injuria mulierum Sabinarum (Liv.), *the wrong done to the Sabine women.*
memoria nostri tua (Fam. xiii. 17), *your memory of us.*
consensio divinarum humanarumque rerum (Læl. 6), *the harmony of divine and human things.*
vim suorum pro suo periculo defendebant (B.C. iii. 110), *they parried the attack on their comrades as if it were their own peril.*

Occasionally possessive adjectives are used in the same way (see § **47**, 5, *c*).

b. Adjectives requiring an object of reference (*relative adjectives*) govern the genitive.

These are — 1. Adjectives denoting *desire, knowledge, memory, fulness, power, sharing, guilt*, and their opposites; 2. Verbals in **ax**; 3. Participles in **ns** when used to denote a *disposition* and not a particular act, so that they become adjectives: as,

avidus laudis, *greedy of praise.*
fastidiosus literarum, *disdaining letters.*
juris peritus, *skilled in law.*
habetis ducem memorem vestri oblitum sui (Cat. iv. 9), *you have a leader who thinks of you and forgets himself.*
plena consiliorum inania verborum (De Or. i. 9), *full of wisdom, void of words.*
rationis et orationis expertes (Off. i. 16), *devoid of reason and speech.*
virtutis compos (id.), *possessed of virtue.*
paternorum bonorum exheres (De Or. i. 38), *ousted from his father's estate.*
rei capitalis affinis (2 Verr. ii. 43), *accessory to a capital crime.*
justum ac tenacem propositi virum (Hor. Od. iii. 3), *a man just and steadfast to his purpose.*

si quem tui amantiorem cognovisti (Q. Fr. ix. 1), *if you have known any more fond of you.*
multitudo insolens belli (B. C. ii. 36), *a crowd unused to war.*
sitiens sanguinis, *thirsting for blood.* But,
Tiberius sitiens sanguinem (Tac.), *Tiberius* [then] *thirsting for blood.*

c. Some other adjectives of similar meaning occasionally take the genitive; and the poets and late writers use almost any adjective with a genitive of *specification:* as,

callidus rei militaris (Tac. H. ii. 31), *skilled in soldiership.*
pecuniæ liberales (Sall. C. 7), *lavish of money.*
virtutum sterile seculum (id. i. 3), *a century barren in virtue.*
pauper aquarum (Hor.), *scant of water.*
prodigus æris (id.), *a spendthrift of wealth.*
notus animi, *of known bravery.*
fessi rerum (Virg.), *weary of toil.*
læta laborum (id.), *glad of work.*
modicus voluptatis, *moderate in pleasure.*
integer vitæ scelerisque purus (Hor.), *upright in life, and clear of guilt.*
docilis modorum (id.), *teachable in measures.*

REMARK. — **Animi** (strictly a locative, plural **animis**), is added to adjectives of *feeling:* as,

æger animi, *sick at heart.*
confusus animi, *disturbed in spirit.*

d. A few adjectives of *likeness, nearness, belonging* — requiring the dative as such — take the possessive genitive: these are, **aequalis, affinis, communis, finitimus, par, propinquus, proprius** (regularly), **similis, vicīnus.**

REMARK. — One noun limiting another is regularly used in the genitive, and not with a preposition, — prepositions being originally *adverbs,* and requiring a verb. Sometimes, however, one noun has another connected with it by a preposition. This happens with nouns of *action, feeling, and motion;* some relations of place *to* or *in which* or *from which* (including *origin*); *accompaniment,* &c.: as,

odium in Cæsarem (*or* odium Cæsaris), *hate of Cæsar.*
merita erga me (Cic.), *services to me.*
auxilium adversus inimicos (id.), *help against enemies.*
reditus in cælum (id.), *return to heaven.*
impetus in me (id.), *attack on me.*
excessus e vitâ (id.), *departure from life.*
e proelio nuntius, *a messenger from the battle.*
castra ad Bagradam (Cæs.), *camp near the Bagrada.*
invidia ob scelera (Sall.), *odium for his crimes.* So,
domum reditionis spes (id.), *the hope of returning home.*

4. Genitive after Verbs. The genitive is used as the object of several classes of Verbs.

a. Verbs of Remembering, Forgetting, and Reminding, take the genitive of the object when they are used *of a continued state of mind,* but the accusative when used *of a single act:* as,

pueritiæ memoriam recordari (Arch. i.), *to recall the memory of childhood.*
animus meminit præteritorum (Div. i. 30), *the soul remembers the past.*
venit mihi in mentem illius diei, *I bethought me of that day.*
obliviscere cædis atque incendiorum (Cat.), *turn your mind from slaughter and conflagrations.*
bona præterita non meminerunt (Fin. ii. 20), *they do not remember past blessings.*
memineram Paullum (Cat. M. 2), *I remembered Paulus.*
memini etiam quæ nolo (Fin. ii. 33), *I remember even what I would not.*
totam causam oblitus est (Brut. 60), *he forgot the whole case.*

REMARK. — The above distinction is unimportant as to verbs of reminding, which take the genitive except of neuter pronouns: as, **hoc te admoneo,** *I warn you of this.* The accusative is always used of a person or thing *remembered by an eye-witness.* **Recordor** is almost always construed with an accusative, or with a phrase or clause.

b. Verbs of Accusing, Condemning, and Acquitting, take the genitive of the *charge* or *penalty:* as,

arguit me furti, *he accuses me of theft.*
peculatûs damnatus (pecuniæ publicæ damnatus) (Flac. 18), *condemned for embezzlement.*
capitis damnatus, *condemned to death.*

Peculiar genitives, under this construction, are —

capitis (damnare capitis, *to sentence to death*);
majestatis, *treason* (crime against the dignity of the State);
repetundarum, *extortion* (lit. of an action for *claiming back* money wrongfully taken);
voti (damnatus or **reus voti,)** *bound* to the payment of one's vow, i.e. *successful* in one's effort).

REMARK. — The crime may be expressed by the ablative with **de**; the punishment by the ablative alone: as,

de vi et majestatis damnati (Phil. i.), *condemned of assault and treason.*
vitia autem hominum atque fraudes damnis, ignominiis, vinculis, verberibus, exiliis, morte damnantur (De Or. i. 43), *but the vices and crimes of men are punished with fines, dishonor, chains, scourging, exile, death.*

But, **inter sicarios accusare (defendere),** *to accuse of murder.*

c. Many verbs of Emotion take the genitive of the object which excites the feeling (Gen. of *source*). These are —

1. Verbs of *pity*, as **misereor** and **miseresco**: as,

miserescite regis (Æn. viii. 573), *pity the king.*
miserere animi non digna ferentis (id. ii. 144), *pity a soul that endures unworthy things.*

But **miseror, commiseror,** *bewail,* take the accusative.

2. The impersonals **miseret, piget, poenitet, pudet, taedet** (or **pertaesum est**), which take also the accusative of the person affected (§ 39, 2): as,

hos homines infamiæ suæ neque pudet neque tædet (Verr. i. 12), *these men are neither ashamed nor weary of their dishonor.*

REMARK. — An infinitive or clause may be used with these verbs instead of the genitive of a noun: as,

me pœnitet hæc fecisse, *I repent of having done this.*

Sometimes they are used personally: as,

nonne te hæc pudent (Ter. Ad.), *do not these things shame you?*

d. The impersonals **interest** and **rēfert,** *it concerns,* takes the genitive of the person affected, — the subject of the verb being a neuter pronoun or a substantive clause: as,

Clodi intererat Milonem perire (Mil. 21), *it was the interest of Clodius that Milo should die.*

But instead of the genitive of a *personal pronoun* the possessive is used in the ablative singular feminine: as,

quid tuâ id refert? — magni (Ter. Ph.), *how does that concern you? much.*

refert is seldom used in any other way; but it takes, rarely, the *dativus commodi* (Hor. Sat. i. 1, 49). The object of **interest** is sometimes in the accusative with **ad**: as,

magni ad honorem nostrum interest (Fam. xvi. 1), *it is of consequence to our honor.*

NOTE. — The word **interest** may be used (1) impersonally with the genitive, as above; (2) personally with the dative: as, **interest exercitui,** *he is present with the army;* (3) with the accusative and prepositions: as, **interest inter exercitum et castra,** *he is between* — or, *there is a difference between* — *the army and camp.*

e. Some verbs of plenty and want govern the genitive (rarely, except **egeo** and **indigeo,** *need*): as,

quid est quod defensionis indigeat? (Rosc. Am. 12), *what is there that needs defence?*
satagit rerum suarum, *he has his hands full with his own affairs.*

Also, sometimes, **potior**, *get possession of;* as always in the phrase **potiri rerum,** *to be master of affairs.* But these verbs more commonly take the ablative.

REMARK. — The genitive is also used after the adverbs **pridie,** *the day before;* **postridie,** *the day after;* **tenus,** *as far as:* as,

postridie ejus diei (B. G. v. 10), *the next day.*

51. DATIVE.

The Dative is used of the object *indirectly affected* by the action, which is usually denoted in English by TO or FOR (*Indirect Object*).

NOTE. — The dative seems to have the primary meaning of *towards,* and to be closely akin to the Locative. But this meaning is lost in Latin, except in some adverbial forms (**eo, illo,** &c.) and in the poets. In most of its derived meanings, it denotes an object not merely (like the Accusative) as *passively affected* by the action, or *caused* by it; but as reciprocally *sharing* in the action, or *receiving it actively.* Thus, in **dedit mihi librum,** *he gave me a book,* or **fecit mihi injuriam,** *he did me an injury;* it is I that *receive* the book or *feel* the wrong. Hence persons, or objects personified, are most likely to be in the dative. So in the Spanish, the dative is used whenever a Person is the object of an action: as, **yo veo al hombre,** *I see the man.*

As this difference between the accusative and dative (direct and indirect object) depends on the view taken by the writer, verbs of similar meaning in different languages, or even in the same, differ in the case of the object. In English, especially, owing to the loss of its cases, many verbs are construed as transitive, which in Latin require the dative. Thus *believe,* which in English originally governed the genitive, has become transitive; while the corresponding verb in Latin, **credo** (a compound of **cred** and **do** (DHA), *to place confidence in*) takes the dative.

1. *Dative with Transitives.* Transitive verbs, whose meaning permits it, take the dative of the *indirect object,* with the accusative of the *direct.*

These are, especially, verbs of Giving, Telling, Sending, and the like: as,

do tibi librum, *I give you a book.*
valetudini tribuamus aliquid (Tusc. i. 118), *let us allow something to health.*
illud tibi affirmo (Fam. i. 7), *this I assure you.*
Pompeio plurimum debebam (id. i. 9), *I owed much to Pompey.*
id omne tibi polliceor ac defero (Man. 24), *all this I promise you and bestow.*

6

commendo tibi ejus omnia negotia (Fam. i. 1), *I put all his affairs in your hands.*
amico munusculum mittere (id. ix. 12), *to send a slight tribute to a friend.*
illi inimico servum rem. (Deiot. ii.), *to him, his enemy, he returned a slave.*
dabis profecto misericordiæ quod iracundiæ negavisti (id. 14), *you will surely grant to mercy what you refused to wrath.*
Karthagini bellum denuntio (Cat. M. 6), *I announce war to Carthage.*
curis gaudia misces (Catull. — only poet.), *thou minglest joy with care.*

a. In the passive, such verbs retain the dative of the indirect object: as,

hæc nobis nuntiantur, *these things are told us.*

b. When the idea of *motion* is distinctly conveyed, a preposition is used (except by poetic use): as,

has litteras ad te mitto, *I send you this letter.*

c. A few verbs of this class — under a different view of the action — may take the accusative of a *person*, with an ablative of *means.*

Such verbs are **dono, impertio, induo, exuo, adspergo, inspergo, circumdo, circumfundo, prohibeo, intercludo.** Thus —

donat coronas suis, *he presents wreaths to his men;* or,
donat suos coronis, *he presents his men with wreaths.*
pomis se induit arbos (G. iv. 143), *the tree decks itself with fruits.*
copiis (dat.) armis exutis (B. G. iii. 6), *the forces being stripped of arms.*
aram sanguine adspergere (N. D. iii. 36), *to sprinkle the altar with blood.*

2. *Dative after Intransitives.* Intransitive verbs take the dative of the *indirect object* only: as,

cedant arma togæ (Phil. i. 8), *let arms give way to the gown.*
quid homini potest turpius usuvenire (Quinct. 15), *what more shameful can befall a man?*
respondi maximis criminibus (Phil. i. 14), *I have answered the heaviest charges.*
ut ita cuique eveniat (id. 46), *that it may so turn out to each.*
manent ingenia senibus (Cat. M. 7), *old men keep their powers of mind.*
vento et fluctibus loqui (Lucr. iv. 491), *to talk to wind and wave.*

nec quereris patri (Juv. ii. 131), *you complain not to a father.*
non cuivis homini contingit adire Corinthum (Hor. Ep. i. 17), *it is not every man's luck to go to Corinth.*

a. Most verbs signifying to *favor, help, please, serve, trust,* and their contraries, — also, to *believe, persuade, command, obey, envy, threaten, pardon,* and *spare,* — take the Dative in Latin, though transitive in English.

These include, among others, the following: **adversor, credo, faveo, fido, ignosco, impĕro, invĭdeo, irascor, noceo, parco, pareo, placeo, servio, studeo, suādeo (persuadeo)**: as,

cur mihi invides, *why do you envy me?*
civitati serviebat, *he served the state.*
tibi favemus, *we favor you.*
mihi parcit atque ignoscit, *he spares and pardons me.*
sontibus opitulari poteram (Fam. iv. 13), *I was able to help the guilty.*
bonis invident (Sall.), *they envy the good.*
Catoni resistimus (Fam. i. 1); *we withstand Cato.*
non omnibus servio (id. xvi. 13), *I am not a servant to every man.*
cum ceteris tum mihi ipsi displiceo (id. iv. 13), *I dissatisfy other people and myself too.*
non parcam operæ (id. xvi. 13), *I will spare no pains.*
sic mihi persuasi (Cat. M. 21), *so I have persuaded myself.*
huic legioni Cæsar confidebat maxime (B. G. i. 40), *in this legion Cæsar had special confidence.*
ex quo efficitur hominem naturæ obedientem homini nocere non posse (Off. iii. 5), *whence it appears that a man while obeying Nature cannot harm a fellow-man.*

REMARK. — **1.** Some verbs of the same meanings take the accusative: as, **juvo, adjŭvo,** *help;* **laedo,** *injure;* **jubeo,** *order;* **deficio,** *fail.*

2. Some take the dative or accusative indifferently: as, **adūlor,** *flatter;* **aemŭlor,** *rival;* **comĭtor,** *attend;* **despēro,** *despair;* **praestōlor,** *await;* **medeor, medicor,** *heal.*

3. Some take the dative or accusative according to their meaning: as,

parti civium consulunt (Off. i. 25), *they consult for a party of the citizens.*
cum te consuluissem (Fam. xi. 29), *when I had consulted you.*
metuens pueris (Plaut. Am. v. 1), *anxious for the boys.*
nec metuunt deos (Ter. Hec. v. 2), *they fear not even the gods* (so also *timeo.*)
ei cavere volo (Fam. iii. 1), *I will have a care for him.*
caveto omnia (id. xi. 21), *beware of everything.*

prospicite patriæ (Cat. iv. 2), *have regard for the state.*
prospicere sedem senectuti (Liv. iv. 49), *to provide a habitation for old age* [so also *providere*].
nequeo mihi temperare (Plin. xviii. 6), *I cannot control myself.*
rempublicam temperare (Tusc. i. 1), *to govern the state* [so also *moderor*].

See Lexicon, under **convenio, cupio, fido** (abl.), **insisto, maneo, praesto, praeverto, recipio, renuntio, solvo, succedo**.

b. The dative is used after the Impersonals **libet, licet**; after verbs compounded with **satis, bene**, and **male**; together with the following : — **gratificor, gratulor, haereo** (rarely), **jungo, medeor, medicor, misceo** (poetic), **nubo, permitto, plaudo, probo, studeo, supplico**; and the phrases **auctor esse, gratias agere (habere), morem gerere (morigeror), supplex (dicto audiens) esse**: as,

quod mihi maxime lubet (Fam. i. 18), *what most pleases me.*
Di isti Segulio male faciant (id. xi. 21), *may the gods send evil upon that Segulius.*
mihi ipsi nunquam satisfacio (id. 17), *I never satisfy myself.*
virgo nupsit ei (Div. i. 46), *a maiden married him.*
Pompeio se gratulari putent (id. i. 1), *they suppose they are doing Pompey a service.*
sed tibi morem gessi (id. ii. 18), *but I have deferred to you.*
tibi permitto respondere (N. D. iii. 1), *I give you leave to answer.*
armatus adversario maledixi (Fam. vi. 7), *in arms I cursed the foe.*
voluptati aurium morigerari (Or. 48), *to humor the lust of the ears.*
habeo senectuti maximam gratiam (Cat. M. 14), *I owe old age much thanks.*
maximas tibi gratias ago, *I return you the warmest thanks.*

c. Many verbs of the above classes take an accusative of the *thing*, with a dative of the *person:* as,

cui cum rex crucem minitaretur (Tusc. i. 43), *when the king threatened him with the cross.*
invident nobis optimam magistram (id. iii. 2), *they grudge us our best of teachers* [Nature].
frumento exercitui proviso (B. G. v. 44), *when the army was supplied with corn.*
puerum [vocare] cui cenam imperaret (Ros. Am. 21), *to call a boy and order supper of him.*
imperat oppidanis decem talenta, *he exacts ten talents of the townspeople.*
omnia sibi ignoscere (Vell. ii. 30), *to pardon one's self everything.*

d. Most verbs compounded with **ad, ante, con, in, inter, ob, post, prae, pro, sub, super** — and some with **circum** — take the dative of the object on account of their acquired meaning (many take also the accusative, being originally transitive): as,

> neque enim assentior iis (Læl. 3), *for I do not agree with them.*
> tempestati obsequi artis est (Fam. i. 9), *it is a point of skill to yield to the weather.*
> omnibus negotiis non interfuit solum sed præfuit (id. i. 6), *he not only had a hand in all matters, but took the lead in them.*
> pueritiæ adulescentia obrepit (Cat. M.), *youth steals upon childhood.*
> [Archiæ] antecellere omnibus contigit (Arch. 3), *it was his good fortune to outvie all.*
> quantum natura hominis pecudibus antecedit (Off. i. 30), *so far as man's nature is superior to brutes.*
> nos ei succedimus (Fam. vii. 31), *we succeed him.*
> criminibus illis pro rege se supponit reum (Deiot. 15), *he takes those charges upon himself in the king's behalf.*
> nec unquam succumbet inimicis (id. 13), *he will never bend before his foes.*
> illis libellis nomen suum inscribunt (Arch. 13), *they put their own name to those papers.*
> tibi obtempera (F. ii. 7), *restrain yourself.*
> hibernis Labienum præposuit (Cæs.), *he set Labienus over the winter-quarters.*
> cur mihi te offers, ac meis commodis officis et obstas (Ros. Am. 38), *why do you put yourself in my way, to hinder and withstand my advantage?*

So **excello**: as,

> tu longe aliis excellis (De Or. ii. 54), *you far excel others.*

REMARK. — 1. Some of the above compounds acquire a transitive meaning, and take the accusative: as, **aggredior**, *approach*; **adire**, *go to*; **antecedo, anteeo, antegradior**, *precede* (both cases); **convenio**, *meet*; **ineo**, *enter*; **obeo**, *encounter*; **offendo**, *hit*; **oppugno**, *oppose*; **subeo**, *go under* (take up): as,

> nos oppugnat (Fam. i. 1), *he opposes us.*
> quis audeat bene comitatum aggredi, *who would dare encounter a man well-attended?*
> munus obire (Læl. 2), *to attend to a duty.*

2. The adjective **obvius** — also the adverb **obviam** — with a verb takes the dative: as,

> si ille obvius ei futurus non erat (Mil. 18), *if he was not intending to get in his way.*
> mihi obviam venisti (Fam. ii. 16), *you came to meet me.*

e. Many compounds of **ab, de, ex**, with **adimo**, take the dative (especially of *persons*) instead of the ablative of separation, — the action being more vividly represented as done *to* the object affected by it: as,

    vitam adulescentibus vis aufert (C. M. 19), *force deprives young men of life.*
    nihil enim tibi detraxit senectus (id. 1), *for age has robbed you of nothing.*
    nec mihi hunc errorem extorqueri volo (id. 23), *nor do I wish this error wrested from me.*
    cum extorta mihi veritas esset (Or. 48), *when the truth had been forced from me.*

REMARK. — The distinct idea of *place*, — and, in general, names of *things*, — require the ablative with a preposition; or both constructions may be used together: as,

    illum ex periculo eripuit (B. G. iv. 12), *he dragged him out of danger.*
    victoriam eripi sibi e manibus, *that victory should be wrested from his hands.*

f. Intransitive verbs governing the dative can be used in the Passive only *impersonally:* as,

    cui parci potuit (Liv. xxi. 12), *who could be spared?*
    non modo non invidetur illi aetati verum etiam favetur (Off. ii. 13), *that age* [youth] *is not only not envied, but is even favored.*
    mihi quidem persuaderi nunquam potuit (C. M. 22), *I for my part could never be persuaded.*
    resistendum senectuti est (id. 11), *we must resist old age.*
    plaudi tibi non solere (Deiot. 12), *that you are not wont to be applauded.*
    tempori serviendum est (Fam. ix. 7), *we must serve the time.*

g. The dative is often used by the poets in constructions which would strictly require another case with a preposition: as,

    differt sermoni (Hor.), *differs from prose* [a sermone].
    tibi certet (Virg.). *may vie with you* [tecum].
    lateri abdidit ensem (id.), *buried the sword in his side* [in latere].
    solstitium pecori defendite (Ecl. vii. 47), *keep the noontide from the flock* [a pecore].

Here the poets regard the acting as done *to* the thing affected, for greater vividness of expression.

3. Dative of Possession. The dative is used after **esse** and similar words to denote the Owner: as,

    est mihi liber, *I have a book.*

REMARK. — The Genitive or a possessive with **esse** emphasizes the *possessor;* the Dative the fact of *possession:* as, **liber est meus,** *the book is mine* (and no one's else); **est mihi liber,** *I have a book* (among other things). This is the usual form to denote simple *possession;* **habeo,** *I have,* generally signifying *hold,* often with some secondary meaning: as,

> legionem quam secum habebat (B. G. i. 8), *the legion which he had with him.*
> domitas habere libidines (De Or.), *to keep the passions under.*

a. Compounds of **esse** take the dative (excepting **abesse** and **posse**; for other compounds, see above, 2, *d*).

b. After **nomen est,** and similar expressions, the name is usually put in the dative by a kind of apposition with the *person:* as,

> puero ab inopiâ Egerio inditum nomen (Liv. i. 34), *the boy was called Egerius from his poverty.*
> cui Africano fuit cognomen (Liv. xxv. 2), *whose surname was Africanus.*

But the name may be in apposition with **nomen**; or in the genitive (§ 50, 1,*f*): as,

> cui nomen Arethusa (Verr. iv. 52), [a fount] *called Arethusa.*
> nomen Mercurî est mihi (Plaut. Am.), *my name is Mercury.*

4. *Dative of Agency.* The dative is used, after some passive forms, to denote the *agent:* viz.

a. Regularly with the Gerund or Gerundive, to denote the person on whom the necessity rests: as,

> hæc vobis provincia est defendenda (Man. 6), *this province is for you to defend* [to be defended by you].
> mihi est pugnandum, *I have to fight* [i.e., the need of fighting is mine; compare *mihi est liber*].

b. The dative is often used after *perfect participles,* especially when used in an adjective sense, — rarely after other parts of the verb: as,

> mihi deliberatum et constitūtum est (Rull. i. 8), *I have deliberated and resolved.*
> oratori omnia quæsita esse debent (De Or. iii. 14), *an orator should search everything.*
> acceptus mihi, *acceptable to me.*

c. By the poets and later writers it is used in this way after almost any passive verb: as,

> neque cernitur ulli (Æn. i. 440), *nor is seen by any.*
> felix est dicta sorori (Fast. iii.), *she was called happy by her sister.*

REMARK. — The dative is regularly used after the passive of **video** (usually to be rendered *seem*) : as,

 videtur mihi, *it seems* (or *seems good*) *to me*.

5. *Dative of Service.* The dative is used to denote the *purpose* or *end;* often with another dative of the person or thing affected: as,

reipublicæ cladi sunt (Jug. 85), *they are ruin to the State.*
rati sese dîs immortalibus curæ esse (id. 75), *thinking themselves to be the special care of the gods.*
magno usui nostris fuit (B. G. iv. 25), *it was of great service to our men.*
tertiam aciem nostris subsidio misit (id.), *he sent the third line as a relief to our men.*
omnia deerant quæ ad reficiendas naves erant usui (id. 29), *all things were wanting which were of use for repairing the ships.*

REMARK. — In this use the dative is nearly equivalent to a noun in apposition with the subject or object of the verb. It is common with the words **cordi**, *a delight* (lit. *to the heart*) ; **dono**, *a gift;* **emolumento**, *a gain;* **usui**, *an advantage;* **vitio**, *a fault.* The indeclinable adjective **frugi** is properly a dative of service.

6. *Dative of Nearness, &c.* The dative is used after Adjectives and Adverbs, to denote that to which the given quality is directed, or for which it exists.

Such are especially words of *fitness, nearness, likeness, service, inclination*, and their opposites: as,

nihil est tam naturæ aptum (Læl. 5), *nothing is so fitted to nature.*
carus omnibus exspectatusque venies (F. xvi. 7), *you will come loved and longed for by all.*
locum divinæ naturæ æternitatique contrarium (Cat. M. 21), *a point opposed to the divine nature and eternity.*
nihil difficile amanti puto (Or. 10), *I think nothing hard to a lover.*
pompæ quam pugnæ aptius (id. 13), *fitter for a procession than a battle.*
consentaneum tempori et personæ (id. 22), *adapted to the time and the party.*
rebus ipsis par et æqualis oratio (id. 36), *a speech equal and level with the subject.*

Also, in poetic and colloquial use, **idem**, *the same:* as,

 in eadem arma nobis (Cic.), *to the same arms with us.*

a. Adjectives of Usefulness or Fitness take oftener the accusative with **ad**, but sometimes the dative: as,

aptus ad rem militarem, *fit for a soldier's duty.*
locus ad insidias aptior (Mil. 20), *a place fitter for lying-in-wait.*
ad amicitiam idoneus (Læl. 17), *apt to friendship.*
castris idoneum locum deligit (B. G. vi. 10), *he selects a suitable camping-ground.*

b. Adjectives and nouns of *inclination* may take the accusative with **in** or **erga**: as,

comis in uxorem (Hor. Ep. ii. 2), *kind to his wife.*
divina bonitas erga homines (N. D. ii. 23), *the divine goodness towards men.*

c. The following may take also the possessive genitive: —
aequalis, affinis, amīcus, cognatus, communis, consanguineus, dispar, familiaris, inimīcus, necessarius, par, peculiaris, proprius, superstes.

REMARK. — After **similis**, *like*, with early writers, the genitive is more usual; Cicero uses the genitive of *persons*, and the genitive or dative of *things*.

d. The following take the accusative: — **propior, proximus** (sometimes), **propius, proxime** (more commonly) — as if prepositions, like **prope**.

e. Verbal nouns take (rarely) the dative, like the verbs from which they are derived: as,

invidia consuli (Sall.), *ill-will against the consul.*
ministri sceleribus (Tac.), *servants of crime.*
obtemperatio legibus (Leg. i. 15), *obedience to the laws.*
sibi ipsi responsio (De Or. iii. 54), *an answer to himself.*

7. *Dative of Advantage.* The dative is often required not by any particular word, but by the general meaning of the sentence (*dativus commodi et incommodi*).

NOTE. — In these cases there may be only one word in the sentence; but they are distinguished by the fact that the meaning of the verb is complete without the dative, while in the preceding cases it is required to complete the sense of some particular word.

tibi aras (Pl. Merc. i. 1), *you plough for yourself.*
non solum nobis divites esse volumus sed liberis (Off. iii. 15), *it is not for ourselves alone but for our children that we would be rich.*
res tuas tibi habe (formula of divorce), *keep your goods.*
laudavit mihi fratrem, *he praised my brother* [out of regard for me; *laudavit fratrem meum* would imply no such motive].

a. The dative of advantage is often used instead of the possessive genitive: as,

> iter Pœnis vel corporibus suis obstruere (Cat. M. 20), *to block the march of the Carthaginians even with their bodies.*
> se in conspectum nautis dedit (Verr. vi. 33), *he put himself in sight of the sailors.*
> versatur mihi ante oculos (id. 47), *it comes before my eyes.*

b. The dative of advantage is used in relations of *direction*, answering to the English *as you go in* (on the right, in the front, &c.): as,

> oppidum primum Thessaliæ venientibus ab Epiro (B. C. iii. 80), *the first town of Thessaly as you come from Epirus.*
> lævâ parte sinum intrantibus (Liv. xxxvi. 26), *on the left as you sail up the gulf.*

c. The dative of advantage is used, rarely (by a Greek idiom), with the participle of **volo** or **nolo**, and similar words: as,

> ut quibusque bellum invitis aut volentibus erat (Tac. Ann. i. 59), *as they might receive the war reluctantly or gladly.*
> ut militibus labos volentibus esset (Jug. 100), *that the soldiers might assume the task willingly.*

***d.* Ethical Dative.** The dative of the personal pronouns is used to show a certain interest felt by the person referred to (*dativus ethicus:* compare "I'll rhyme you so eight years together." — *As you Like it.*) : as,

> quid mihi Celsus agit (Hor.), *pray what is Celsus doing?*
> at tibi repente venit mihi Cominius (F. ix. 2), *but, look you, of a sudden comes to me Cominius.*
> hem tibi talentum argenti (Pl. Trin. v. 1), *hark ye, a talent of silver.*
> quid tibi vis? *what would you have?*
> avaritia senilis quid sibi velit non intelligo (Cat. M. 18), *I do not understand what an old man's avarice means.*

REMARK. — To express FOR — meaning *instead of, in defence of, in behalf of* — the ablative with **pro** must be used, not the dative: as,

> pro patriâ mori (Hor. Od. iii. 2), *to die for one's country.*
> pro rege, lege, grege (prov.), *for king, law, people.*
> ego ibo pro te (Pl. Most.), *I will go instead of you.*
> non pro me sed contra me (De Or. iii. 20), *not for me but against me.*

52. Accusative.

The Accusative denotes that which is immediately affected by the action of a verb (*Direct Object*).

1. *General Use*. The Accusative is the case of the *direct object* of a transitive verb: as,

> **legationem suscepit**, *he undertook the embassy.*
> **Caesar vicit Pompeium**, *Cæsar conquered Pompey.*

REMARK.—The Object of a transitive verb in the active voice becomes its Subject in the Passive, and is put in the nominative: as,

> legatio suscipitur, *the embassy is undertaken.*
> Pompeius a Cæsare victus est, *Pompey was overcome by Cæsar.*

a. Many verbs which express Feeling, apparently intransitive, may take an accusative in Latin: as,

> fidem supplicis erubuit (Virg.), *he respected* [blushed at] *the faith of a suppliant.*
> flebat mortuos vivosque, *he wept the dead and living.*
> meum casum luctumque doluerunt (Sest. 69), *they grieved* [at] *my calamity and sorrow.*
> horreo conscientiam (Fin. i. 16), *I shudder at conscience.*

Such verbs may accordingly be used in the passive: as,

> ridetur ab omni conventu (Hor.), *he is laughed* [at] *by the whole assembly.*

b. **Cognate Accusative.** A neuter verb often takes an accusative of kindred meaning (almost always modified by an adjective, or in some other manner): as,

> vivere eam vitam (Cic.), *to live that kind of life.*
> ætatem tertiam vivebat, *he was living his third age.*

Similarly, in such phrases as **vincere judicium**, *to gain one's case at court*, and in poetic use: as,

> saltare Cyclopa (Hor. Sat. v. 1), *to dance the Cyclops.*
> Bacchanalia vivere (Juv. ii. 2), *to live in revels.*

c. Verbs of taste, smell, &c., take an accusative of the quality: as,

> vinum redolens (Cic.), *smelling of wine.*
> herbam mella sapiunt (Plin.), *the honey tastes of grass.*

d. Verbs of motion, and a few others, compounded with prepositions, especially compounds of **circum** and **trans**, frequently become transitive, and take the accusative: as,

    mortem obire, *to die.*
    consulatum ineunt (Livy iii. 6), *they assume the consulship.*
    neminem conveni (Fam. ix. 14), *I met no one.*
    tectum subire, *to enter* [go under] *a place of shelter.*
    colloquium haud abnuit (Livy xxx. 29), *he did not refuse the interview.*
    si insulam adisset (B. G. iv. 20), *if he should go to the island.*
    cives qui circumstant senatum (Cat. i. 8), *the citizens who throng about the senate.*

***e.* Constructio Praegnans.** The accusative is used in certain phrases *constructively*, the real object of the verb being something understood: as,

    coire societatem, *to* [go together and] *form an alliance.*
    ferire fœdus, *to strike a treaty* [i.e. to sanction by striking down the victim].
    mare navigare, *to sail the sea* [i.e. to sail a ship upon the sea].

f. The accusative is used after the Impersonals **decet**, *it becomes;* **delectat, juvat**, *it delights;* **oportet**, *it behooves;* **fallit**, *it deceives;* **fugit, praeterit**, *it escapes:* as,

    te non praeteriit (Fam. i. 8), *it has not escaped your notice.*

(For Accusative and Genitive after Impersonals, see § **50**, 4, *c*.)

2. *Two Accusatives.* Several classes of verbs, besides the direct object, take another accusative, either in apposition or as a secondary object.

a. The accusative is used in apposition after verbs of *naming, choosing,* &c. (See § **46**.)

b. A second accusative is sometimes used after transitive verbs compounded with prepositions: as,

    Hiberum copias trajecit (Liv. xxi. 23), *he threw his forces across the Ebro.*

But with these verbs the preposition is oftener repeated.

c. Verbs of *asking and teaching* govern two accusatives, either of which may be regarded as the direct object of the action: as,

    hoc vos doceo (Cic.), *I teach you this.*
    hoc te vehementer rogo (id.), *this I urgently beg of you.*

REMARK. — The accusative of the *thing* may remain, in this construction, after a passive: as, **rogatus sententiam**; while the *person* will be, after verbs of asking, in the ablative with the preposition **ab** or **ex**: as, **hoc a te rogatur**. The preposition is always used, to denote the person after **peto, postulo** (ab), **quaero** (**ex** or **de**): as,

pacem ab Romanis petere (Caes.), *to beg peace of the Romans.*

d. The transitive **celo**, *conceal,* and the usually neuter **lateo**, *lie hid*, take the accusative of the person: as,

hoc me celavit, *he hid this from me.* ℟. *Cic. pro Clu.* 66
latet plerosque (Plin.), *it is hid from most.*

3. *Adverbial Accusative.* The accusative is used *adverbially*, or for specification. This is found—

a. With many verbs usually intransitive, which take a neuter pronoun or adjective in the accusative: as,

quid moror, *why do I delay?*
pauca milites hortatus (Sall.), *having briefly exhorted the men.*
dulce loquentem (Hor. Od. i. 22), *sweetly speaking.*
acerba tuens (Æn. ix. 793), *looking cruelly.*
torvum clamat (id. vii. 599), *he cries harshly.*
idem gloriari, *to boast the same thing.*

NOTE. — Many of these are *cognate accusative.*

b. In a few adverbial phrases, such as **id temporis**, *at that time;* **meam vicem**, *on my part;* **quod si**, *but (as to which) if.*

c. In the so-called *synecdochical* or Greek accusative, used by the poets to denote the part affected: as,

caput nectentur (Virg.), *their head shall be bound* [they shall be bound about the head].

The part is strictly in apposition with the whole, and remains (as above) after the passive.

REMARK. — The accusative after passive verbs used *reflexively* is sometimes wrongly referred to this construction: as,

inutile ferrum cingitur (Virg.), *he girds on the useless steel.*

4. *Special Uses.* Peculiar uses are the following:—

a. The accusative is used in Exclamations: as,

O fortunatam rempublicam (Cic.), *O fortunate republic!*
O me miserum! *Ah wretched me!*

b. The subject of the Infinitive Mood is in the accusative. This is especially frequent after verbs of *knowing, thinking,* and *telling* (**verba sentiendi et declarandi**, § 67, 1). In all cases, the accusative is strictly the Object of the leading verb.

c. Time *how long,* and Distance *how far,* are in the accusative. (See § **55**.)

For the Accusative with Prepositions, see § **56**.

53. Vocative.

The Vocative is the form of direct Address: as,

Tiberine pater, te sancte precor (Liv. ii. 103), *O father Tiber! thee, holy one, I pray.*

NOTE. — The Vocative can hardly be called a case, as it properly has no case termination, and forms no part of the sentence.

a. Sometimes the nominative of a noun is used instead of the vocative, in apposition with the subject of the Imperative: as,

audi tu, populus Albanus (id. i. 24), *hear, thou people of Alba.*

b. Sometimes the vocative of an adjective is used instead of the nominative, where the verb is of the second person: as,

censorem trabeate salutas (Pers.), *robed you salute the censor.*

So in the phrase,

macte [= magne, root MAG] virtute esto (Hor.), *be enlarged in manliness* [bravo, well done].

54. Ablative.

The Ablative is used to denote the relations expressed in English by the prepositions *from, in, at, with, by.*

NOTE. — The Ablative *form* contains three distinct cases, — the ablative proper, expressing the relation FROM; the locative, IN; and the instrumental, WITH or BY. This confusion has arisen partly from phonetic decay, by which the cases have become identical in form, and partly from the development by which they have approached one another in meaning. Compare, for the first, the like forms of the dative and ablative plural, the old dative in e of the fifth declension, and the loss of the original **d** in the ablative; and, for the second, the phrases **a parte dextra,** ON *the right;* **quam ob causam,** FROM *which cause;* **ad famam,** AT (in consequence of) *the report.*

The relative of FROM includes *separation, source, cause, agent,* and *comparison;* that of IN or AT, *place, time, circumstance;* that of WITH or BY, *accompaniment, instrument, means, manner, quality,* and *price.* It is probable that, originally, the idea of *accompaniment* had a separate case, which became confounded with the *instrumental* before the Latin was separated from the kindred tongues.

1. Ablative of Separation. Verbs meaning to *remove, set free, be absent, deprive,* and *want,* are followed by the ablative: as,

> levamur superstitione, liberamur mortis metu (Fin. i. 19), *we are relieved from superstition, freed from fear of death.*
> oculis se privavit (id. v. 29), *he deprived himself of eyes.*
> consilio et auctoritate orbari (Cat. M. 6), *to be bereft of counsel and authority.*
> legibus solutus, *relieved from the obligation of laws.*
> ea philosophia quæ spoliat nos judicio, privat approbatione, omnibus orbat sensibus (Acad. ii. 19), *that philosophy which despoils us of judgment, deprives of approval, bereaves of every sense.*
> omni Galliâ interdicit Romanos (B. G. i. 46), *he* [Ariovistus] *bars the Romans from the whole of Gaul.*
> ei aquâ et igni interdicitur (Vall. Pat. ii. 45), *he is debarred the use of fire and water.*
> [cives] calamitate prohibere (Manil. 7), *to keep the citizens from ruin.*
> carere febri (Fam. xvi. 16), *to be free from fever.*
> voluptatibus carere (Cat. M. 3), *to lack enjoyments.*
> non egeo medicinâ (Læl. 3), *I want no physic.*
> magno me metu liberabis (Cat. i. 5), *you will relieve me of great fear.*
> Ephorus calcaribus eget (Quint.), *Ephorus needs the spur.*

a. Compounds of **a, ab, de, ex,** take the ablative when used *figuratively;* but in their literal meaning, implying *motion,* they usually follow the rules of *place from which* (see § **55,** 3): as,

> conatu desistere (B. G. i. 8), *to desist from the attempt.*
> exsolvere se occupationibus (Fam. vii. 1), *to get clear of occupation.*
> prius quam ea cura decederet patribus (Liv. ix. 29), *before that anxiety left the fathers.*
> desine communibus locis (Ac. ii. 25), *quit commonplaces.*
> abire magistratu, *to leave the office.*
> abscedere incepto, *to relinquish the undertaking.*
> abstinere injuriâ, *to refrain from wrong.*
> exire ære alieno, *to get out of debt.*

b. More rarely, the ablative is used after verbs without a preposition to denote the *place from which:* as,

> cessisset patriâ (Mil. 25), *he would have left his country.*
> loco movere (Liv. i. 35), *to move from its place.*
> patriâ pellere, *to drive out of the country.*
> Galliâ arcere (Phil. v. 13), *to keep out of Gaul.*
> manu mittere, *to emancipate* [let go from the hand].

c. Adjectives denoting *freedom* and *want* are followed by the ablative: as,

> liber curâ et angore (Fin. i. 15), *free from care and anguish.*
> vacuos curis (ib. ii. 14), *void of care.*
> urbs nuda præsidio (Att. vii. 13), *the city naked of defence.*
> immunis militiâ (Liv. i. 43), *free of military service.*
> plebs orba tribunis (Leg. iii. 3), *the people deprived of tribunes.*

d. **Opus** and **usus** signifying *need* (with **esse**) are followed by the ablative (often by the ablative of the *perfect participle*, with or without a noun): as,

> magistratibus opus est (Leg. iii. 2), *there is need of magistrates.*
> curatore usus est (id. 4, — chiefly ante-clássical), *there is need of a manager.*
> properato opus esset (Mil. 19), *there were need of haste.*
> ut opu'st facto (Ter. Heaut.), *as there is need to do.*

REMARK. — The nominative is often used with **opus** in the predicate: as,

> multi opus sunt boves (Varro R. R. i. 18), *there is need of many cattle.*
> dux nobis et auctor opus est (Fam. ii. 6), *we need a chief and adviser.*

e. **Egeo** and **indigeo** are often followed by the genitive: as,

> ne quis auxili egeat (B. G. vi. 11), *lest any require aid.*
> quæ ad consolandum majoris ingeni et ad ferendum singularis virtutis indigent (Fam. vi. 4), [sorrows] *which for comfort need more ability, and for endurance unusual courage.*

REMARK. — With all words of separation and want, the poets frequently, by a Greek idiom, use the genitive (see § **50**, 3, *c*): as,

> desine mollium tandem querelarum (Hor. Od. ii. 9), *cease at length from weak complaints.*
> abstineto irarum (id. iii. 27), *abstain from wrath.*
> operum solutis (id. 17), *free from toils.*

2. *Ablative of Source.* The ablative is used to denote the source from which anything is derived, or the material of which it consists.

a. Participles denoting *birth* or *origin* are followed by the ablative. Such participles are **natus, satus, editus, genitus, ortus**: as,

> Jove natus et Maiâ (N. D. iii. 22), *son of Jupiter and Maia.*
> ortus equestri loco (Leg. Agr. i. 9), *born of equestrian rank.*
> edite regibus (Hor. Od. i. 1), *descendant of kings.*
> quo sanguine cretus (Æn. ii. 74), *born of what blood.*

REMARK. — A preposition (**ab, de, ex**) is usually expressed with the name of the *mother*, and with that of distant ancestors.

b. Rarely, the *place of birth* is expressed by the ablative: as,

desideravit C. Felginatem Placentiâ, A. Granium Puteolis (B. C. iii. 71), *he lost C. F. of Placentia, A. G. of Puteoli.*

c. The ablative is used with **constare** and similar verbs, to denote *material* (but with other verbs a preposition is generally used, except by the poets): as,

animo constamus et corpore (Fin. iv. 8), *we consist of soul and body.*

NOTE. — The ablative with **consistere** and **contineri** is *locative* (see below, 10).

d. The ablative of *material* is used with **facere, fieri,** and similar words: as,

quid hoc homine facias (Verr. ii. 16), *What are you going to do with this man?*
quid Tulliolâ meâ fiet (Fam. xiv. 4), *what will become of my dear Tullia?*
quid te futurum est (Verr. ii. 64), *what will happen to you?*

3. *Ablative of Cause.* The ablative (with or without a preposition) is used to express the *cause*.

NOTE. — The cause, in the Ablative, is considered as *source*, as is shown by the use of **ab, de, ex**; while with **ad, ob**, the idea of cause arises from *nearness*. But occasionally it is difficult to distinguish between *cause* and *means* (which is instrumental) or *circumstance* (either locative or instrumental).

nimio gaudio pæne desipiebam (Fam. i. 13), *I was almost a fool with excess of joy.*
negligentiâ plectimur (Læl. 22), *we are chastised for negligence.*
cæcus avaritiâ (Liv. v. 51), *blind with avarice.*
gubernatoris ars utilitate non arte laudatur (Fam. i. 13), *the pilot's skill is praised as service not as skill.*

a. The ablative is used with the adjectives **dignus, indignus,** and with the verbs **dignor, laboro** (also with **ex**), **exsilio, exsulto, triumpho, lacrimo, ardeo.**

vir patre, avo, majoribus suis dignissimus (Phil. iii. 10), *a man most worthy of his father, grandfather, and ancestors.*
doleo te aliis malis laborare (Fam. iv. 3), *I am sorry that you suffer with other ills.*
ex ære alieno laborare (B. C. iii. 22), *to labor under debt.*
exsultare lætitiâ ac triumphare gaudio cœpit (Clu. 5), *she began to exult in gladness, and triumph in joy.*

b. The motive which influences the mind of the person acting is expressed by the ablative alone; the object exciting the emotion often by **ob** or **propter** with the accusative: as,

> non ob prædam aut spoliandi cupidine (Tac. H. i. 63), *not for booty or through lust of plunder.*

c. The ablatives **causā** and **gratiā**, *for the sake of*, are used with a genitive preceding, or with a possessive in agreement: as,

> eâ causâ, *on account of this*; meâ causâ, *for my sake.*
> et ipsorum et reipublicæ causâ (Manil. 2), *for their own sake and the republic's.*
> sui purgandi gratiâ, *for the sake of clearing themselves.*

With possessives the use of **gratia** in this sense is rare.

4. *Ablative of Agent.* The voluntary agent after a passive verb is put in the ablative with **ab** (see § 56, 4): as,

> laudatur ab his, culpatur ab illis (Hor. Sat. i. 2), *he is praised by these, blamed by those.*
> ab animo tuo quidquid agitur id agitur a te (Tusc. i. 22), *whatever is done by your soul is done by yourself.*

a. This construction is sometimes used after neuter verbs having a passive sense: as,

> perire ab hoste, *to be slain by an enemy.*

b. The agent, considered as instrument or means, is expressed by **per** with the accusative, or by **operā** with a genitive or possessive: as,

> per Antiochum (Liv.), *by means of Antiochus.*
> meâ operâ (Cic.), *by my means.*

So **per vim**, as well as **vi** (B. G. i. 14), *by force.*

5. *Ablative of Comparison.* The Comparative degree is followed by the ablative (signifying THAN): as,

> quis me beatior (Tusc. i. 4), *who more blest than I?*
> quid nobis duobus laboriosius est (Mil. 2), *what more burdened than we two?*

NOTE. — Here the object of comparison is the *starting-point* from which we reckon, as itself possessing the quality in some degree. That this is the true explanation is shown by the ablative in Sanskrit, and the genitive in Greek.

a. **Quam** with the same case as the adjective may also be used, and must regularly be used when the adjective is not either nominative or accusative. But the poets sometimes use the ablative even then: as, pane egeo jam mellitis potiore placentis (Hor. Ep. i. 10), *I want bread better than honey-cakes.*

REMARK. — **Quam** is never used in this construction with relative pronouns having a definite antecedent.

b. Particularly the idiomatic ablatives **opinione, spe, solito, dicto, aequo, credibili,** and **justo,** are used instead of a clause: as,

celerius opinione (Fam. iv. 23), *faster than one would think.*
amnis solito citatior (Liv. xxii. 19), *a stream swifter than its wont.*

c. **Plus, minus, amplius, longius,** are often used with words of measure or number without affecting their case (being in a kind of apposition) : as,

plus septingenti capti (Liv. xli. 12), *more than 700 were taken.*
plus tertiâ parte interfectâ (Cæs.), *more than a third part being slain.*
spatium non amplius sexcentorum pedum (id.), *a space of not more than 600 feet.*

NOTE. — **Alius** is used by the poets with the ablative, perhaps in imitation of the Greek; but the construction is found also in Sanskrit, and is probably original: as, *alium sapienti bonoque* (Hor. Ep. i. 16). Under comparatives belong the adverbs **antea, antidea, postilla, postea, præterea,** *earlier than this,* &c. (see § 56, 3).

[For Ablative of Difference, see below, 6, *e.*]

6. *Ablative of Means.* The ablative is used to denote *accompaniment, means,* or *instrument:* as,

vultu Milonis perterritus (Mil. 15), *scared by the face of Milo.*
animum appellat novo nomine (Tusc. i. 10), *he calls the mind by a new name.*
probabilia conjecturâ sequens (id. 9), *following probabilities by conjecture.*
excultus doctrinâ (id. 2), *thoroughly trained in learning.*
fidibus canere (id.), *to sing to the lyre.*
Fauno immolare agnâ (Hor. Od. i. 4), *to sacrifice to Faunus with a ewe-lamb.*
pol pudere quam pigere præstat totidem literis (Plaut. Trin. 345), *by Pollux better shame than blame, although the letters count the same* [lit. with as many letters].

a. The ablative of *accompaniment* regularly takes **cum** (except sometimes in military phrases, and a few isolated expressions, especially in the early writers): as,

cum funditoribus sagittariisque flumen transgressi (B. G. ii. 19), *having crossed the river with the slingers and archers.*
subsequebatur omnibus copiis (ib.), *he followed close with all his forces.* [*out.*
hoc præsidio profectus est (Verr. ii. 34), *with this convoy he set*

REMARK. — **Misceo** and **jungo**, with their compounds, may take the ablative of accompaniment, without **cum**, or sometimes the dative.

b. Words of *contention* require **cum** (but often take the dative in poetry): as,

> armis cum hoste certare (Cic.), *to fight with the enemy in arms.*
> est mihi tecum certamen (id.), *I have a controversy with you.*
> solus tibi certat Amyntas (Ecl. v. 8), *Amyntas alone vies with you.*

c. The ablative of *means* is used with words of *filling, abounding,* and the like: as,

> Deus bonis omnibus explevit mundum (Univ. 3), *God has filled the world with all good things.*
> dialecticis imbutus (Tusc. i. 7), *tinctured with logic.*
> circumfusi caligine (id. 19), *overspread with darkness.*
> opimus prædâ (Verr. i. 50), *rich with spoil.*
> vita plena et conferta voluptatibus (Sext. 10), *a life full and crowded with delights.*
> Forum Appî differtum nautis (Hor. Sat. i. 5), *Forum Appii crammed with bargemen.*

REMARK. — These verbs and adjectives take the genitive in the poets by a Greek idiom: as,

> terra scatet ferarum (Lucr. v. 41), *the land abounds in wild creatures.*
> explere ultricis flammæ (Æn. ii. 586), *fill with avenging flame.*

Compleo, impleo, and **plenus,** often take the genitive in prose.

d. The deponents **utor, fruor, fungor, potior, vescor,** with several of their compounds, govern the ablative: as,

> utar vestrâ benignitate (Cic.), *I will avail myself of your kindness.*
> Numidæ plerumque lacte et ferinâ carne vescebantur (Jug. 88), *the Numidians fed mostly on milk and game.*

Potior also takes the genitive, as always in the phrase **potiri rerum,** *to get the power.* In early Latin, the accusative is sometimes found with these verbs.

e. The ablative is used with comparatives and words implying comparison, to denote the *degree of difference:* as,

> duobus milibus plures, *more numerous by* 2000.
> quinque milibus passuum distat (Liv.), *it is five miles distant.*

REMARKS. — This use is especially frequent with the ablatives **eo ... quo; quanto ... tanto** (see § **22,** *c*): as,

> quo minus cupiditatis eo plus auctoritatis (Liv. xxiv. 28), *the less greed the more weight.*

7. Ablative of Quality. The ablative is used, with an adjective or limiting genitive, to denote *manner* and *quality*: as,

> animo meliore, *of better mind.*
> more hominum, *after the manner of men.*
> non quæro quantā memoriā fuisse dicatur (Tusc. i. 24), *I do not ask how great a memory he is said to have had.*

a. The ablative of description (with adjectives) is always used to denote *physical characteristics* (other qualities may be in the genitive): as,

> vultu sereno, *of calm face.*
> capillo sunt promisso (B. G. v. 14), *they have long hanging locks.*

b. The ablative of *manner* more commonly takes **cum**, unless it has a modifying adjective: as,

> minus cum curā (Plaut.), *less carefully.*
> hoc onus feram studio et industriā (Rosc. Am. 4), *I will bear this burden with pains and diligence.*

But words of manner, **modo, ratione, viā,** &c. — with such expressions as **silentio**, *in silence*, **injuriā**, *wrongfully* — hardly ever have **cum**.

8. Ablative of Price. The price of a thing (or that which is given in exchange) is put in the ablative: as,

> agrum vendidit sestertiûm sex milibus, *he sold the field for 6000 sesterces.*
> exsilium patriā sede mutavit (Q. C. iii. 8), *he exchanged his native land for exile.*

a. Certain genitives of Quantity are used to denote *indefinite value*. Such genitives are **magni, parvi, tanti, quanti, pluris, minoris**: as,

> est mihi tanti (Cat. ii. 7), *it is worth my while.*
> meā magni interest, *it is of great consequence to me.*

REMARK. — With verbs of buying and selling, the ablative of price (**magno**, &c.) must be used, except the following genitives: **tanti, quanti, pluris, minoris.**

b. The genitive of certain nouns is used in the same way: as,

> non flocci faciunt (Pl. Trin.), *they care not a straw.*

The genitives so used are **nihili**, *nothing;* **assis**, *a farthing;* **flocci**, *a lock of wool,* and a few others (see § 50, 1, *i*).

[For the Ablative of Penalty, see § **50**, 4, *b*, Rem.]

9. Ablative of Specification. The ablative denotes that *in respect to which* anything is said to be or be done, or *in accordance with which* anything happens: as,

> virtute præcedunt (B. G. i. 1), *they excel in courage.*
> incluta bello mœnia (Æn. ii. 24), *walls famous in war.*
> claudus altero pede (Nep. Ages.), *lame of one foot.*
> linguâ hæsitantes, voce absoni (De Or. i.), *hesitating in speech, harsh in voice.*
> tanta caritas patriæ est, ut eam non sensu nostro sed salute ipsius metiamur (Tusc. i. 37), *such is our love of country, that we measure it not by our own feeling, but by her own welfare.*

10. Locative Ablative. The ablative of the *place where* is retained in many figurative expressions: as,

> jure peritus, *skilled in law* [compare Sanskrit usages].
> pendemus animis (Tusc. i. 40), *we are in suspense of mind.*
> socius periculis vobiscum adero (Jug. 85), *I will be present with you a companion in dangers.*
> premit alto corde dolorem (Æn. i. 209), *he keeps down the pain deep in his heart.*
> confertâ legione (B. G. iv. 33), *as they were in close order.*
> pedibus prœliantur (id. 34), *they fight on foot.*
> quibus rebus (id. 35), *under these circumstances.*

a. The verbs **acquiesco, delector, laetor, gaudeo, glorior, nitor, sto, maneo, fido (confido), consisto, contineor,** — with the verbals **fretus, contentus, laetus,** — are followed by the ablative: as,

> spe niti (Att. iii. 9), *to rely on hope.*
> prudentiâ fidens (Off. i. 33), *trusting in prudence.*
> lætari bonis rebus (Læl. 13), *to rejoice in good things.*

REMARK. — The above verbs also take the preposition **in**.

b. **Ablative Absolute.** A noun or pronoun, with a participle, is put in the ablative, to define the *time* or *circumstances* of an action (compare § 72). An adjective, or another noun, may take the place of the participle.

> vocatis ad se undique mercatoribus (B. G. iv. 20), *having called to him the traders from all quarters.*
> exiguâ parte æstatis reliquâ (id.), *when but a small part of the summer was left.*
> M. Messalâ et M. Pisone consulibus (id. i. 2), *in the consulship of Messala and Piso.*

NOTE. — In this use the noun is equivalent to the Subject, and the participle to the Predicate, of *a subordinate clause;* and so they should generally be translated. But, as the copula **esse** has no participle in Latin, a noun or adjective is often found alone as predicate, while the participle is found, in this construction, in Sanskrit and Greek. The noun originally denotes *circumstance*, considered as *place* or *time* (locative); then, being modified by a participle, it becomes fused with it into a single idea, equivalent to that contained in a subordinate clause (compare **ab urbe condita**, lit. *from the city built*).

c. Sometimes a participle or adjective (under the construction of the ablative absolute) is put in agreement with a phrase or clause, or is used adverbially : as,

incerto quid peterent, *since it was uncertain what they sought.*
auspicato (Tac. H. i. 84), *after taking the auspices* [the auspices having been taken].
consulto et cogitato (Off i. 8), *on purpose and with reflection* [the matter having been deliberated and thought on].
sereno (Liv. xxxi. 12), *under a clear sky.*

d. The ablative is often used to denote the *place where*, or the *time when* (see § 55, 1 ; 3, *f*).

[For the government of the Ablative by Prepositions, see § 56.]

55. Time and Place.

1. *Time.* Time *when* (or *within which*) is put in the Ablative ; time *how long* the Accusative : as,

constitutâ die, *on the set day.*
quotâ horâ? *at what o'clock?*
tribus proxumis annis (Jug. 11), *within the last three years.*
dies continuos triginta, *for a month together.*
paucis post diebus (*or* paucos post dies), *after a few days.*
 [Here **diebus** is the ablative of *difference* (§ 54, 6, *e*), and **post** an adverb (§ 56, 2, *d*).]

Note. — The ablative of time is *locative ;* the accusative is the same as that of *extent of space* (see below), **heri vespari**).

a. The use of a preposition gives greater precision and clearness : as,

in diebus proximis decem (Sall.), *within the next ten days.*
ludi per decem dies (Cat. iii. 8), *games lasting ten days.*

b. The ablative is rarely used to express duration of time : as,

milites quinque horis proelium sustinuerant (B. C. i. 47), *the men had sustained the fight five hours.* [This use is *locative.*]

2. Space. Extent of space is put in the Accusative: as,

fossas quindecim pedes latas (B. G. vii. 72), *trenches 13 feet broad.*

NOTE.— This accusative is the object *through* or *over which* the action takes place, and is kindred with the accusative of the *end of motion.*

a. Measure is often expressed as a quality by the Genitive (§ **50,** 1, *h*) : as,

vallo pedum duodecim (B. G. ii. 30), *in a rampart of 12 feet* [in height].

b. Distance is put in the Accusative (as *extent of space*), or Ablative (as *degree of difference*) : as,

quinque dierum iter abest (Liv. xxx. 29), *it is distant five days' march.*
triginta milibus passuum infra eum locum (B. G. vi. 35), *thirty miles below that place.*
tanto spatio secuti (B. G. iv. 35), *having followed over so much ground.*

3. Place. To express relations of Place, prepositions are necessary, except with the names of Towns and small Islands; except also with **domus, rus,** and a few other words in special relations.

NOTE.— Originally these relations were expressed with all words by the *cases alone,* — the Accusative denoting the end of motion as in a certain sense the *object* of the action; and the Ablative (in its proper meaning of *separation*) denoting the place from which. For the place *where* there was a special case, the Locative, the form of which was partially retained and partially merged in the Ablative (see Note, p. 134). The Prepositions (originally Adverbs) were added to define more exactly the *direction* of the motion, and by long usage at length became necessary, except in the cases given above.

a. The name of the place *from which* is in the Ablative: as,

Româ profectus, *having set out from Rome.*
rure reversus, *having returned from the country.*

b. The name of the place *to which* is in the Accusative: as,

Romam rediit, *he returned to Rome.*
rus ibo, *I shall go into the country.*

REMARK.— The old construction is retained in the phrases **exsequias ire,** *to attend a funeral;* **infitias ire,** *to make denial;* **pessum ire,** *to go to ruin;* **pessum dare,** *to undo;* **venum dare (vendere),** *to set to sale;* **venum ire,** *to be set to sale;* **foras,** *out of doors;* and the Supine in **um** (see § **74,** 1).

c. The name of the place *where* takes the Locative form, which in the first and second declensions singular is the same as the *genitive;* in the plural, and in the third declension, the same as the *dative:* as,

Romae, *at Rome;* **Corinthi,** *at Corinth;* **Lanuvi,** *at Lanuvium;* **Karthagini,** *at Carthage;* **Athenis,** *at Athens;* **Curibus,** *at Cures.*

REMARK. — In names of the third declension the ablative is often found, especially where the metre requires it in poetry: as,

Tibure vel Gabiis (Hor. Ep. ii. 2), *at Tibur or Gabii.*

d. The words **domi** (rarely **domui**), *at home;* **belli, militiae** (in contrast to **domi**), *abroad in military service;* **humi,** *on the ground;* **ruri,** *in the country;* **foris,** *out-of-doors;* **terrā marique,** *by land and sea,* are used like names of towns, without a preposition; also **heri, vesperi, infelici arbori** (Liv.).

e. A possessive, or **alienus,** may be used with **domus** in this construction; but when it is modified in any other way, a preposition is generally used: as,

domi suæ (Mil. 7), *at his own house.*
in M. Læcæ domum (Cat. i. 4), *to Læca's house.*

f. The ablative is used without a preposition to denote the *place where,* in many general words — as **loco, parte** — regularly; frequently with nouns when qualified by adjectives (regularly where **totus** is used); and in poetry in any case: as,

quibus loco positis (De Or. iii. 38), *when these are put in their places.*
quâ parte victi erant (Att. ix. 11), *on the side where they were beaten.*
se oppido tenet (id.), *keeps himself within the town.*
mediâ urbe (Liv. i. 33), *in the midst of the city.*
totâ Siciliâ (Verr. iv. 23), *throughout Sicily.*
litore curvo (Æn. iii. 16), *on the bending shore.*

REMARK. — To denote the neighborhood of a place (*to, from, in* the neighborhood), prepositions must be used.

4. The way *by which* is put in the Ablative (of *instrument*): as,

viâ breviore equites præmisi (Fam. x. 9), *I sent forward the cavalry by a shorter road.*
Ægeo mari trajecit (Liv. xxxvii. 14), *he crossed by way of the Ægean sea.*

56. Use of Prepositions.

1. Prepositions govern either the Accusative or Ablative.

a. The following govern the Accusative: — **ad, adversus, adversum, ante, apud, circa,** or **circum, circiter, cis, citra, contra, erga, extra, infra, inter, intra, juxta, ob, penes, per, pone, post, praeter, prope, propter, secundum, supra, trans, ultra, versus.**

b. The following govern the Ablative: — **a, ab, abs, absque, coram, cum, de, e, ex, prae, pro, sine, tenus.**

c. **In** and **sub** take the Accusative when they denote *motion;* when *rest*, the Ablative: as,

in contionem venit (Off. iii. 11), *he came into the meeting.*
dixit in contione (ib.), *he said in the meeting.*
sub jugum mittere (Cæs.), *to send under the yoke.*
sub monte consedit (id.), *he halted below the hill.*

REMARK. — The verbs of *placing*, — such as **pono** and its compounds (except **impono**), **loco, statuo,** &c., — though implying motion, take in Latin the construction of the place *in which:* as,

qui in sede ac domo collocavit (Parad. iii. 2), *who put one into his place and home.*

d. When it means *concerning*, **super** takes the Ablative; otherwise the Accusative (unless in poetry): as,

hac super re (Cic.), *concerning this thing.*
super culmina tecti (Virg.), *above the house-top.*

e. After **subter**, the Accusative is used, except sometimes in poetry: as,

subter togam (Liv.), *under his mantle.*
subter litore (Catull.), *below the shore.*

f. In Dates, the phrase **ante diem (a. d.)** with an ordinal, or the ordinal alone, is followed by an accusative, like a preposition; and the phrase itself may be governed by a preposition: as,

is dies erat a.d. quintum kalendas Aprilis (B. G. i. 6), *that day was the 5th before the calends of April* [March 28].
in a.d. v. kal. Nov. (Cat. i. 3), *to the 5th day before the calends of November* [Oct. 28].
xv. kal. Sextilis, *the 15th day before the calends of August* (July 18). [Full form, *quinto die ante.*]

g. **Tenus** (which follows its noun) regularly takes the Ablative: as,

Tauro tenus (Mil. 13), *as far as Taurus.*
capulo tenus (Æn. v. 55), *up to the hilt.*

REMARK.—**Tenus** is found especially with the feminine of the adjective pronouns, in an adverbial sense: as,

hactenus, *hitherto;* quatenus, *so far as,* &c.

Sometimes it takes the Genitive: as,

Corcyræ tenus (Liv. xxv. 24), *as far as Corcyra.*

2. Many words may be construed either as Prepositions or as Adverbs: thus —

a. The adverbs **pridie, postridie, propius, proxime, usque** — also (less frequently) the adjectives **propior** and **proximus** — may be followed by the Accusative: as,

pridie Nonas Junias (Cic.), *the day before the Nones of June* (June 4).
postridie ludos (id.), *the day after the games.*

b. The adverbs **palam, procul, simul,** may take the Ablative: as,

palam populo (Liv.), *in the presence of the people.*

c. The adverb **clam** may take either case (very rare): as,

clam matrem suam (Plaut.), *unbeknown to the mother.*
clam mihi (id.), *in secret from me.*
clam vobis (Cæs.), *without your knowledge.*

d. Prepositions often retain their original meaning as Adverbs. This is especially the case with **ante** and **post,** in relations of *time;* **adversus, contra** (*on the other hand*), **circiter, prope,** and, in general, those ending in **ā. Clam** and **versus** are often excluded from the list of Prepositions.

[For the use of prepositions in Composition, see § **42,** 3.]

3. Some prepositions or adverbs which imply *comparison* are followed, like comparatives, by **quam,** — several words, or even clauses, sometimes coming between: as,

neque ante dimisit eum quam fidem dedit (Liv. xxxix. 10), *nor did he let him go until he gave a pledge.*

Such words are **ante, prius, post, pridie, postridie.**

4. The ablative, with **a** or **ab,** is regularly used after passive verbs to denote the Agent, if a person, or if spoken of as a person (§ **54,** 4): as,

jussus a patre, *bidden by his father.*

REMARK. — The ablative of the *agent* (which requires the preposition) must be carefully distinguished from the ablative of *instrument*, which stands by itself: as,

> occisus gladio, *slain by a sword;* but,
> occisus ab hoste, *slain by an enemy.*

5. The following prepositions sometimes follow their noun: —
**ad, citra, circa, contra, inter, penes, propter, ultra, tenus;
e, de, juxta.**

[For the so-called Dative of the Agent, with the Gerundive, see §§ **51,** 4, *a*.]

III. Syntax of the Verb.

57. USE OF MOODS.

(See § **24.**)

The MOODS of a Latin Verb are the Indicative, Subjunctive, Imperative, and Infinitive.

NOTE. — The Infinitive is not strictly a mood, being only the oblique case of a noun; but it is most conveniently treated along with the moods.

1. *Indicative.* The Indicative is the mood of direct assertions or questions; and is used when no special construction requires one of the others.

2. *Subjunctive.* The Subjunctive is used in special constructions, both in dependent and independent clauses, viz.: —

a. **Independent Clauses.** **1.** In independent clauses, the subjunctive is used to denote an Exhortation or Command (*hortatory subjunctive*); a Wish (*optative subjunctive*); a Concession (*concessive subjunctive*); or a Doubtful Question (*dubitative subjunctive*).

2. It is also used to denote the conclusion of a Conditional sentence (*apodosis*), which is, grammatically, an independent clause, though logically depending on a condition expressed or implied (see §§ **59, 60**).

b. **Dependent Clauses.** In dependent clauses, the subjunctive is used to denote a Purpose (§ **64**), or a Result (§ **65**). It is used, idiomatically, in Temporal Clauses (§ **62**), in Indirect Discourse (§ **67**), in Indirect Questions (id.), and in Intermediate Clauses (§ **66**).

[For Subjunctive after Particles of Comparison, see § **61**.]

[For the so-called Subjunctive of Cause, see § **63**.]

NOTE. — The Present Subjunctive contains two distinct forms, — the Subjunctive and Optative of the "Indo-European" tongue. Both these forms had originally a *future* meaning; and from these future meanings all the uses of this mood in Latin are developed. The *subjunctive proper* was originally a Present, denoting *continued action*, which became Future in sense (compare conative present and present for future, § 58, 2, *b*); and afterwards, in many uses, Imperative (compare future for imperative). The *optative* contains, in composition, a past tense of the root I (whence eo, εἶμι, *go*); so that it had a *futurum in præterito* meaning, which developed into a *conditional future*, and into an expressive of *wish* and *command*; and, in Latin, lost its connection with past time.

The other tenses of the Subjunctive are compounds formed (in Latin alone) to remedy the confusion of optative and subjunctive. The Subjunctive has, therefore, the uses of both the optative and subjunctive of the cognate languages.

3. Hortatory Subjunctive. The subjunctive is used in the Present — less commonly in the Perfect — to express a command or exhortation: as,

> hos latrones interficiamus (B. G. vii. 38), *let us kill these robbers.*
> aut bibat aut abeat (Tusc. v. 41), *let him quaff or quit.*
> caveant intemperantiam, meminerint verecundiæ (Off. i. 34), *let them shun excess and cherish modesty.*
> Epicurus hoc viderit (Acad. ii. 7), *let Epicurus look to this.*
> his quoque de rebus pauca dicantur (Off. i. 35), *of this, too, let a few words be said.*

NOTE. — The Perfect represents an action as *complete in the future;* but in most cases it can hardly be distinguished from the Present.

a. The Second Person is used only of an *indefinite subject*, except in prohibition, in early Latin, and in poetry: as,

> injurias fortunæ, quas ferre nequeas, defugiendo relinquas (Tusc. v. 41), *the wrongs of fortune, which you cannot bear, you will leave behind by flight.*
> nihil ignoveris (Mur. 31), *pardon nothing.*
> amicus populo Romano sis (Liv. xxvi. 50), *be a friend to the Roman people.*

b. In *prohibitions*, the Perfect is more common than the Present: as,

>hoc facito: hoc ne feceris (Div. ii. 61), *thou shalt do this: thou shalt not do that.*
>nec mihi illud dixeris (Fin. i. 7), *do not say that to me.*
>ne territus fueris (Tac. H. i. 16), *be not terrified.*

c. The hortatory subjunctive is used — sometimes with **modo, modo ne, tantum, tantum ne,** or **ne** alone — to denote a *proviso:* as,

>valetudo modo bona sit (Brut. 16), *if only the health be good.*
>aliam condicionem tantummodo æquam (Jug. 79), *another condition, provided it were just.*
>modo ne sit ex pecudum genere (Off. i. 30), *provided only he be not of brutish stock.*
>tantummodo Gnæus noster ne Italiam relinquat (Q. F. iii. 9), *if only Pompey will not forsake Italy.*
>manent ingenia senibus, modo permaneat studium et industria (Cat. M. 7), *old men retain their mind if they only retain their zeal and diligence.*

d. The Imperfect and Pluperfect of the hortatory subjunctive denote an *obligation in past time,*—the latter more clearly representing the time for the action as past: as,

>moreretur, inquies (Rab. Post.), *he should have died you will say.*
>ne poposcisses (Att. ii. 1), *you should not have asked.*
>potius diceret (Off. iii. 22), *he should rather have said.*
>saltem aliquid de pondere detraxisset (Fin. iv. 20), *at least he should have taken something from the weight.*

4. *Optative Subjunctive.* The subjunctive is used to denote a Wish,—the Present, a wish conceived as *possible;* the Imperfect, an unaccomplished one in the *present;* the Pluperfect, one unaccomplished in the *past:* as,

>ita vivam (Att. v. 15), *so may I live* [as true as I live].
>ne vivam si scio (id. iv. 16), *I wish I may not live if I know.*
>di te perduint (Deiot.), *the gods confound thee!*
>valeant, valeant, cives mei; valeant. sint incolumes (Mil. 34), *farewell* [he says], *my fellow-citizens; may they be secure from harm.*

a. The Perfect in this use is antiquated: as,

>male di tibi faxint (Plaut. Curc. 131), *may the gods do thee a mischief.*

b. The particles **uti** (ut), **utinam**, **O si**, often precede the Subjunctive of *wish:* as,

> falsus utinam vates sim (Liv. xxi.), *I wish I may be a false prophet.*
> ut pereat positum rubigine telum (Hor. Sat. ii. 1), *may the unused weapon perish with rust.*
> utinam me mortuum vidisses (Q. Fr. i. 3), *would you had seen me dead.*

NOTE. — In this use, the particle has no effect on the grammatical construction, except that **O si** is probably a *Protasis*.

c. **Velim** with the present subjunctive, and **vellem** with the imperfect or pluperfect — with their compounds — (strictly, *conditional sentences* with the wish in a dependent clause) are often used instead of a proper optative subjunctive: as,

> de Menedemo vellem verum fuisset, de reginâ velim verum sit (Att. iv. 16), *about Menedemus I wish it had been true; about the queen I hope it may be.*
> nollem accidisset tempus (Fam. iii. 10), *I wish the time never had come.*

5. Concessive Subjunctive. The subjunctive is used to express a *concession*, either with or without **ut**, **quamvis**, **quamlibet**, and similar words.

REMARK. — In this use, the Present refers to *future* or *indefinite* time; the Imperfect to *present* or *past* time, — the concession being impliedly untrue; the Perfect to *past* time or *completed future* time; the Pluperfect to *completed action in past time* (usually untrue): as,

> nemo is unquam fuit : ne fuerit (Or. 29), *there never was such a one you will say: granted.*
> quamvis comis in amicitiis tuendis fuerit (Fin. ii. 25), *amiable as he may have been in keeping his friendships.*
> sit Scipio clarus, ornetur Africanus, erit profecto aliquid loci nostræ (Cat. iv. 10), *let Scipio be glorious, and Africanus honored, yet surely there will be some room for our fame.*
> dixerit hoc idem Epicurus ... non pugnem cum homine (Fin. v. 27), *though Epicurus may have said the same, I would not contend with the man.*
> ne sit summum malum dolor, malum certe est (Tusc. ii. 5), *granted that pain is not the greatest evil, at least it is an evil.*
> fuerit aliis : tibi quando esse cœpit (Verr. i. 41). *suppose he was [so] to others, when did he begin to be to you ?*

6. The Present, and rarely the Perfect Subjunctive, are used in questions implying doubt, indignation, or an impossibility of the thing being done (*dubitative subjunctive*) : as,

> sed quid faciamus (Att. viii. 23), *but what can we do?*
> quid loquar plura (Pis. 32), *why should I say more?*
> quid hoc homine faciatis (Verr. ii. 16), *what are you to do with this fellow?*
> cui ego exspectem dum tabellae diribeantur (Pis. 40), *what, shall I wait till the ballots are counted?*
> quis enim celaverit ignem (Ov. Her. xv. 7), *who could conceal the flame?*

The Imperfect denotes the same idea in past time: as,

> an ego non venirem (Phil. ii. 2), *what, should I not have come?*
> quid dicerem (Att. vi. 3), *what was I to say?*

7. *Imperative.* The Imperative is used in Commands; also, by early writers and poets, in Prohibitions: as,

> consulite vobis, prospicite patriae, conservate vos (Cat. iv. 2), *have care for yourselves, guard the country, preserve yourselves.* [*much.*
> nimium ne crede colori (Ecl. ii. 17), *trust not complexion over-*
> ad me fac venias (Fam. xiv. 4), *do come to me.*

a. Prohibitions are regularly (in classical Latin) expressed by **ne** with the second person singular of the Perfect Subjunctive; by **noli** with the Infinitive; or by **cave** (colloquially **fac ne**) with the Present or Perfect Subjunctive: as,

> ne territus fueris (Tac. H. i. 16), *be not frightened.*
> noli putare (Brut. 33), *do not suppose.*
> cave faxis (Ter. Heaut. 187), *do not do it.*
> fac ne quid aliud cures (Fam. xvi. 11), *pray attend to nothing else.*

b. In early Latin, in poetry, and in general prohibitions, the Present Subjunctive is also used: as,

> Albi ne doleas (Hor. Od. i. 33), *grieve not, Albius.*
> denique isto bono utare dum adsit: cum absit ne requiras (Cat. M. 10), *in short, use this good while present; when wanting, do not regret it.*

REMARK. — The *third person* of the Imperative is antiquated or poetic.

> ollis salus populi suprema lex esto (id.), *the safety of the people shall be their first law.*
> justa imperia sunto, iisque cives modeste parento (Leg. iii. 3), *let the commands be just, and let the citizens strictly obey them.*

c. The Future Imperative is used where there is a distinct reference to the *future time:* viz.

1. In connection with a *future* or *future-perfect;*

2. With adverbs or other expressions of *time;*

3. In *general directions*, as Precepts, Statutes, Edicts, and Wills : as,

> cum valetudini consulueris, tum consulito navigationi (Fam. xvi. 4), *when you have attended to your health, then look to your sailing.*
> rei suæ ergo ne quis legatus esto (Leg.), *no one shall be ambassador in his own affair.*

REMARK. — The future form of the imperative is regularly used of **scio, memini,** and **habeo** (in the sense of *consider*) : as,

> filiolo me auctum scito (Att. i. 2), *learn that I am blessed with a little boy.*
> sic habeto, mi Tiro (Fam. xvi. 4), *so understand it, my good Tiro.*
> de pallâ memento, amabo (Pl. Asin.), *pray, dear, remember the gown.*

d. The Future is sometimes used for the imperative ; and **quin** (*why not?*) with the present indicative may have the force of an imperative : as,

> si quid acciderit novi, facies ut sciam (Fam. xiv. 8), *you will let me know if anything new happens.*
> quin accipis? (Ter. Heaut. iv. 7), *here, take it.*

8. *Infinitive.* The Infinitive denotes the action of the verb as an *abstract noun*, differing, however, from other abstract nouns in the following points : — (1) It admits, in many cases, of the distinction of *tense;* (2) It is modified by *adverbs* and not by *adjectives;* (3) It *governs* the case of its verb ; (4) It is only used in special constructions.

NOTE. — The Infinitive is properly the *Dative case* of an abstract noun, denoting Purpose, which has developed in Latin, in many cases, into a substitute for a finite verb. Hence the variety of its use. Its Subject is, strictly, the Object of some other verb, which has become attached to it : as, **jubeo te valere,** lit., *I command you for being well* (i.e. that you may be well) ; just as, in Purpose-clauses, the purpose becomes the object of command (compare Purpose Clauses, § 64).

a. Infinitive as Subject. The infinitive, with or without a subject accusative, may be used as the Subject of a verb (or in predicate apposition), and, rarely, as the Object : as,

> nihil est aliud [hominem] bene et beate vivere, nisi honeste et recte vivere (Parad. i. 6), *to live well and happily, is nothing else than to live honorably and rightly.*
> invidere non cadit in sapientem (Tusc. iii. 10), *envy does not belong to a wise man.*
> est humanitatis vestræ . . . prohibere (Man. 7), *it is for your humanity to hold safe*, &c.
> nam istuc ipsum *non esse* cum fueris miserrimum puto (Tusc. i. 6), *for I think this very thing most wretched, not to be when one has been.*

In this use, the infinitive is found chiefly with **esse** and impersonal verbs, — rarely with others.

b. The infinitive is used with many Impersonal verbs and expressions, partly as *subject* and partly as *complement* (see Note below) : as,

> te abundare oportet præceptis (Off. i. 1), *you must abound in maxims.*
> id primum in poetis cerni licet (De Or. iii. 7), *this may be seen first in poets.*
> reperiebat quid dici opus esset (Brut. 59), *he found what needed to be said.*
> hæc præscripta servantem licet magnifice vivere (Off. i. 26), *one who observes these precepts may live nobly.*
> proponis quam sit turpe me adesse (Att. ix. 2), *you make it clear how base it is for me to be present.*

c. **Complementary Infinitive.** The infinitive, without a subject, is used with verbs which require *another action of the same subject* to complete their meaning. Such are verbs denoting *to be able, dare, undertake, remember, forget, be accustomed, begin, continue, cease, hesitate, learn, know how, fear*, and the like : as,

> hoc queo dicere (Cat. M. 10), *this I can say.*
> mitto quærere (Rosc. Am), *I omit to ask.*
> vereor laudare præsentem (N. D. i. 21), *I fear to praise in one's own presence.*
> oro ut matures venire (Att. iv. 1), *pray make haste to come.*

NOTE. — The mark of this construction is that no Subject of these infinitives is admissible or conceivable; though the same verbs, in other senses, may take an infinitive with a subject.

d. The infinitive is used optionally with many verbs which also take a *subjunctive clause* (§ **70**) : such are those signifying *willingness, necessity, propriety, resolve, command, prohibition, effort,* and the like. The subject is usually, though not always, omitted, when it is the same as that of the principal verb : as,

> quos tueri debent deserunt (Off. i. 9), *they forsake those whom they should protect.*
> Atticos volo imitari (Brut. 82), *I wish to imitate the Attics.*

> student excellere (Off. i. 32), *they aim to excel.*
> istum exheredare in animo habebat (Rosc. Am. 18), *he had it in mind to deprive him of the inheritance.*
> cupio me esse clementem [= cupio esse clemens] (Cat. i. 2), *I desire to be merciful.*

Some of these verbs — **jubeo** and **veto** regularly — may take the infinitive with another subject: as,

> signa inferri jubet (Liv. xlii. 59), *he orders the standards to be borne forward.*

NOTE.—This construction, though in many cases different from the two preceding, shades off imperceptibly into them. In none of the uses is the infinitive strictly Subject or Object; but its meaning is developed from the original one of *purpose*. Hence the distinction between the uses is not always clearly marked.

e. **With Subject Accusative.** The infinitive, with subject accusative, is regularly used after verbs of *knowing, thinking, telling,* and the like (**verba sentiendi et declarandi,** § 67, 1): as,

> dicit montem ab hostibus teneri (B. G. i. 22), *he says that the hill is held by the enemy.*

NOTE.—The Infinitive may thus represent, in *indirect discourse,* a finite verb in *direct discourse,* admitting all the variations of the verb except number and person (see § 67).

REMARK.—1. With verbs which govern the dative, the subject of the action may be in the dative. With **licet** regularly, and with others rarely, the predicate may also be in the dative: as,

> nemini certare cum eo necesse fuit (Liv. xxi. 11), *there was need for none to strive with him.*
> non libet mihi deplorare vitam (Cat. M. 23), *I have no desire to bewail life.* [*gent.*
> mihi negligenti esse non licet (Att. i. 17), *I must not be negli-*
> non est stantibus omnibus necesse dicere (Marc. 11), *it is not necessary for all to speak standing.*
> expedit bonas esse vobis (Ter. Heaut. ii. 4), *it is for your interest to be good.*

So with the *dativus commodi:* as,

> quid est tam secundum naturam quam senibus emori (Cat. M. 19), *what is so according to nature as for old men to die?*

2. When the subject of the infinitive is not expressed, a predicate (except after impersonals) takes the case of the subject: as,

> si esset in iis fides in quibus summa esse debebat (Fam. i. 1), *if there were faith in those in whom it ought to be greatest.*

So, by a Greek idiom, even in Indirect Discourse: as,

> vir bonus et sapiens ait esse paratus (Hor. Ep. i. 7), *a good and wise man says he is prepared,* &c.

sensit medios delapsus in hostes (Æn. ii. 377), *he found himself fallen amongst the foe.*

f. In a few cases, the infinitive retains its original meaning of purpose: viz.

1. With **habeo, do, ministro,** in isolated passages: as,

tantum habeo polliceri (Fam. i. 5), *so much I have to promise.*

2. After the adjectives **paratus, suetus,** and their compounds.

id quod parati sunt facere (Quin. 2), *which they are ready to do.*

3. In poetry and later writers with any verb or adjective: as,

durus componere versus (Hor. Sat. i. 4), *harsh in composing*
furit te reperire (Hor. Od. i. 15), *he rages to find thee.* [*verse.*
cantari dignus (Ecl. v. 54), *worthy to be sung.*

REMARK.—Rarely, in poetry, the infinitive is used to denote *result.*

g. The infinitive, with subject-accusative, may be used in Exclamations (compare § **52**, 4): as,

mene incepto desistere victam (Æn. i. 37), *what! I desist beaten from my purpose?*
te in tantas ærumnas propter me incidisse (Fam. xiv. 1), *alas! that you should fall into such grief for me.*

NOTE.—This construction is elliptical: that is, the thought is quoted in Indirect Discourse, though no verb of Saying, &c., appears, or perhaps is thought of (compare the French **dire que**).

***h.* Historical Infinitive.** The Infinitive is often used for the tenses of the Indicative in narration, and takes a subject in the nominative: as,

tum Catilina polliceri novas tabulas (Sall. Cat. 21), *then Catiline promised abolition of debts* [clean ledgers].
ego instare ut mihi responderet (Verr. ii. 77), *I pressed him to answer.*

This usage is most frequent where many verbs are crowded together in rapid narrative: as,

pars cedere, alii insequi; neque signa neque ordines servare; ubi quemque periculum ceperat, ibi resistere ac propulsare; arma, tela, equi, viri, hostes atque cives permixti; nihil consilio neque imperio agi; fors omnia regere (Jug. 51), *a part give way, others press on; they hold neither to standards nor ranks; where danger overtook, there each would stand and fight; weapons, missiles, horses, men, foe and friend, were mixed; nothing went by counsel or command; chance ruled all.*

58. Use of Tenses.

The TENSES are the Present, Imperfect, Future (of *incomplete action*), and the Perfect, Pluperfect, Future Perfect (of *completed action*).

1. *Tenses of the Indicative.* The tenses of the Indicative denote *absolute time;* that is, present, past, or future, in reference to the Speaker.

2. *Present.* The Present denotes an action or state, as *now existing*, as *incomplete*, or as *indefinite* without reference to time: as,

> agitur salus sociorum (Manil. 2), *the safety of our allies is at stake.*
> Senatus hæc intellegit, consul videt, hic tamen vivit (Cat. i. 1), *the Senate knows this, the consul sees, yet this man lives.*
> nihil est victoriâ dulcius (Verr. vi. 26), *nothing is sweeter than victory.*
> tu actionem instituis, ille aciem instruit (Mur. 9), *you arrange a case, he arrays an army.*

a. The present, with expressions of duration of time, denotes an action begun in the past but continuing in the present: as,

> patimur jam multos annos (Verr. vi. 48), *we suffer now these many years.*
> anni sunt octo cum ista causa versatur (Clu. 30), *it is now eight years that this case has been in hand.*

b. **Conative Present.** The present sometimes denotes an action not completed at all, but only attempted: as,

> Quintus frater Tusculanum venditat (Att. i. 14), *my brother Quintus is trying to sell the place at Tusculum.*

(So the present Infinitive and Participle.)

c. The present, especially in colloquial language, is sometimes used for the *future:* as,

> imusne sessum (De Or. iii. 5), *shall we take a seat?*
> ecquid me adjuvas? (Clu. 26), *won't you give me a little help?*
> in jus voco te. non eo. non is? (Pl. As. 480), *I summon you to the court. I won't go. You won't?*
> si reus condemnatur, desinent homines dicere his judiciis pecuniam plurimum posse (Verr. i. 2), *if the prisoner is convicted, men will no longer say that money is the chief power in the courts.*

(See also under cum, antequam, dum § 62.)

***d*. Historical Present.** The present in lively narrative is often used for the historical perfect: as,

> affertur nuntius Syracusas; curritur ad prætorium; Cleomenes, quamquam nox erat, tamen in publico esse non audet; includit se domi (Verr. vi. 35), *the news is brought to Syracuse; they run to head-quarters; Cleomenes, though it was night, does not venture to be abroad; he shuts himself up at home.*

***e*.** The present is regularly used with **dum**, *while*, though referring to past time: as,

> hæc dum aguntur, interea Cleomenes jam ad Elori litus pervenerat (id.), *while this is going on, Cleomenes meanwhile had come down to the coast at Elorum.*

But when the time referred to is *contrasted with some other*, the past tenses must be used: as,

> nec enim dum eram vobiscum animum meum videbatis (Cat. M. 22), *for even when I was with you, you did not see my soul.*

***f*.** The present is regularly used of writers whose works are extant: as,

> Epicurus vero ea dicit (Tusc. ii. 7), *but Epicurus says such things.*
> apud illum Ulysses lamentatur in vulnere (id. 21), *in him [Sophocles] Ulysses bewails over his wound.*

3. *Imperfect*. The Imperfect denotes an action or condition continued or repeated in past time: as,

> hunc audiebant antea (Man. 5), *they used to hear him before.*
> Socrates ita censebat itaque disseruit (Tusc. i. 30), *Socrates thought so* [habitually] *and so he spoke* [then].
> C. Duilium redeuntem a cenâ senem sæpe videbam (C. M. 13), *I would often see Duilius, then old, coming home from dinner.*

***a*.** Hence the imperfect is used in *descriptions*: as,

> erant omnino itinera duo . . . mons altissimus impendebat (B. G. i. 6), *there were in all two ways . . . a very high mountain overhung.*

***b*.** The imperfect is sometimes used in the sense of a pluperfect and imperfect combined (see above, 2, *a*): as,

> copias quas diu comparabant (Fam. i. 13), *the forces which they had long been getting ready.*

***c*.** The imperfect sometimes denotes an action merely attempted, but never accomplished (compare conative present, 2, *b*): as,

in exsilium eiciebam quem jam ingressum esse in bellum videbam (Cat. ii. 6), *was I sending into exile one who I saw had already gone into war?*
consules sedabant tumultus (Liv. iii. 15), *the consuls busied themselves to calm the tumult.*
si licitum esset veniebant (Verr. vi. 49), *they were coming if it had been allowed.*

d. The imperfect is sometimes used to express a certain surprise at the *present* discovery of a fact already existing: as,

O tu quoque hic aderas, Phormio (Ter. Ph. v. 6), *O, you are here too, Phormio.*
ehem pater mi, tu hic eras? (Pl. id. v. 7), *what, you here, father?*
ah miser! quantâ laborabas Charybdi (Hor. Od. i. 27), *unhappy boy, what a whirlpool you are struggling in* [and I never knew it].

e. The imperfect is often used in narration by the comic poets, where later writers would employ the perfect: as,

ad amicum Calliclem quoi rem aibat mandâsse hic suam (Trin. 956), *to his friend Callicles, to whom, he said, he had intrusted his property.*
præsagibat animus frustra me ire quom exibam domo (Aul. 222), *my mind mistrusted when I went from home that I went in vain.*

The Imperfect Indicative in Apodosis, *contrary to fact*, regularly refers to present time (see § **59**, 3, *d*).

4. Future. The Future denotes an action or condition that will occur hereafter.

[For Future instead of the Imperative, see § **57**, 7, *d*.]

5. Perfect. The Perfect *definite* denotes an action as now completed; the Perfect *historical*, as having taken place indefinitely, in past time: as,

ut ego feci, qui Græcas litteras senex didici (C. M. 8), *as I have done, who have learned Greek in my old age.*
tantum bellum extremâ hieme apparavit, ineunte vere suscepit, mediâ æstate confecit (Man. 12), *so great a war he made ready for at the end of winter, undertook in early spring, and finished by midsummer.*

[For the difference between the Perfect and Imperfect in *narration*, see Note, page 53.]

a. The perfect is sometimes used emphatically to denote that something no longer exists: as,

> fuit ista quondam in hac re publicâ virtus (Cat. i. 1), *there was once such virtue in this commonwealth.*
> fuimus Troes, fuit Ilium (Æn. ii. 325), *we were Trojans, Ilium did exist.*
> habuit, non habet (Tusc. i. 36), *he had, he has no longer.*

b. The perfect is sometimes used of indefinite time in connection with a general present: as,

> qui in compedibus corporis semper fuerunt, etiam cum soluti sunt tardius ingrediuntur (Tusc. i. 31), *they who have always been in fetters of the body, even when released move more slowly.*

c. The perfect is sometimes used of a general truth, especially with negations: as,

> qui studet contingere metam multa tulit fecitque (Hor. A. P. 412), *he who aims to reach the goal, first bears and does many things.*
> non æris acervus et auri deduxit corpore febres (id. Ep. i. 2), *the pile of brass and gold removes not the fever from the frame.*

d. The perfect is often used in expressions containing or implying a *negation*, where in affirmation the imperfect would be preferred: as,

> dicebat melius quam scripsit Hortensius (Or. 38), *Hortensius spoke better than he wrote.* [Here the negative is implied in the comparison: compare the use of **quisquam, ullus,** &c. (foot of p. 48), and the French **ne** after comparatives and superlatives.]

[For Perfect in apodosis of future conditions, see § 59, 4, *e*; for Perfect after **ubi,** &c., § 62, 2, *a.*]

REMARK. — The Perfect and Pluperfect of a few verbs are equivalent to the Present and Imperfect of kindred verbs (**novi,** *I know;* **coepi,** *I begin;* **memini,** *I remember;* **cognoveram,** *I knew;* **venerat** (= **aderat**), *he was at hand* (see § 36, 1): as,

> qui dies æstus maximos efficere consuevit (B. G. iv. 29), *which day generally makes the highest tides.*
> cujus splendor obsolevit (Quinc. v. 18), *whose splendor is now out of date.*

6. *Pluperfect.* The Pluperfect is used to denote an action completed in time past; sometimes, also, repeated in indefinite time: as, neque vero cum aliquid mandaverat confectum putabat (Cat. iii. 7), *for when he had given a thing in charge he did not look on it as already done.*

quæ si quando adepta est id quod ei fuerat concupitum, tum fert alacritatem (Tusc. iv. 15), *if it* [desire] *ever has gained what it had desired, then it produces joy.*

7. *Future Perfect.* The Future Perfect denotes an action as completed in the future: as,

ut sementem feceris ita metes (Or. ii. 65), *as you sow, so shall you reap.*

REMARK. — The Future Perfect is used (as above) with much greater exactness in Latin than in English, and may even be used instead of the Future, from the fondness of the Latins for representing an action as completed: as,

quid inventum sit paulo post videro (Acad. ii. 24), *what has been found out I will see presently.*

ego certe meum officium præstitero (B. G. iv. 25), *I at least shall have done my duty.*

8. *Epistolary Tenses.* In Letters, the perfect (*historical*) or imperfect may be used for the present, and the pluperfect for past tenses, as if the letter were *dated* at the time it is supposed to be *received:* as,

neque tamen, cum hæc scribebam, eram nescius quantis oneribus premerere (Fam. v. 12), *nor while I write this am I ignorant under what burdens you are weighed.*

ad tuas omnes [epistulas] rescripseram pridie (Att. ix. 10), *I* [have] *answered all your letters yesterday.*

9. *Tenses of the Subjunctive.* The tenses of the Subjunctive denote Absolute time only in *independent clauses.* In these the Present always refers to *future time;* the Imperfect to either *past or present;* the Perfect to either *future or past;* the Pluperfect always to *past.*

In *dependent clauses,* the tenses of the Subjunctive denote Relative time, not with reference to the speaker, but *to the action of some other verb.*

10. *Sequence of Tenses.* The forms which denote *absolute time* may be used in any connection. But those denoting *relative time* follow special rules for the Sequence of Tenses. For this purpose, tenses are divided into two classes: viz.,

1. **Primary,** including the Present, both Futures, and Perfect (*definite*);

2. **Secondary,** including the Imperfect, Perfect (*historical*), and Pluperfect.

RULE.— In compound sentences, a Primary tense in the leading clause is followed by a Primary tense in the dependent clause; and a Secondary tense is followed by a Secondary: as,

scribit ut nos moneat, *he writes to warn us.*
scribet ut nos moneat, *he will write to warn us.*
scripsit ut nos moneat, *he has written to warn us.*
scribe (scribito) ut nos moneas, *write that you may warn us.*
scripsit ut nos moneret, *he wrote to warn us.*
scribit quasi oblitus sit, *he writes as if he had forgotten.*
scripsit quasi oblitus esset, *he wrote as if he had forgotten.*

REMARK.— The Rule appears in the following Diagram:—

TENSES OF THE SUBJUNCTIVE.

	Primary.	*Secondary.*
1. Action not complete (time relatively *present* or *future*).	PRESENT.	IMPERFECT.
2. Action complete (time relatively *past*).	PERFECT.	PLUPERFECT.

In applying the rule for the Sequence of Tenses, consider (1) whether the leading verb is *primary* or *secondary*; (2) whether the dependent verb is required to denote *complete* action (i.e. relatively past), or *incomplete* (relatively present or future). By taking the corresponding tense, as given above, the correct usage will generally be found.

Notice that the FUTURE PERFECT denotes relatively *completed* action, and hence is represented in the Subjunctive by the PERFECT or PLUPERFECT.

a. The perfect *definite* is properly a primary tense; but as its action is (at least) commenced in past time, it is more commonly followed by secondary tenses: as,

ut satis esset præsidi provisum est (Cat. ii. 12), *provision has been made that there should be ample guard.*
adduxi hominem in quo satisfacere exteris nationibus **possetis** (Verr. i. 1), *I have brought a man in whose person you can make satisfaction to foreign nations.*

b. The perfect subjunctive is regularly used to denote any past action (either as Perfect *definite* or *historical*) depending on a verb in a primary tense: as, ex epistulis intellegi licet quam frequens **fuerit** Platonis auditor (Or. 4), *it may be understood from his letters how constant a hearer he was of Plato.*

c. In clauses of Result, the perfect subjunctive is very often (the present rarely) used after secondary tenses: as,

Hortensius ardebat dicendi cupiditate sic ut in nullo unquam flagrantius studium **viderim** (Brut. 88), *Hortensius was so hot with desire of speaking that I never saw a more burning ardor in any man.*

Siciliam Verres per triennium ita vexavit ac perdidit, ut ea restitui in antiquum statum nullo modo **possit** (Verr. i. 4), *for three years* [Verres] *so racked and ruined Sicily, that she can in no way be restored to her former state.*

REMARK.—This construction gives more emphasis to the fact stated as a result; while the regular one gives more prominence to the main clause. The perfect, thus used, can stand only for a *perfect* indicative, not an *imperfect;* and, in general, the perfect is often represented by the perfect subjunctive, contrary to the general rule: as,

Thorius erat ita non superstitiosus ut illa plurima in suâ patriâ et sacrificia et fana contemneret; ita non timidus ad mortem ut in acie sit ob rem publicam interfectus (Fin. ii. 20), *Thorius was so little superstitious that he despised* [contemnebat] *the many sacrifices and shrines in his country, so little timorous about death that he was killed* [interfectus est] *in battle, in defence of the state.*

Zeno nullo modo is erat qui nervos virtutis inciderit [compare 5, *d*]; sed contra qui omnia in unâ virtute poneret (Acad. i. 10), *Zeno was noway one to cut the sinews of virtue; but one, on the contrary, who made everything depend on virtue alone.*

d. A general truth after a past tense follows the connection of tenses in Latin (though not usually in English): as,

ex his quæ tribuisset sibi quam mutabilis **esset** reputabat (Q. C. iii. 9), *from what she* [Fortune] *had bestowed on him, he reflected how inconstant she is.*

ibi quantam vim ad stimulandos animos ira **haberet**, apparuit (Liv. xxxiii. 37), *here it appeared what power anger has to goad the mind.*

e. The historical present, or the present with **dum**, may be followed by either primary or secondary tenses, but more commonly by secondary: as,

rogat ut **curet** quod dixisset (Quinct. 5), *he asks him to attend to the thing he had spoken of.*

castella communit quo facilius prohiberi **possent** (B. G. i. 8), *he strengthens the forts that they might be more easily kept off.*

f. When the secondary tenses of the subjunctive are used in protasis and apodosis, they may stand after any tense: as,

> quia tale sit, ut vel si ignorarent id homines, &c. (Fin. ii. 15),
> *because it is such that even if men were ignorant.*

g. The imperfect subjunctive, in protasis or apodosis, even when it refers to present time, is regularly followed by secondary tenses: as,

> si solos eos diceres miseros quibus moriendum **esset**, neminem exciperes (Tusc. i. 5), *if you called only those wretched who must die, you would except no one.*

h. After the present, when a past tense appears to be in the writer's thought, secondary tenses sometimes follow by a kind of *Synesis*: as,

> sed tamen ut **scires** hæc tibi scribo (Fam. xiii. 47), *but yet that you may know, I write thus* [as if Epistolary Imperfect].
> cujus præcepti tanta vis est ut ea non homini cuipiam sed Delphico deo **tribueretur** (Leg. i. 22), *such is the force of this precept, that it was ascribed not to any man, but to the Delphic god* [the precept was an old one].

11. *Infinitive.* The tenses of the Infinitive are present, past, or future, relatively to the time of the verb on which they depend: as,

> nostros non esse inferiores intellexit (B. G. ii. 8), *he ascertained that our men were not inferior.*
> quam Juno fertur terris magis omnibus coluisse (Æn. i. 15), *which Juno, 'tis said, cherished above all lands.*
> sperant se maximum fructum esse capturos (Læl. 21), *they hope they shall receive the greatest advantage.*

a. The present infinitive, after a verb in the past, must often be rendered by the perfect infinitive in English: as,

> scire potuit (Milo, 17), *he might have known.*
> qui videbatur omnino mori non debuisse (Arch. 8), *who seemed* [one that] *ought not to have died at all.*

REMARK. — This is most frequent with verbs of necessity, propriety, and possibility (**potui, debui, oportuit**); and occurs because the tenses of the corresponding verbs in English have lost their original past signification (compare " one whom he ought [owed] a grudge unto," A.D. 1597).

b. **Memini** and a few other verbs, stating what the speaker has personally witnessed, take the present infinitive: as,

> memini Catonem mecum disserere (Læl. 3), *I remember Cato's discoursing with me* (So *dicere aiebat*, De Or. ii. 3.)

Compare Greek present infinitive for imperfect (G. 203, N. 1).

REMARK. — The infinitive **posse** is used also in the sense of a future.

c. Except in Indirect Discourse the present infinitive only is generally used, with no distinct reference to time : as,

> est adulescentis majores natu vereri (Off. i. 34), *it is the duty of the young to reverence their elders.*
> de quibus dicere aggrediar (Off. ii. 1), *of which I will undertake to speak.*

d. After verbs of *wishing, necessity,* and the like, the perfect passive infinitive is often used instead of the present : as,

> domesticâ curâ te levatum [esse] volo (Q. F. iii. 9), *I wish you relieved of household care.*
> liberis consultum volumus propter ipsos (Fin. iii. 17), *we wish regard paid to children on their own account.*
> quod jampridem factum esse oportuit (Cat. i. 2), *which ought to have been done long ago.*

REMARK. — In early Latin, and in poetry, the perfect active is also used, and even after other verbs than those of wishing : as,

> commisisse cavet (Hor. A. P. 168), *he is cautious of doing.*
> edixerunt ne quis quid fugæ causâ vendidisse neve emisse vellet (Liv. xxxix. 17), *they* [the old laws] *declared that none should sell or buy to escape obligation.*
> haud equidem premendo alium me extulisse velim (id. xxii. 59), *I would not by crushing another exalt myself.*
> sunt qui nolint tetigisse (Hor. Sat. i. 2), *there are those who would not touch.*
> nollem dixisse (Verr. v. 20), *I would not say.*

e. The perfect infinitive is used, especially by poets, to denote a completed action after verbs of *feeling ;* also with **satis est (habeo), melius est, contentus sum,** and in a few other cases where this distinction is important : as,

> quiêsse erit melius (Liv. iii. 48), *it will be better to have kept quiet.*
> non pœnitebat intercapedinem scribendi fecisse (Fam. xvi. 21), *I was not sorry to have made a respite of writing.*
> pudet me . . . non præstitisse (id. xiv. 3), *I am ashamed not to have shown.*
> sunt quos curriculo pulverem Olympicum collegisse juvat (Hor. Od. i. 1), *there are those who delight, &c.*
> majus dedecus est parta amittere quam omnino non paravisse (Jug. 31), *it is more discredit to have lost one's gains than never to have gained at all.*
> nil ego si peccem possum nescisse (Ov. Her. xvii. 47), *if I go wrong, I cannot have done it in ignorance.*

f. The future infinitive is often expressed by **fore** or **futurum esse ut** (§ 70, 4) : as,

> spero fore ut contingat id nobis (Tusc. i.), *I hope that will be our happy lot.*

59. Conditional Sentences.

A Conditional Sentence (or Clause) is one beginning with IF, or some equivalent.

1. *Protasis and Apodosis*. In a conditional sentence, the clause containing the *condition* is called the Protasis; and that containing the *conclusion* is called the Apodosis: as,

> si qui exire volunt [PROTASIS], conivere possum [APODOSIS] (Cat. ii. 12), *if any wish to depart, I can keep my eyes shut.*

a. The **Protasis** is regularly introduced by the conditional particles **si**, *if;* **sin**, *but if;* **nisi** (ni), *unless.* But a clause introduced by an Indefinite Relative (as **quisquis**, *whoever*), a Relative or Concessive Conjunction (**cum**, *since*, **quamvis**, *although*), a Participle, or an Imperative, is treated as a conditional clause: as,

> quæcunque causa vos huc attulisset, lætarer (De Or. ii. 4), *I should be glad, whatever cause had brought you here* [i.e. if any other, as well as the one which did].
> philosophia, cui qui pareat, omne tempus ætatis sine molestia possit degere (Cat. M. 1), *philosophy, which IF any one obeys, he will be able to spend his whole life without vexation.*
> virtutem qui adeptus erit ubicunque erit gentium a nobis diligetur (N. D. i. 44), *if any one shall have attained virtue, &c.*

[For Implied Conditions, see § **60**.]

NOTE. — The Indefinite Relative, *whoever, whatever, whenever,* may be regarded as a conditional expression, equivalent to *if any one, if at any time,* &c., as is seen in the analogy of the Greek ὅς ἄν, ὅταν, and in the structure of relative as compared with conditional clauses. In the Statutes of Massachusetts, for instance, the phrase "Whoever shall" has been substituted for the old form "IF any person shall," &c.

b. The **Apodosis**, being the main clause, depends in form on the grammatical structure of the sentence, which may require a Participle, Infinitive, or Phrase: as,

> quod si præterea nemo sequatur, tamen se cum solâ decimâ legione iturum (B. G. i. 40), *but if no one else would follow, he would go with the tenth legion alone.*
> si quos adversum prœlium commoveret, hos reperire posse (id.), *if the loss of a battle alarmed any, they might find.*
> sepulturâ quoque prohibituri, ni rex humari jussisset (Q. C. viii. 2), *intending also to deprive him of burial, unless the king had ordered him to be interred.*

2. *Particular and General Conditions.* The supposition contained in a Protasis may be either *particular* or *general*.

a. A Particular supposition refers to a *definite act* (or a definite series of acts) occurring at some *definite time:* as,

> si hæc condicio consulatûs data est ... feram libenter (Cat. iv. 1), *if this condition has been imposed on the consulship, I will bear it willingly.*

b. A General supposition refers to *any one* of a class of acts, which may occur (or may have occurred) *at any time:* as,

> si vero habet aliquod tamquam pabulum studi atque doctrinæ, nihil est otiosâ senectute jucundius (Cat. M. 14), *indeed, if it have some sustenance (as it were) of study and learning, nothing is more cheerful than an old age of leisure.*

NOTE. — These two classes of conditions are distinguished *logically;* and in most languages are also distinguished *grammatically,* — but only as to Present and Past Conditions. In Latin, in *particular conditions,* present or past tenses of the Indicative are regularly used in Protasis, where no opinion is intimated of its truth or falsity; and the Apodosis may take any form of the verb which can be used in an independent sentence. In *general conditions,* also, referring to Present or Past time, the Indicative is for the most part used both in Protasis and Apodosis. (Compare Goodwin's Greek Grammar, § 220.)

c. **Classification.** The principal forms of Conditional Sentences may be exhibited as follows: —

1. PRESENT OR PAST CONDITIONS.

(a) Simple statement (nothing implied as to fulfilment):
- **si adest bene est,** *if he is* [now] *here, it is well.*
- **si aderat (adfuit) bene erat,** *if he was* [then] *here, it was well.*

(b) Supposition contrary to fact (condition not fulfilled):
- **si adesset bene esset,** *if he were* [now] *here, it would be well.*
- **si adfuisset bene fuisset,** *if he had* [then] *been here, it would have been well.*

2. FUTURE CONDITIONS.

(a) More vivid (probable):
- **si aderit bene erit,** *if he is* [shall be] *here, it will be well.*

(b) Less vivid (improbable):
- **si adsit bene sit,** *if he should* [hereafter] *be here, it would be well.*

3. GENERAL SUPPOSITIONS.

(a) Indefinite subject:
- **si hoc dicas bene est,** *if one says this, it is well.*

(b) Repeated Action:
- **si hoc diceret bene erat** (rare), *if* [whenever] *he said this, it was well.*

3. *Present and Past Conditions*. A present or past condition may be simply stated, implying nothing as to its fulfilment; or it may be stated so as to imply that it *is not* or *was not* fulfilled.

a. In the statement of a condition *whose falsity is* NOT *implied*, the present and past tenses of the Indicative are used in Protasis; the apodosis expressing simply what *is*, *was*, or *will be*, the result of the fulfilment (G. 221) : as,

 si tu exercitusque valetis, bene est (Fam. v. 2), *if you and the army are well, it is well.*
 si justitia vacat, in vitio est (Off. i. 19), *if justice be wanting, it* [bravery] *is in fault.*
 si placet . . . videamus (Cat. M. 5), *if you please, let us see.*
 fuerit hoc censoris, si judicabat (Div. i. 16), *grant that it was the censor's duty if he judged, &c.*
 quicquid jurârunt ventus et unda rapit (Prop. ii. 28), *whatever they have sworn* [i.e. if they have sworn anything], *the winds and waves sweep away.*

b. In the statement of a supposition *known to be false*, the Imperfect and Pluperfect subjunctive are used,—the imperfect referring to *present time*, the pluperfect to *past* (G. 222) : as,

 quæ si exsequi nequirem, tamen me lectulus oblectaret meus (Cat. M. 11), *if I could not* [now] *follow this* [an active life], *yet my couch would afford me pleasure.*
 nisi tu amisisses, nunquam recepissem (id. 4), *unless you had lost it, I should not have recovered it.*
 si meum consilium auctoritasque **valuisset**, tu hodie **egeres**, nos liberi **essemus**, respublica non tot duces et exercitus **amisisset** (Phil. ii. 15), *if my judgment and authority had prevailed* [as they did not], *you would this day be a beggar, we should be free, and the republic would not have lost so many leaders and armies.*

NOTE.—The implication of falsity, in this construction, is not inherent in the Subjunctive; but comes from *the transfer of a future condition to past time.* Thus the time for the happening of the condition has, at the time of writing, already passed; so that, if the condition remains *a condition*, it must be contrary to fact. So forms implying a future frequently take the place of the subjunctive in apodosis in this construction (see *c*, below).

c. In many cases the imperfect refers to past time, both in protasis and apodosis, especially when a *repeated or continued action* is denoted, or when the condition *if true would still exist :* as,

 hic si mentis **esset** suæ, ausus esset educere exercitum (Pis. 21), *if he were of sane mind would he have dared to lead out the army?*

non concidissent, nisi illud receptaculum classibus nostris **pateret** (Verr. ii. 1), [the power of Carthage] *would not have fallen, unless that station had been open to our fleets.*

d. The past tenses of the indicative in Apodosis (after a subjunctive in Protasis) may be used to express what *ought* to have been done, or is *intended*, or is already *begun:* as,

si Romæ privatus esset hoc tempore, tamen is **erat** deligendus (Manil. 17), *if he* [Pompey] *were at this time a private citizen in Rome, yet he ought to be appointed,*
quod esse caput debebat, si probari posset (Fin. iv. 9), *what ought to be the main point if it could be proved.*
si licitum esset matres veniebant (Verr. vi. 49), *the mothers were coming if it had been allowed.*
in amplexus filiæ ruebat, nisi lictores obstitissent (Ann. xvi. 32), *he was about rushing into his daughter's arms, unless the lictors had opposed.*

REMARK. — In this use, the imperfect indicative corresponds in time to the imperfect subjunctive, and the perfect or pluperfect indicative to the pluperfect subjunctive (the tenses of the subjunctive may, however, be used as well; see Note, above) : as,

satius erat (esset), *it were better.*

e. This use is regular with all verbs and expressions denoting the *necessity, propriety, desirableness, duty, possibility,* of an action — including the two periphrastic conjugations (see page 83) — where it is implied that what was necessary, &c., *has not been done.* It is sometimes carried still further in poetry: as,

nam nos decebat lugere (Tusc. i. 47), *it would befit us to mourn.*
si non alium jactaret odorem, laurus erat (Georg. ii. 133), *it were a laurel, but for giving out a different odor.*

NOTE. — Observe that all these expressions contain the idea of Futurity. Compare note under *b.*

e. So the participle in **urus** with **fui** is equivalent to a *pluperfect subjunctive.* Hence, when the Apodosis is itself a *dependent clause,* requiring the subjunctive, a *pluperfect subjunctive* may be represented by the Future Participle with the *subjunctive* of **esse** (compare apodosis in Indirect Discourse, § **67**, 1, *c*) : as,

quid enim futurum fuit [= fuisset], si ... (Liv. ii. 1), *what would have happened, if,* &c.
neque ambigitur quin ... id facturus fuerit, si ... (ib.), *and no doubt he would have done it, if,* &c.
ex quo intellegi potest quam acuti naturâ sint, qui hæc sine doctrinâ credituri fuerint (Tusc. i. 21), *hence it may be understood how keen they are by nature, who, without instruction, would have believed this.* [Here the condition is contained in the words *sine doctrinâ.*]

adeo parata seditio fuit, ut Othonem **rapturi fuerint**, ni incerta noctis timuissent (Tac. H. i. 26), *so far advanced was the conspiracy, that they would have seized upon Otho, had they not feared the hazards of the night* [in the direct discourse, *rapuissent ni timuissent*].

4. *Future Conditions*. A Future condition may either make a *distinct supposition* of a future case, the apodosis expressing what *will be* the result; or the supposition may be less distinct and vivid, the apodosis expressing what *would be* the result in the case supposed.

a. If the condition is stated vividly, so as to be conceived as *actually about to take place*, the Future Indicative is used in both protasis and apodosis (G. 223): as,

sanabimur si volemus (Tusc. iii. 6), *we shall be healed if we wish.*
quod si legere aut audire voletis ... reperietis (Cat. M. 6), *if you will read or hear, you will find.*

b. The Present subjunctive expresses a future condition *less vividly*, or as *less probable*, than when the future indicative is used (G. 224): as,

hæc si tecum patria loquatur, nonne impetrare debeat (Cat. i. 8), *if thy country should thus speak with thee, ought she not to prevail?*
quod si quis deus mihi largiatur ... valde recusem (Cat. M. 23), *but if some god were to grant me this, I should earnestly refuse.*

REMARK. — The present subjunctive sometimes stands in protasis with the future in apodosis.

c. If the conditional act is regarded as *completed* before that of the apodosis begins, the future perfect is substituted for the *future*, and the perfect subjunctive for the present: as,

sin, cum potuero, non venero, tum erit inimicus (Att. ix. 2), *but if I do not come when I can, he will be unfriendly.*
si non feceris, ignoscam (Fam. v. 19), *if you do not do it, I will excuse you.*

REMARK. — This is a very common construction in Latin, owing to the tendency of the language to represent an action as *completed*, rather than as *in progress*.

d. Any form denoting future time may stand in the apodosis of a future condition (so the participles in **dus** and **rus**, and verbs of *necessity, possibility,* and the like): as,

non possum istum accusare si cupiam (Verr. v. 41), *I cannot accuse him if I should desire.*

alius finis constituendus est si prius quid maxime reprehendere Scipio solitus sit dixero (Læl. 16), *another limit must be set if I shall first state what Scipio was most wont to blame.*

e. Rarely the perfect is used (rhetorically) in apodosis with a present or even future in protasis, representing the conclusion as *already accomplished:* as,

> si hoc bene fixum in animo est, vicistis (Liv. xxi. 44), *if this is well fixed in your minds, you have conquered.*
> si eundem [animum] habueritis, vicimus (id. 43), *if you shall have kept the same spirit, we have conquered.*

f. Frequently the present subjunctive of a future condition becomes imperfect by the sequence of tenses or some other cause (retaining the same force relatively to past time): as,

> non poterat nisi vellet (B. C. iii. 44), *was not able unless he wished.*
> Cæsar si peteret... non quicquam proficeret (Hor. Sat. i. 2), *if even Cæsar were to ask he would gain nothing.* [Here the construction is not contrary to fact, but is simply *si petat non proficiat,* thrown into past time.]
> tumulus apparuit... si luce palam iretur hostis præventurus erat (Liv. xxii. 24), *a hill appeared... if they should go openly by light the enemy would prevent.* [Independent of *apparuit,* this would be, *si eatur, præventurus est,* for *præveniat.*]

5. General Conditions. General conditions are distinguished in Latin in only two cases: viz.

a. **Indefinite Subject.** The subjunctive is used in the *second person singular,* to denote the act of an indefinite subject (*you = any one*). Here the present Indicative of a *general truth* may stand in the apodosis (G. 225): as,

> mens prope uti ferrum est: si exerceas conteritur; nisi exerceas, rubiginem contrahit (Cato de Mor.), *the mind is very like iron: if you use it, it wears away; if you don't use it, it gathers rust.*
> virtutem necessario gloria, etiamsi tu id non agas, consequitur (Tusc. i. 38), *glory necessarily follows virtue, even if that is not one's aim.*
> si prohibita impune transcenderis, neque metus ultra neque pudor est (Ann. iii. 54), *if you once overstep the bounds with impunity, there is no fear nor shame any more.*
> si cederes placabilis (Tac. Ann.), [*he was*] *easily appeased if one yielded.*

b. **Repeated Action.** In later writers (not in Cicero), the imperfect and pluperfect subjunctive are used in protasis, with the imperfect indicative in apodosis, to state a *repeated or customary action*: as,

>accusatores, si facultas incideret, pœnis adficiebantur (Ann. vi. 30), *the accusers, whenever opportunity offered, were visited with punishment.*
>quemcunque lictor prehendisset, tribunus mitti jubebat (Liv. iii. 11), *whomever the lictor had seized, the tribune ordered to be let go.*

c. In all other cases, General Suppositions — including those introduced by Indefinite Relatives — take the *indicative.*

60. Implied Conditions.

In many sentences properly conditional, the subordinate member is not expressed *as a conditional clause;* but is stated in some other form of words, or is implied in the nature of the thought.

1. *Condition Disguised.* The condition is often contained in some other form of words than a regular Protasis, in the same clause or sentence.

a. The condition may be contained in a relative, participial, or other qualifying clause: as,

>facile me paterer — vel ipso quærente, vel apud Cassianos judices — pro Sex. Roscio dicere (Rosc. Am. 30), *I would readily allow myself to speak for Roscius,* IF *he, &c.*
>non mihi, nisi admonito, venisset in mentem (De Or. ii. 42), *it would not have come into my mind, unless* [I had been] *admonished* [= nisi admonitus essem].
>nulla alia gens tantâ mole cladis non obruta esset (Liv. xxii. 54), *there is no other people that would not have been crushed by such a weight of disaster* [i.e. IF it had been any other people].
>nemo unquam, sine magnâ spe immortalitatis, se pro patriâ offerret ad mortem (Tusc. i. 15), *no one, without great hope of immortality, would ever expose himself to death for his country.*
>quid hunc paucorum annorum accessio juvare potuisset (Læl. 3), *what good could the addition of a few years have done him?* [if he had had them.]

b. The condition may be contained in a wish, or expressed as a command, by the imperative or hortatory subjunctive: as,

>utinam quidem fuissem! molestus nobis non esset (Fam. xii. 3), *I wish I had been* [chief]: *he would not now be troubling us* [i.e. if I had been].

roges enim Aristonem, neget (Fin. iv. 25), *for ask Aristo, and he would deny.*
tolle hanc opinionem, luctum sustuleris (Tusc. i. 13), *remove this notion, and you will have done away grief.*
naturam expellas furcâ, tamen usque recurret (Hor. Ep. i. 10), *drive out nature with a pitchfork, still she will ever return.*
manent ingenia senibus, modo permaneat studium et industria (Cat. M. 7), *old men keep their mental powers, only let them keep their zeal and diligence.*

NOTE. — This usage is probably the origin of the use of the subjunctive in Protasis; the subjunctive being used first, as in § 57, 3, while the conditional particle is a form of an indefinite pronoun.

c. Rarely, the condition is stated in an independent clause: as,
rides: majore cachinno concutitur (Juv. iii. 100), *you laugh: he shakes with louder laughter.*
de paupertate agitur: multi patientes pauperes commemorantur (Tusc. iii. 24), *we speak of poverty: many patient poor are mentioned.*

2. *Condition Omitted.* The condition is often wholly omitted, but may be inferred from the course of the argument.

REMARK. — Under this head belong all the apparently independent uses of the subjunctive not mentioned in § **57**, 2. In this use the perfect subjunctive is especially common, in the same sense as the present, referring to the *immediate future;* the imperfect to *past time* (not to *present,* as in § **57, 3**).

a. **Potential Subjunctive.** The present and perfect subjunctive (often with **forsitan** or the like) are used to denote an action as *possible;* also, the second person singular of all the tenses, denoting an *indefinite subject:* as,
hic quærat quispiam (N. D. ii. 53), *here some one may ask.*
ut aliquis fortasse dixerit (Off. iii. 6), *as one may perhaps say.*
forsitan hæc illi mirentur (Verr. v. 56), *they may perchance marvel at these things.*
tum in lecto quoque videres susurros (Hor. Sat. ii. 8), *then on each couch you might see whisperings.*

b. The subjunctive is used in cautious, modest, or hypothetical statement (*conjunctivus modestiæ*): as,
pace tuâ dixerim (Mil. 38), *I would say by your leave.*
haud sciam an (De Or. i. 60), *I should incline to think.*
tu velim sic existimes (Fam. xii. 6), *I would like you to think so.*
vellem adesset M. Antonius (Phil. i. 7), *I wish Anthony were here* [here *vellem* implies an impossible wish in present time].
hæc erant fere quæ tibi nota esse vellem (Fam. xii. 5), *this is about what I want you to know* [here *vellem* is simply *velim* transferred to past time on account of *erat*, by connection of tenses, and does not imply an impossible wish].

c. The Indicative of verbs signifying *necessity, propriety*, and the like, may be used in the apodosis of implied conditions, either future or contrary to fact: as,

> longum est [sit] ea dicere, sed ... (in Pison. 10), *it would be tedious to tell, &c.*
> illud erat aptius, æquum cuique concedere (Fin. iv. 1), *it would be more fitting to yield each one his rights.*
> ipsum enim exspectare magnum fuit (Phil. ii. 40), *would it have been a great matter to wait for himself?*
> quanto melius fuerat (Off. iii. 25), *how much better it would have been.*
> quod contra decuit ab illo meum [corpus cremari] (Cat. M.), *whereas on the other hand mine ought to have been burnt by him.*
> nam nos decebat domum lugere ubi esset aliquis in lucem editus (Tusc. i. 48), *for it were fitting to mourn the house where a man has been born* [but we do not].
> nunc est bibendum ... nunc Saliaribus ornare pulvinar deorum tempus erat dapibus sodales (Hor. Od. i. 37), i.e. *it would be time* [if it were for us to do it, but it is a public act].

REMARK. — Notice that, in this construction, the imperfect indicative refers to *present time;* the pluperfect to *simply past* time, like the perfect. Thus **oportebat** means *it ought to be* [now], *but is not;* **oportuerat** means *it ought to have been, but was not.*

d. The omission of the protasis often gives rise to mixed constructions: as,

> peream male si non optimum erat (Hor. Cat. ii. 1), *may I perish if it would not be better.* [Here the protasis and apodosis come under § **59**, 3, *d.* Optimum erat is itself an apodosis with the protasis omitted.]
> quod si in hoc mundo fieri sine deo non potest, ne in sphærâ quidem eosdem motus Archimedes sine divino ingenio potuisset imitari (Tusc. i. 25). [Here the protasis of *potuisset* is in *sine divino ingenio.*]

61. CONDITIONAL PARTICLES.

Certain Particles implying a Condition are followed by the Subjunctive, but upon several different principles.

1. *Comparative Particles.* The particles of *comparison* — **tamquam, quasi, quam si, acsi, utsi, velutsi, veluti,** and poetic **ceu** — introduce conditional clauses, of which the conclusion is omitted or implied; and take the subjunctive.

REMARK. — Contrary to the English idiom, the *present and perfect subjunctive* are regularly used with these particles, except where the connection of tenses requires secondary tenses: as,

tamquam clausa sit Asia (Fam. xii. 9), *as if Asia was closed.*
tamquam si claudus sim (Plaut. Asin. 2), *just as if I were lame.*
quasi vero non specie visa judicentur (Acad. ii. 18), *as if forsooth visible things were not judged by their appearance.*
velut si coram adesset (B. G. i. 32), *as if he were there present.*
similiter facis ac si me roges (N. S. iii. 3), *you do exactly as if you asked me.*
æque ac si mea negotia essent (Fam. xiii. 43), *as much as if it were my own business.*
ceu cetera nusquam bella forent (Æn. ii. 438), *as if there were no fighting elsewhere.*
magis quam si domi esses (Att. vi. 4), *more than if you were at home.*
ac si ampullam perdidisset (Fin. iv. 12), *as if he had lost the bottle.*

2. Concessive Particles. The particles of *concession* — *although, granting that* — sometimes take the subjunctive, but under various constructions: viz.,

Quamvis and **ut** (except in later writers) take the *hortatory subjunctive* (§ 57, 2); **licet** is a verb, and is followed by an object-clause (§ 70, 3); **etsi** has the same constructions as **si** (§ 59); **cum** has a special construction (§ 62, 1); **quanquam** takes the indicative (59, 3, *a*): as,

quamvis ipsi infantes sint, tamen ... (Or. 23), *however incapable themselves of speaking, yet, &c.*
ut neminem ali alium rogâsset (Mil. 17), *even if I had asked no other.*
licet omnes in me terrores periculaque impendeant (Rosc. Am. 11), *though all terrors and perils should menace me.*
etsi abest maturitas (Fam. vi. 18), *though ripeness of age is wanting.*
etsi nihil aliud abstulissetis (Sull. 32), *even if you had taken away nothing else.*

3. A Proviso, introduced by **modo, dum, dummodo,** requires the Subjunctive: as,

valetudo modo bona sit (Brut. 16), *provided the health is good.*
modo ne sit ex pecudum genere (Off. i. 30), *provided it [pleasure] be not after the manner of cattle.*

oderint dum metuant (Off. i. 28), *let them hate, if only they fear.*
dum de patris morte quaereretur (Rosc. Am. 41), *let the inquiry only be of a father's death.*
dummodo inter me atque te murus intersit (Cat. i. 5), *provided only the city wall is between us.*

NOTE. — The Subjunctive with **modo** is a hortatory Subjunctive; with **dum** and **dummodo**, a development from the Subjunctive in temporal clauses.

4. The use of some of the more common Conditional Particles may be stated as follows: —

a. **Si** is used for *affirmative*, **nisi** and **si non** for *negative* conditions. With **nisi**, the negative belongs rather to the Apodosis, — i.e. the conclusion is true except in the case supposed; with **si non**, the Protasis is negative, — i.e. the conclusion is *limited* to the case supposed. (The difference is often only one of emphasis.) **Nisi** is never used if the clause has a *concessive* force. **Ni** is an old form, reappearing in poets and later writers, and in a few conventional phrases. Sometimes **nisi si** occurs.

b. **Nisi vero** and **nisi forte** — sometimes **nisi** alone — regularly introduce an *objection*, or *exception*, ironically, and take the Indicative.

c. **Sive ... sive (seu)** introduce conditions in the form of an *alternative.* They have no peculiar construction, but may be used with any kind of condition, or with different kinds in the two branches, often also without a verb.

d. Of the concessive particles, the compounds of **si** are used in all the forms of protasis; **quanquam** regularly introduces only *conceded facts*, and hence takes the Indicative; **quamvis, quantumvis, quamlibet, ut, cum,** and **libet,** take idiomatic constructions corresponding to their original meaning. Later writers, however, frequently use all these particles like the compounds of **si**, connecting them with the Indicative or Subjunctive according to the nature of the condition. Even Cicero occasionally uses **quanquam** with the Subjunctive.

62. RELATIONS OF TIME.

Temporal clauses are introduced by particles which are almost all of *relative* origin; and are construed like other relative clauses, except where they have developed into special constructions.

Temporal Particles are the following: — **ubi, ut** (**ut primum, ut semel**), **simul atque** (**simul ac** or **simul** alone), **cum** (**quom**), **antequam, priusquam, postquam** (**posteāquam**), **dum, donec, quoad, quamdiu, quando.**

1. The particles **ubi, ut, cum, quando,** either alone or compounded with **-cunque,** are used as *indefinite relatives,* and have the constructions of Protasis (§ **59**) : as,

> cum rosam viderat, tum incipere ver arbitrabatur (Verr. v. 10), *whenever he had seen a rose, he thought Spring was begun* [general condition].
> cum id malum esse negas (Tusc. ii. 12), *when you* [the individual disputant] *deny it to be an evil.*
> cum videas eos ... dolore non frangi (id. 27), *when you see* [indefinite subject] *that those are not broken by pain, &c.*
> quod profecto cum me nulla vis cogeret, facere non auderem (Phil. v. 18), *which I would surely not venture to do, as long as no force compelled me* [supposition contrary to fact].
> id ubi dixisset, hastam in fines eorum emittebat (Liv. i. 32), *when he had said this, he* [used to] *cast the spear into their territories* [repeated action].

REMARK. — So **est cum, fuit cum,** &c., are used in general expressions like **est qui, sunt qui** (§ **65**).

2. Temporal clauses of *absolute time* take the Indicative; those of *relative time*, the Subjunctive.

(For the definition of absolute and relative time, see § **58**, 1, 9.)

NOTE. — This distinction is not made in other languages, but it may be made clear in the two following expressions: 1. When was the great fire in London? *Ans.* When Charles II. was king (*absolute time*). 2. When Charles II. was king (*relative time*), a great fire broke out in London. In the first case the reign of Charles is referred to as an *absolute fixed date,* known to the hearer; while in the second the time is not so fixed, but is given as *relative to the event narrated by the main verb,* which alone denotes absolute time. In this construction, the Subjunctive describes the time by its *characteristics* (as in § 65, 2), and thus is a branch of the Subjunctive of *result.* Hence this *qualitative* character of the temporal clause often reappears and occasions the Subjunctive, where the idea of relative time would not naturally be expected: as, *tum, cum* HABERET *hæc respublica Luscinos,* &c. ... *et tum, cum* ERANT *Catones,* &c. Here the former clause describes *the character of the age* by its men (at *a* time when there were such men); in the latter, *the individual men* are present to the mind (at *the* time of the Catos, &c.).

a. The particles **postquam** (**posteāquam**), **ubi, ut** (**ut primum, ut semel**)**, simul atque** (**simul ac** or **simul** alone), introduce clauses of *absolute time,* and take the Indicative (usually the narrative tenses, the *perfect* and the *historical present*): as, milites postquam victoriam adepti sunt, nihil reliqui victis fecêre (Sall. Cat. 11), *when the armies had won the victory, they left nothing to the vanquished.*

Pompeius ut equitatum suum pulsum vidit, acie excessit (B. C. iii. 94), *when Pompey saw his cavalry beaten, he left the army.*

REMARK. — 1. Those particles may also take the *imperfect*, denoting a continued state of things, and the *pluperfect*, denoting the result of an action completed, in the Indicative: as,

postquam instructi utrimque stabant, duces in medium procedunt (Liv. i. 23), *when they stood in array on both sides, the generals advance into the midst.*

P. Africanus posteaquam bis consul et censor fuerat (Div. in Caec. 21), *when Africanus had been* [i.e. had the dignity of having been] *twice consul and censor.*

postquam id difficilius visum est, neque facultas perficiendi dabatur, ad Pompeium transierunt (B. C. iii. 60), *when this seemed too hard, and no means of effecting it were given, they passed over to Pompey.*

post diem quintum quam barbari iterum male pugnaverant (= victi sunt), legati a Boccho veniunt (Jug. 110), *the fifth day after the barbarians were beaten the second time, envoys came from Bocchus.*

2. Rarely these particles denote *relative time*, and take the Subjunctive: as,

posteaquam maximas aedificâsset ornâssetque classes (Manil. 4), *having built and equipped mighty fleets.*

b. **Cum** (**quom**), TEMPORAL, meaning *when*, introduces both absolute and relative time, and takes either mood, — the Indicative of the *present and perfect*, the Subjunctive of the *imperfect and pluperfect*: as,

cum occiditur Sex. Roscius, ibidem fuerunt servi (Rosc. Am. 61), *when Roscius was slain, the slaves were on the spot.*

nempe eo [lituo] regiones direxit tum cum urbem condidit (Div. i. 17), *he traced with it the quarters* [of the sky] *at the time he founded the city.*

cum servili bello premeretur (Manil. 11), *when she* [Italy] *was under the load of the Servile war.*

inde cum se in Italiam recepisset (id. 12), *when he had returned thence to Italy.*

cum incendisses cupiditatem meam . . . tum discedis a nobis (Fam. xv. 21), *while you had inflamed my eagerness, yet you withdrew from us.*

NOTE. — The Present takes the Indicative because present time is generally, from its very nature, defined in the mind; and it is only when the circumstances are described as causal or adversative (see below, § 65, 2, *e*) that the Subjunctive is used. The Perfect takes the Indicative as the tense of narrative, as with **postquam**, &c. The Imperfect and Pluperfect are, from their nature, fitter to denote relative time.

REMARK. — 1. But the imperfect and pluperfect may denote *absolute time*, and then are in the Indicative: as,

> res cum hæc scribebam erat in extremum adducta discrimen (Fam. xii. 6), *at the time I write* [epistolary] *the affair was brought into great hazard.*
> quem quidem cum ex urbe pellebam, hoc providebam animo (Cat. iii. 7), *when I was about forcing him* [conative imperfect] *from the city, I looked forward to this.*
> fulgentes gladios hostium videbant Decii cum in aciem eorum irruebant (Tusc. ii. 24), *the Decii saw the flashing swords of the enemy when they rushed upon their line.*
> tum cum in Asia res magnas permulti amiserant (Manil. 7), *at that time, when many had lost great fortunes in Asia.*

2. When the clauses are inverted, so that the real temporal clause becomes the main clause, and *vice versa*, the Indicative must be used: as,

> dies nondum decem intercesserant, cum ille alter filius infans necatur (Clu. 9), *ten days had not yet passed, when the other infant son was killed.*
> hoc facere noctu apparabant, cum matres familiæ repente in publicum procurrerunt (B. G. vii. 26), *they were preparing to do this by night, when the women suddenly ran out into the streets.*

3. With Future tenses, there is no distinction of absolute or relative time; and hence the Indicative is used: as,

> non dubitabo dare operam ut te videam, cum id satis commode facere potero (Fam. xiii. 1), *I shall not hesitate to take pains to see you, when I can do it conveniently.*
> longum illud tempus cum non ero (Att. xii. 18), *that long time when I shall be no more.*

In the other tenses, the distinction is of late origin: hence in Plautus **quom** always takes the Indicative except where the Subjunctive is used for other reasons.

c. In narration **antequam** and **priusquam** — also, in late writers, **dum** and **donec** — have the same construction as **cum**: as,

> antequam tuas legi litteras (Att. ii. 7), *before I read your letter.*
> nec ante finis fuit quam concessêre (Liv. viii. 13), *there was no end until they yielded* [regular with non ante quam, &c.].
> antequam homines nefarii de meo adventu audire potuissent, in Macedoniam perrexi (Planc. 41), *before those evil men could learn of my coming, I arrived in Macedonia.*
> nec obstitit falsis donec tempore ac spatio vanescerent (Tac. Ann. ii. 82), *nor did he contradict the falsehoods till they died out through lapse of time.*

REMARK. — In reference to future time, these particles take the present and future perfect indicative; rarely the future indicative and present subjunctive: as,

> prius quam de ceteris rebus respondeo, de amicitiâ pauca dicam (Phil. ii. 1), *before I reply to the rest, I will say a little of friendship.*
> non defatigabor ante quam illorum ancipites vias percepero (De Or. iii. 36), *I shall not weary till I have traced out their doubtful ways.*

In a few cases the subjunctive of protasis seems to be used: as,

> priusquam incipias consulto et ubi consulueris mature facto opus est (Sall. Cat. 1), *before beginning you need reflection, and after reflecting, prompt action.*
> tempestas minatur antequam surgat (Sen. Ep. 103), *the storm threatens before it rises.* [Compare § 59, 5, a.]

d. **Dum, donec,** and **quoad,** implying purpose, take the subjunctive (§ **64**); otherwise, except in later writers, the indicative. **Dum** and **dummodo,** *provided,* take the subjunctive: as,

> dum hæc geruntur (B. G. i. 46), *while this was going on.*
> donec rediit silentium fuit (Liv. xxiii. 31), *there was silence until he returned.*
> dum res maneant, verba fingant (Fin. v. 29), *so long as the facts remain, let them fashion words.*
> hoc feci dum licuit, intermisi quoad non licuit (Phil. iii. 13), *I did this so long as it was allowed, I discontinued so long as it was not.*
> dummodo sit polita, dum urbana, dum elegans (Brut. 82), *provided it be polished, refined, elegant.*

REMARK. — With all temporal particles, the Subjunctive is often found, depending on other principles of construction.

e. **Cum** — CAUSAL, meaning *since, while,* or *although* — takes the subjunctive (often emphasized by **ut, utpote, quippe, praesertim**): as,

> cum solitudo ... insidiarum et metûs plena sit (Fin. i. 20), *since solitude is full of treachery and fear.*
> cum primi ordines ∴.. concidissent, tamen acerrime reliqui resistebant (B. G. vii. 62), *though the first ranks had fallen, still the others resisted vigorously.*
> nec reprehendo: quippe cum ipse istam reprehensionem non fugerim (Att. x. 3), *I do not blame it: since I myself did not escape that blame.*

But frequently in the sense of **quod,** *on the ground that,* it takes the Indicative: as,

> gratulor tibi cum tantum vales apud Dolabellam (Fam. xi 14), *I congratulate you that you are so strong with Dolabella.*

NOTE. — This *causal* relation is merely a variation of the idea of *time,* where the attendant circumstances are regarded as the cause.

f. **Cum ... tum,** signifying *both ... and,* usually take the Indicative; but when **cum** approaches the sense of *while* or *though,* it may have the Subjunctive: as,

> cum multa non probo, tum illud in primis (Fin. i. 6), *while there are many things I do not approve, there is this in chief.*
> cum res tota ficta sit pueriliter, tum ne efficit quidem quod vult (ib.), *while the whole thing is childishly got up, he does not even make his point.*

63. Cause or Reason.

Causal clauses may take the Indicative or Subjunctive according to their construction; the idea of Cause being contained *not in the mood itself,* but in the form of the argument, or the connecting particles.

1. The Causal Particles **quod, quia, quoniam, quando** —and in early Latin **cum** (*causal*)—take the Indicative: as,

> quia postrema ædificata est (Verr. iv. 53), *because it was built last.*
> utinam illum diem videam, cum tibi agam gratias quod me vivere coëgisti (Att. iii. 3), *O that I may see the day when I may thank you that you have forced me to live.*
> quoniam de utilitate jam diximus, de efficiendi ratione dicamus (Or. Part. 26), *since we have now spoken of* [its] *advantage, let us speak of the method of effecting it.*
> quando ita vis di bene vortant (Trin. 573), *since you so wish, may the gods bless the undertaking.*
> quom tua res distrahitur utinam te redîsse salvam videam (id. 617), *since your property is torn in pieces, oh, that I may see you returned safely!*

2. Clauses introduced by these particles, like any other dependent clause, take the Subjunctive of Indirect Discourse (see § **67,** 1).

a. A relative clause of *characteristic,* with its verb, in the subjunctive, may have the force of a causal sentence (see § **65,** 2).

b. The particle **cum,** when used in a causal sense, idiomatically takes the Subjunctive (§ **62, 2,** *e*).

64. Purpose.

1. FINAL CLAUSES, or those expressing *purpose*, take the Subjunctive after relatives (**qui** = **ut is**), or the conjunction **ut** (uti), *in order that* (negatively **ut ne** or **ne**, *lest*): as,

> ab aratro abduxerunt Cincinnatum, ut dictator esset (Fin. ii. 4), *they brought Cincinnatus from the plough, that he might be dictator.*
> scribebat orationes quas alii dicerent (Brut. 56), *he wrote speeches for other men to deliver.*
> huic ne ubi consisteret quidem contra te locum reliquisti (Quinct. 22), *you have left him no ground even to make a stand against you.*
> nihil habeo quod scribam, *I have nothing to write.*
> habebam quo confugerem (Fam. iv. 6), *I had* [a retreat] *whither I might flee.*
> ut ne sit impune (Mil. 12), *that it be not with impunity.*
> ne qua ejus adventûs procul significatio fiat (B. G. vi. 29), *that no sign of his arrival may be made at a distance.*

REMARK. — Sometimes the relative or conjunction has a correlative in the main clause: as,

> legum **idcirco** omnes servi sumus, ut liberi esse possimus (Clu. 53), *for this reason we are subject to the laws, that we may be free.*
> eâ causâ ... ne, *for this reason, lest,* &c.

NOTE. — As **ut** (**uti**) is of relative origin, the construction with ut is the same as that of relatives. That with **ne** is perhaps, in origin, a *hortatory* subjunctive.

a. The ablative **quo** (= **ut eo**) is used as a conjunction in final clauses, especially with *comparatives*: as,

> libertate usus est, quo impunius dicax esset (Quinct. 3), *he availed himself of liberty, that he might bluster with more impunity.*

Compare **quominus** (= **ut eo minus**), after verbs of *hindering* (§ 65, 1, *a*).

b. The Principal clause, upon which a final clause depends, is often to be supplied from the context: as,

> ac ne longum sit ... jussimus (Cat. iii. 5), *and, not to be tedious, we ordered,* &c. [strictly, "not to be tedious, I say."]
> sed ut ad Dionysium redeamus, ... (Tusc. v. 22), *but to return to Dionysius,* &c.
> satis inconsiderati fuit, ne dicam audacis (Phil. xiii. 5), *it was the act of one rash enough, not to say daring.*

REMARK. — To this principle belongs **nedum**, *still less, not to mention that*, with which the verb itself is often omitted: as,

nedum ... salvi esse possimus (Clu. 35), *much less could we be safe.*

nedum isti ... non statim conquisituri sint aliquid sceleris et flagitii (Leg. Ag. ii. 35), *far more will they hunt up at once some sort of crime and scandal.*

nedum in mari et viâ sit facile (Fam. xvi. 8), *still less is it easy at sea, and on a journey.*

c. Final clauses easily become the object of verbs of *wishing, commanding,* &c. (see § **68**).

2. The Purpose of an action is expressed in Latin in various ways; but never (except rarely in poetry) by the simple Infinitive, as in English. The sentence, *they came to seek peace,* may be rendered —

(1) venerunt ut pacem peterent ... [final clause with **ut**];
(2)   ,,   qui pacem peterent [final clause with Relative];
(3)   ,,   ad petendum pacem (rare) [gerund with **ad**];
(4)   ,,   ad petendam pacem [gerundive with **ad**];
(5)   ,,   pacem petendi causâ * [gerund with **causa**];
(6)   ,,   pacis petendæ causâ [gerundive with **causa**];
(7)   ,,   pacem petituri [future participle (not in Cicero)];
(8)   ,,   pacem petitum [former supine].

* Or gratiâ.

65. CONSEQUENCE OR RESULT.

1. CONSECUTIVE CLAUSES, or those expressing *result,* take the Subjunctive after relatives or the conjunction **ut**, *so that* (negatively, **ut non**): as,

nemo est tam senex, qui se annum non putet posse vivere (Cat. M. 7), *no one is so old as not to think he can live a year.*

nam est innocentia affectio talis animi, quæ noceat nemini (Tusc. iii. 8), *for innocence is such a quality of mind as to do harm to no one.*

sunt aliæ causæ quæ plane efficiant (Top. 15), *there are other causes, such as to bring to pass.*

REMARK. — A negative result is expressed by **ut non**. Sometimes, when the result is regarded as *intended* (though not a purpose), **ut ne** or **ne** is used: as,

[librum] ita corrigas ne mihi noceat (Fam. vi. 7), *correct the book so that it may not hurt me.*

hoc est ita utile ut ne plane illudamur ab accusatoribus (Rosc. Am. 20), *this is so useful, that we are not utterly mocked by the accusers* [*i.e.*, only on this condition].

a. The subjunctive with **quominus** (= **ut eo minus**) may be used, to express a result, after verbs of *hindering*: as,

nec aetas impedit quominus agri colendi studia teneamus (Cat. M. 17), *nor does age prevent us from retaining an interest in tilling the ground.*

b. A clause of result is introduced by **quin** after general negatives, where **quin** is equivalent to **qui (quae, quod) non**; also after clauses denoting *hindrance, resistance, doubt,* and *suspension of effort* (when these clauses are also negative): as,

non dubito quin, *I do not doubt that* [dubito an, *I doubt whether*].
aegre (vix) abstinui quin, *I hardly refrained from, &c.*
nihil impedit quin . . ., *there is nothing to prevent, &c.*
abesse non potest quin (Or. 70), *it cannot be but that.*
nihil est illorum quin [=quod non] ego illi dixerim (Plaut. Bac. iii. 9), *there is nothing of this that I have not told him.*

REMARK. — The above clauses of *result* easily pass into Substantive Clauses, for which see § 70.

2. A relative clause of Result is often used to indicate a *characteristic* of the antecedent, even where the idea of result can be no longer perceived. This is especially common where the antecedent is otherwise undefined: as,

neque enim tu is es, qui qui sis nescias (Fam. v. 12), *for you are not such a one, as not to know who you are.*
multa dicunt quae vix intelligant (Fin. iv. 1), *they say many things such as they hardly understand.*
paci quae nihil habitura sit insidiarum semper est consulendum (Off. i. 11), *we must always aim at a peace which shall have no plots.*
unde agger comportari posset, nihil erat reliquum (B. C. ii. 15), *there was nothing left, from which an embankment could be put together.*

NOTE. — These cases of *result* are to be distinguished from the Indefinite Relative in *protasis* (§ 59, 1).

Such relative clauses of *characteristic* are used in several idiomatic constructions: viz., —

a. After general expressions of *existence* and *non-existence,* including questions implying a negative: as,

erant qui Helvidium miserarentur (Ann. xvi. 29), *there were some who pitied Helvidius.*

quis est qui id non maximis efferat laudibus (Lael. 7), *who is there that does not extol it with the highest praises?*
sunt aliae causae quae plane efficiant (Top. 15), *there are other causes which clearly effect, &c.*

b. After **unus** and **solus**: as,

nil admirari prope res est una solaque quae possit facere et servare beatum (Hor. Ep. i. 6), *to wonder at nothing is almost the sole and only thing that can make and keep one happy.*

c. After comparatives followed by **quam**: as,

majores arbores caedebant quam quas ferre miles posset (Liv. xxviii. 5), *they cut larger trees than what a soldier could carry.*
Canachi signa rigidiora sunt quam ut imitentur veritatem (Brut. 18), *the statues of Canachus are too stiff to represent nature.*

d. In expressions of *restriction* or *proviso*, introduced by Relatives: as,

quod sciam, *so far as I know.*
Catonis orationes, quas quidem invenerim (Brut. 17), *the speeches of Cato, at least such as I have discovered.*
servus est nemo, qui modo tolerabili condicione sit servitutis (Cat. iv. 8), *there is not a slave, at least in any tolerable condition of slavery.*

e. When the quality indicated is connected with the action of the main clause, either as Cause on account of which (*since*), or as Hindrance in spite of which (*although*): as,

O virum simplicem qui nos nihil celet (Or. 69), *oh, guileless man, who hides nothing from us!*
egomet qui sero Graecas litteras attigissem tamen complures Athenis dies sum commoratus (De Or. 18), *I myself, though I began Greek literature late, yet, &c.* [lit., *a man who*].

f. **Dignus, indignus, aptus, idoneus,** take a clause of result with a relative (rarely with **ut**); in the poets the Infinitive: as,

idoneus qui impetret (Manil. 19), *fit to obtain.*
dignum notari (Hor. Sat. i. 3), *worthy to be stigmatized.*

66. Intermediate Clauses.

A Relative or other subordinate clause takes the Subjunctive, when it expresses the thought of *some other person* than the speaker or writer, or when it is an integral part of a Subjunctive clause or equivalent

1. The Subjunctive is used in intermediate clauses to express the thought of some other person —

   a. In subordinate clauses in Indirect Discourse (see § **67**).

   b. When the clause depends upon another containing a *wish*, a *command*, or a *question* expressed indirectly, though not indirect discourse proper: as,

> animal sentit quid sit quod deceat (Off. i. 6), *an animal feels what it is that is fit.*
>
> hunc sibi ex animo scrupulum, qui se dies noctesque stimulet ac pungat, ut evellatis postulat (Rosc. Am. 2), *he begs you to pluck from his heart this doubt that goads and stings him day and night.* [Here the relative clause is not a part of the Purpose expressed in *evellatis*, but is an assertion made by the subject of *postulat*.]

   c. When the main clause of a quotation is merged in the verb of *saying*, or some modifier of it: as,

> nisi restituissent statuas, vehementer iis minatur (Verr. iii. 67), *he threatens them violently unless they should restore the statues.* [Here the main clause, "that he will inflict punishment," is contained in *minatur*.]
>
> prohibitio tollendi, nisi pactus esset, vim adhibebat pactioni (id. iv. 14), *the forbidding to take away unless he came to terms gave force to the bargain.*

   d. With a *reason* or an *explanatory fact* introduced by a relative or by **quod** (rarely **quia**): as,

> Favonius mihi quod defendissem leviter succensuit (Att. iii. 1), *Favonius gently chided me for my defence.*
>
> Paetus omnes libros quos pater suus reliquisset mihi donavit (id.), *Paetus presented me all the books his father had left.*

REMARK. — Under this head, even what the speaker himself thought under other circumstances may have the subjunctive. So also with **quod**, even the verb of *saying* may take the subjunctive. To this use also belong **non quia, non quod**, introducing a reason *expressly to deny it.* **Non quo, non quin**, introduce a *result clause,* but with nearly the same meaning as **non quod**: as,

> pugiles ingemiscunt, non quod doleant, sed quia ... (Tusc. ii. 23), *boxers groan not with pain, but, &c.*
>
> non quia philosophia ... percipi non posset (id. i. 1), *not that philosophy cannot be found, &c.*
>
> non quoniam hoc sit necesse (Verr. ii. 9), *not that this is necessary.*

NOTE. — This usage probably originates in apodosis, the condition being the supposed truth of the speaker, the main subject.

2. A clause depending upon another subjunctive clause (or equivalent Infinitive) will also take the subjunctive if it is regarded *as an integral part of that clause:* as, non pugnabo quominus utrum velis eligas (Div. C. 18), *I will not oppose your taking which you will.*

imperat, dum res adjudicetur, hominem ut asservent: cum judicatum sit, ad se adducant (Verr. iv. 22), *he orders them while the affair is under judgment, to keep the man; when he is judged, to bring him to him.*

etenim quis tam dissoluto animo est, qui hæc cum videat, tacere ac neglegere possit (Rosc. Am. 11), *for who is so reckless of spirit, that when he sees these things, he can keep silent and pass them by?*

si tibi hoc Siculi dicerent, nonne id dicerent quod cuivis probare deberent (Div. C. 6), *if the Sicilians said this to you, would they not say a thing which they must prove to everybody?*

mos est Athenis laudari in contione eos qui sint in prœliis interfecti (Or. 44), *it is the custom at Athens for those to be publicly eulogized who have been slain in battle.*

NOTE. — The subjunctive in this use is either a Protasis or Apodosis, and partakes of the nature of the clause on which it depends, — or at least of its original nature. In all cases except *purpose* and *result*, this is clearly seen. In these, the case is undoubtedly the same; as the Purpose has, of course, a future sense, and the Result is a branch of *apodosis*. (See "Essay on the Latin Subjunctive," page 27.)

It is often difficult to distinguish between this construction and the preceding. Thus, in *imperat ut ea fiant quæ opus essent*, **essent** may stand for **sunt**, and then will be Indirect Discourse (under 1, *b*); or it may stand for **erunt**, and will then be Protasis (under 2).

67. INDIRECT DISCOURSE.

A Direct Quotation is one which gives the exact words of the original speaker or writer. An Indirect Quotation is one which adapts the original words to the construction of the sentence in which they are quoted.

REMARK. — The term INDIRECT DISCOURSE (**oratio obliqua**) is used to designate all clauses — even single clauses in a sentence of different construction — which indirectly express the word or thought of any person other than the speaker or writer, or even his own under other circumstances. But it is more strictly used to include those cases only in which the form of Indirect Quotation is given to some *complete proposition or citation*, which may be extended to a narrative or address of any length, — as found in the Speeches of Cæsar and Livy, — the form being dependent on some word of *saying*, &c., with which it is introduced.

The term DIRECT DISCOURSE (**oratio recta**) includes all other forms of expression, whether narration, question, exclam—

1. *Indirect Narrative.* In a Declaratory Sentence in indirect discourse, the principal verb is in the Infinitive, and its subject in the Accusative. All subordinate clauses take the Subjunctive: as,

> esse nonnullos quorum auctoritas plurimum valeat (B. G. i. 17), *there are some, whose influence most prevails.* [In direct discourse, *sunt nonnulli . . . valet.*]
> nisi jurâsset, scelus se facturum [esse] arbitrabatur (Verr. i. 47), *he thought he should incur guilt, unless he should take the oath* [direct, *nisi juravero, faciam*].
> Stoici negant quidquam esse bonum, nisi quod honestum sit (Fin. ii. 21), *the Stoics assert that nothing is good but what is right.* [The verb **nego** is used in preference to **dico** with a negative.]

***a.* Subject-Accusative.** The subject of the infinitive in Indirect Discourse must regularly be expressed, even though it is wanting in the Direct: as,

> orator sum, *I am an orator;* [dicit] se esse oratorem, [he says] *he is an orator.*

But rarely, it is omitted, when it would be easily understood: as,

> ignoscere imprudentiæ dixit (B. G. iv. 27), *he said he pardoned their rashness.*
> rogavi pervenissentne Agrigentum: dixit pervenisse (Verr. iv. 12), *I asked whether they* [the curtains] *had come to Agrigentum: he answered that they had.*

REMARK. — After a relative, or **quam** (*than*), where the verb would be the same as that of the main clause, it is usually omitted, and its subject is attracted into the accusative: as,

> te suspicor eisdem rebus quibus meipsum commoveri (Cat. M. 1), *I suspect that you are disturbed by the same things as I.*

***b.* Relative Clauses.** A subordinate clause *merely explanatory*, and containing statements which are regarded as true independently of the quotation, takes the Indicative. It often depends merely upon the feeling of the writer whether he will use the indicative or subjunctive: as,

> quis neget hæc omnia quæ videmus deorum potestate administrari (Cat. iii. 9), *who can deny that all these things we see are ruled by the power of the gods?*
> cujus ingenio putabat ea quæ gesserat posse celebrari (Arch. 9), *by whose genius he thought that those deeds which he had done could be celebrated.* [Here the fact expressed by *quæ gesserat*, though not explanatory, is felt to be true without regard to the quotation: *quæ gessisset* would mean, what Marius *thought* he had done.]

Remark. — Some clauses introduced by relatives are really independent, and take the accusative and infinitive. Rarely, also, subordinate clauses take this construction. The infinitive construction is regularly continued after a comparative with **quam**: as,

Marcellus requisivisse dicitur Archimedem illum, quem cum audisset interfectum permoleste tulisse (Verr. iv. 58), *Marcellus is said to have sought for Archimedes, and when he heard that he was slain, to have been greatly distressed.*

unumquemque nostrum censent philosophi mundi esse partem, ex quo [= et ex eo] illud naturâ consequi (Fin. iii. 19), *the philosophers say that each one of us is a part of the universe, from which this naturally follows.*

quemadmodum si non dedatur obses pro rupto se fœdus habiturum, sic deditam inviolatam ad suos remissurum (Liv. ii. 13), [he says] *as in case the hostage is not given up he will consider the treaty as broken, so if given up he will return her unharmed to her friends.*

addit se prius occisum iri ab eo quam me violatum iri (Att. ii. 20), *he adds that he himself will be killed by him, before I shall be injured.*

The subjunctive with or without **ut** also occurs with **quam** (see § **70**).

c. **Conditional Sentences.** In a conditional sentence, the Indicative in Apodosis is in any case represented by the corresponding tense of the Infinitive. The Subjunctive is represented by the Future Participle with **fuisse** for the pluperfect, and the Future Infinitive for the other tenses (compare the use of the participle in **urus** with **fui** for the *pluperfect subjunctive*). The Protasis, as a dependent clause, is in all cases Subjunctive: as,

se non defuturum [esse] pollicetur, si audacter dicere velint (B. C. i. 1), *he promises not to fail, if they will speak their minds boldly* [non deëro si voletis].

Note. — The future infinitive, representing the imperfect subjunctive in Protasis, is for some reason very rare, and only four or five examples occur in classic authors. On the contrary, the form with **fuisse** is quite common.

d. **Questions.** A Question coming *immediately after* a verb of asking or the like is treated as an Indirect Question (see below, 2); but questions — generally rhetorical — coming in course of a long indirect discourse are treated like Declaratory Sentences: as,

num etiam recentium injuriarum memoriam [se] deponere posse (B. G. i. 14], *could he lay aside the memory of recent wrongs?* [num possum?]

quem signum daturum fugientibus? quem ausurum Alexandro succedere (Q. C. iii. 5), *who will give the signal on the retreat? who will dare to succeed Alexander?*

Remark. — Generally *real* questions, expecting an answer (chiefly in the *second person*), take the subjunctive. Questions asked by the dubitative subjunctive must retain the subjunctive (see 2, *b*) : as,

quid sibi vellent (B. G. i. 44), *what did they want?* [quid vultis?]

2. Indirect Questions. An Indirect Question takes its verb in the Subjunctive: as,

quid ipse sentiam exponam (Div. i. 6), *I will explain what I think* [direct, *quid sentio*].
id possetne fieri consuluit (id. 7), *he consulted whether it could be done* [direct, *potestne*].
quam sis audax omnes intellegere potuerunt (Rosc. Am. 31), *all could understand how bold you are.*
doleam necne doleam nihil interest (Tusc. ii. 12), *it is of no account whether I suffer or not.*
incerti quidnam esset (Jug. 49), *uncertain what it was.*

Remark. — An Indirect Question is any sentence or clause, introduced by an interrogative word (pronoun, adverb, or particle), depending immediately on a verb, or on any expression implying uncertainty or doubt.

In grammatical form, exclamatory sentences are not distinguished from interrogative, as in the third example given above.

a. The Future Indicative is represented in indirect questions by the participle in **urus** with the subjunctive of **esse**, — rarely by the simple subjunctive: as,

prospicio qui concursus futuri sint (Div. in Caec.), *I foresee what throngs there will be* [erunt].
quid sit futurum cras, fuge quaerere (Hor. Od. i. 9), *forbear to ask what will be on the morrow* [erit; *or* futurum est].

b. The Dubitative Subjunctive referring to future time remains unchanged except in tense: as,

[quaeritur] utrum Carthago diruatur, an Carthaginiensibus reddatur (De Inv. i. 12), [*the question is*] *shall Carthage be destroyed, or restored to the Carthaginians.*
nec quisquam satis certum habet, quid aut speret aut timeat (Liv. xxii. 7), *nor is any one assured what he shall hope or fear.* [Here the participle with **sit** could not be used.]
incerto quid peterent aut vitarent (Liv. xxviii. 36), *since it was doubtful* [abl. abs] *what they should seek or shun.*

c. The Subject of an indirect question is often, in colloquial usage and in poetry, attracted into the main clause as Object (*accusative of anticipation*): as,

nôsti Marcellum quam tardus sit (Fam. viii. 10), *you know how slow Marcellus is.* — In like manner,

potestne igitur earum rerum quare futuræ sint ulla esse præ-
sensio (Div. ii. 5), *can there be, then, any foreknowledge as
to those things, why they will occur ?*

REMARK. — In some cases the Object becomes Subject by a
change of *voice*, and an apparent mixture of relative and interrogative construction is the result: as,

quidam sæpe in parvâ pecuniâ perspiciuntur quam sint leves
(Læl. 17), *it is often seen, in a trifling matter of money, how
unprincipled some people are.*
quemadmodum Pompeium oppugnarent a me indicati sunt
(Leg. Ag. i. 2), *it has been shown by me in what way they
attacked Pompey.*

d. In early Latin and poetry, questions which elsewhere would
have the Subjunctive as indirect often have the Indicative: as,

non reputat quid laboris est (Amph. 172), *he does not consider
what a task it is.*
vineam quo in agro conseri oportet sic observato (Cato R.R 6),
in what soil a vineyard should be set you must observe thus.

NOTE. — These cases are usually considered Direct questions; but
they occur (as above) where the question cannot be translated as
direct without distortion of the meaning.

e. A few expressions properly interrogative are used idiomatically as *indefinites*, and do not take a subjunctive: such are **nescio
quis**, &c., **mirum** (or **nimirum**) **quam** or **quantum**, **immane
quantum**, &c. : as,

qui istam nescio quam indolentiam magnopere laudant (Tusc.
iii. 6), *who greatly extol that painlessness (whatever it is).*
mirum quantum profuit (Liv. ii. 1), *it helped marvellously.*

f. Occasionally, a virtual indirect question is introduced by **si**
in the sense of *whether* (like *if* in English) : as,

circumfunduntur hostes, si quem aditum reperire possent
(B. G. vi. 37), *the enemy pour round* [to see] *if they can find
entrance.*
visam si domi est (Heaut. 118), *I will go see if he is at home.*

3. *Indirect Commands*. All Imperative forms of speech
take the Subjunctive in indirect discourse: as,

reminisceretur veteris incommodi populi Romani (B. G. 13),
remember [said he] *the ancient disaster*, &c. [reminiscere].
ne committeret ut (ib.), *do not* [said he] *bring it about* [ne
commiseris].
finem orandi faciat (id. 20), *let him make an end of entreaty*

The following example may serve to illustrate some of the foregoing principles in a connected address:—

Indirect Discourse.

Si pacem populus Romanus cum Helvetiis *faceret*, in eam partem *ituros* atque ibi *futuros Helvetios*, ubi eos Cæsar *constituisset* atque esse *voluisset:* sin bello persequi *perseveraret*, *reminisceretur* et veteris incommodi populi Romani, et pristinæ virtutis Helvetiorum. Quod improviso unum pagum adortus *esset*, cum ii qui flumen *transissent* suis auxilium ferre non *possent*, ne ob eam rem aut *suæ* magno opere virtuti *tribueret*, aut *ipsos despiceret:* se ita a patribus majoribusque *suis didicisse*, ut magis virtute quam dolo *contenderent*, aut insidiis *niterentur*. Quare ne *committeret*, ut *is* locus ubi *constitissent* ex calamitate populi Romani et internecione exercitûs nomen *caperet*, aut memoriam *proderet*.—B. G. i. 13.

Direct Discourse.

Si pacem populus Romanus cum Helvetiis *faciet*, in eam partem *ibunt* atque ibi *erunt, Helvetii*, ubi eos Cæsar *constituerit* atque esse *voluerit:* sin bello persequi *perseverabit*, *reminiscere* [inquit] et veteris incommodi populi Romani, et pristinæ virtutis Helvetiorum. Quod improviso unum pagum adortus *es*, cum ii qui flumen *transierant* suis auxilium ferre non *possent*, ne ob eam rem aut tuæ magno opere virtuti *tribueris*, aut *nos despexeris: nos* ita a patribus majoribusque *nostris didicimus*, ut magis virtute quam dolo *contendamus*, aut insidiis *nitamur*. Quare, ne *commiseris*, ut *hic* locus ubi *constitimus* ex calamitate populi Romani et internecione exercitûs nomen *capiat*, aut memoriam *prodat*.

68. Wishes and Commands.

1. Wishes are expressed by the Subjunctive, often strengthened by the particles **ut, utinam, O si** (early Latin), **qui**; the primary tenses being used in reference to future time, the secondary to express a hopeless wish,—the imperfect in present time, the pluperfect in past (see § 57, 4).

Remark.—A periphrasis with **velim, vellem**, &c., is sometimes used (57, 4, *c*).

2. Commands are expressed by the Imperative or Subjunctive (§ 57, 3, 7); Prohibitions by the Subjunctive, or by a periphrasis with **noli** or **cave** (§ 57, 7, *a*). The object of the command is given in a *purpose-clause* (§ 70, 3) with **ut** or **ne**, except after **jubeo** and **veto** (§ 70, 2).

3. Indirectly quoted, all these forms of speech take the Subjunctive (see § 67, 3).

69. Relative Clauses.

1. A simple relative, merely introducing a descriptive fact, takes the Indicative.

2. The Subjunctive appears more or less frequently in many relative clauses (which have been already treated). These relatives always either — (1) are general relatives of Protasis; or (2) express some *logical connection* between the relative and antecedent, or (3) have no effect at all upon the construction. These constructions are —

1. General or Future Conditions in Protasis (§§ **59, 60, 61**).
2. *a.* Final Clauses (§ **64**).
  b. Consecutive Clauses (§ **65**).
  c. Relatives of Characteristic (§ **65, 2**).
  d. Relatives implying Cause or Hindrance (§ **65, 2, *e***).
  e. Temporal Clauses of relative time (**62, 2**).
3. *a.* Intermediate Clauses (§ **66**).
  b. Clauses in Indirect Discourse (§ **67**).

70. Substantive Clauses.

A Substantive Clause is one which, like a noun, is the subject or object of a verb, or in apposition with a subject or object.

REMARK. — The Infinitive with the Accusative, though not strictly a Clause, is equivalent to one, and may be treated as such.

When a substantive clause is used as Subject, the verb to which it is subject is called Impersonal (§ **39**), and its sign, in English, is IT; when it is used as Object, it generally follows some verb of *knowing*, &c. (§ **67**, 1) or of *wishing* or *effecting*, and its sign, in English, is THAT, or TO (Infinitive).

1. *Classification.* Substantive Clauses are of four kinds: — 1. The Accusative with the Infinitive, denoting an idea as *thought* or *spoken* (§ **67**, 1); 2. Indirect Questions (**67, 2**); 3. The Subjunctive with **ut, ne, quo, quin,** or

quominus, denoting *purpose* or *result;* 4. The Indicative with **quod**, denoting a *fact.* But the Infinitive alone may take the place of either 1 or 3.

2. *Accusative and Infinitive.* The Accusative with the Infinitive is used as the Object — 1. Of all verbs and expressions of *knowing, thinking, and telling* (Indirect Discourse, § 67, 1); 2. Of **jubeo** and **veto**, and rarely of other verbs of *commanding, requesting, admonishing,* and the like; 3. Sometimes of verbs of *wishing:* as,

> dicit montem ab hostibus teneri (B. G. i. 22), *he says that the height is held by the enemy.*
> negat ullos patere portus (Liv. xxviii. 43), *he says that no ports are open.*
> Labienum jugum montis adscendere jubet (id. 21), *he orders Labienus to ascend the ridge of the hill.*
> judicem esse me non doctorem volo (Ov. 33), *I wish to be a judge, not a teacher.*

a. **After Passives.** If the main verb is changed to the passive, either (1) the Subject of the infinitive (like other objects of active verbs) becomes *nominative,* and the infinitive is retained; or (2) the passive is used *impersonally,* and the clause retained as its Object. With verbs of *saying,* &c., the former construction is more common, especially in the tenses of incomplete action; with **jubeo** and **veto** it is always used: as,

> primi traduntur arte quadam verba vinxisse (Or. 13), *they first are related to have joined words with a certain skill.*
> jussus es renuntiari consul (Phil. ii. 32), *you were under orders to be declared consul.*
> in lautumias Syracusanas deduci imperantur (Verr. v. 27), *they are ordered to be taken to the stone-pits of Syracuse.*
> hic accusare non est situs (Sest. 44), *he was not allowed to accuse.*
> prædicari de se ac nominari volunt (Arch. 10), *they wish to be talked of and known by name.* [Here the passive is used impersonally.]
> voluntariâ morte interîsse creditus est (Tac. H. iv. 67), *he was thought to have perished by voluntary death.*
> nuntiatur piratarum naves esse in portu (Verr. v. 24), *it is told that the ships of the pirates are in port.*

b. The poets extend the use of the passive to verbs which are not properly **verba sentiendi**: as,

> colligor dominæ placuisse (Ov. Am. ii. 6, 61), *it is gathered* [from this memorial] *that I pleased my mistress.*

c. Such indirect discourse may depend on any word *implying* speech or thought, though not strictly a verb of *saying*, &c.: as,

eos redire jubet: se in tempore adfuturum esse (Liv. xxiv. 13), *he orders them to return* [promising] *that he will be at hand in season.*

orantes ut urbibus saltem — jam enim agros *deploratos esse* — opem senatus ferret (id. xvi. 6), *praying that the senate would bring aid to the cities — for the fields* [they said] *were already given up as lost.*

d. Verbs of *promising, expecting, threatening, swearing,* and the like, regularly take the construction of Indirect Discourse, contrary to the English idiom (§ **67,** 1, *a*); but sometimes a simple complementary infinitive: as,

me spero liberatum [esse] metu (Tusc. ii. 27), *I trust I have been freed from fear.*
minatur sese abire (Asin. iii. 3), *he threatens to go away.* [Direct, abeo, *I am going away.*]
ex quibus sperant se maximum fructum esse capturos (Læl. 21), *from which they hope to gain the utmost advantage.*
quem inimicissimum futurum esse promitto ac spondeo (Mur. 41), *who I promise and warrant will be the bitterest of enemies.*
dolor fortitudinem se debilitaturum minatur (Tusc. v. 27), *pain threatens to wear down fortitude.*
pollicentur obsides dare (B. G. iv. 21), *they promise to give hostages* [compare Greek aorist infinitive after similar verbs.]

3. *Clauses of Purpose.* The clause with **ut** (negative **ne**), developed from PURPOSE, is used as the Object of all verbs denoting an action *directed towards the future.* Such are —

a. Verbs of *commanding, asking, admonishing, urging,* and in general those denoting an *influence* upon some one (§ **64**). These verbs rarely take the Infinitive (except **jubeo** and **veto**, which take it regularly): as,

his uti conquirerent imperavit (B. G. i. 2), *he ordered them to search.*
monent ut omnes suspiciones vitet (id. 20), *he warns him to avoid all suspicion.*

b. Verbs of *wishing* and the like. These take also the simple Infinitive; more commonly when the subject remains the same, less commonly when it is different (see 2, above): as,

cupio ut impetret (Capt. i. 2), *I wish he may get it.*
cum nostri perspici cuperent (B. G. iii. 21), *when our men wished it to be seen.*

mallem Cerberum metueres (Tusc. i. 6), *I would rather you feared Cerberus.*
quos non tam ulcisci studeo quam sanare (Cat. ii. 8), *whom I do not care so much to punish as to cure.*

  c. Verbs of *permission, concession,* and *necessity.* These take also the Infinitive: as,

permisit ut partes faceret (De Or. ii. 90), *permitted him to make divisions.*
vinum importari non sinunt (B. G. iv. 2), *they do not allow wine to be imported.*
nullo se implicari negotio passus est (Lig. 3), *he suffered himself to be tangled in no business.*
sint enim oportet si miseri sunt (Tusc. i. 6), *they must exist, if they are wretched.*

REMARK. — The clause with **licet** (usually without **ut**) is regularly used to express a concession in the sense of *although.*

  d. Verbs of *determining, resolving, bargaining,* which also take the Infinitive. Those of *decreeing* often take the participle in **dus**, on the principle of *indirect discourse:* as,

edicto ne quis injussu pugnaret (Liv. v. 19), *having commanded that none should fight without orders.*
pacto ut victorem res sequeretur (id. xxviii. 21), *having bargained that the property should belong to the victor.*
Regulus captivos reddendos non censuit (Off. i. 13), *Regulus voted that the captives should be returned.* [He said, in giving his opinion, *captivi non reddendi sunt.*]

  e. Verbs of *caution* and *effort.* Those denoting an *effort to hinder* may also take **quominus** or **ne**: as,

cura et provide ut nequid ei desit (Att. ii. 3), *take care and see that he lacks nothing.*
non deterret sapientem mors quominus ... (Tusc. i. 38), *death does not deter the wise man from, &c.*
ne facerem impedivit (Fat. i. 1), *prevented me from doing.*

  f. Verbs of *fearing* take the Subjunctive, with **ne** affirmative and **ne non** or **ut** negative: as,

ne animum offenderet verebatur (B. G. i. 19), *he feared he should offend the mind, &c.*
vereor ut tibi possim concedere (De Or. i. 9), *I fear I cannot grant you.*
haud sane periculum est ne non mortem optandam putet (Tusc. v. 40), *there is no danger of his not thinking death desirable.*

REMARK. — The particle **ut** or **ne** is often omitted, — generally after verbs of *wishing, necessity, permission*; with **cave, dic, fac**; and in indirect discourse, frequently after verbs of *commanding* and the like.

g. With any verbs of the above classes, the poets may use the Infinitive: as,

hortamur fari (Æn. ii. 74), *we exhort* [him] *to speak.*

4. *Clauses of Result.* The clause with **ut** (negative **ut non**, &c.), developed from RESULT, is used as the Object of verbs denoting the *accomplishment of an effort:* as,

commeatus ut portari possent efficiebat (B. G. ii. 5), *he made it possible that supplies could be bought.* [Lit., he effected that, &c.]

a. The substantive clause becomes the Subject of such verbs in the passive; and hence is further used as the subject of verbs denoting *it happens, it remains, it follows,* and the like; and even of the simple **esse** in the same sense, and other phrases: as,

sequitur ut doceam (N. D. ii. 32), *the next thing is to show, &c.*
accidit ut esset plena luna (B. G. iv. 29), *it chanced to be full moon.*
accedit ut conturber (Deiot. 1), *besides this I am troubled.*
reliquum est quarta virtus ut sit ipsa frugalitas (id.), *it remains that the fourth virtue is thrift.*
quando fuit ut quod licet non liceret (Cæl. 20), *when was it that what is now allowed was not allowed?*

b. A result clause, with or without **ut**, frequently follows **quam**, after a comparative: as,

perpessus est omnia potius quam indicaret (Tusc. i. 22), *he endured all, rather than betray, &c.*

c. A result clause with **ut** is often used elliptically, in exclamations, with or without **-ne** (compare § 57, 8, *g*): as,

quanquam quid loquor? te ut ulla res frangat (Cat. i. 9), *yet why do I ask? that anything should bend you!*
egone ut te interpellem (Tusc. ii. 18), *what, I interrupt you?*

REMARK. — The infinitive, in exclamations, usually refers to something actually occurring; the subjunctive to something contemplated.

d. The phrase **tantum abest**, *it is so far* [from being the case], besides a subject-clause (*substantive*) with **ut**, regularly takes another **ut**-clause (of *result*) depending on **tantum**: as,

tantum abest **ut** nostra miremur, **ut** usque eo difficiles ac morosi simus, **ut** nobis non satisfaciat ipse Demosthenes (Or. 29), *so far from admiring our own matters, we are difficult and captious to that degree, that not Demosthenes himself satisfies us.* [Here the first **ut**-clause depends directly on *abest;* the second on *tantum;* and the third on *usque eo.*]

e. The expressions **facere ut, committere ut,** often form a periphrasis for the simple verb (compare **fore ut** for the future infinitive): as,

> invitus feci ut Flamininum e senatu eicerem (Cat. M. 12), *it was with reluctance that I expelled, &c.*

f. Rarely, a thought or idea is considered as a result, and takes the subjunctive with **ut** instead of the accusative and infinitive (in this case a demonstrative usually precedes): as,

> altera est res, ut... (Off. i. 20), *the second point is that, &c.*
> praeclarum illud est, ut eos... amemus (Tusc. iii. 29), *this is a noble thing, that we should love, &c.*
> quae est igitur amentia, ut... *what folly is there then in demanding, &c.*

g. Verbs and other expressions which imply *hindering* and the like, may take **quin** *when the main verb is negative*, formally or virtually: as,

> facere non possum quin... (Att. xii. 27), *I cannot avoid, &c.*
> nihil praetermisi quin scribam... (Q. F. iii. 3), *I have left nothing undone to write.*
> ut nullā re impedirer quin (Att. iv. 2), *that I might be hindered by nothing from, &c.*
> non humana ulla neque divina obstant quin (Sall. Ep. Mith. 17), *no human or divine laws prevent, but that, &c.*

REMARK. — This usage is found especially with the phrase **non dubito** and similar expressions making a kind of indirect discourse: as,

> non dubitabat quin ei crederemus (Att. vi. 2), *he did not doubt that we believed him.*
> illud cave dubites quin ego omnia faciam (Fam. v. 20), *do not doubt that I will do all.*
> quis ignorat quin (Flacc. 27), *who is ignorant that, &c. ?*
> neque ambigitur quin Brutus pessimo publico id facturus fuerit si priorum regum alicui regnum extorsisset (Livy, ii. 1), *nor is there any question that Brutus, if he had wrested the kingdom from any one of the former kings, would have done it with the worst results to the state* [direct discourse, *fecisset*].

h. Some verbs and expressions may be used either as verbs of *saying* as well as of *commanding* or *effecting* and the like, and may be construed accordingly: as,

> sequitur illico esse causas immutabiles (Fat. 12), *it follows directly that there are unalterable causes.* [The regular construction with *sequor* used of a logical sequence.]
> laudem sapientiae statuo esse maximam (Div. v. 13), *I hold that the glory of wisdom is the greatest.*

statuunt ut decem milia hominum mittantur (B. G. xii. 21), *they resolve that 10,000 men shall be sent.*
res ipsa monebat tempus esse (Att. x. 8), *the thing itself warned that it was time* [monere ut, *warn to do something*].
fac mihi esse persuasum (N. D. i. 27), *suppose that I am persuaded of that* [facere ut, *accomplish that*].
hoc volunt persuadere non interire animos (B. G. vi. 13), *they wish to convince that souls do not perish.*
huic persuadet uti ad hostes transeat (B. G. iii. 18), *persuades him to pass over to the enemy.*

NOTE. — The infinitive, with a subject, in this construction is indirect discourse, and is to be distinguished from the simple infinitive sometimes found with these verbs.

5. *Indicative with* quod. The clause in the Indicative with **quod** is used (more commonly as Subject) when the statement is *regarded as a fact:* as,

alterum est vitium, quod quidam nimis magnum studium conferunt (Off. i. 6), *it is another fault, that some bestow too much zeal, &c.* [Here **ut** with the subjunctive could be used, meaning that they *should*, or the accusative and infinitive, meaning *to* more abstractly; **quod** makes it a fact that men *do*, &c.]
inter inanimum et animal hoc maxime interest, quod animal agit aliquid (Ac. ii. 12), *there is this chief difference, &c., that an animal has an aim.*
quod rediit nobis mirabile videtur (Off. iii. 31), *that he* [Regulus] *returned seems wonderful to us.* [Redisse would mean he *should have returned.*]

a. In colloquial language, the clause with **quod** appears as an *accusative of specification*, corresponding to the English WHEREAS: as,

quod de domo scribis (Fam. xiv. 2), *as to what you write of the house.*
quod mihi de nostro statu gratularis, minime miramur te tuis praeclaris operibus laetari (Att. i. 5), *as to your congratulating me on our condition, no wonder you are pleased with your own noble works.*

b. Verbs of *feeling* and its expression take either **quod** (**quia**) or the accusative and infinitive (Indirect Discourse) : as,

quod scribis ... gaudeo (Q. F. iii. 1). *I am glad that you write.*
quae perfecta esse vehementer laetor (Rosc. Am. 47), *I greatly rejoice that this is finished.*
facio libenter quod eam non possum praeterire (Leg. i. 24). *I am glad that I cannot pass it by.*

REMARK. — Rarely, an apparent substantive clause, with **miror** and similar expressions, is introduced by **si** (really a Protasis) : as,

miror si quemquam amicum habere potuit (Lael. 15), *I should wonder if he could ever have a friend.*

71. Questions.

Questions are introduced by Interrogative Pronouns, Adverbs, or Particles, and are not distinguished by the order of words, as in English.

The Interrogative Particles are, **an, utrum, num,** and the enclitic **-ne** (see page 86). For other interrogative words, see list, page 49.

1. *Interrogative Particles.* The enclitic **-ne** is used in questions asked *for information merely;* **nonne,** when the answer *yes,* and **num** when the answer *no,* is expected or implied: as,

> meministine me in senatu dicere (Cat. i. 3), *do you remember my saying in the senate?*
> nonne animadvertis quam multi salvi pervenerint (N. D. iii. 37), *do you not observe how many have come through safe?*
> num dubium est (Rosc. Am. 37), *there is no doubt, is there?*

REMARK. — The interrogative particle is sometimes omitted: as,

> patere tua consilia non sentis (Cat. i. 1), *do you not see that your plans are manifest?*

a. In Indirect Questions, **num** loses its peculiar force: as,

> quæro num aliter evenirent (Fat. 3). *I ask whether they would turn out differently.*

b. The form of Indirect questions is the same as that of Direct; the difference being only in the verb, which regularly takes the subjunctive (§ **71,** 2).

REMARK. — In English, indirect questions are introduced by interrogatives, or by the particle *whether.*

c. The enclitic -ne is often added to interrogative words when not required: as, **utrumne, numne, anne.**

d. The expressions **nescio an, dubito an,** and the like, incline to the Affirmative, — *I don't know but.*

2. *Double Questions.* In Double or Alternative Questions, **utrum** or **-ne,** *whether,* stands in the first member; **an, anne,** *or;* **annon, necne,** *or not,* in the second: as,

> utrum nescis, an pro nihilo id putas (Fam. x. 26), *don't you know? or do you think nothing of it?*

quæro servosne an liberos (Rosc. Am. 27). *I ask whether slaves or free.* [Here *servos aut liberos* would mean, *were there any*, either slaves or free.]

REMARK. — In direct questions, **annon** is more frequently found in the alternative; in indirect, **necne**.

a. The interrogative particle is often omitted in the first member; when **-ne (anne, necne)** may stand in the second: as,

Gabinio dicam anne Pompeio (Manil. 19), *shall I say to Gabinius or to Pompey?*
sunt hæc tua verba necne (Tusc. iii. 18), *are these your words or not?*

b. Sometimes the first member is omitted or implied; and **an (anne)** alone asks a question — usually with indignation or surprise: as,

an tu miseros putas illos (Tusc. i. 7), *what! do you think those men wretched?*

c. The second member may be omitted, when **utrum** asks a question to which there is no alternative: as,

utrum in clarissimis est civibus is quem. . . . (Flacc. 19), *is he among the noblest citizens, whom, &c.*

d. The following exhibits the various forms of alternative questions: —

utrum . . . an
—— . . . an (anne)
-ne . . . an
—— . . . ne

3. *Question and Answer.* As there is no word in Latin meaning simply *yes* or *no*, in answering a question the verb is generally repeated: as,

valetne, *is he well?* valet, *yes* (*he is well*).
eratne tecum, *was he with you?* non erat, *no* (*he was not*).

a. An intensive or negative particle is sometimes used in answer to a direct question: thus **immo** (*nay but*), **vero** (*in truth*), or **etiam** (*even so*) may have the meaning of *yes*; and **non** (*not*), or **minime** (*least-of-all*), of *no*.

b. In the answer to an alternative question, one member of the alternative must be repeated: as,

tune an frater erat, *was it you or your brother?*
ego [eram], *it was I.*

NOTE. — *Tune aut pater* would mean, *was it either of you?*

72. PARTICIPLES.

The Participle expresses the action of the verb in the form of an adjective; but has a partial distinction of tense, and generally governs the case of its verb.

1. *Distinctions of Tense.* The Present participle denotes the action as *not completed;* the Perfect as *completed;* the Future as *still to take place.*

a. **Present.** The Present participle has several of the irregular uses of the present indicative (compare § 58, 2): as,

> quærenti mihi jamdiu certa res nulla veniebat in mentem (Fam. iv. 13), *though I had long sought, no certain thing came to my mind* (cf. ib. *a*).
> C. Flaminio restitit agrum Picentem dividenti (Cat. M. 4), *he resisted Flaminius while attempting to divide, &c.* (cf. *b*).
> iens in Pompeianum bene mane hæc scripsi (Att. iv. 9), *I write this when about going to my place at Pompeii* (cf. *c*).

Hence it is used in late writers to denote *purpose.*

b. **Perfect.** The Perfect participle of a few deponent verbs is used nearly in the sense of a Present. Such are, regularly, **ratus, solitus, veritus;** commonly, **fisus, ausus, secutus,** and occasionally others, especially in later writers: as,

> cohortatus milites docuit (B. C. iii. 80), *encouraging the men, he showed, &c.*
> iratus dixisti (Mur. 30), *you spoke in a passion.*
> oblitus auspicia (Phil. i. 13), *forgetting the auspices.*
> insidias veritus (B. G. ii. 11), *fearing ambuscade.*
> imperio potitus (Liv. xxi. 2), *holding the command.*
> ad pugnam congressi (id. iv. 10), *meeting in fight.*
> rem incredibilem rati (Sall. C. 48), *thinking it incredible.*

c. The present participle, wanting in the Passive, is usually supplied by a clause with **dum** or **cum**; rarely by the participle in **dus**: as,

> Dic, hospes, Spartæ, nos te hic vidisse jacentes,
>   Dum sanctis patriæ legibus obsequimur.
> *Tell it, stranger, at Sparta, that we lie here obedient to our country's sacred laws.* [Here *dum obsequimur* is a translation of the Greek πειθόμενοι.]
> crucibus adfixi aut flammandi (Ann. xv. 44), *crucified or set on fire* [compare note under § **73**].

2. *Adjective use*. The present and perfect participles are used sometimes as attributes, nearly like adjectives: as,

> cum antiquissimam sententiam tum comprobatam (Div. i. 5), *a view at once most ancient and approved.*
> signa nunquam fere ementientia (id. 9), *signs hardly ever deceitful.*
> auspiciis utuntur coactis (id. 15), *they use forced auspices.*

a. Thus they are used, like adjectives, as nouns: as,

> sibi indulgentes et corpori deservientes (Leg. i. 13), *the self-indulgent, and slaves to the body.*
> recte facta paria esse debent (Par. iii. 1), *right deeds ought to be like in value.*
> male parta male dilabuntur (Phil. ii. 27), *ill got, ill spent.*
> consuetudo valentis (De Or. ii. 44), *the habit of a man in health.*

b. So, also, they are connected with nouns by **esse** and similar verbs: as,

> videtis ut senectus sit operosa et semper agens aliquid et moliens (Cat. M. 8), *you see how busy old age is, always aiming and trying at something.*
> Gallia est omnis divisa (B. G. i. 1), *all Gaul is divided.*
> locus qui nunc sæptus est (Liv. i. 8), *the place which is now enclosed.*

c. From this adjective use arise the compound tenses of the passive, — the participle of *completed action* with the incomplete tenses of **esse** developing the idea of past time: as,

> interfectus est, *he was* (or *has been*) *killed*, lit., *he is having-been-killed* [i.e., *already slain*].

d. In the best writers (as Cicero) this participle, when used with the tenses of *completed action*, retains its proper force; but in later writers the two sets of tenses (as, **amatus sum** or **fui**) are often used indiscriminately: as,

> [leges] cum quæ latæ sunt tum vero quæ promulgatæ fuerunt (Sest. 25), *the laws, both those which were proposed, and those which were published.* [The *proposal* of the laws was a single act: hence *latæ sunt* is a pure perfect. The *publishing*, or *posting*, was a continued state, which is indicated by *promulgatæ*, and *fuerunt* is the pure perfect.]
> arma quæ fixa in parietibus fuerant, humi inventa sunt (Div. i. 34), *the arms which had been fastened on the walls were found upon the ground.* [Compare *occupati sunt et fuerunt* (Off. i. 17): the difference between this and the preceding is, that *occupatus* can be used only as an adjective.]

3. *Predicate use*. The Present and Perfect participles are often used as a predicate, where in English a clause would be used to express *time, cause, occasion, condition, concession, characteristic, manner, circumstance:* as,

> vereor ne turpe sit dicere incipientem (Mil. 1), *I fear it may be a dishonor* [to me] *when beginning to speak.*
> salutem insperantibus reddidisti (Marc. 7), *you have restored a safety which we did not hope.*
> nemo ei neganti non credidisset (Mil. 19), *no one would have disbelieved him when he denied.*

REMARK. — This use is especially frequent in the Ablative Absolute (see § 54, 10, *b* and Note). A co-ordinate clause is sometimes compressed into a perfect participle; and a participle with a negative expresses the same idea which in English is given by *without:* as,

> imprudentibus nostris (B. G. v. 15), *while our men were not looking.*
> miserum est nihil proficientem angi (N. D. iii. 5), *it is wretched to vex one's self without effecting anything.*
> instructos ordines in locum æquum deducit (Sall. C. 59), *he draws up the lines, and leads them to level ground.*
> ut hos transductos necaret (B. G. v. 5), *that he might carry them over and put them to death.*

a. A noun and passive participle are often so united that the participle and not the noun contains the main idea (compare the participle in indirect discourse in Greek: G. 280): as,

> ante conditam condendamve urbem (Liv. Pref.), *before the city was built or building.*
> illi libertatem civium Romanorum imminutam non tulerunt; vos vitam ereptam negligetis (Manil. 5), *they did not endure the infringement of the citizens' liberty; will you disregard the destruction of their life?*

So with **opus**: as,

> opus est viatico facto (Plaut. Trin.), *there is need of laying in provision.*
> maturato opus est (Livy viii. 13), *there is no need of haste.*
> [Here there is no noun, as the verb is used impersonally.]

b. The perfect participle with **habeo** (rarely with other verbs) is almost the same in meaning as a perfect active: as,

> fidem quem habent spectatam jam et diu cognitam (Div. C. 4), *my fidelity, which they have proved and long known.*

(Hence the perfect with *have* in modern languages.)

c. The perfect participle, with verbs of *effecting, effort,* or the like (also with **volo** where **esse** may be understood, cf. § 70, 3, *b*), expresses more forcibly the idea of the verb: as,

> præfectos suos multi missos fecerunt (Verr. iv. 58), *many discharged their officers.*

hic transactum reddet omne (Capt. 345), *he will get it all done.*
me excusatum volo (Verr. i. 40), *I wish to be excused.*

d. The present participle is sometimes nearly equivalent to an infinitive, but expresses the action more vividly (after **facio, induco**, and the like, used of authors, and after verbs of *sense*): as,

Xenophon facit Socratem disputantem (N. D. i. 11), *Xenophon represents Socrates disputing.*

4. *Future Participle.* The Future Participle (except **futurus** and **venturus**) is rarely used in simple agreement with a noun, except by later writers.

a. The future participle is chiefly used with **esse** in a periphrastic conjugation (see § **40**, *a*): as,

morere, Diagora, non enim in cælum adscensurus es (Tusc. i. 46), *die, for you are not likely to go to heaven.*
conclave illud ubi erat mansurus si ... (Div. i. 15), *that chamber where he would have staid if, &c.*
sperat adolescens diu se victurum (Cat. M. 19), *the young man hopes to live long* (§ **67**, 1).
neque petiturus unquam consulatum videretur (Off. iii. 20), *and seemed unlikely ever to seek the consulship.*

By later writers it is also used in simple agreement to express likelihood or purpose, or even an apodosis: as,

cum leo regem invasurus incurreret (Q. C. viii. 1), *when a lion rushed on to attack the king.*
rediit belli casum de integro tentaturus (Liv. xvii. 62), *he returned to try the chances of war anew.*
ausus est rem plus famæ habituram (Liv. ii. 10), *he dared a thing which would have more repute.*

[See also examples in § **59**, 1, *b*.]

b. With past tenses of **esse**, the future participle is often equivalent to the pluperfect subjunctive (§ **59**, 3, *e*).

5. *Gerundive.* The Gerundive, in its participial or adjective use, denotes *necessity* or *propriety.*

a. The gerundive is sometimes used, like the present and perfect participles, in simple agreement with a noun: as,

fortem et conservandum virum (Mil. 38), *a brave man, and worthy to be preserved.*

b. The most frequent use of the gerundive is with **esse** in a second periphrastic conjugation (§ **40**, *b*): as,

non agitanda res erit (Verr. vi. 70), *will not the thing have to be agitated?*

REMARK. — The gerundive in this construction is *passive* in meaning. But in early Latin, and occasionally elsewhere, it is used impersonally, governing the accusative ; and it is regularly so used with **utor, fruor,** &c., governing the ablative (sometimes called the nominative of the gerund): as,

via quam nobis ingrediendum sit (Cat. M. 2), *the way we have to enter.*

agitandumst vigilias (Trin. 869), *I have got to stand guard.*

[Compare Greek verbal in -τέος, G. 281.]

c. It is also used to denote purpose after verbs signifying *to give, deliver, agree for, have, receive, undertake, demand:* as,

redemptor qui columnam illam conduxerat faciendam (Div. ii. 21), *the contractor who had undertaken to make that column* [the regular construction with this class of verbs].

ædem Castoris habuit tuendam (Verr. ii. 50), *he had the temple of Castor to take care of.*

naves atque onera diligenter adservanda curabat (id. vi. 56), *he took care that the ships and cargoes should be kept.*

For the Gerundive after verbs of *decreeing,* see § **70**, 3, *d.*

For the AblatIVE Absolute, see § **54**, 10, *b.*

73. Gerund and Gerundive.

1. *Gerund.* The Gerund is a verbal noun, retaining the government of the verb, and modified by adverbs, but in grammatical construction following the same rules as nouns.

REMARK. — The use of the Gerund, in the oblique cases, corresponds to the use of the Infinitive as Subject (§ **57**, 8, *a*), its nominative form being found only in the impersonal use of the participle in **dus:** as,

ars bene disserendi et vera ac falsa dijudicandi (De Or. ii. 38), *the art of discoursing well, and distinguishing the true and false.* [Here the verbal nouns *discoursing* and *distinguishing,* if used in the nominative, would be expressed by the infinitive *disserere* and *dijudicare.*]

juveni parandum, seni utendum est (Sen. Ep. 36), *it is for the young to get, for the old to enjoy* (compare § **51**, 3, 4).

2. *Gerundive.* When the gerund would have an object in the accusative, the Gerundive is generally used instead, agreeing with the noun, and in the case which the gerund would have had: as,

paratiores ad omnia pericula subeunda (B. G. i. 5), *readier to undergo all dangers.* [Here *subeunda* agrees with *pericula,* which is itself governed by *ad:* the construction with the gerund would be, *ad subeundum, &c.; ad* governing the gerund, and the gerund governing the accusative *pericula.*]

exercendæ memoriæ gratiâ (Off. i. 15), *for the sake of training the memory.* [Here the gerund construction would be, *exercendi memoriam.*]

REMARK. — The verbs **utor, fruor,** &c. (§ **54,** 6, *d*), are treated like verbs governing the Accusative, as they do in early Latin: as,

expetuntur divitiæ ad perfruendas voluptates (Off. i. 8), *riches are sought for the enjoyment of pleasure.*

NOTE. — The gerundive construction is probably the original one. The Participle in **dus** seems to have had a present passive force as in *secundus* (from *sequor*), *rotundus, volvendis, annis* (Virg.), *flammandi* (Tac.), from which the idea of necessity was developed through that of futurity, as in the development of the subjunctive. *Consilium urbis delendæ* would thus have meant a plan of a city being destroyed [in process of destruction], then about to be destroyed, then to be destroyed, then a plan of destroying the city, the two words becoming fused together as in *ab urbe conditâ.* The gerund is simply an impersonal use of the participle, in its original present sense, retaining the case of its verb, as in *agitandum est vigilias; quid opus est facto?*

3. Construction. The Gerund (if of transitive verbs, with a noun in government) and the Gerundive (with a noun in agreement) are used, in the oblique cases, in the constructions of nouns, as follows: —

a. **Genitive.** The Genitive is used after nouns or adjectives in the constructions of the *objective genitive* (§ **50,** 3); more rarely in the predicate after **esse,** or as a genitive of *quality:* as,

neque consilii habendi neque arma capiendi spatio dato (B. G. iv. 14), *time being given neither for forming plans nor for taking arms* [objective genitive after *spatio*].
ne conservandæ quidam patriæ causâ (Off. i. 45), *not even in order to save the country.*
vivendi finis est optimus (Cat. M. 20), *it is the best end of life.*
non tam commutandarum rerum quam evertendarum cupidos (id. ii. 1), *desirous not so much of changing as of destroying the state.*
quæ res evertendæ reipublicæ solent esse (Verr. iii. 53), *which things generally tend to the overthrow of the commonwealth.*
cognoscendæ antiquitatis (Ann. ii. 59), *to study old times.* [Here *gratiâ* is, by a rare construction, omitted.]

The genitive of the Gerund is, in a few cases, used (like a noun) with the genitive of an object agreeing neither in gender nor number: as,

ejus videndi cupidus (Ter. Hec.), *eager to see her.*
reiciendi trium judicum potestas (Inv. ii. 2), *the power of challenging three jurors.*

REMARK. — In the genitive, the construction of the gerund and gerundive are about equally common.

***b*. Dative.** The Dative is used after the adjectives (and rarely nouns) which are followed by the dative of nouns (§ **51,** 6); also, in a few expressions after verbs: as,

> præesse agro colendo (Rosc. Am. 18), *to take charge of tillage.*
> esse solvendo, *to be able to pay.*
> genus armorum aptum tegendis corporibus (Liv. xxxii. 10), *a sort of armor suited to the defence of the body.*
> reliqua tempora demetiendis fructibus et percipiendis accommodata sunt (Cat. M. 19), *the other seasons are fitted to reap and gather in the harvest.*
> diem præstituit operi faciendo (Verr. ii. 56), *he appointed a day for doing the work.*

It is also used in certain phrases belonging to the civil law, after nouns meaning officers, offices, elections, &c.: as,

> comitia consulibus rogandis (Div. i. 17), *elections for nominating consuls.*
> triumvirum coloniis deducundis (Jug. 42), *a triumvir for leading out colonies.*

***c*. Accusative.** The Accusative is used after the prepositions **ad, inter, circa, ob** (rarely **in** and **ante**); most frequently after **ad,** denoting *purpose* (compare § **72,** 4): as,

> vivis non ad deponendam sed ad confirmandam audaciam (Cat. i. 2), *you live, not to put off, but to confirm your daring.*
> inter agendum (Ecl. ix. 24), *while driving.*
> me vocas ad scribendum (Or. 10), *you call me to write.*

***d*. Ablative.** The Ablative is used to express *means* or *instrument;* also *manner* (often by later writers, in a sense equivalent to the present participle); after *comparatives;* and after the prepositions **ab, de, ex, in,** and (rarely) **pro** and **cum:** as,

> multa pollicendo persuadet (Jug. 46), *he persuades by large promises.*
> his ipsis legendis (Cat. M. 7), *by reading these very things.*
> nullum officium referendâ gratiâ magis necessarium est (Off. i. 15), *no duty is more important than gratitude.*
> in re gerendâ versari (Cat. M. 6), *to be employed in affairs.*
> Latine loquendo cuivis par (Brut. 34), *equal to any man in speaking Latin.*
> nullis virtutis præceptis tradendis (Off. i. 2), *without giving any precepts of virtue.*
> obscuram atque humilem conciendo ad se multitudinem (Liv. i. 8), *calling to them a mean and obscure multitude.*

REMARK. — The gerund is occasionally found in apposition with a noun: as,

> ad res diversissimas, parendum atque imperandum (Livy, xxi. 3), *for the most widely different things obeying and commanding.*

NOTE. — From the ablative of manner comes the Italian and Spanish form of the participle, the true participle form becoming an adjective.

74. Supine.

The Supine is a verbal noun, having no distinction of tense or person, and is limited to two uses.

NOTE. — The Supine is a verbal abstract of the fourth declension. The form in **um** is the accusative of the *end of motion*. The form in **u** is probably dative of *purpose*, though possibly ablative.

1. *Former Supine*. The Supine in **um** is used after verbs of *motion* to express the purpose of the motion; it governs the case of its verb, and is modified by adverbs: as,

quid est, imusne sessum? etsi admonitum venimus te, non flagitatum (De Or. iii. 5), *how now, shall we be seated? though we have come to remind not to entreat you.*
nuptum collocâsse (B. G. i. 18), *to establish in marriage.*
venerunt questum injurias (Liv. iii. 25), *they came to complain of wrongs.*

REMARK. — The supine in **um** is used especially after **eo**; and with the passive infinitive **iri** forms the future infinitive passive (see § **55**, 3, *b*, Rem.): as,

fuêre cives qui rempublicam perditum irent (Sall. C. 36), *there were citizens who went about to ruin the republic.*
non Graiis servitum matribus ibo (Æn. ii. 786), *I shall not go in slavery to the Grecian dames.*
si scîsset se trucidatum iri (Div. ii. 9), *if he [Pompey] had known that he was going to be murdered.*

2. *Latter Supine*. The Supine in **u** is used only after a few adjectives, and the nouns **fas, nefas**, and **opus**, to denote that in respect to which the quality is asserted: as,

O rem non modo visu fœdam, sed etiam auditu (Phil. ii. 25), *a thing not only shocking to see, but even to hear of!*
quærunt quid optimum factu sit (Verr. ii. 27), *they ask what is best to do.*
humanum factu aut inceptu (Andr. 236), *a human thing to do or undertake.*
si hoc fas est dictu (Tusc. v. 13), *if this is lawful to say.*

So rarely with verbs: as,

pudet dictu (Agric. 32), *it is shame to tell.*

REMARK. — The supine in **u** is found especially with such adjectives as indicate an effect on the senses or the feelings, and those which denote *ease, difficulty*, and the like. But with **facilis, difficilis, jucundus**, the construction of **ad** with the gerund is more common. The Infinitive is often used in the same signification, by the poets, with all these adjectives.

75. General Rules of Syntax.

1. Nouns meaning the same thing agree in *case* (§ 46).
2. Adjectives agree with Nouns in *gender, number,* and *case* (47).
3. Possessive Adjectives are used for the genitive, and in any case may have a genitive in agreement (47, 5).
4. Relatives agree with their antecedents in *gender* and *number;* their *case* depending on the construction of their clause (48).
5. A Verb agrees with its Subject in *number* and *person* (49).
6. Two or more singular subjects — also collective nouns, with **quisque** and **uterque** — may take a plural verb (49, 1).
7. The Subject of a finite verb is in the Nominative (49, 2).
8. A Noun used to limit or define another is in the Genitive (50).
9. The Genitive is used to denote the *author, owner, source,* and (with adjectives) *measure* or *quality* (50, 1).
10. Words denoting a *part* are followed by the genitive of the *whole* to which the part belongs (50, 2).
11. Certain adjectives of Quantity are used in the genitive to express indefinite Value (50, 1, *i*).
12. Many words of *memory* and *feeling, knowledge* or *ignorance, fulness* and *want,* — also verbals and participles used as adjectives, — govern the genitive (50, 3).
13. Verbs of *accusing, condemning,* and *acquitting* take the genitive of the charge or penalty (50, 4, *b*).
14. The Dative is the case of the Indirect Object (51).
15. Words of *likeness, fitness, nearness, service,* or *help* are followed by the dative (51, 5, 6).
16. Verbs meaning to *favor, help, please, serve, trust,* and their contraries, — also to *believe, persuade, command, obey, envy, threaten, pardon,* and *spare,* — govern the dative (51, 2, *a*).
17. The Dative is used after **esse,** *to be,* to denote the Owner (51, 3).
18. Most verbs compounded with **ad, ante, con, in, inter, ob, post, præ, pro, sub, super,** govern the Dative (51, 2, *d*).
19. Verbs of *giving, telling, sending,* and the like — and sometimes of *comparing* and *taking away* — govern the accusative and dative (51, 1).
20. The dative is used to denote the *purpose* or *end;* often with another dative of the person or thing affected (51, 5).
21. The Accusative is the case of the Direct Object (52).
22. The subject of the Infinitive mood is in the accusative (52, 4, *b*).
23. Time *how long* and Distance *how far* are in the accusative.
24. The accusative is used *adverbially,* or for specification (52, 3).
25. Verbs of *naming, choosing, asking,* and *teaching* govern two accusatives (52, 2).

26. The ABLATIVE is used of *cause, manner, means, instrument, quality, specification,* and *price* (**54**).
27. The Voluntary Agent after a passive verb is in the ablative with **ab** (**54**, 4).
28. Words denoting *separation* and *plenty* or *want* — also **opus** and **usus** signifying *need* — govern the ablative (**54**, 1).
29. Participles denoting *birth* or *origin* govern the ablative (**54**, 2, *a*).
30. The adjectives **dignus, indignus**, — with many verbals, as **contentus, fretus, lætus, præditus**, — govern the ablative (**54**, 3, *a*; 10, *a*).
31. The deponents **utor, fruor, fungor, potior, vescor**, and their compounds, govern the ablative (**54**, 6, *d*).
32. Comparatives may take the ablative instead of **quam**, *than*.
33. Degree of Difference is put in the ablative (**54**, 6, *e*).
34. Time *at* or *within which* is put in the ablative (**55**, 1).
35. **Ablative Absolute.** A Subject and Predicate in the ablative are used to define the *time* or *circumstances* of an action.
36. The name of the Town *where* is in form like the Genitive of singular names in **us, a, um**, otherwise Dative or Ablative; that *whither* in the Accusative, and *whence* in the Ablative.
    So of *domus, rus* (also *humi, belli, militiæ*), and many names of Islands.
37. With other words (including names of Countries) Prepositions are used to denote *where, whither,* or *whence*.
38. The Infinitive is used like a neuter noun, as the Subject or Object, or to complete the action of a verb (**57**, 8, *a*).
39. The Infinitive, with subject-accusative, is regularly used after verbs of *knowing, thinking, telling,* and the like (**57**, 8, *e*).
40. **Historical Infinitive.** The Infinitive is often used for tenses of the indicative in narration (**57**, 8, *h*).
41. The Gerund, governing the case of its verb, or the Gerundive in agreement with a noun, has the construction of a *verbal noun*.
42. The Supine in **um** is used after verbs of *motion;* the Supine in **u** after adjectives.
43. The Subjunctive is used independently to denote a *wish, command,* or *concession* (**57**, 2).
44. Relatives or Conjunctions implying *purpose* or *result*, — also relative clauses of *characteristic*, — require the Subjunctive.
45. Indirect Questions take a verb in the subjunctive (**67**, 2).
46. The Subjunctive present and perfect are used in *future* conditions; the imperfect and pluperfect in those *contrary to fact*.
47. Dependent clauses in Indirect Discourse, or in a subjunctive construction, take the subjunctive.
48. In the sequence of Tenses, primary tenses are followed by primary, and secondary by secondary (**58**, 10).

76. Arrangement.

In Latin the words do not follow the order of construction, yet they have a regular arrangement. This, however, is constantly modified for emphasis, harmony, and clearness.

1. *Normal Order.* Regularly the subject stands *first*, followed by its modifiers; the verb *last*, preceded by the words which depend upon it: as,

> civis Romanus sum (*not* sum civis Romanus).
> voluptates blandissimæ dominæ majores partes animi a virtute detorquent (Off. ii. 10).

a. A predicate nominative, as the most important part of the predicate, is often placed after the copula: as,

> qui Athenis est mortuus (id. 24).
> hæc ad judicandum sunt facillima (id. iii. 6).

b. The forms of **esse** meaning *there is*, &c., often come first in the sentence: as,

> sunt quædam officia quæ aliis magis quam aliis debeantur (Off. i. 18).

c. A numeral adjective, or one essential to the meaning of the phrase, goes before its noun; one simply descriptive commonly follows: as,

> omnes homines decet.
> est viri magni rebus agitatis punire sontes (Off. i. 24).
> omnis actio vacare debet temeritate et neglegentiâ (id. 29).
> cum aliquâ perturbatione (id. i. 38).
> Lælius et sapiens et amicitiæ gloriâ excellens (Læl. 1).

d. A Demonstrative pronoun precedes the noun, Relatives stand first in their sentence or clause, Adverbs stand directly before the word they qualify.

2. *Emphasis.* Inversion of the above order gives emphasis.

a. Particularly the verb comes first and the subject last. This makes either or both emphatic: as,

> dicebat idem C. Curio (Off. ii. 17).

b. Any word closely connected with the preceding sentence comes first, and with the following last: as,

> ac duabus iis personis quas supra dixi tertia adjungitur (Off. i. 32).

objecit [Cato] ut probrum M. Nobiliori quod is in provinciam poëtas duxisset; duxerat autem consul ille in Ætoliam ut scimus Ennium (Tusc. i. 2).

maxime perturbantur officia in amicitiis; quibus et non tribuere quod recte possis, et tribuere quod non sit æquum, contra officium est (Off. iii. 10).

c. A word or phrase inserted between the parts of compound tenses becomes emphatic: as,

ille reprehensus a multis est (N. D. ii. 38).

d. A modifier of a noun and adjective or participle is often placed between them. So in the gerundive construction: as,

de communi hominum memoriâ (Tusc. i. 24).
de uno imperatore contra prædones constituendo (Manil. 17).

e. Sometimes a noun and its attribute are separated as far as possible, so as to include less important words: as,

objurgationes etiam nonnunquam incidunt necessariæ (Off. i. 38).

f. One pair of ideas is set off against another, either in the same order or in exactly the opposite order. The latter, which is very common, is called *chiasmus* from the Greek X on account of the *cross* arrangement. Thus,

rerum copia verborum copiam gignit (De Or. iii. 3, 31).
pro vitâ hominis nisi hominis vita reddatur (B. G. vi. 16).
leges supplicio improbos afficiunt, defendunt ac tuentur bonos (Fin. iii. 3).
non igitur utilitatem amicitia, sed utilitas amicitiam consecuta est (Læl. 14). [Here the arrangement of cases only is chiastic, that of ideas is regular.]

g. Different forms of the same word are often placed together, also words from the same root.

h. A favorite order with the poets is the interlocked, by which the attribute of one pair comes between the parts of the other. This is often joined with chiasmus: as,

et superjecto pavidæ natârunt æquore damæ (H. Od. i. 2, 11).
arma nondum expiatis uncta cruoribus (id. ii. 1, 5).

3. *Special Rules.*

a. Prepositions regularly precede their nouns (except **tenus** and **versus**), but they are often placed between a noun and adjective: as,

quem ad modum; quam ob rem; magno cum metu; omnibus cum copiis; nullâ in re.

b. **Itaque** regularly comes first in its sentence, or clause; **enim, autem, vero, quoque,** never first, but usually second, sometimes third if the second word is emphatic; **quidem** never first, but after the emphatic word: **ne ... quidem** include the emphatic word or words.

c. **Inquam, inquit,** &c., **credo, opinor, quaeso,** used parenthetically, always follow one or more words.

d. The negative precedes the word it especially affects; but if it belongs to no one word, it begins the sentence.

4. *Structure.* Latin expresses the relation of words to each other by *inflection,* rather than by *position,* like modern languages. Hence its structure not only admits of great variety in the arrangement of words, but is especially favorable to that form of sentence which is called a Period. In a period, the sense is expressed by the sentence *as a whole,* and is held in suspense till the delivery of the last word, which usually expresses the main action or motive.

An English sentence does not often admit this form of structure. It was imitated, sometimes with great skill and beauty, by many of the early writers of English prose; but its effect is better seen in poetry, in such a passage as the following: —

> "High on a throne of royal state, which far
> Outshone the wealth of Ormus and of Ind,
> Or where the gorgeous East with richest hand
> Showers on her kings barbaric pearl and gold,
> Satan exalted sat."
>
> *Paradise Lost,* Book II. 1-5.

PART THIRD.

RULES OF VERSE (PROSODY).

77. RHYTHM.

1. The Poetry of the ancients was not composed, like modern poetry, according to accent and rhyme; but was measured, like music, by the length of the syllables, or vowel sounds. The measured flow of verse is called Rhythm.

2. Each syllable is considered as either long or short, — in Quantity or *length* (not in Quality or *sound*, as we speak of the long or short vowel-sounds in English); a long syllable being reckoned in length equal to two short ones (see p. 3).

REMARK. — The quantity of radical or stem-syllables — as of short **a** in păter or of long **a** in māter — can be learned only by observation or practice, unless determined by the general rules of Quantity. Most of the rules of Prosody are only arbitrary rules for the purposes of memory; the syllables being long or short *because the ancients pronounced them so*. In those cases which cannot be conveniently grouped, the quantity is shown by the actual practice of the ancients, and is said to be determined *by the authority of the Poets*, — the principal means we have of learning it. In some inscriptions, however, the long vowels are distinguished in various ways by marks over the letters, or by doubling.

Owing to the practice of Roman poets of borrowing very largely from the poetry and mythology of the Greeks, numerous Greek words, especially proper names, make an important part of Latin poetry. These words are generally employed in accordance with the Greek and not the Latin laws of quantity. Where these vary in any important point, they will be noticed in the rules given below.

78. RULES OF QUANTITY.

1. *General Rules.*

a. A vowel before another vowel is *short:* as, vĭa, trăho.

REMARK. — The aspirate h, as in the example above, is not reckoned as a Consonant in the rules of prosody (See § 1, I, Note).

EXCEPTIONS. — 1. In the genitive form ius (§ 16, 1, b), i is long. It is, however, sometimes made short in verse.

2. In the fifth declension (genitive and dative singular), e is long between two vowels: as, diēi; but is short after a consonant, as in fidĕi.

3. In fio (§ 37, 4), i is long except when followed by er: as, fīo, fīebam, fīam, fīeri, fĭerem.

4. In the terminations āius and ēius, a and e are long: as in Cāius, Pompēius; also in the verb āio, and genitives in āī.

5. In many Greek proper names, the vowel in Latin represents a long vowel or diphthong, and is consequently long: as, Trōĕs, Thălĭa, hērōăs. But many Greek words are more or less Latinized in this respect as Academĭa, chorĕa.

b. A Diphthong is *long:* as, foēdus, cūī, caēlum, deīnde.

EXCEPTION. — The preposition prae in compounds is generally short before a vowel (as in præustis, Æn. vii. 524).

c. A vowel formed by contraction (*crasis*) is *long:* as i in nīl (for nĭhĭl); currūs (genitive for currŭīs). But not where the vowels are united by *synæresis*, as in parĭĕtibus (*par-yetibus*).

d. A syllable in which a short vowel comes before two consonants or a double consonant — also before the letter j — is *long:* as, māgnus, rēx, pējor, ēt vēntis ocior, (but ădhuc). But if the two consonants are a mute followed by l or r, the syllable is common, — that is, it may be either long or short in verse: as, alăcris, pătribus, rēfluo.

REMARK. — Sometimes the y or v resulting from synæresis has the effect of a consonant: as, flūviōrūm rēx (G. i. 482).

e. In early Latin s at the end of words was not sounded, and hence does not make position with another consonant. In many other cases in the comic poets two consonants do not make position, especially in pronouns and particles: as, īlle, ĭste, nĕmpe.

REMARK. — A short syllable, made long under this rule, is said to be long by Position: as, in docĕtne. In docēsne, the same syllable is long by the general rule (2, *h*, below). The rules of Position do not, in general, apply to *final vowels*.

2. *Final Syllables.*

a. Words of one syllable ending in a vowel are *long:* as, mē, tū, hī, nē.

The attached particles -nĕ, -quĕ, -vĕ, -cĕ, ptĕ, and rĕ- (rĕd-) are short; sē- is long: as, sēcedit, exercitumquĕ rĕducit.

b. Nouns of one syllable are *long*: as, sōl, ōs (ōris), bōs, vīs.

EXCEPTIONS.— cŏr, fĕl, mĕl, ŏs (ossis), vĭr.

c. Final a in words declined by cases is *short*, except in the ablative singular of the first declension; in all other words it is *long*: as, eă stellă (nominative), cum eā stellā; frustrā, vocā (imperative), posteā, trigintā; also, quā (plural).

EXCEPTIONS. — eiă, ită, quiă, pută (*suppose*); and, in late use, trigintă, &c.

d. Final e is *short*, except (1) in nouns of the fifth declension; (2) in adverbs formed from adjectives of the first and second declension, with others of like form; (3) in the imperative singular of the second conjugation: as, nubĕ, ducitĕ, fidē, famē (§ 11, *b*, 3), quārē (quā rē), hŏdiē (hoc die), monē, monētĕ, saepĕ, saepissimē.

EXCEPTIONS. — benĕ, malĕ; ferē, fermē; also (rarely), cavĕ, habĕ, tacĕ, valĕ, vidĕ; infernĕ, supernĕ.

e. Final i is *long*: as in turrī, filī, audī. But it is *common* in mihi, tibi, sibi, ibi, ubi; and *short* in nisĭ, quasĭ, cŭĭ (when making two syllables), and in Greek vocatives, as Alexĭ.

f. Final o is *common*; but long in datives and ablatives; also, usually, in verbs.

EXCEPTIONS. — citŏ, modŏ, ilicŏ, profectŏ, dummodŏ, immŏ, egŏ, duŏ, octŏ.

g. Final u is *long*; final y is *short*.

h. Final as, es, os, are *long*; final is, us, ys are *short*: as, nefās, rupēs, servōs, honōs; hostĭs, amicŭs, Tethўs.

EXCEPTIONS. — as is short in Greek plural accusatives, as lampadăs; and in anăs.

es is short in nouns of the third declension (lingual) increasing short: as milĕs (ĭtis), obsĕs (ĭdis), — except abiēs, ariēs, pariēs, pēs; in the present of esse (ĕs, adĕs); in the preposition penĕs; and in the plural of Greek nouns.

os is short in compos, impos; in some Greek endings, as barbitŏs; also o for later u in the second declension, as servŏs (nominative).

is in plural cases is long, as in bonīs, omnīs (accusative plural); in sīs, vīs, velīs, malīs, nolīs; in gratīs, forīs (properly plurals); in the second person singular of the fourth conjugation, as audīs (where it is the stem-vowel); and sometimes in the forms in -erīs (perfect subjunctive), where it was originally long.

us is long in the genitive singular and nominative and accusative plural of the fourth declension; and in nouns of the third declension having ŭ long in the stem: as **virtūs** (**ūtis**), **incūs** (**ūdis**).

i. Of other final syllables, those ending in a consonant, except **c**, are short: as, **ăd, āc, istŭc, amăt, amatŭr.**

EXCEPTIONS. — **donĕc, făc, nĕc,** sometimes **hĭc; ēn, nōn, quĭn, sĭn; crās, plūs; cūr, pār.**

3. *Penultimate Syllables.*

a. Increment. A Noun is said to *increase*, when in any case it has more syllables than in the nominative singular.

Thus **stella** is said to increase *long* in **stellārum**; and **corpus** to increase *short* in **corpŏris**.

NOTE. — The rules of increment are purely arbitrary, as the syllables are long or short according to the proper quantity of the stem or the formative terminations. The quantity of noun stems appears in the schedule of the third declension (§ 11, iv. 3), and that of terminations, under the various inflections where it is better to learn them.

A Verb is said to increase, when in any part it has more syllables than in the stem (inclusive of the final vowel).

Thus **amo** is said to increase *long* in **amātis**; and **rego** to increase *short* in **regĭtis**.

The final syllable of an inflected word is called the *termination*; that immediately preceding is called the *increment*.

Thus, in the examples given above, the penultimate syllable is called the increment. In **itĭnĕrĭbus, amāvĕrĭtis,** the syllables marked are called the first, second, and third increments of the noun or verb.

b. Nouns. In the increment of Nouns and Adjectives, **a** and **o** are generally *long*; **e, i, u, y,** generally short (see list, pp. 25–27): as, **aetātis, honōris, servōrum; opĕris, carmĭnis, murmŭris, pecŭdis, chlamўdis.** Exceptions are: —

ă: — baccar (ăris), hepar (ătis), jubar (ăris), lar (lăris), mas (măris), nectar (ăris), par (păris), sal (sălis), vas (vădis), daps (dăpis), fax, anthrax (ăcis).

ŏ: — neuters of third declension (except ōs, ōris); arbor (ŏris), scrobs (scrŏbis), ops (ŏpis).

78 : 3.] RULES OF QUANTITY. 219

ē :—increments of fifth declension; heres (ēdis), lex (lēgis), locuples (ētis), merces (ēdis), plebs (plēbis), quies (ētis), rex (rēgis), ver (vĕris).

ī :—most nouns and adjectives in **ix**: as, felīcis, radīcis (except filix, nix, strix); dis (dītis), glis (glīris), lis (lītis), vis (vīres), Quirītes, Samnītes.

ū :—forms from nouns in **ūs**: as, palūdis, tellūris, virtūtis; also lux (lūcis), frux (frūgis).

c. Verbs. In the increment of Verbs (see Tables of Inflection, pp. 66-74), the characteristic vowels are as follows:—

Of the first conjugation ā: as, **amāre, amātur.**

Of the second conjugation ē: as, **monēre, monētur.**

Of the third conjugation ĕ, ĭ: as, **regĕre, regĭtur.**

Of the fourth conjugation ī: as, **audīre, audītur.**

Exc.—do and its compounds have ă: as, **dăre, circumdăbat.**

In other increments —

ā is always *long:* as, **moneāris, regāmus.**

ē is *long* in tense-endings: as, **regēbam, audiēbar.** But it is *short* before **ram, rim, ro**; in the future personal endings -**bĕris, bĕre**; and sometimes in the perfect -**ĕrunt** (as **stĕtĕruntque comae,** Æn. ii. 774).

ī is *long* in forms after the analogy of the fourth conjugation: as, **petīvi, lacessītus** (in others short: as, **monĭtus**); also in the subjunctive present of **esse** and **velle**, and (rarely) in the endings -**rīmus, -rītis**; but short in the future forms **amabĭtis**, &c.

ō is found only in imperatives, and is always *long.*

ŭ is short in **sŭmus, volŭmus, quaesŭmus**; in the supine and its derivatives it is long: as, **solūtūrus.**

d. Perfects and supines of two syllables lengthen the stemsyllable: as, **jŭvo, jūvi, jūtum; vĭdeo, vīdi, vīsum; fŭgio, fūgi.**

EXCEPTIONS.—**bĭbi, dĕdi (do), fĭdi (findo), scĭdi (scindo), stĕti (sto), stĭti (sisto), tŭli (fero)**;—**cĭtum (cieo), dătum (do), ĭtum (eo), lĭtum (lino), quĭtum (queo), rătum (reor), rŭtum (ruo), sătum (sero), sĭtum (sino), stătum (sto or sisto).** In some compounds of **sto, stātum** is found long, as **prostātum.**

e. Reduplicated perfects shorten both syllables: as, **cĕcĭdi (cădo), dĭdĭci (disco), cĕcĭni (căno)**; but **cĕcīdi** from **caedo, pepēdi** from **pēdo.**

f. Forms from the same STEM retain the original quantity: as, ămo, ămavisti, gĕnus, gĕneris.

EXCEPTIONS. — 1. bōs, lār, mās, pār, pēs, sāl, vās — also arbōs (not arbŏr) — have a long vowel in the nominative from short stems.

2. Nouns in **or**, genitive **ōris**, have the vowel shortened before the final **r**: as, honŏr. (But this shortening is comparatively late, so that in Plautus and some inscriptions these nominatives are often found long.)

3. Many verb-forms with original long vowel shorten it before final **t**: as, amĕt, dicerĕt (compare amēmus), audĭt, fĭt. (The final syllable in **t** of the perfect seems to have been originally long, but to have been shortened under this rule.)

g. Forms from the same ROOT often vary in quantity from *vowel-increase* (see §§ 1, 3, *a*; 5, 2; **44**, 1, *a*); as, dīco (cf. maledĭcus), dūco (dŭcis), fīdo (perfĭdus), vōcis (vŏco), lēgio (lĕgo).

h. COMPOUNDS retain the quantity of the words which compose them: as, occīdo (cădo), occĭdo (caedo), inīquus (aequus). Greek words compounded with προ have **o** short, as prŏphēta, prŏlŏgus. Some Latin compounds of **pro** have **o** short, as prŏficiscor, prŏfiteor. Compounds with **ne** vary: as, nĕfas, nĕgo, nĕqueo, nēquis, nēquam. So dejĕro and pejĕro from jūro.

[For the quantity of Penultimate Syllables in regular Derivatives, see § **44**, pages 97–99.]

79. FEET.

1. The most natural division of musical time is into intervals, consisting of either two or three equal parts, making what is called double or triple time; but the ancients also distinguished five equal parts. These intervals are in music called Measures; in prosody, they are called Feet.

2. The feet most frequently employed in Latin verse consist either of two or three syllables; and may be represented by musical notation, as follows: —

a. Of Two Syllables.

1. $\frac{2}{8}$ | ♪♪ | *Pyrrhic* (˘ ˘): as, **bŏnŭs**.
2. $\frac{3}{8}$ | ♩♪ | *Trochee* or *Choree* (¯ ˘): as, **cārŭs**.
3. $\frac{3}{8}$ | ♪♩ | *Iambus* (˘ ¯): as, **bŏnōs**.
4. $\frac{2}{4}$ | ♩♩ | *Spondee* (¯ ¯): as, **cārōs**.

b. Of Three Syllables.

1. $\frac{2}{4}$ | ♩♪♪ | *Dactyl* (¯ ˘ ˘): as, **dētŭlĭt**.
2. $\frac{2}{4}$ | ♪♪♩ | *Anapæst* (˘ ˘ ¯): as, **dŏmĭnōs**.
3. $\frac{2}{4}$ | ♪♩♪ | *Amphibrach* (˘ ¯ ˘): as, **ămīcŭs**.
4. $\frac{3}{8}$ | ♪♪♪ | *Tribrach* (˘ ˘ ˘): as, **hŏmĭnĭs**.
5. $\frac{3}{4}$ | ♩♩♩ | *Molossus* (¯ ¯ ¯): as, **fūgērūnt** (rare).

Of three syllables, but more than three units of time.

6. | ♩♪♩ | *Amphimacer* or *Cretic* (¯ ˘ ¯): as, **ēgĕrānt**.
7. | ♪♩♩ | *Bacchius* (˘ ¯ ¯): as, **rĕgēbānt**.

c. Of Four Syllables.

1. *Choriambus* (trochee, iambus): as, **dētŭlĕrānt**.
2. *Greater Ionic* (spondee, pyrrhic): as, **dējēcĕrăt**.
3. *Lesser Ionic* (pyrrhic, spondee): as, **rĕtŭlīssēnt**.
4. The first, second, third, or fourth *Epitritus* has a short syllable in the first, second, third, or fourth place with three long syllables.
5. The first, second, third, or fourth *Pæon* has a long syllable in the first, second, third, or fourth place with three short syllables.
6. The *Proceleusmatic* consists of four short syllables, as **ŏpĕrĭbŭs**.

NOTE.—Narrative poetry was written for rhythmical recitation, or chant; and Lyrical poetry for rhythmical melody, or music, often to be accompanied by measured movements or dance. But in reading, it is not usual, though it is better, to keep the strict measure of time; and often accent is substituted for rhythm, as ●●nglish poetry.

d. In general, feet of the same *time* can be substituted for each other, and two short syllables may stand for a long one. In the latter case, the long syllable is said to be *resolved*.

Thus the Spondee may take the place of the dactyl or anapæst, the Tribrach of the trochee or iambus; the Proceleusmatic, or a Dactyl standing for an anapæst, is the resolution of a spondee.

When a long syllable having the *ictus* is resolved, the ictus properly belongs to both the short syllables; but the accent to indicate it is placed on the first: as,

Núnc experiar | sítne aceto | tíbi cor acre in | péctore.
BACCH. 405.

3. *Arsis and Thesis.* The accented syllable of each foot is called the Arsis; and the unaccented part the Thesis.

NOTE. — The name Arsis meant originally the *raising* of the foot in beating time ("upward beat"), and Thesis the *putting down* ("downward beat"); but these terms came, in later use, to signify respectively the raising and depression of the voice. (See Mar. Vict. Chap. ix.)

4. *Ictus.* Accent, in prosody, is called Ictus, — that is, the *beat* of the foot, as in a dance or march.

5. *Cæsura.* The end of a word interrupting a foot is called Cæsura; and when this coincides with a rhetorical break in the sense, it is called *the* Cæsura of the verse.

NOTE. — The position of the principal Cæsura is important, as affecting the melody or rhythm. See description of verses below.

80. SCANNING.

1. *Verse.* A single line in poetry, or a series of feet set in metrical order, is called a Verse (i.e. a *turning back*).

To divide the verse, in reading, into its appropriate feet, according to the rules of quantity and versification, is called Scanning or Scansion (i.e. *climbing,* or advance by steps).

A verse lacking a syllable at the beginning is called Acephalous (*headless*); lacking a syllable at the end, it is called Catalectic (*stopped*); complete, Acatalectic. Sometimes a verse appears to have a superfluous syllable, and is then called Hypercatalectic.

The word Verse (**versus**, *a turning*) is opposed to Prose (**prorsus** or **pro-**◼︎**us**, *straight ahead*).

2. *Elision*. In scanning, a vowel or diphthong at the end of a word (unless an interjection) — sometimes even at the end of a verse — is dropped, when the next word begins with a vowel or with h. This is called Synalœpha (*smearing*), or Elision (*bruising*); or, at the end of a verse, Synapheia (*binding*).

A final **m**, with the preceding vowel, is dropped in like manner: this is called Ecthlipsis. (Hence a final syllable in **m** is said to have no quantity of its own; its vowel, in any case, being either elided, or else made long by position.) Thus in the verse: —

Monstr*um* horrend*um* inform*e* ingens cui lumen ademptum.
Æn. iii. 658.

NOTE. — The practice of Elision is followed in Italian and French poetry, and is sometimes adopted in English, particularly in the older poets: as,

T' inveigle and invite th' unwary sense. — *Comus*, 538.

In early Latin poetry, a syllable ending in **s** was often elided, even before a consonant: as,

Senio confectu' quiescit. — *Ennius* (quoted in Cat. M. 5).

3. *Hiatus*. Elision is sometimes omitted when a word ending in a vowel has a special emphasis, or is succeeded by a pause. This is called Hiatus (*gaping*). *Ecl. iii. 6*

4. A final syllable, regularly short, is sometimes lengthened before a pause: it is then said to be long by Cæsura. (This usage is comparatively rare, most cases where it appears being caused by the retention of an original long quantity.)

Nostror*um* obruimūr, oriturque miserrima cædes. — *Æn.* ii. 411.

5. The last syllable of any verse may be indifferently long or short (except in some forms of Anapæstic and Ionic verse).

81. METRE.

1. Metre is the regular combination of feet in verse, and is named from its most frequent and ruling foot: as, Dactylic, Iambic, Trochaic, Anapæstic, Choriambic.

Note. — The ruling foot, so called, always consists of a combination of *long* and *short syllables*, and is therefore never a pyrrhic or spondee.

The shorter feet (Iambus, Trochee) are counted not by single feet, but by pairs (dipodies), so that six Iambi make a *trimeter*, &c.

2. A Verse consists of a given number of feet arranged metrically. It is named from the number of feet (or pairs) it contains, as Hexameter, Trimeter.

3. A Stanza, or Strophe, consists of a definite number of verses ranged in a fixed order. It is often called from the name of some poet, as Sapphic, Alcaic, Horatian.

82. Forms of Verse.

1. *Dactylic*. The most common forms of dactylic verse are the Hexameter and Pentameter.

a. **Hexameter.** The Hexameter, called also Heroic verse, is used in narrative and pastoral poetry. It consists of six feet, of which the last is always incomplete (a trochee or spondee), the fifth generally a dactyle, and the rest indifferently dactyles or spondees. The fifth foot is rarely a spondee, in which case the verse is called *spondaic*. The principal Cæsura falls after the *arsis* (sometimes in the *thesis*) of the third foot or after the arsis of the fourth. In the last case there should be another in the third.

The introductory verses of the Æneid, divided according to the foregoing rules, will be as follows, the principal Cæsura in each verse being marked by double lines: —

ārmă vĭ|rūmquĕ că|nō ‖ Trō|jæ quī | prīmŭs ăb | ōrīs
Ĭtāl|ĭăm fā|tō prŏfŭ|gūs ‖ Lā|vīnĭăquĕ | vēnĭt-
lītŏră, | mūlt*e* ill*e* | ēt tēr|rīs ‖ jăc|tātŭs ĕt | āltō
vī sŭpĕ|rūm sæ|væ ‖ mĕmŏ|rēm Jū|nōnĭs ŏb | īram ;
mūltă quŏ|qu*e* ēt bēl|lō pās|sūs ‖ dūm | cŏndĕrĕt | ūrbem,
īnfēr|rētquĕ dĕ|ōs Lătĭ|ŏ, ‖ gĕnŭs | ūndĕ Lă|tīnum,
Ālbā|nīquĕ pă|trēs, ‖ ātqu*e* āltæ | mœnĭă | Rōmæ.

Another form of cæsura is seen in the following: —

Hōc făcĭ|ēns vī|vām mĕlĭ|ūs ‖ sīc | dūlcīs ă|mīcis.

Hor. Sat. I. 4, 135.

The Hexameter verse has been illustrated in English thus: —

"Strongly it | bears us a|long, ‖ in | swelling and | limitless | billows,
Nothing be|fore and | nothing be|hind, ‖ but the | sky and the | ocean."

b. **Pentameter.** The Pentameter consists of five feet, and is used alternately with the hexameter to form the Elegiac stanza. It must be scanned as two half-verses, of which the latter always has two dactyls, and each ends in a long syllable or half-foot. There is no cæsura; but the first half-verse must always end with a word: as,

cūm sŭbĭt | īllī|ūs trīs|tīssĭmă | nōctis ĭ|māgo
quā mĭhĭ | sūprē|mūm ‖ tēmpŭs ĭn | ūrbĕ fŭ|ĭt,
cūm rĕpĕ|tō nōc|tēm quā | tōt mĭhĭ | cāră rĕ|līquī,
lābĭtŭr | ēx ŏcŭ|līs ‖ nūnc quŏquĕ | gŭttă mĕ|īs.
jām prŏpĕ | lūx ădĕ|rāt, quā | mē dīs|cēdĕrĕ | Cæsăr
fīnĭbŭs | ēxtrē|mæ ‖ jūssĕrăt | Ausŏnĭ|æ.
                      Ov. Trist. I. El. 3, 1–6.

The Elegiac Stanza has been illustrated thus: —

"In the hex|ameter | rises the | fountain's | silvery | column,
In the pent|ameter | still ‖ falling in | melody | back."

c. Rarely, other dactylic verses, or half-verses, combined with trochees or iambs, are used by the lyric poets: viz., —

Dactylic pentameter:

ārbŏrĭ|būsquĕ cŏ|mæ. — Hor. Od. IV. 7.

Dactylic tetrameter:

crās īn|gēns ĭtĕ|rābĭmŭs | æquŏr. — Od. I. 7.

Archilochian heptameter:

solvitur | acris hi|ēmps, grā|tā vĭcĕ | vērĭs | ēt Fă|vōnī.
                      Od. I. 4.

2. *Iambic*. The most common forms of Iambic verse are the Trimeter (*Senarius*), and Tetrameter (*Septenarius* or *Octonarius*).

a. **Trimeter.** The Iambic Trimeter is the ordinary verse of dramatic dialogue. It consists of three measures, each containing a double iambus. In the first half-measure (odd places), the Spondee or its equivalents (anapæst or dactyl) may be regularly substituted. In the comic poets, these substitutions may be made in any foot except the last: as,

> O lūcǐs āl|mě rēctŏr ‖ ēt | cāelī děcǔs !
> qui āltērnă cūr|rū spătǐă ‖ flām|mǐfěro āmbiens,
> īllūstrě lāē|tīs ‖ ēxsěrǐs | tērrīs cǎpǔt.
>
> HERC. FUR. 592-94.

> hŏmō s*um:* hūmā|nī ‖ nihīl ā m*e* ălǐ|ēnūm pǔtō.
> vēl mē mŏnē|r*e* hŏc ‖ vēl pērcōn|tārī pǔtā.
>
> HEAUT. 77, 78.

REMARK.— The choliambic (lame Iambic) substitutes a trochee for the last Iambus: as,

> sēd nōn vǐdē|mūs māntǐcæ | quŏd īn tērg*o* ēst.
>
> CATULL. XXII. 21.

***b*. Tetrameter.** The Iambic Tetrameter *catalectic* (Septenarius) consists of seven iambic feet, with the same substitutions as the above. It is used in more lively dialogue: as,

n*am* īdcīrc*o* ārcēs|sōr, nūptǐās | quŏd m*i* ādpǎrā|rī sēnsǐt.
quǐbǔs quǐděm quām fǎcǐ|lě pǒtǔěrāt | quǐēscī si hīc | quǐēsset !
ANDRIA, 690-91.

The iambic tetrameter *acatalectic* (Octonarius) consists of eight full iambic feet with the same substitutions. It is also used in lively dialogue: as,

hŏcǐnēsthūmā|nǔm fāct*u* aūt | īn 'cēpt*u* ? hŏcǐnēst ōf|fǐcǐum pǎtrǐs ?
quǐd ǐllǔd ēst ? prō | děǔm fǐdēm, | quǐd ēst, s*i* hōc nōn cōn|-
tǔmēlǐāst ?   ANDRIA, 236-7.

***c*. Dimeter.** The Iambic Dimeter consists of either four (*acatalectic*) or three and a half (*catalectic*) iambic feet. The former is used in combination with a longer verse, and the latter only in choruses: as,

> běātǔs il|lě quī prŏcūl | něgōtǐǐs,
> ǔt prīscǎ gēns | mōrtālǐum,
> pǎtērnǎ rū|rǎ būbǔs ēx|ērcēt sǔīs,
> sǒlūtǔs ōm|nī fēnǒrě ;
> něqu*e* ēxcǐtā|tūr clāssǐcō | mīlēs trǔcī,
> něque hōrrět ī|rātūm mǎrě ;
> fǒrūmquě vī|tǎt, ēt sǔpēr bǎ cīvǐum
> pǒtēntǐō|rūm līmǐnǎ.
>
> HOR. EPOD. II. 1-8.

quōnām crŭēn|tă Mænās,
præcĕps ămō|rĕ sævō,
răpĭtūr quŏd īm|pŏtēntī
făcĭnūs părāt | fŭrōrĕ?
                                    MEDEA, 850-53.

3. *Trochaic*. The most common form of Trochaic verse is the Tetrameter *catalectic* (Septenarius), consisting of seven complete feet with an additional syllable. Strictly, the spondee and its resolutions can be substituted only in the even places; but the comic poets allow the substitution in every foot but the last: as,

Itĭd*em* hăbēt pĕtă|s*um* āc vēstītūm : | tām cōnsĭmĭlīst | ātqu*e* ĕgŏ.
sūră, pēs, stă|tūră, tōnsŭs, | ŏcŭlī, nāsūm, | vēl lăbră,
mālæ, mēntūm, |. bārbă, cōllŭs : | tōtŭs ! quĭd vēr|bĭs ŏpūst ?
sī tērgūm cĭ|cātrīcōsūm, | n*i*hĭl hōc sĭmĭlīst | sĭmĭlĭŭs.
                                    AMPHITR. 443-46.

4. *Anapœstic*. Anapæstic verses of various lengths are found in dramatic poetry. The spondee, dactyl, or proceleusmatic may be substituted for the anapæst: as,

hĭc hŏmōst | ŏmnĭ*um* hŏmĭ|nūm præ|cĭpŭŏs
vŏlŭptā|tĭbŭs gaū|d*i*īsqu*e* ān|tĕpŏtēns.
Ĭtă cōm|mŏdă quæ | cŭpĭ*o* ē|vĕnĭūnt,
quŏd ăgō | sŭbĭt, ād sĕcŭē | sĕquĭtūr :
Ĭtă gaū|d*i*īs gaū|dĭŭm sūp|pĕdĭtāt.
                                    TRIN. 1115-19.

Some other forms of trochaic verse are found in the lyric poets, in combination with other feet, either as whole lines or parts of lines: as,

nōn ĕbūr nĕ|qu*e* aūrĕūm [dimeter]
mĕā rĕnī|dĕt īn dŏmō | lăcūnăr.
                                    HOR. OD. II. 18.

5. *Bacchic*. The Bacchius occurs in dramatic poets either in verses of two feet (Dimeter) or of four (Tetrameter). The long syllables may be resolved into short ones, and the molossus substituted: as,

mūltās rēs | sĭmīt*u* īn | mĕō cōr dĕ vōrsō,
mūltum īn cō|gĭtāndō | dŏlōr*em* īn|dĭpīscor.

ĕgŏmēt mē | cŏqu*o* ēt mā|cĕr*o* ēt dē|fĕtīgō :
măgīstēr | mĭhi ēxēr|cĭtōr ănĭ|mŭs nūnc ēst.
Trin. 223-26.

6. *Cretic*. Cretic feet (Amphimacer) occur in the same manner as the Bacchius, with the same substitutions. The last foot is usually incomplete : as,

ămŏr ămī|cūs mĭhī | nē fŭās | ūnquām.
hīs ĕgō | d*e* ārtĭbūs | grātĭām | făcĭō.
nīl ĕg*o* īs|tōs mŏrōr | fæcĕōs | mōrēs.
Trin. 267, 293, 297.

7. *Choriambic*. Choriambic feet are regularly preceded by a spondee or trochee, called a *basis*, and are followed by a *close*, consisting of one or more syllables (see below).

a. The First or Lesser Asclepiadic verse consists of two choriambs preceded by a trochee (in Horace a spondee), and followed by an iambus (8, *d*).

b. The Second or Greater Asclepiadic has three choriambs with the same basis and close (8, *h*) : as,

nēc fāc|t*a* īmpĭă fāl|lācum hŏmĭnūm | cāēlĭcŏlīs | plăcēnt.
Catull. XXX. 4.

c. The Glyconic consists of one choriambus, with the same basis and close (8, *e*).

d. The Pherecratic consists of one choriambus, with the same basis, and one long syllable for close (8, *g*).

e. The Greater Sapphic consists of two choriambs, preceded by a trochaic dipody (*epitritus secundus*), and followed by a bacchius (8, *c*) : as,

Sæpĕ trāns fī|nēm jăcŭlō | nōbĭlĭs ēx pĕdītō.
Hor. Od. I. 8.

f. The Lesser Sapphic consists of one choriambus, with the same basis and close (8, *b*) : as,

īntĕr audā|cēs lŭpŭs ēr|răt āgnōs.
Hor. Od. III. 18, 13.

g. The Adonic consists of one choriambus, followed by a long syllable (8, *b*).

h. The Phalæcian consists of a basis, a choriambus, an iambus, and bacchius: as,

>dīsēr|tĭssĭmĕ Rō|mŭlī | nĕpōtum
>quŏt sūnt | quŏtquĕ fuē|rĕ Mār|cĕ Tulli.
>
>CATUL. XLIX. 1, 2.

i. The lesser Ionic verse consists of pairs of the foot of the same name.

k. Rarely other forms of choriambic verse occur: as, for example —

Aristophanic:
>tēmpĕrăt ō|ră frēnīs.
>
>HOR. OD. I. 8, 7.

Tetrameter:
>ōbstĭpuĭt; | pēctŏrĕ nīl | sīstĕrĕ cōn|sĭlī quīt.
>
>ADELPHI, 613.

8. *Stanzas.* The principal forms of lyric stanza, or strophe, are the following: —

a. ALCAIC STROPHE, consisting of four verses: the first two (greater Alcaic) having each a spondee (or trochee), bacchius and two dactyls; the third a spondee, bacchius, and two trochees, and the fourth into two dactyls and two trochees: as,

>jūst*um* āc | tĕnācēm | prŏpŏsī|tī vĭrŭm
>nōn cī|vĭ*um* ārdōr | prāvă jŭ|bēntĭŭm,
>nōn vūl|tŭs īnstān|tīs ty|rānnī,
>mēntĕ quă|tĭt sŏlī|dā nĕ|qu*e* aūstēr.
>
>HOR. OD. III. 3.

b. LESSER SAPPHIC, consisting of three Lesser Sapphic verses, and one Adonic (see above, 7, *f*, *g*): as,

>jām sătīs tēr|rīs nĭvĭs āt|quĕ dīræ
>grāndĭnīs mī|sĭt pătĕr ēt | rŭbēntĕ
>dēxtĕrā sā|crās jăcŭlā|tŭs ārcēs
>tērrŭĭt ūr|bem.
>
>Id. OD. I. 2, 1-4.

c. GREATER SAPPHIC, consisting of a choriambic dimeter (7, *h*), and a greater Sapphic (7, *e*): as,

>Lydĭă dīc | pĕr ōmnēs
>tē dĕōs ō|rō Sybărīn | cūr prŏpĕrās | ămāndō.
>
>HOR. OD. I. 8.

d. LESSER ASCLEPIADEAN, consisting of single lines (*monostrophon*), of lesser asclepiadics (7, *a*): as,

Mæcē|nās ătăvīs | ēdĭtĕ rē|gĭbŭs
O ēt | præsĭdĭ*um* ēt | dūlcĕ dĕcūs | mĕŭm.

Id. I. 1.

e. SECOND ASCLEPIADEAN, consisting of one Glyconic (7, *e*), and one lesser Asclepiadic: as,

Rōmæ | prīncĭpĭs ūr|bĭŭm
dīgnā|tūr sŭbŏlēs | īntĕr ămā|bĭlēs
vātūm | pōnĕrĕ mē | chŏrōs ;
ēt jām | dēntĕ mĭnŭs | mōrdĕŏr īn|vĭdō.

Id. OD. IV. 3, 13-16.

f. THIRD ASCLEPIADEAN, consisting of three lesser Asclepiadics and one Glyconic: as,

audīs | quō strĕpĭtū | jānŭă quō | nĕmŭs
īntēr | pūlchrā sătūm | tēctā rĕmū|gĭăt
vēntīs | ēt pŏsĭtās | ūt glăcĭēt | nĭvēs
pūrō | nūmĭnĕ Jū|pĭtĕr.

Id. OD. III. 10, 5-8.

g. FOURTH ASCLEPIADEAN, consisting of two lesser Asclepiadics, one Pherecratic (7, *d*), and one Glyconic: as,

hīc bēl|lūm lăcrĭmō|*sum* hīc mĭsĕrām | fămĕm
pēstēm|qu*e* ā pŏpŭl*o* ēt | prīncĭpĕ Cæ|sărĕ ĭn
Pērsās | ātquĕ Brĭtān|nōs
vēstrā | mōtŭs ăgēt | prĕcĕ.

Id. OD. III. 21, 13-16.

h. GREATER ASCLEPIADEAN, consisting of single lines of greater asclepiadics: as,

tū nē | quæsĭĕrīs | scīrĕ nĕfās | quēm mĭhĭ quēm | tĭbĭ.

OD. I. 11, 18; IV. 10.

i. The above forms include upwards of a hundred of the Odes of Horace. In the eighteen not included, he employs twelve different kinds of stanzas, most of which are combinations of the verses already given. They may be briefly indicated as follows: —

1. Hexameter, followed by the last four feet of an hexameter. — OD. I. 7, 28; EPOD. 12.

2. Hexameter, followed by Iambic Dimeter.—Epod. 14, 15.
3. Iambic Trimeter alone.—Epod. 17.
4. Hexameter, followed by Iambic Trimeter.—Epod. 16.
5. Verse of four Lesser Ionics.—Od. III. 12.
6. Hexameter with Dactylic Penthemim (five half-feet):

dīffŭ|gērĕ nĭ|vēs rĕdĕ | ūnt jām | grāmĭnă | cāmpīs
ārbŏrĭ|būsquĕ cŏ|mæ.—Od. IV. 7.

7. Iambic Trimeter; Dactylic Penthemim; Iambic Dimeter.—Epod. 11.
8. Hexameter; Iambic Dimeter; Dactylic Penthemim.—Ed. 13.
9. Archilochian Heptameter; Iambic Trimeter catalectic: as,

sōlvĭtŭr | ācrĭs hĭ|ēms grā|tā vĭcĕ | vērĭs | ēt Fă|vōni
trăhūnt|quĕ sīc|cās mā chĭnæ | cărī|nas.—Od. I. 4.

10. Trochaic Dimeter and Iambic Trimeter, each imperfect: as,

nōn | ĕbūr | nĕqu*e* au|rĕum
mĕā | rĕnī|dĕt īn | dŏmō | lăcū|nar.—Od. II. 18.

k. Other lyric poets use other combinations of the above-mentioned verses.

1. Four Glyconics with one Pherecratic: as,

Dĭā|næ sŭmŭs īn | fĭdĕ
puel|læ ēt pŭĕr*i* īn|tĕgrī:
Dĭā|nām, pŭĕr*i* īn|tĕgrī
pŭēl|læquĕ cănā|mus.—Catull. 34.

2. Sapphics, in series of single lines, closing with an Adonic: as,

An magis diri tremuēre Manes
Herculem? et visum canis inferorum
fugit abruptis trepidus catenis?
fallimur: læte venit, ecce, vultu,
quem tulit Pœas; humerisque tela
gestat, et notas populis pharetras
Herculis heres.
Herc. Œt. 1600-6.

3. Sapphics followed by Glyconics, of indefinite number (Herc. Fur. 830-874, 875-894).

83. EARLY PROSODY.

The prosody of the earlier Latin poets differs in several respects from that of the later.

NOTE. — Before the language was used in literature, it had become very much changed by the loss of final consonants and shortening of final syllables under the influence of accent, which was originally free in its position, but in Latin became limited to the penult and ante-penult. This tendency was arrested by the study of grammar and by literature, but shows itself again in the Romance languages. In many cases this change was still in progress in the time of the early poets.

a. At the end of words **s** was only feebly sounded, so that it does not make *position* with a following consonant, and is sometimes cut off before a vowel. (This usage continues in all poets till Cicero's time: see §§ **1**, 2, 6; **80**, 2, note.

b. The last syllable of any word of two syllables may be made short if the first is short. (This effect remained in a few words like **pŭtă, căvĕ, vălĕ, vĭdĕ**.) Thus:—

ăbĕst (Cist. ii. 1, 12); ăpŭd tēst (Trin. 196); sŏrŏr dīctāst (Enn. 157); bŏnăs (Stich. 99); dŏmī dĕæque (Pseud. 37); dŏmĭ (Mil. 194).

c. The same effect is produced when a short monosyllable precedes a long syllable: as,

ĭd ĕst profecto (Merc. 372), ĕrĭt et tĭbĭ ĕxoptatum (Mil. 1011), sī quĭdem hĕrcle (Asin. 414), quĭd ĕst sĭ hōc (Andria, 237).

d. In a few isolated words position is often disregarded. Such are, **ĭlle, ĭste, ĭnde, ŭnde, nĕmpe, ĕsse** (?). (Scholars are not yet agreed upon the principle in this irregularity, or its extent.) Thus: —

ĕcquĭs his in ædibust (Bacch. 581).

e. In some cases the accent seems to shorten a syllable preceding it in a word of more than three syllables: as in **senĕctūti, Syrăcusae**.

f. At the beginning of a verse, many syllables long by position stand for short ones: as,

ĭdnĕ tu (Pseud. 442); ĕstne consimilis (Epid. v. 1. 18).

g. The original long quantity of many final syllables is retained. Thus: —

1. Final **a** of the first declension is often long: as,

n*e* epístulā quid*em* úlla sit in aédibus (Asin. 762).
Pol hódi*e* alterá jam bis detónsa certost.

2. Final **a** of the neuter plural is sometimes long (though there seems no etymological reason for it): as,

Núnc et amico prósperab*o* et géniō meŏ multā bona faciam (Pers. 263).

3. So also nouns in **-or** with long stem, either with original **r** or original **s**: as,

módo quom dict*a* in m*e* íngerebas ódium non uxōr eram (Asin. 927).
íta m*i* in pector*e* átque corde fácit amōr incéndium (Merc. 590).
atque quanto nóx fuisti lóngiōr hoc próxuma (Amph. 548).

4. So in nouns with vowel lengthened originally by loss of a consonant: as, **milēs, superstitēs**.

5. So all verb-endings in **r** and **t**, where the vowel is elsewhere long in inflection: as,

régrediōr audísse mē (Capt. 1023); átqu*e* ut qui fuerīs et qui nunc (Capt. 248); me nómināt hæc (Epid. iv. 1, 8); faciāt ut semper (Pœn. ii. 42); ínfuscabát, amabo (Cretics, Cist. i. 1, 21); quí amēt (Merc. 1021); ut fīt in bello capitur alter filius (Capt. 25); tibi sīt ad me revísas (Truc. ii. 4, 79).

h. The hiatus is allowed very freely, especially at a pause in the sense, or when there is a change of the speaker. (The extent of this license is still a question among scholars, but in the present state of texts it must sometimes be allowed.)

84. Reckoning of Time.

1. *Date of Year.* The year was dated, in earlier times, by the names of the Consuls; but was afterwards reckoned from the building of the City (*ab urbe conditâ*, or *anno urbis conditæ*), the date of which was assigned by Varro to a period corresponding with B.C. 753. In order, therefore, to reduce Roman dates to those of the Christian era, *the year of the city is to be subtracted from* 754: e.g. A.U.C. 691 (the year of Cicero's consulship) = B.C. 63.

2. *The Roman Year.* Before Cæsar's reform of the Calendar (B.C. 46), the Roman year consisted of 355 days: March, May, Quintilis (July), and October having each 31 days, February having 28, and each of the remainder 29; with an Intercalary month, on alternate years, inserted after February 23, at the discretion of the Pontifices. The "Julian year," by the reformed calendar, had 365 days, divided as at present. Every fourth year the 24th of February (vi. kal. Mart.) was counted twice, giving 29 days to that month: hence the year was called *Bissextilis*. The month Quintilis received the name *Julius* (July), in honor of Julius Cæsar; and Sextilis of *Augustus* (August), in honor of his successor.

The Julian year (see below) remained unchanged till the adoption of the Gregorian Calendar (A.D. 1582), which omits leap-year once in every century.

3. *The Month.* Dates, according to the Roman Calendar, are reckoned as follows:—

a. The *first* day of the month was called **Kalendae** (*Calends*), from **calare**, *to call*,—that being the day on which the pontiffs publicly announced the New Moon in the *Comitia Calata*, which they did, originally, from actual observation.

b. Sixteen days before the Calends,—that is, on the *fifteenth* day of March, May, July, and October, but the *thirteenth* of the other months,—were the **Idus** (*Ides*), the day of Full Moon.

c. Eight days (the ninth by the Roman reckoning) before the Ides,—that is, on the *seventh* day of March, May, July, and October, but the *fifth* of the other months,—were the **Nonae** (*Nones*, or *ninths*).

d. From the three points thus determined the days of the month were reckoned *backwards* (the point of departure being, by Roman custom, counted in the reckoning), giving the following rule for determining the date:—

If the given date be Calends, add *two* to the number of days in the month preceding,—if Nones or Ides, add *one* to that of the day on which they fall,—and from the number thus ascertained subtract the given date:—thus, viii. Kal. Feb. (33—8) = Jan. 25;—iv. Non. Mar. (8—4) = Mar. 4;—iv. Id. Sept. (14—4) = Sept. 10.

e. The days of the Roman month by the Julian Calendar, as thus ascertained, are given in the following Table:—

	January.	February.	March.	April.
1.	KAL. JAN.	KAL. FEB.	KAL. MARTIÆ	KAL. APRILES
2.	IV. Non. Jan.	IV. Non. Feb.	VI. Non. Mart.	IV. Non. Apr.
3.	III. ,, ,,	III. ,, ,,	V. ,, ,,	III. ,, ,,
4.	prid. ,, ,,	prid. ,, ,,	IV. ,, ,,	prid ,, ,,
5.	NON. JAN.	NON. FEB.	III. ,, ,,	NON. APRILES.
6.	VIII. Id. Jan.	VIII. Id. Feb.	prid. ,, ,,	VIII. Id. Apr.
7.	VII. ,, ,,	VII. ,, ,,	NON. MARTIÆ	VII. ,, ,,
8.	VI. ,, ,,	VI. ,, ,,	VIII. Id. Mart.	VI. ,, ,,
9.	V. ,, ,,	V. ,, ,,	VII. ,, ,,	V. ,, ,,
10.	IV. ,, ,,	IV. ,, ,,	VI. ,, ,,	IV. ,, ,,
11.	III. ,, ,,	III. ,, ,,	V. ,, ,,	III. ,, ,,
12.	prid. ,, ,,	prid. ,, ,,	IV. ,, ,,	prid. ,, ,,
13.	IDUS JAN.	IDUS FEB.	III. ,, ,,	IDUS APRILES.
14.	XIX. Kal. Feb.	XVI. Kal. Martias	prid. ,, ,,	XVIII. Kal. Maias
15.	XVIII. ,, ,,	XV. ,, ,,	IDUS MARTIÆ.	XVII. ,, ,,
16.	XVII. ,, ,,	XIV. ,, ,,	XVII. Kal. Aprilis	XVI. ,, ,,
17.	XVI. ,, ,,	XIII. ,, ,,	XVI. ,, ,,	XV. ,, ,,
18.	XV. ,, ,,	XII. ,, ,,	XV. ,, ,,	XIV. ,, ,,
19.	XIV. ,, ,,	XI. ,, ,,	XIV. ,, ,,	XIII. ,, ,,
20.	XIII. ,, ,,	X. ,, ,,	XIII. ,, ,,	XII. ,, ,,
21.	XII. ,, ,,	IX. ,, ,,	XII. ,, ,,	XI. ,, ,,
22.	XI. ,, ,,	VIII. ,, ,,	XI. ,, ,,	X. ,, ,,
23.	X. ,, ,,	VII. ,, ,,	X. ,, ,,	IX. ,, ,,
24.	IX. ,, ,,	VI. ,, ,,	IX. ,, ,,	VIII. ,, ,,
25.	VIII. ,, ,,	V. ,, ,,	VIII. ,, ,,	VII. ,, ,,
26.	VII. ,, ,,	IV. ,, ,,	VII. ,, ,,	VI. ,, ,,
27.	VI. ,, ,,	III. ,, ,,	VI. ,, ,,	V. ,, ,,
28.	V. ,, ,,	prid. ,, ,,	V. ,, ,,	IV. ,, ,,
29.	IV. ,, ,,	[prid. Kal. Mart.	IV. ,, ,,	III. ,, ,,
30.	III. ,, ,,	in leap-year, the	III. ,, ,,	prid. ,, ,,
31.	prid. ,, ,,	vi. Kal. (24th) being	prid. ,, ,,	So June, Sept., Nov.
	(So Aug., Dec.)	counted twice.]	(So May, July, Oct.)	

NOTE.— Observe that a date before the Julian Reform (B.C. 46) is to be found not by the above, but by taking the earlier reckoning of the number of days in the month.

85. MEASURES OF VALUE.

1. The Money of the Romans was in early times wholly of copper, the unit being the **As**. This was nominally a pound, but actually somewhat less, in weight, and was divided into twelve **unciae**. In the third century B.C. the *As* was reduced by degrees to one-twelfth of its original value. At the same time silver coins were introduced; the Denarius = 10 *Asses*, and the Sestertius or *sesterce* (*semis-tertius*, or *half-third*, represented by IIS or HS = *duo et semis*) = $2\frac{1}{2}$ *Asses*.

2. The **Sestertius**, being probably introduced at a time when it was equal in value to the original AS, came to be used as the unit of value: hence **nummus**, *coin*, was used as equivalent to *Sestertius*. Afterwards, by the reductions in the standard, four *asses* became equal to a *sesterce*. Gold was introduced later, the **aureus** being equal to 100 *sesterces*.

The value of these coins is seen in the following Table: —

2½ asses = 1 sestertius or nummus (HS), value about 4 cents.
10 asses or 4 sestertii = 1 denarius . . . ,, ,, 16 ,,
1000 sestertii = 1 sestertium . . . . ,, ,, $40.00.

3. The **Sestertium** (probably the genitive plural of *sestertius*) was a sum of money, not a coin; the word is inflected regularly as a neuter noun: thus, *tria sestertia* = $120.00. When combined with a numeral adverb, *hundreds of thousands* (*centena milia*) are to be understood: thus *decies sestertium* (*decies* HS) = $40,000. In the statement of large sums the noun is often omitted: thus *sexagies* (Rosc. Am. 11) signifies, *sexagies* [*centena milia*] *sestertium* (6,000,000 sesterces) = $240,000.

4. In the statement of sums of money in cipher, a line above the number indicates thousands; lines at the sides also, hundred-thousands. Thus HS. DC. = 600 *sestertii*; — HS. $\overline{\text{DC.}}$ = 600,000 *sestertii*, or 600 *sestertia*; — HS. $|\overline{\text{DC}}|$ = 60,000,000 *sestertii*.

5. MEASURES OF LENGTH.

12 unciæ (*inches*) = 1 Roman Foot (*pes*, 11.65 English inches).
1½ Feet = 1 Cubit. — 2½ Feet = 1 Degree or Step (*gradus*).
5 Feet = 1 Pace (*passus*). — 1000 Paces (*mille passuum*) = 1 Mile.

The Roman mile was equal to 4850 English feet. The **Jugerum**, or unit of measure of land, was an area of 240 (Roman) feet long and 120 broad; a little less than ⅔ of an English *acre*.

6. MEASURES OF WEIGHT.

12 unciæ (*ounces*) = one pound (*libra*, about ¾ lb. avoirdupois).

For fractional parts of the pound, see Lexicon, art. **as.** The Talent was a Greek weight = 60 *libræ*.

7. MEASURES OF CAPACITY.

12 cyathi = 1 sextarius (nearly a pint).
16 sextarii = 1 modius (peck).
6 sextarii = 1 congius (3 quarts, liquid measure).
8 congii = 1 amphora (6 gallons).

APPENDIX.

LATIN was originally the language of the plain of Latium, lying south of the Tiber, the first territory occupied and governed by the Romans. This language, together with the Greek, Sanskrit, Zend (old Persian), the Sclavonic and Teutonic families, and the Celtic, are shown by comparative philology to be offshoots of a common stock, a language once spoken by a people somewhere in the interior of Asia, whence the different branches, by successive migrations, peopled Europe and Southern Asia.

The name Indo-European (or Aryan) is given to the whole group of languages, as well as to the original language from which the branches sprang. By an extended comparison of the corresponding roots, stems, and forms, as they appear in the different branches, the original ("Indo-European") root, stem, or form can in very many cases be determined; and this is used as a model, or type, to which the variations may be referred. A few of these forms are given in the grammar for comparison (see, especially, p. 59). A few are here added for further illustration:

1. *Case Forms* (Stem vāk, *voice*).

		Indo-Eur.	Sanskr.	Greek.	Latin.
SING.	Nom.	vāks	vāks	ὄψ	vox
	Gen.	vākas	vāchas	ὀπός	vocis
	Dat.	vākai	vāche	ὀπί	voci
	Acc.	vākam	vācham	ὄπα	vocem
	Abl.	vākat	vāchas	(gen. or dat.)	voce(d)
	Loc.	vāki	vāchi	(dat.)	(dat.)
	Instr.	vākā	vāchā	(dat.)	(abl.)
PLUR.	Nom.	vākas	vāchas	ὄπες	voces
	Gen.	vākām	vāchām	ὀπῶν	ocum
	Dat.	vākbhyams	vāgbhyas	ὀψί	vocibus
	Acc.	vākams	vāchas	ὄπας	voces
	Abl.	vākbhyams	(as dat.)	(gen. or dat.)	vocibus
	Loc.	vāksvas	vāksu	(dat.)	
	Instr.	vākbhis	vāgbhis	(dat.)	(abl.)

(For Verb-Forms, see p. 59.)

238   APPENDIX.

2. Cardinal Numbers.

74

	Indo-Eur.	Sanskr.	Greek.	Latin.
1	?	[eka]	[εἷς]	[unus]
2	dva	dva	δύο	duo
3	tri	tri	τρεῖς	tres
4	kvatvar	chatur	[τέσσαρες]	quattuor
5	kvankva	panchan	πέντε	quinque
6	ksvaks	shash	ἕξ	sex
7	saptam	saptan	ἑπτά	septem
8	aktam	ashtun	ὀκτώ	octo
9	navam	navan	ἐννέα	novem
10	dakam	dasan	δέκα	decem
12	dvadakam	dva-dasan	δώδεκα	duodecim
13	tridakam	trayo-dasan	τρισκαίδεκα	tredecim
20	dvidakanta	vinsati	εἴκοσι	viginti
30	tridakanta	trinsati	τριάκοντα	triginta
100	kantam	satam	ἑκατόν	centum

3. Familiar and Household Words.

	Indo-Eur.	Sanskr.	Greek.	Latin.
Father.	pătar-	pitri-	πατήρ	păter
Mother.	mātar-	mātri-	μήτηρ	māter
Father-in-law.	çvakura-	çvaçura-	ἑκυρός	socer
Daughter-in-law.	snushā-	snusha-	νυός	nurus
Brother.	bhrātar-	bhrātri-	φράτηρ*	frāter
Sister.	svasar- (?)	svasar-	[ἀδελφή]	soror
Master.	pati-	pati-	πόσις	potis
House.	dama-	dama-	δόμος	domus
Seat.	sadas-	sadas-	ἕδος	sedes
Year.	vatas-	vatsa-	ἔτος	vetus (old)
Field.	agra-	ajra-	ἀγρός	ager
Ox, Cow.	gau-	go-	βοῦς	bos
Sheep (Ewe).	avi-	avi-	ὄϊς	ovis
Swine (Sow).	sū-	sū-	ὗς, σύς	sus
Yoke.	yuga-	yuga-	ζυγόν	jugum
Wagon.	rata-	rata-	[ἅμαξα]	rota (wheel)
Middle.	madhya-	madhya-	μέσος	medius
Sweet.	svādu-	svādu-	ἡδύς	suāvis

The immigrants who peopled the Italian peninsula also divided into several branches, and the language of each branch had its own development, until they were finally crowded out by the dominant Latin. Fragments of some of these dialects have been preserved, in monumental remains, or as cited by Roman antiquarians, though no literature now exists in them; and other fragments were probably incorporated in that popular or rustic dialect which formed the basis of the modern Italian. The most important of these ancient languages of Italy — not including Etruscan, which was

* Clansman.

of uncertain origin — were the Oscan of Campania, and the Umbrian of the northern districts. Some of their forms as compared with the Latin may be seen in the following:

Latin.	Oscan.	Umbrian.	Latin.	Oscan.	Umbrian.
accinere		arkane	neque	nep	
alteri (loc.)	alttrei		per	perum	
argento	aragetud		portet		portaia
avibus		aveis	quadrupedibus		peturpursus
censor	censtur		quatuor	petora	petur
censebit	censazet		quinque	pomtis	
contra, F.	contrud, N.		qui, quis	pis	pis
cornicem		curnaco	quid	pid	
dextra		destru	quod	pod	pod
dicere	deicum	(cf. venum-do)	cui	piei	
dixerit	dicust		quom		pone, pune
duodecim		desenduf	rectori	regaturei	
extra	ehtrad		siquis		svepis
facito	factud		stet	stai•t(stai•et)	
fecerit	fefacust		subvoco		subocau
fertote		fertuta	sum	sum	
fratribus		fratrus	est	i•st	
ibi	ip		sit	set	
imperator	embratur		fuerit	fust	fust
inter	anter	anter	fuerunt	fufans	
liceto	licitud		fuat	fuid	fuia
magistro		mestru	tertium		tertim
medius		mefa	ubi	puf	
mugiatur		mugatu	uterque		puturus pid
multare	moltaum		utrique	puterei•	putrespe

Fragments of early Latin are preserved in inscriptions dating back to the third century before the Christian era; and some Laws are attributed to a much earlier date, — to Romulus (B. C. 750) and Numa (B. C. 700); and especially to the Decemvirs (Twelve Tables, B. C. 450); but in their present form no authentic dates can be assigned to them. Some of these are usually given in a supplement to the Lexicon. (See also Cic. de Legibus, especially ii. 8, iii. 3, 4.)

Latin did not exist as a literary language, in any compositions known to us, until about B. C. 200. At that time it was already strongly influenced by the writings of the Greeks, which were the chief objects of literary study and admiration. The most popular plays, those of Plautus and Terence, were simply translations from Greek, introducing freely, however, the popular dialect and the slang of the Roman streets. As illustrations of life and manners they belong as much to Athens as to Rome. And the natural growth of a genuine Roman literature seems to have been thus very considerably checked or suppressed. Orations, rhetorical works, letters, and histories, — dealing with the practical affairs and passions of politics, — seem to be nearly all that sprang direct from the native soil. The Latin poets of the Empire were mostly court-poets, writing for a cultivated and luxurious class; satires and epistles alone keep the flavor of Roman manners, and exhibit the familiar features of Italian life.

In its use since the classic period, Latin is known chiefly as the language of the Civil Code, which gave the law to a large part of Europe ; as the language of historians, diplomatists, and philosophers during the Middle Age, and in some countries to a much later period ; as the official language of the Church and Court of Rome, down to the present day ; as, until recently, the common language of scholars, so as still to be the ordinary channel of communication among many learned classes and societies ; and as the universal language of Science, especially of the descriptive sciences, so that many hundreds of Latin terms, or derivative forms, must be known familiarly to any one who would have a clear knowledge of the facts of the natural world, or be able to recount them intelligibly to men of science. In some of these uses it may still be regarded as a living language ; while, conventionally, it retains its place as the foundation of a liberal education.

During the classical period of the language, Latin existed not only in its literary or urban form, but in several local dialects, known by the collective name of *lingua rustica*, far simpler in the forms of inflection than the classic Latin. This, it is probable, was the basis of modern Italian, which has preserved many of the ancient words without aspirate or case-inflection, as *orto* (*hortus*), *gente* (*gens*). In the colonies longest occupied by the Romans, Latin — often in its ruder and more popular form — grew into the language of the common people. Hence the modern languages called "Romance" or "Romanic"; viz., Italian, Spanish, Portuguese, and French, together with the Catalan of Northeastern Spain, the Provencal or Troubadour language of the South of France, the "Rouman" or Walachian of the lower Danube (Roumania), and the "Roumansch" of some districts of Switzerland.

A comparison of words in several of these tongues with Latin will serve to illustrate that process of phonetic decay to which reference has been made in the body of this Grammar, as well as the degree in which the substance of the language has remained unchanged. Thus, in the verb *to be* the general tense-system has been preserved from the Latin in all these languages, together with both of the stems on which it is built, and the personal endings, somewhat abraded, which can be traced throughout. The following exhibit the verb-forms with considerably less alteration than is found in the other Romanic tongues: —

Latin.	Italian.	Spanish.	Portuguese.	French.	Provençal.
sum	sono	soy	sôu	suis	son (sui)
es	sei	eres	és	es	ses (est)
est	è	es	hé	est	es (ez)
sumus	siamo	somos	sômos	sommes	sem (em)
estis	siete	sois	sôis	êtes	etz (es)
sunt	sono	son	saõ	sont	sont (son)
eram	era	era	era	étais	era
eras	eri	eras	eras	étais	eras
erat	era	era	era	était	era
eramus	eravamo	éramos	éramos	étions	eram
eratis	eravate	erais	ĕreis	étiez	eratz
erant	érano	eran	eraõ	étaient	eran
fui	fui	fui	fui	fus	fui
fuisti	fosti	fuiste	fôste	fus	fust
fuit	fù	fuè	fôi	fut	fo (fou)
fuimus	fummo	fuimos	fômos	fûmes	fom
fuistis	foste	fuisteis	fôstos	fûtes	fotz
fuerunt	fúrono	fueron	fôraõ	furent	foren
sim	sia	sea	seja	sois	sia
sis	sii	seas	sejas	sois	sias
sit	sia	sea	seja	soit	sia
simus	siamo	seamos	sejâmos	soyons	siam
sitis	siate	seais	sejais	soyez	siatz
sint	siano	sean	séjaõ	soient	sian
fuissem	fossi	fuese	fôsse	fusse	fos
fuisses	fossi	fueses	fôsses	fusses	fosses
fuisset	fosse	fuese	fôsse	fût	fossa (fos)
fuissemus	fóssimo	fuésemos	fôssemos	fussions	fossem
fuissetis	foste	fueseis	fôsseis	fussiez	fossetz
fuissent	fóssere	fuesen	fôssem	fussent	fossen
es	sii	se	sê	sois	sias
esto	sia	sea	seja	soit	sia
este	siate	sed	sêde	soyez	siatz
sunto	siano	sean	séjaõ	soient	sian
esse	éssere	ser	sêr	être	esser
[sens]	essendo	siendo	sêndo	étant	essent

PRINCIPAL ROMAN WRITERS.

	B.C.
T. Maccius Plautus, *Comedies*	254–184
Q. Ennius, *Annals, Satires, &c.* (Fragments)	239–169
M. Porcius Cato, *Husbandry, Antiquities, &c.*	234–149
M. Pacuvius, *Tragedies* (Fragments)	220–130
P. Terentius Afer (Terence), *Comedies*	195–159
L. Attius, *Tragedies* (Fragments)	170–75
C. Lucilius, *Satires* (Fragments)	148–103
M. Terentius Varro, *Husbandry, Antiquities, &c.*	116–28
M. Tullius Cicero, *Orations, Letters, Dialogues*	106–43
C. Julius Cæsar, *Commentaries*	100–44
T. Lucretius Carus, *Poem "De Rerum Naturâ"*	95–52
C. Valerius Catullus, *Miscellaneous Poems*	87–47
C. Sallustius Crispus (Sallust), *Histories*	86–34
Cornelius Nepos, *Lives of Famous Commanders*	c. 100–28
P. Vergilius Maro, *Eclogues, Georgics, Æneid*	70–19
Q. Horatius Flaccus, *Satires, Odes, Epistles*	65–8
Albius Tibullus, *Elegies*	54–18
Sex. Aurelius Propertius, *Elegies*	51–15
T. Livius Patavinus (Livy), *Roman History*	59–A.D. 17
P. Ovidius Naso (Ovid), *Metamorphoses, Fasti, &c.*	43–A.D. 18
Phædrus, *Fables*	–41
Valerius Maximus, *Anecdotes, &c.*	–31
C. Velleius Paterculus, *Roman History*	19–31
Pomponius Mela, *Husbandry & Geography*	–50
A. Persius Flaccus, *Satires*	A.D. 34–62
L. Annæus Seneca, *Philos. Letters, &c.; Tragedies*	B.C. 3(?)–65
M. Annæus Lucanus, *Historical Poem "Pharsalia"*	39–65
Q. Curtius Rufus, *History of Alexander*	–54 ?
C. Plinius Secundus (Pliny), *Nat. Hist., &c.*	23–79
C. Valerius Flaccus, *Heroic Poem, "Argonautica"*	–88
P. Papinius Statius, *Heroic Poems, "Thebais," &c.*	61–96
C. Silius Italicus, *Heroic Poem, "Punica"*	25–100
D. Junius Juvenalis (Juvenal), *Satires*	40–120
L. Annæus Florus, *Hist. Abridgment*	–120
M. Valerius Martialis (Martial), *Epigrams*	43–104
M. Fabius Quintilianus, *Rhetoric*	40–118
C. Cornelius Tacitus, *Annals, History, &c.*	60–118
C. Plinius Cæcilius Secundus (Pliny Junior) *Letters*	61–115
C. Suetonius Tranquillus, *Biographies*	70–
Apuleius, *Philos. Writings, "Metamorphoses" &c.*	110–
A. Gellius, *Miscellanies, "Noctes Atticæ"*	about –180
† Q. Septimius Florens Tertullianus, *Apologist*	160–240
† M. Minucius Felix, *Apol. Dialogue*	about –250
† Firmianus Lactantius, *Theology*	250–325
† D. Magnus Ausonius, *Miscellaneous Poems*	–400.3
Ammianus Marcellinus, *Roman History*	–400.3
Claudius Claudianus, *Poems, Panegyrics, &c.*	–410 4
† Aurelius Prudentius Clemens, *Christian Poems*	348–410
† Aurelius Augustinus, *Confessions, Discourses, &c.*	354–430
Anicius Manlius Boëthius, *Philos. Dialogues*	470–520

† Christian writers.

aecilius Statius (Ruf. 163) 210+ —168 (Mom. II. 5

(om. IV. 719)   (Ruf. c. 93-23 ?F

'and 2)
L. I. P. (Ruf. 594)   INDEX. C. I. P. (Biog. III. 13
f.)
(630)   Columella (L. Junius Moderatus)

INDEX.

NOTE.—The Figures refer to *pages;* the Letters to the *upper, middle,* or *lower* part of the page.

AB, preposition 88 c, with agent, after passives 138 b.
Abbreviations of prænomens 32.
Ablative 12 a, ending 13 b, in -ABUS 14 c, in I 18 b, 35 c, 37 c, in IS (3d decl.) 21 b, in -UBUS 28 c, neuter used adverbially 84 c, EO and QUO 49 c, after prepositions 88, with AB or DE for partitive gen. 116 b, of crime or punishment 119 c, with dat. after verbs 122 b, with PRO for defence &c. 130 c, syntax of 134-143, of separation 135 a, of place from which 135 c, of source 136 c, of material 137 b, of cause 137 b, with adjectives &c. 137 c, of agent 138 b, after comparatives 138 c, after PLUS &c. 139 a, of means 139 b, of accompaniment 139 c, after UTOR &c. 140 b, of degree of difference 140 c, of quality 141 a, of manner 141 a, of price 141 b, of specification 142 a, location 142 b, 143 b, absolute 142 c, used adverbially 143 a, of time 143 b, time *how-long* 143 c, of distance 144 a, place *from which* 144 c, for locative 145 a, place *where* 145 c, way *by which* 145 c, with prepositions 145 a, with AB for *agent* 147 c, distinguished from abl. of *instrument* 148 a.
ABSQUE 89 a.
Abstract nouns in plur. 30 c, with neut. adj. 106 a, expressed by neut. adj. 107 c.
AC see ATQUE; AC SI with subj. 174 c.
Accent 7 c.
Accompaniment abl. of 139 c.
Accusative 11 c, endings 13 a, in IM 18 b, 35 c, in IS 19 a, 37 c, neut. used as adv. 83 c (gen. 85 a), after prep. 88, 145 a, with verbs of remembering &c. 119 a, with impers. 120, 132 b, with dat. 123 c, 124 c, after compounds of preps. 125 c, after AD for dat. 128 c, after adj. 129 c, construction of 131, as div. obj. 131 a, with verbs of feeling 131 b, cognate 131 c, verbs of taste &c. 131 c, after compounds 132 a, constructive 132 a, two acc. 132 b, adverbial 133 a, syncedochical 133 b, in exclamations 133 c, as subj. of infin. 133 c, of duration 133 c, 143 c, of space 133 c, 144 a, of distance 133 c, 144 a, place whither 144 c, in ind. disc. 188 a, of anticipation 190 c, in subst. clauses 194 a, after passives 194 b, after verbs of promising &c. 195 a.
Action, nouns of 96 b, 97 c, governing genitive 117 a.
AD 88 b, following noun 148 a.
Adjectives 33, of two termin. 35 a, of one termin. 36 a, of common gender 38 a, used as adv. 38 a, deriv. of 96 b, 98 a, compound 100 b, modifying 102 a, adj. phrase 102 b, agreement of 105, in appos. 105 b, in agr. with appos. 106 b, with part. 106 c, used as nouns 106 c, neuter 107 b, used for gen. 108 a, 114 a, qualifying act 108 c, for obj. gen. 108 b, in rel. clause 111 b, neut. used partitively 115 c, relat. gov. gen. 117 c, of feeling with ANIMI 118 b, gov. gen. and dat. 118 c, 129 a, followed by dat. or acc. with AD 128 c, dat. or acc. 129 b, of want with abl. 136 a, DIGNUS &c. with abl. 137 c.
ADMODUM 41 a.
Adverbs 9 c, 84, compar. of 40 b, compound 100 c, numeral 43 c, correl. 49 c, classif. of 85, 86, modifying 102 a, phrase 102 b, qualifying noun 107 b, rel. or dem. equiv. to pron. 111 c, partitive use 116 a, formed with TENUS 147 a, used as prepos. 147 b, followed by QUAM 147 c.
Adverbial phrase 102 b, accus. 133 b, in abl. absolute 143 a.
Adversative conjunctions 94 a.
ADVERSUS 89 b, as adverb 147 b.
Affix, close and open 96.
Agency, nouns of 96 b, 97 c, governing gen. 117 a.
Agent 138 b, abl. with AB 147 c.
Agnomen 32 b.
Agreement 103 b, nouns in for part. gen. 116 c.
AIO 81 c.
Alcaic strophe,
ALIENUS with DOMUS 145 b.
ALI- (stem of ALIUS) 48 b.
ALIUS infl. of 34 c, with abl. 139 b.
Alphabet, classification of 1 b.
AMBO, infl. 42 b.
AMPLIUS, constr. of 139 a.

AN, ANNE, ANNON, interrog. particles 200 c.
ANTE 89 b, om. in dates 146 c, as adv. 147 b, followed by QUAM 147 c, ANTE DIEM 146 c.
Antecedent of relative 110 a, implied 110 b, in both clauses 110 c, omitted 111 a.
Antepenult 7 c.
ANTEQUAM with relat. clauses 179 c.
Aorist 53 b.
APAGE 82 b.
Apodosis 166 a, c.
Appositive 102 a, 104 a, adjectives 105 b, neut. adj. 107 c, in periphr. form 112 a, expr. by gen. 115 a, with NOMEN EST, 127 a, after verbs of naming 132 c.
APUD 89 c.
APTUS followed by rel. and subj. 185 c.
Arsis and Thesis 222 b.
AS, the unit of value 235 c.
Asclepiadic verse 230.
Asking, verbs of, with two acc. 132 c.
Aspirate 1 c, 115 c.
Assimilation of consonants 36, in prepos. 4 a.
AT 95 b, AT VERO 96 a.
ATQUE 95 a.
Attraction of Relative 110.
Attributive adj. 105 b.
AUDEO 77 a.
AUSIM 77 b.
AUT 95 b, in questions 201 c.
AUTEM 95 b, position, 96 a.
AVE 82 b.

BELLI (locative) 145 a.
Birth, place of in abl. 137 a.
BOS, decl. of 22 b, c.

C and G 2 a, for QU 2 b, interchanged with T 4 b, pronunciation of 6 a.
Cæsura 222 b.
Calendar, Roman 235 a.
Cardinal numbers 41 b, declined 42 b.
CARO, decl. 25 c.
Cases 11 b, endings 13 b, forms (see declensions) construction of 113 b.
Catalectic verse,
CAUSA with gen. 115 b, 138 a.
Causal conjunctions 94 b, clauses 102 c, with subjunct. 181 b.
Causative verbs 99 a.
Cause, with subjunctive 185 b.
CAVE in prohibitions 192 c.
-CE enclitic 45 b.
CELO with two accusatives 133 a.
CEDO (defective) 82 b.
CERTE and CERTO 87 b.
CEU with subjunct. 174 c.
Choliambic verse 226 b.
Choriambic verse 228 b.
CIRCA, CIRCITER, CIRCUM, CIS 89 c.
CIRCITER as adv. 147 b.
Cities, gender of 10 c.
CITRA 89 c, following noun 148 a.

CLAM as prepos. 147 b.
Clauses 102 b, adv. use 84 b, with neut. in appos. 107 c, limited by gen. 114 b, with impersonals 120 a, dependent, in seq. of tenses 162 a.
Close syllables 5 c, affixes 9 b, in compounds 65 a.
Commands in subjunct. 149 c, imperative 51 b, 152 b.
CŒPI 81 b.
Cognomen 32 b.
Collective nouns with plur. verbs 112 c.
Combinations of consonants 5 a, 192 c.
Commands, indirect 191 c.
Common gender 11 a, of adj. 38 a.
Comparative conjunctions 94 b.
Comparatives, declensions 37 a, use 40 c, partitive 115 c.
Comparison, forms of 38 b, irregular 39 b, defective 39 c, of adverbs 40 b, in appos. 104 b, of qualities, 108 c.
Complementary acc. 104 b, infin. 154 b.
Complete action, tenses of 53 c, 159 c, favorite use 170 c.
Compounds of verbs 65 a, of FACIO 80 a, of FIO 81 c, of NON 86 a, stems 96 b, words 100 a, of preps. governing acc. 132 a, with two acc. 132 c, with abl. 135 b, quantity of 220 b.
Conditional conjunctions 94 b, clauses 102 b, 103 a, 166, classified 167 c.
Conditions, partic. and gen. 167, present and past 168, future 170 a, general 171 c, implied 172 b, omitted 173 b, in indirect discourse 89 b.
Conjugation 9 b, 60, the four regular 66-75.
Conjunctions 92, correlative 49 c, classes of 93.
Connectives 103 b.
Consecutive clauses 102 c, 103 a, subjunctive 183 c.
Consonants 1 b, stems 12 c, 36 a.
Constructio prægnans 132 a.
CONTRA 90 a, as adv. 147 b, following noun 148 a.
Contraction 3 a, shown by circumflex, 7 a.
Co-ordinate clause 102 c.
Correlatives 49.
Countries, gender of 10 c.
Crime, expressed by ablative 119 c.
CUM (prep.) 90 a, as enclitic 44 c, 47 c.
CUM (conj.) 95 c, with subjunct. 176 c, 178 c, as indef. relat. 177 a, causal w. subj. 180 c, 181 c, like QUOD with indic. 180 c, CUM TUM with indic. 181 a, causal with indicative 181, for pres. pass. part. 202 c.

Dactylic Verse 224 b.
Dative 11 c, ending 13 b, in -ABUS 14 c, in IS (3d decl.) 21 b, -UBUS 28 c, in I 34 b, construction 121, with transitives 121 c, after verbs of motion (poet.) 122 b, with abl. id., after intrans. 122 c, 123, with acc. 123 c, 124 c, after impersonals 124 b, after com-

pounds 125, 126, in poetry 126 c, of possession id., after comp. of ESSE 127 a, with NOMEN EST id., of agency 127 b, after participles and passives id., of service 128 a, of nearness 128 b, after nouns 129 b, of advantage 129 c, used for gen. 130 a, for direction id., of volens &c. 130 b, ethical id., with infinitive of verbs governing dative 155 b.
Declaratory sentence 101.
Declension 12 c, general rules 13 a.
Defective nouns, 29, 30, adj. 37, tenses 50 b, verbs 81.
-DEM, enclitic 45 b.
Denominative verbs 99 a, c.
Deponents 75 c, semi-deponents 77 a.
Derivation 96–100.
Derivative verbs 77 b, 99.
DIGNUS with abl. 137 c, with QUI and subj. 185 c.
Diphthongs 1 b, 6 a, long 7 a.
Diptotes 31 a.
Distance (acc.) 133 c (acc. or abl.) 144 a.
Distributives 43 b.
DOMI (loc.) 145 a.
DONEC with subjunctive 180 b.
Doubtful gender 11 a.
Dual 42 b.
DUBITO 184 b, 198 b, 200 c.
DUM with pres. 158 a, id. followed by secondary tenses 163 c, (provided) with subj. 175 c, 180 b, (until) with subj. 180 b, for pass. part. 202 c.
DUMMODO with subj. 175 c, 180 b.

Early forms, alphabet 2, prosody.
EDO 80 a.
EGEO with gen. 120 c, 136 b.
Ellipsis 101 c.
Emphasis as dependent on arrangement 212 c.
Enclitics, intensive 45 a, CUM 44 c.
ENIM 95 b, 96 a.
Epicene nouns 11 a.
Epistolary tenses 161 b.
ESCIT, 59 c.
ESSE 57 c, comparative forms 59 c, compounds 60, omitted 113 b, compounds with dative 127 a.
ET . . . ET 95 c.
ETIAM 87 a, in answers 201 c.
ETSI 175 b.
Etymology 1–100.
Euphonic changes 2 c, 3 b.
EX 90 c, following noun 148 a, compounds of, with dative 126 a.
Exclamations (accus.) 133 c.
Exclamatory sentences 101 b, accusative with infinitive 156 b.

FACIO 80 c, compounds 100 c, facio ut in periphr. 198 a.
FARI 82 a.
Feeling, nouns of, with genitive 117 a, verbs of, with acc. 131 b.

Feminine forms lacking masc. 34 b, abl. in o 34 b, in A of adj. of 3d decl. 37 a, abl. as adv. 85 a.
Festivals, names of, plural 30 c.
FERO 78 b.
FIDO 77 a.
Filling, verbs of, with abl. or genitive 140 b.
Final clauses 102 c, 103 a, 182, 195.
Finite verb 113 a.
FIO 80 c, defective comp. 82 c.
Foot (in prosody) 220 e, classif. 221.
FORE UT for fut. inf. pass. 55 c, 165 c.
FORIS (loc. form) 145 a.
Frequentative verbs 77 c, 99 c.
FRUOR and FUNGOR with abl. 140 b.
Future tense 53 a, endings 54 c, 61 b, c, of subj. 83 c, for imperative 153 b, syntax 159 b, has no relative time 179 b, infin. expr. by FORE UT 165 c, participle 202 a.
Future Perfect 53 a, syntax 161 a, used for future id., how repr. in subjunctive 162 b, in protasis 170 c.
Future infin. pass. (sup. with IRI) 55 c.

Games, names of, plural 30 c.
GAUDEO 77 a.
Gender 9 c, grammatical 10 a, of apposition 104 c, of adjective 105 c.
General truth in seq. of tenses, 163 c.
Genitive 11 c, plural ending 13 b, in AI and AS 14 b, in IUM 19 a, c, in IUS 34 b, in appos. with possessive 105 a, 108 b, construction 113 c, subjective 114 a, in pred. b, with phrase id., of adj. for neuter noun 114 c, of substance id., for noun in apposition 115 a, of quality and measure id., of value id. b, partitive id., after adj. for noun 116 b, two gen. with one noun 117 a, objective 117 a, of specification 118 a, after verbs 119 a, (of remembering &c. 119 a, of accusing &c. b, of emotion 120 a, impersonals 120, of plenty and want 120 c, 136 b, 140 b, with POTIOR 121 a, 127 a, of price 141 c.
Gentiles, names of, 8 b.
Gerund 50 a, 52 b, syntax 206 c.
Gerundive 52 a, ending 55 b, periphr. form 83 c, with dative of agent 127 c, syntax 205 c, 206, origin 207 a.
Glyconic verse 228 b.
Government 103 c.
GRATIA with gen. 115 b, 138 a.
Greek accus. (synecd.) 133 b.

H (aspirate) 1 c, used with c 4 c, omitted 4 c, not reckoned in position, 215 c.
HABEO, imperative 153 b, with perf. part. 204 c.
Heteroclites 31 b.
Heterogeneous nouns 31 c.

Hexameter verse.
HIC 45, 46.
Hindrance, subject of 185 b.
HUMI (loc.) 145 c.

I in perf. 55 a, added to root 62 c, lost in 3d conj. 63 c, suffix 96 c.
Iambic verse.
ID QUOD, 111 b.
IDCIRCO 95 c.
IDEM 46, deriv. 45 b.
IDONEUS with QUI and subj. 185 c.
-IER in infin. pass. 65 c.
IGITUR 95 c, position 96 a.
ILLE 45, 46.
-IM in present subjunctive 65 c.
IMMO 201 c.
Imperative 51 b, termin. 54 b, a weakened 63 a, drops termin. 65 a, sentence 101 a, in commands 152 b, 3d person antiq. 152 c, future 153 a, equiv. to condition 172 c.
Imperfect 53 a, lengthens vowel 63 a, of subj. 64 c, of hortat. subj. 150 b, optat. subj. 150 c, concess. subj. 151 c, syntax 158 b, in descriptions 158 c, for plup. id., of surprise 159 a, for perf. 159 b, in epist. style 161 b, subj. in unfulfilled cond. 168 b, in temp. clauses 178 a, 179 a, subjunctive referring to present time 164 a.
Impersonal verbs 82, with gen. 120 a, used personally 120 b, with dative 121 b, passive of verbs governing dative 126 b, with acc. 132 b, with infin. 154 b, with subst. clause 193 c.
Impure syllable 5 c.
IN 90 c, construction of 87 b, 146 a.
Inceptive forms 62 c, verbs (inchoative) 77 b, 99 c.
Incomplete tenses 53 c.
Increment 218.
Indeclinable nouns 31 a, gender 10 c, adjective 37 c, 49 c.
Indefinite subj. omitted 113 a, relative, equiv. to condition 166 c.
Indicative 51 a, 61, 63, syntax 148 b, tenses of 157, in cond. clauses 167 b, 168 a, in apod. of unfulf. cond. 169 a, in fut. cond. 170 a, in apod. of implied condition 174 a, absolute time 177 b, in inverted clauses 179 a, with CUM 180 c, in causal clauses 181 b, with QUOD in subst. clauses 199 b.
INDIGEO with génitive 120 c, 136 b.
INDIGNUS, with relative and subjunc. 185 c, with ablative 137 c.
Indirect discourse 187 c, subj. of infin. om. 155 c, subjunct. in subord. clause 186 a, example 192.
Infinitive 51 b, endings 55 b, c, pass. in -IER 65 c, syntax 153 c, as subj. id., with impers. 154 b, complementary 154 b, for subst. clause 154 c, with subj. acc. 155 b, of purpose and result 156 a, in exclam. 156 b, 197 c, historical 156 c, tenses 164 b, only used in present 165 a, with acc. in

subst. clauses 194 a, with acc. after passives 194 b, after verbs of wishing 195 c, verbs of permission 196 a, of determining 196 b, used by poets 197 a.
Inflection 8 a.
INQUAM 81 c.
INSTAR with gen. 115 b.
Intensive verbs 77 c, 99 c.
INTEREST 120 b.
Interjections 9 c, 95 a.
Intermediate clauses 102 c, with subjunctive 185 c.
Interrogative particles 9 c, 86 b, 200 a, omitted 200 b, 201 a, sentences 101 b.
IPSE (IPSUS) 45, 46 c.
Irregular nouns 30 b, verbs 78.
IS 45, 46 c.
Islands, gender of, 10 c.
ISTE 45, 46.
ITAQUE 95, accent 7 c (ergo, 96 a).
ITER, declined 22 b.

JAM 87 b.
JECUR, decl. 22 b.
JUDEO, constr. 155 a, 194 a.
JUCUNDUS, constr. of 209 c.
JUNGO with abl. 140 a.
JUPPITER, decl. 22 b.
JUXTA 91 b, following noun 148 a.

L doubled (3d conj.) 62 b.
Labial stems 20 b, gender of 24 b, 26 b.
LATEO with acc. 133 a.
-LIBET 48 a.
LICET with dat. of pred. 155 b, with subj. 175 b, 176 c, 196 a.
Lingual stems 20 c, gender 24 b, 26 b.
Liquid stems 19 b, gender 24 a, 25.
Locative case 12 b, as adverb 85 a, in appos. 104 c, for place 145 a.
LOCO without prep. 145 c.
LONGIUS, constr. of, 139 a.

MAGIS in compar. 39 a, 109 a.
MALO 79 b.
Masculine adj. 38 a.
Material, gen. of, 114 c, abl. 137 b.
MAXIME, in comp. 39 a.
Means, abl. of, 139 b.
Measure, gen. of, 115 a, 144 a.
Meditative verbs 78 c, 99 c.
MEMINI 81 b, imperative form, 153 b.
-MET, enclitic, 45 a.
Metre 223 c.
MILITIÆ (loc.) 145 a.
MILLE, decl. and constr. 43 a.
MINIME 41 a, in answers 201 c.
MINORIS (of value) 141 c.
MINUS 41 a, constr. of 139 a.
MIRUM QUAM 191 b.
MISCEO with abl. 140 a.
MISERET 83 a, 120 a.
Modification of subj. or pred. 102 a.
MODO with hort. subj. 150 a, 175 c.
Monoptotes 31 a.

Months, gender of 10 c, in -BER 35 c, construction 146 c, division 234 b.
Moods 50 a, 51, syntax of, 148 b.
Motion, preps. with acc. 122 b, verbs of (comp.) with acc. 132 c.
Motive with OB or PROPTER 138 a.
Mountains, gender of, 10 c.
Multiplication 43 b.
Multiplicatives 43 c.
Mute stems 20 a.

N of stem lost 19 b, inserted in 3d conj. 62 b.
NAM, NAMQUE 35 b, 96 a.
Names of men and women 32.
NE with hort. subj. 150 a, in final clauses 182 a, in consec. 183 c, with verbs of caution 196 b, of fearing 196 c, omitted id.
-NE (enclitic) 200 a, with HIC 45 b, added to interrog. words 200 c, in double questions id.
NECNE 200 c.
NEDUM 183 a.
Negative particles 9 c, 86 c, two equal to affirmative 87 a.
NEGO for DICO NON 188 a.
NEQUEO 82 b.
NE . . . QUIDEM 87 c, 214 a.
NESCIO AN 200 c, NESCIO QUIS 191 b.
Neuter passives 77 a.
Neuters, like cases 13 a, in AL and AR 17 c, of adj. in S 36 c, acc. as adv. 84 c, of adj. with abstr. nouns 106 a, as noun 107 b, partitive use 115 c.
Neuter verbs, with agent 138 b.
Neutral passives 77 b.
NI, NISI 176 b, 166 b.
NIX, decl. 22 c.
NOLO 79 b, NOLI 192 c.
NOMEN 32 b, with dative 127 a.
Nominative 11 b, formed from stems 12 c, in adj. 36 a, as subj. of verb 113 a, used for voc. 134 a, with opus 136 b.
NONNE 200 a.
Nouns 14–32, used as adj. 38 a, 107 b, verbal 50 a, irreg. 30 b, derived 96 a, compound 100 b, agreement of 103 c, in relative clause 110 c, understood with gen. 114 a, governing dat. 129 c.
NUM 200 a.
Number of appositive 104 c, of adj. 105 b, of verb 112 b.
Numerals 41 b, partitive use 115 c.
Numeral adverbs 43 c.
NUNC 86 b.

O SI with subjunct. of wish 151 a.
O for U after U 2 b, in verb-stems 62 c.
Object 101 c, indir. 121 b, direct 131 a.
Oblique cases 12 a.
OBVIUS with dativo 125 c.
ODI 81 b.
Open syllables 5 c, pron. 6 a, affix 9 b, in compounds 65 a.
OPERA with gen. 138 b.

OPUS with abl. 136 a, with perf. part. 204 c.
Oratio Obliqua, see Indirect Discourse.
Order of words 212.
Ordinal numbers 41 b, how formed, 42 b, declined 42 c.
OS for US 15 c.
OS, OSSIS, decl. 22 c.

P inserted before M 3 c, 20 b, 72 b.
PALAM 147 b.
Palatal 1 b, stems 21 c, gender 24 b, 27 b, verbs 62 c.
Parisyllabic nouns 17 b, adj. 35 a.
PARTE, without prepos. 145 c.
Participial clause, equiv. to condition 172 b.
Participles 50 a, 51 c, abl. in I 20 b; 37 b, compared 39 a, future of purpose 51 c, 205 b, perfect as adj. 25 a, 82 c, with HABEO 204 c, active 52 a, periphr. use 53 c, 83 b, ending 55 b, pres. of ESSE 57 c, of deponents 76 b, 51 a, present as adj. 83 c, in NS with gen. 17 c, with dative of agent 127 c, of source with abl. 136 c, in URUS with FUI plup. subj. 169 c, in RUS or DUS in future apod. 170 c, syntax 202, adj. and pred. 203.
Particles 9 c, 84–96, in compounds 100 c, conditional, with subj. 174 c, interrogative 200 a.
Partitive genitive 115 b.
PARUM 41 a.
Passive voice 50 c, reflex. use id. 83 b, with acc. 133 b, termin. 54 b, infin. in IER 65 c, participles of deponents 76 c, of impersonals 83 b, followed by dative 122 a, of agent 127 c, subject 131 a, of verbs of feeling 131 b, of asking, &c., with acc. 132 c, of saying, &c., with accusative and infinitive 194 b.
Patronymics 98 b.
Peculiar forms, 3d decl. 22 a, genders 25 a, 26 a, 27 b.
PENES 91 c, following noun 148 a.
Penult 7 c, quantity of 218–220.
PER 91 c, in compos. 41 a, for agent 138 b.
Perfect tense, meaning, 53 b, endings 54 b, 55 a, syncop. 65 b, subjunct. in prohib. 150 a, 152 b, of subj. antiquated 150 c, concess. subj. 151 c, in quest. 152 a, syntax 159 c, implies discontin. 160 a, in negatives 160 b, for pres. in epist. style 161 b, followed by imp. subj. 162 c, subj. for past act. after primary tenses 162 c, used for sec. tenses in result 163 a, with fut. prot. 117 a, infin. for pres. 165 a, after verbs of feeling 165 c, participle in pass. tenses 52 a, of depon. id. syntax 202 b.
Period 214 b.
Personal endings 54 a.
Persons of verbs 54 a, 112 b, with relat. 110 a, 2d in subjunct. 149 c, 171 c, 3d of imperative antiquated 152 c.

PERTÆSUM EST 120 a.
PETO with prepos. 133 a.
Pherecratic verse 228 c.
Phonetic decay 2 c, 3 a.
Phrases, gender 10 c, as adv. 85 b, modifying 102 b, limited by gen. 114 b.
PIGET 120 a.
Place, relations of 144 b, abl. of 142 b, 143 b, whence 144 c, whither id., where 145, verbs of, constr. 146 b.
Plants, gender of, 10 c, 2d and 4th decl. 29 a.
Plautus, use of QUAL with indic. 179 b, prosodial forms 23 b.
Pluperfect 53 a, of subjunctive, how formed 64 b, use 150 b, opt. subj. 150 c, conc. subj. 151 c, syntax 160; for imp. in epist. style 161 b, of subj. in false cond. 168 b, in temp. clauses 178 a, 179 a.
Plural acc. used as adv. 85 b.
Pluralia tantum 30 c, with distrib. 43 b.
PLURIS, gen. of value 141 c.
PLUS, decl. of 37 b, constr. 139 a.
PŒNITET 120 a.
PONE 91 c.
Position in prosody 216 c.
Possessives in appos. with gen. 105 a, 108 a, as nouns 107 a, for gen. 108 b, 114 a, neuter 114 c, abl. with REFERT &c. 138 a, with DOMI 145 b.
POSSUM 60 b, infin. as future 164 c.
POST 91 c, with QUAM 147 c.
POSTQUAM with temp. clauses 177 c.
POSTULO with prep. 133 a.
POSTRIDIE with gen. 121 a, with acc. 147 b, with QUAM 147 c.
Potential mood 51 a.
POTIOR with gen. 121 a, with abl. 140 b.
PRÆ 91 c, in comp. 41 a.
Prænomen 32 b.
PRÆSERTIM, strengthening CUM 180 c.
PRÆTER 92 a.
Predicate 101 c, nom. 104 a, adj. 105 b, gender 106 a, after infin. 155 c.
Prepositions, assimil. 4 a, classif. and meaning 88–93, in comp. 93 a, 100 c, comp. with dative 125, 126, with acc. 125 c, 132 a, c, with verbs of asking 132 c, after words of origin 137 a, of time 143 c, of place 142 c, 144 b, for neighborhood 145 c, constr. 146, as adv. 147 b, followed by QUAM 147 c, following noun 148 a.
Present stem 53 c.
Present tense 53 a, endings 54 c, vowel 61, 62 b, of subjunct. 150–152, syntax 157 b, curative 157 c, for future id., historical 158 a, with DUM 158 a, hist. followed by sec. tenses 163 c, infin. after past verb 164 b, of memory 164 c, participle 202 a, supplied in passive 52 a, 202 c.
Preteritive verbs 81 b, 160 c.
Price, abl. or gen. 141 c.
PRIDIE with genitive 121 a, with acc. 147 b, with QUAM 147 c.
PRIMO and PRIMUM 87 c.

Principal parts of verbs 64 b, combined 65 a.
PRIUS with QUAM 147 c.
PRIUSQUAM in relative clauses 179
PRO 92 a, *for* 130 c.
PROCUL with abl. 147 b.
Prohibitions, subj. with NE 149 c, regular constr. 152 b.
Pronouns 44, old forms 44 b, gen. in I 44 c, omitted 113 a, reflexive 44 b, 46 c, possessive 44 b, 47 b, 105 c, CUJUS 48 c, reciprocal 44 c, 109 c, demonstr. 45 a, as nouns 107 a, as antecedent 111 a, intensive 46 c, relative 47, 109 c, agreement 110, as connective 111 c, interrog. and indef. 47.
Pronunciation, 5, 6.
PROPE 92 a, with acc. 147 b, as adv. id.
Proper names 32 b, in plural 30 c.
PROPTER 92 a, following noun 148 a.
PROSUM 60 a.
Protasis 166 a (see Condition).
-PTE (-pse), encl. 45 a.
PUDET 120 a.
Punishment, abl. of, 119 c.
Pure syllable 5 c.
Purpose, infinitive of, 156 a, UT 182 a, ways of expressing 183 b.

QUÆ RES 111 b.
QUÆSO 82 a.
Quality, genitive of, 115 a.
-QUAM (-pan) 48 a.
QUAM with superl. 40 c, etym. 48 c, in comparisons 109 a, 138 c, after prep. 147 c, followed by subj. 185 a, by infinitive 188 b, by result clause 197 b.
QUAM SI with subj. 174 c.
QUAMLIBET, QUANQUAM, QUAMVIS, 48 a, 151 b, 174 b, 176 c.
QUANDO 95 c, as indef. rel. 177 a, with ind. 181 b.
QUANTI, gen. of value 141 c.
Quantity 6 c, notes of 215–220.
QUANTUM VIS with subj. 176 c.
QUASI with subj. 174 c.
-QUE (encl.), forming universals 48 c.
QUEO 82 b.
Questions 200, indirect 190 a, 200 b, in ind. disc. 189 c, indic. in 191 b.
QUI adverbial 47 b.
QUIA 95 c, with ind. 181 b, with subj. 186 b.
QUIDEM 87 c, 214 a.
QUIN with subj. 104 a, NON QUIN 186 a, in subst. clause 198 b.
QUIPPE with CUM 180 c.
QUISQUAM with neg. 48 c.
QUISQUE with superl. 41 a, with plur. verb 112 c.
QUO in final clauses 182 b, NON QUO 186 c.
QUOAD, *until*, with subj. 180 b.
QUOD 95 c, with ind. 181 b, with subj. 186 b, in subst. clause 199 b, as acc. of specif. 199 b, with verbs of feeling 199 c.

QUOM 95 c.
QUOMINUS with subjunc. 184 a, after verbs of caution, &c. 196 b.
QUONIAM 95 c, with indic. 181 b.
QUOQUE 87 a.

R doubled in third conjugation 62 b.
REAPSE 45.
Reduplication 61 b, 62 a, b, 63 b, lost in compounds 65 a, 96 b, quantity 219 c.
REFERT 120 b.
Reflexive pronouns 44 b, verbs 76 b, 50 c, with acc. 133 b.
Relative pronouns 47, clauses 102 b, classif. of 193, equiv. to condition 172 b, 166 c, of purpose 182 a, 195, of result 183 c, 197, of characteristic 184 b.
Result, infin. of, 156 a, perf. subj. 163 a, subjunctive 183 c, 197 a, elliptical 197 b.
Rhythm 215,
Rivers, gender 10 c.
Root 8 c, 96, of ESSE 59 c, of third conjugation 62 b.
RURI, RURE, 145 a.
RUS, constr. of 144 b.

S elided 2 b, 232 a, becomes R 3 a, 19 b, termin. of nom. 12 c, 13 a, in perf. stem 62 a, 63 b, 64 b, syncop. 65 b.
SE added 62 c.
SALVE 82 b.
SATIS, NON SATIS 41 a.
SCIN' 5 b.
SCIO, imperative form 65 c, 153 b.
SECUNDUM 92 b.
SED 95 b.
SEMI-DEPONENTS 77 a.
SEMI-VOWELS 1 c, I and U 2 a.
SENEX, decl. 22 c.
Separation, with dat. 126 a, abl. 134 a.
Sequence of tenses 161 c.
Sesterces 101 b.
Sestertius 32 a, 236.
SEU (see SIVE).
SI 166 b, whether 191 c, SI NON 176 b, MIROR SI 199 c.
SIEM 59 c.
Signs of quantity 76, of accent 8 a.
SIM in perf. subj. 65 c.
SIMUL with abl. 147 b.
SIMUL ATQUE 177 c.
SIN 166 b.
SINE 92 b.
Singularia tantum 30 c.
SIS (SIVIS) 5 b.
SIVE 95 b, 176 b.
SO in future perfect 65 c.
SODES (SI AUDES) 56, 77 b.
SOLEO 77 a.
SOLUS with subj. 185 a.
Space, acc. of, 133 c, 144 a.
Specification, acc. of, 133 a, abl. 142 a.
Spelling, various, 4 c.
Stem 86, 96, of nouns 12 c, 96 b, incorrect use 13 c, of adj. 33 b, of verbs 53 c, 60 c, changes 54 c, vowel 61, present 64 b, third conj. 62 b, in U 62 c, perf. 64 b, third conj. 63 b, supine 64 b, quantity of 220 a.
SUB in compos. 41 a, constr. 87 b, 146 a.
Subject 101 c, of verb 113 a, of passive 131 a, of infin. 133 c.
Subjunctive 51 a, present (vowel-change) 61 a, 63 c, inserts E 61 c, syntax 148 c, hortat. 149 b, as condition 172 c, optat. 150 c, concess. 151 b, 175 b, dubit. 152 a, in prohib. 152 b, tenses 161 c, in false condition 164 a, 168 b, in fut. cond. 170 b, pres. becomes imperf. 171 b, third person for indef. subjunc. 171 c, repeated action id., potential 173 b, cautious 173 c, with cond. and compar. particles 174 c, relative time 177 b, after CUM 178 c, of protasis after ANTEQUAM &c. 180 a, after DUM, b, of cause 181 b, 185 c, in ind. disc. 181 c, 186 a, in final clauses 182 a, after NEDUM 183 a, of result 183 c, after QUIN and QUOMINUS 184 a, of characteristic 184 b, after UNUS and SOLUS 185 a, after QUAM id., of restriction 185 b, after DIGNUS &c. 185 c, in intermed. clauses id., after UT in subst. clauses 195 c, 197 a, after verbs of commanding 195 c, of happening 197 a, after QUAM 197 b, in exclamations 197 c, in indirect questions 190, 200 b.
Subordinate clauses 102 c.
Substantive clauses 102 c, syntax 193.
SUPER, SUPRA 92 c.
SUBTER 92 b, constr. 87 b, 146 b.
Superlative of eminence 40 c, of participle 109 b, used partitively 115 c.
Supine 29 a, 50 a, 52 b, stem 53 c, 55 b, acc. of place whither 144 c, syntax 209.
Syllables, division of 5 b, pure, open &c. 5 c.
Synesis 103 b, of adj. 106 b, verbs 112 c, of secondary tenses 166 a.
Synopsis 64 c.
Syntax 101-214, general rules 210, 211.

T for D 2 b, intercl. with C 4 b, ending 54 c, 61 b, 62 a, c.
TÆDET 120 a.
TAMEN, position 96 a.
TAMQUAM with subj. 174 c.
TANTI, gen. of value 141 c.
TANTUM as correl. 49 b, with hort. subj. 150 a.
TANTUM ABEST UT 197 c.
TE, enclitic 45 c.
Teaching, verbs of 2, acc. 133 c.
Temporal conjunctions 94 c, clauses 102 c, 176 c.
-TER, suffix 34 c.
Tenses 50 a, 52 c, syntax 157, sequence 151 c.
TENUS 92 c, construction 146 c, following noun 148 a.

TERRA MARIQUE 145 a.
Time, absolute and relative, 157 a, 161 c, how long (acc.) 133 c, 143 b, when (abl.) 143 b.
Towns, gender 10 c, in US, fem. 16 a, in E 18 c, names of, constr. 144 b.
TRANS 92 c.
Trees, gender 10 c.
TRES 42 c.
Triptotes 31 a.
Trochaic verse 227 a.
TUM, TUNC, 87 b, with CUM 95 c, 181 a.

U stems (verbs) 62 c, 64 a, 96 c.
UBI as indef. rel. 177 a, c.
ULLUS with neg. 48 c.
ULTRA 93 a, following noun 148 a.
UNQUAM with neg. 48 c.
UNUS 42 b, with rel. and subj. 185 a.
USQUAM with neg. 48 c.
USQUE with acc. 147 b.
USUS with abl. 136 a.
UT with concess. subj. 151 b, 175 b, 176 c, as indef. rel. 177 a, UT CUM 180 c, in final clauses 182 a, consec. do. 183 c, subst. do. 195 b, 197 a, with verbs of fearing 196 c, omitted id.
UTERQUE with plur. verb 112 c, with nouns and pronouns 116 c.
UTI, UTINAM, with subj. of wish 151 a, 192 c.
UTOR with abl. 140 c.
UTSI with subj. 174 c.
UTRUM 200 c, used alone 201 b.

V 2 a, 6 a, syncop. 65 b.
VALDE 41 a.
Value, genitive of 115 b.
VAPULO 77 b.
Variable nouns 31 b, adj. 37 c.

-VE, VEL, 95 b.
VELIM, VELLEM, with subj.
VELUTI, VELUTSI 174 c.
VENEO 77 b, 80 a.
Verbs 50–83, forms 54, 56, end special forms and parallel ponent 75 c, irreg. 78, d impers. 82, deriv. of 99, c 100 b, syntax 112, 113, omitted 113 b, of rememb 119 a, of accusing &c. 1 emotion with gen. 120 a, c &c. 120 c.
Verbals in AX 98 b, with ge
VERO 96 a, in answers 201 c.
Verse 222 c, forms of 224–231
VERSUS 93 a, as adv. 147 b.
VERUM 95 b.
VESCOR with abl. 140 b.
VETO, constr. of 155 a, 194 a
VIM 5 b, VIS 48 a.
Vocative 12 a, 13 a, of noun 16 b, construction 134, of nom. 134 b.
Voices 50 a.
VOLO 79.
Vowels 1 b, strengthened 62 encl. 63 a.
Vowel change in verbs 56, 63 a, subj. 53 c, in compou
Vowel increase 2 c, 61 a, 62 b,
Vowel scale 2 c.
Vowel stems 12 c, 17 b, 19 a, der of 24.

Winds, gender 10 c.
Wishes and commands 192.
Women, names of, 32 c.

Y in root of third conj. 62 c,

ERRATA.

Page 9, paragraph 8, omit the third line.
„ 143, Note, erase the last two words.

www.ingramcontent.com/pod-product-compliance
Lightning Source LLC
Chambersburg PA
CBHW032142230426
43672CB00011B/2418